The PRICE of
GOVERNMENT

ALSO BY DAVID OSBORNE

The Reinventor's Fieldbook (2000) (with Peter Plastrik)

The Reinventing Government Workbook (1998) (with Victor Colon Rivera)

Banishing Bureaucracy (1997) (with Peter Plastrik)

Reinventing Government (1992) (with Ted Gaebler)

Laboratories of Democracy (1988)

The PRICE of GOVERNMENT

Getting the Results
We Need in an Age of
Permanent Fiscal Crisis

DAVID OSBORNE AND

PETER HUTCHINSON

BASIC
BOOKS

A Member of the Perseus Books Group
New York

Books published by Basic Books are available at special discounts for
bulk purchases in the United States by corporations, institutions, and
other organizations. For more information, please contact the
Special Markets Department at the Perseus Books Group, 11 Cambridge Center,
Cambridge, MA 02142, or call (617) 252-5298, (800) 255-1514 or e-mail
special.markets@perseusbooks.com.

Library of Congress Cataloging-in-Publication Data
Osborne, David.
The price of government : getting the results we need in an age of
permanent fiscal crisis / David Osborne and Peter Hutchinson.
p. cm.
Includes index.
ISBN 0-465-05363-7 (alk. paper)
1. Fiscal policy—United States—States. 2. Budget—United States—
States. 3. United States—Appropriations and expenditures.
4. United States—Politics and government. I. Hutchinson, Peter, 1949–
II. Title.
HJ275.O83 2004
352.4'213'0973—dc22
2004000540

Design by Jane Raese
Set in 9.5-point Utopia

04 05 06 07 08 / 10 9 8 7 6 5 4 3 2

In loving memory of my wife, Rose

—DAVID OSBORNE

To Armi—who was there at the beginning

To Karla, Julia and Emily, who have paid the price, with love

—PETER HUTCHINSON

CONTENTS

ACKNOWLEDGMENTS

Books like this one don't write themselves. Nor are they the products of solitary efforts by those whose names grace their covers. Books like this are collaborations, in every sense of the word. They have a long gestation period: They start with ideas that get tested and nurtured, enriched by other ideas, refined, and finally used, challenged, and adapted in many different settings by many different people. After enough time those ideas become a body of thinking and experience that can be recorded. So it has been with this book.

We owe an enormous debt of gratitude to all those who have joined us in this journey—those who share our passion for the public sector and its potential so much that they have been willing to help us hatch, grow, and refine these ideas. First among these are our friends in the Public Strategies Group. PSG is not only our consulting firm, it is our family of friends and partners, who have provided us with extraordinary support for more than a decade. Babak Armajani, CEO, and Jeff Zlonis, COO, made this work a PSG investment. Anna Schmalzbauer, Bill Lofy, and Steve Struthers provided extraordinary assistance, doing research, compiling data, and answering unending questions. Camille Barnett, Anne Kinney, Connie Nelson, and Beverly Stein went to enormous lengths to help with our research. Lorraine Chang, Doug Farbrother, Larry Grant, Rick Heydinger, Ellen Hutchinson, Jeff Kober, Lisa Mallory-Hodge, Laurie Ohmann Schley, Bob Stone, Chuck and Mary Lofy, Mia Morris-Tucker, Jennifer Spencer, Peter Beck, and Taavo Smith offered encouragement, examples, and answers to our late night requests for help.

The late Governor Rudy Perpich was the first elected official to embrace the "price of government" as an idea. John James, Babak Armajani, Tom Stinson, Charlie Bieleck and Bill Blazar were present at its birth and nurtured it along.

Our friends in the state of Washington showed all of us the immense power of Budgeting for Outcomes. We are grateful to them for their faith and willingness to show the way, including Governor Gary Locke, Fred Kiga, Joe Dear, Marty Brown, Wolfgang Opitz (and the whole budget staff at OFM), Lynne McGuire, Candace Espeseth, Jim Hedrick, Mary Campbell (and her team of facilitators), Ed Penhale, Irv Lefberg, Richard Davis, Phil Bussey, William Vogler, Paul Parker, Dema Harris, and Don Brunell.

We have also learned a great deal from our work with Governor Tom Vilsack and his staff in Iowa. Our sincere thanks go to Governor Vilsack, Cindy Eisenhauer, Jesse Rasmussen, Jim Chrisinger, and Bob Rafferty. From the Minneapolis Public Schools we are grateful to Louise Sundin, David Heistad, David Dudycha and the School Board, who gave PSG the opportunity to make a real difference. In New York State, both Joe Boardman and Ruth Walters have been a great help.

As we composed this book, we turned to many veteran reinventors with questions. We tapped their knowledge, their contacts, and their vast experience in the fields of reinvention. For their continual willingness to take our phone calls and answer our e-mails, we thank John Kamensky, Elaine Kamarck, Lyle Wray, John Gunyou, Jay Kiedrowski, Tim Penny, Bob O'Neill, Neal Johnson, Jay Fountain, Buddy MacKay, Bob O'Leary, Ted Kolderie, Dennis McKenna, Paul Taylor, and Curt Johnson. Many others, too numerous to name, have given us their time and wisdom over the years, and we are deeply grateful to all of them.

We owe a special thanks to our friend Bill Patrick, who helped us crank this book out in record time. He was there with us the day we started writing. Along the way he researched, drafted, edited, and made our ideas and examples both cleaner and clearer. His spirit is very much a part of this book.

Pete Plastrik's voice is also in this book. Through two previous books, David Osborne and Peter Plastrik explored the frontiers of reinvention together. For his extraordinary help with one chapter in this book, and for his collaboration and friendship over the years, we are deeply in his debt.

We are grateful to the team at Basic Books, who saw the potential of *The Price of Government* and brought it to fruition in record time: Bill Frucht, our editor; David Shoemaker, his assistant; Christine Marra, our production coordinator, and David P. Kramer, our copy editor.

And as always, our sincere thanks go to Kristine Dahl, the best literary agent in the world.

We offer our deepest thanks and love to our children, for their love and support; to Sylvia Wolf, for her extraordinary support through a tough year; and to Karla Ekdahl, who makes dreams come true.

Finally, we want to acknowledge one another. Writing is intense and very personal. We are even better friends because we did this. Thanks.

David Osborne
Essex, Massachusetts

Peter Hutchinson
Minneapolis, Minnesota

PREFACE

During the presidential election of 1992, candidate Bill Clinton often derided the "brain-dead politics of left and right."

At the same, Ross Perot led both President Bush and candidate Clinton in the polls until he dropped out in late June. Why? Precisely because Perot had managed to go beyond the brain-dead politics Clinton condemned. He spoke for the radical center—for Americans who were fed up with politics as usual, deeply worried about budget deficits that were ballooning toward $300 billion, and desperate for economic and fiscal sanity.

More than a decade later, American politics seems stuck in the same place. Again we face mega deficits as far as the eye can see—only this time, as we will, the fiscal crisis is permanent. Yet both sides keep mouthing the same old platitudes. From the right, all we hear is "no new taxes," "cut spending," and "starve the beast"—as if conservatives did not see public school students struggling while their school budgets are slashed, homeless populations growing, police and fire departments shrinking despite the threat of terrorism, and 44 million Americans without health insurance.

Traditional liberals see these problems but have little more to offer. They still issue the same calls for new programs, and they still talk of raising taxes—as if they were blind to the very real resistance to higher taxes and the very real depth of this fiscal crisis.

When they have to face the fiscal music, both sides end up using accounting gimmicks to push the reckoning off for one more year, and when that proves insufficient, borrowing billions to push it off for one more generation.

Meanwhile, too much of the media has degenerated into blind ignorance and partisan entertainment. The people who offer quips on television and radio—the Bill O'Reillys and Rush Limbaughs, the Michael Moores and Al Frankens—have no clue how to actually solve our problems.

And the American people are immensely frustrated. They pay the price of government, and they want a government that is worth what they pay.

It is time to move beyond the outworn ideologies of left and right. This book offers solutions for a new era in which fiscal crisis will be a permanent feature. It shows how we can turn fiscal crisis into an opportunity to wring far more value out of our public institutions. The first step is to turn the budget process on its head, so that it starts with the results we demand and the price we are willing to pay rather than the programs we have and the costs they incur. The second is to build the budget by deciding to buy only those programs that deliver the results we want and leave the rest behind. Then we must cut government down to its most effective size and shape, through strategic reviews, consolidation, and rightsizing; use competition to squeeze more value out of every tax dollar; make every program, organization, and employee accountable for results; use technology to empower customersand save money; and reform how government works on the inside (its management systems and bureaucratic rules) to improve its performance on the outside. *The Price of Government* will help public leaders get smarter about budgeting, sizing, spending, management, and, finally, leadership and politics.

When it was published in 1992, *Reinventing Government* launched waves of change in American (and other) governments (and since then in governments all over the world) with a similar message. But a great deal has changed since 1992. Ideas that were then considered controversial or impractical—empowering customers, measuring results, and using competition, to name three—are now in the mainstream. The frontier of reinvention has moved on, and this book will bring readers up to date on some of the most profound advances along that frontier.

But *The Price of Government* differs from *Reinventing Government* in two other ways. First, it focuses specifically on the fiscal crisis, providing solutions to the painful dilemmas it poses. And second, it is far more prescriptive than *Reinventing Government*. That book described experiments going on throughout the public sector, at all levels, and argued that a new, post-bureaucratic model of government—more flexible, innovative, and entrepreneurial—was emerging. Today we are well beyond the experimental phase. The strategies and tools we write about have proven their value in many different public contexts (and in many countries). It is clear to all that they work, and in this book we argue that any leader worth his or her salt should waste no time in implementing them.

The Price of Government does not offer all the detail leaders will need to do so. In the years since *Reinventing Government* was published, David Osborne and Peter Plastrik have published two books that do offer that kind of guidance: *Banishing Bureaucracy* (Addison-Wesley, 1997) outlines the five

Introduction

The usual, political way to handle a projected deficit is to take last year's budget and cut. It is like taking last year's family car and reducing its weight with a blowtorch and shears. But cutting $2 billion from this vehicle does not make it a compact; it makes it a wreck. What is wanted is a budget designed from the ground up.

—*The Seattle Times*
November 17, 2002

American government is waist deep in its worst fiscal crisis since World War II.

On April 7, 2003, the mayor of New York announced the layoff of 3,400 city employees and the closure of eight firehouses. The following day, the city's Department of Education cut another 3,200 jobs. America's largest city faced a budget shortfall of $3.5 billion, despite an 18.5 percent increase in the city property tax and the elimination of 14,000 city jobs since Mayor Bloomberg took office.

Nationwide, 16 percent of cities and towns were forced to cut police positions in 2002 and 38 percent of large cities predicted cuts in police services—even as crime rose and pressure to improve homeland security increased. Portland, Oregon's largest city, cut its police budget by more than 10 percent over three years. Station houses now close at night, the city is turning nonviolent criminals free because it can't afford to provide public defenders, and the county had to stop prosecuting drug and property crimes, like burglary and auto theft. Crime is already up sharply.

Many school districts in Oregon had to end school weeks early in 2003, because of state funding cuts. Oklahoma City had to close seven schools and dismiss 600 teachers. Birmingham, Alabama, closed nine schools,

1

Boston five. Some 100 local school districts across the country shut down schools one day a week to save money.

But local government problems are dwarfed by those of the states. Collectively, the states faced a budget shortfall of $82 billion as they approached fiscal 2004—"the most dire fiscal situation since World War II," according to the National Governors Association (NGA). "The stress is just huge," said longtime NGA executive director Ray Sheppach, "by far the worst we've ever seen."

In fiscal 2002, 38 states cut their budgets by nearly $13.7 billion. In 2003, 40 states—the most ever recorded by the NGA's *Fiscal Survey*—cut another $11.8 billion. Connecticut laid off prosecutors; Kentucky and Washington released prison inmates. Every state in the union has cut Medicaid: either throwing poor people off the rolls, cutting benefits, limiting payments to health providers, raising co-payments, or limiting prescription drug coverage. Texas cut 275,000 children from its health-care rolls, while Nebraska raised the eligibility threshold for Medicaid by 30 percent.

Most states have cut spending for higher education. As a result, the University of Arizona hiked tuition by 39 percent in the fall of 2003, the University of Oklahoma by 28 percent. Massachusetts, Missouri, Iowa, and Texas have all raised tuition at least 20 percent. Meanwhile, programs are disappearing: The University of Illinois eliminated 1,000 classes; the University of Colorado dropped programs in journalism, business, and engineering; the University of California delayed the opening of an entire campus.

The future looks even bleaker. State governments have just begun to pass their problems down to cities and counties, with deep cuts in local aid. And the federal government is digging a fiscal hole so rapidly that further cuts and unfunded mandates for states and localities are inevitable.

Scheppach argues, correctly, that the public sector has entered an era of "perpetual fiscal crisis." He describes the convergence of forces swelling to buffet public finance as "a perfect storm." Most prominent among these are a colossally irresponsible president and Congress, an obsolete tax structure, an aging population, an ineluctable rise in the cost of health care, and continuing resistance to major tax increases. Economic recovery will ease the pain, but it will not eliminate it.

The president's tax cuts and spending increases, passed enthusiastically by Republicans in Congress, have blown a hole in fiscal policy that will be difficult to close. The 2004 deficit is expected to weigh in at *$521 billion*. Federal revenues in 2003 were the lowest, as a percentage of gross domestic product (GDP), since the 1950s. In January 2004, the Congressional Budget Office forecast that at current spending and tax levels, President Bush's plan to make most of his tax cuts permanent would increase the national debt by *$4.1 trillion* over the next decade—a *60 percent* increase in just 10 years. This would create a future obligation of $37,450 for every living American.

At the state level, other factors are at play. In fiscal 2002, per capita tax collections were down almost *10 percent,* when adjusted for inflation—the first year they had fallen since the NGA began tracking them almost 60 years ago. Total revenues (adjusted for inflation and tax increases) dropped for eight straight quarters. The recession, by historical standards quite mild, was only a part of the problem. A second element was the transformation of capital gains into losses as the stock market bubble burst; a third, the tax cuts passed by many states during the flush years of the late 1990s; and the final element, a sudden drop in performance bonuses, which have emerged as a much greater portion of income over the past decade.

These problems will pass, though not quickly: Tax revenues lag economic recoveries by several years. But more fundamental problems will persist, because our tax base is, to use the NGA's word, "deteriorating." In the Information Age, we cling to an Industrial Era tax base, capturing less and less of the economy. Corporations can avoid taxes by moving money to offshore tax havens with the press of a button. Most states don't tax services, which now account for almost 60 percent of consumer spending. Congress and the Supreme Court forbid taxation of Internet access, as well as Internet and catalog orders from companies that have no physical presence in the purchaser's state. Imagine that we had said, when we first imposed sales taxes in the 1930s, "We have to protect this new industrial economy, so we'll tax only agricultural products." When we refuse to tax services and Internet sales, we do the equivalent today.

Will the fiscal storm force us to modernize our tax systems? To a degree, yes. But because we now live in a global economy, in which businesses can easily shift investments across state or national boundaries, it is more difficult than ever to broaden the tax base. Every attempt is met with the argument that new taxes will slow the economy, because corporations will relocate and investors will take their money elsewhere. Around the world, the new economy has put a lid on tax revenues.

The third pressure system in the perfect storm is our aging population. With average life spans pushing 80, we spend ever greater portions of our income on the elderly. In 1975, Social Security and Medicare consumed 23 percent of the federal budget; today the figure is 34 percent. The Congressional Budget Office projects that under current law, even if the historical growth of Medicare slows a bit, those two programs will rise from about 6.6 percent of GDP to almost 15 percent by 2030 and about 22 percent by 2050.

To put this in perspective, *total* federal expenditures have averaged about 20 percent of GDP for the past 50 years.

At current tax levels, both Social Security and Medicare are headed for insolvency. Thanks to the baby boom, the number of people 65 and older is expected to double over the next 30 years, while the number under 65—who must pay Social Security and Medicare taxes—will increase only 15 percent. That demographic reality paints a frightening picture. By 2003, reserves plus the long-term value of all Social Security taxes to be paid by current workers over their lifetimes totaled $3.5 trillion. But benefits owed retirees and these same workers over that period totaled *$14 trillion.*

And Social Security is only the tip of the iceberg. Public pension funds are also in trouble. Of the 123 largest funds monitored by the Wilshire Group, 79 percent are underfunded. Nine states have liabilities that exceed their annual budgets, and the total shortfall could be as high as $1 trillion within seven years. With all other state, municipal, and county funds added in, the number could be $2 trillion.

But the real time bomb hidden in our ever-longer life spans is the cost of health care, which has been rising by 10 percent a year since 1960. It now eats up 15 percent of GDP, and governments pay 45 percent of that total. The rise appears both inevitable, because of our aging population, and unstoppable, because the American people wouldn't have it any other way. When technology can give us longer life spans—with new hearts and hips and knees, new drugs for cancer and heart disease and AIDS, new machines to scan our insides for problems—we will continue to shell out for the best medicine has to offer. And because we refuse to junk our aging loved ones as if they were worn-out machines, we will spend an ever-rising portion of our health care dollars on the elderly.

Skyrocketing health-insurance premiums are bad enough. Because they consume an ever-increasing share of our profits and paychecks, however, they also erode our ability to pay taxes to support public spending on health care. Yet that very spending is exploding. In 1985, Medicaid cost $40 billion and consumed 11 percent of state budgets; today it costs $230 billion and consumes 20 percent. (Health insurance for state employees and the non-Medicaid poor takes another 10 percent.)

It's not hard to see why. The elderly made up less than 10 percent of Medicaid recipients in 2000, but they consumed 28.3 percent of spending. Medicare, which is exclusively for the elderly, cost $278 billion in 2003, nearly 10 times what it cost in 1970, even after adjusting for inflation. The cost of care associated with the graying of our population is simply eating government alive.

Meanwhile, other pressures give budget makers few places to cut. Education spending has risen steadily for 40 years; today it consumes 33 percent of the average state budget. But we can't compete in the global economy without better education, so our leaders resist major reductions. In an effort to reduce crime, we have imprisoned more than two million Americans—a *fourfold* increase in 25 years. But no one wants to see felons released onto the streets, so we won't make deep cuts in prison spending. And our public infrastructure of roads, bridges, airports, and water and sewer systems is in no condition to absorb cuts; if anything, we have deferred maintenance for so long that future costs will rise.

Since the fiscal storm broke, many governments have flailed about, grabbing any solution that could keep them afloat for another year. The tidal wave of red ink has triggered accounting gimmicks worthy of Enron: shifting next year's revenue into this fiscal year; pushing this year's spending onto next year's books; borrowing against future revenue to pay current costs. At least 20 states have sold their huge, 30-year tobacco settlement revenues at deep discounts to plug current deficits. As former congressman Bill Frenzel put it, "Politicians have more tricks than the CFO of Enron." Some government financial officers have even admitted, off the record, "If we were in the private sector, we'd be in jail."

When sleight of hand is no longer enough, our leaders have turned to across-the-board cuts, which weaken every program equally, regardless of its impact on citizens. When these are exhausted and real choices must be made, legislatures typically cut in an ad hoc and highly political fashion, based largely on which interest groups have the most muscle and scream the loudest. This process inevitably victimizes the weakest members of society, who have the least political clout. This is what the *Seattle Times* likened to "taking last year's family car and reducing its weight with a blowtorch and shears."

But as shortsighted or thoughtless as these tactics may be, they all obscure the fundamental flaw in the conventional approach to fiscal crisis. The true outrage is that traditional budget cutting focuses entirely on what we cut (or hide), while ignoring what we keep. It does little to improve the effectiveness of the 85 or 90 percent of public dollars that continue to be spent. It never broaches the question of how to maximize the value of the tax dollars we do collect.

Some conservatives are happy with this situation; they don't mind beggaring government. Many liberals plead for higher taxes to protect spending for the poor and other core constituencies. But virtually all ignore the 90 percent that remains. Few ask the most fundamental question: How can citizens get the most value for the taxes they do pay? Addressing this issue is neither liberal nor conservative—it is just plain common sense.

THE WASHINGTON STATE EXPERIENCE

Consider the recent experience of Washington State. In fiscal 2002 and 2003, the state's general-fund revenue declined for the first time in 30 years. Halfway through this period, Democratic governor Gary Locke and the legislature had to trim $1.5 billion and eliminate 1,340 jobs. The governor and his staff were extremely frustrated by the process.

"Every step we took, we asked ourselves, 'Why aren't we asking the right questions; why are we so focused on the cuts and not on the keeps?'" says Marty Brown, director of the Office of Financial Management (OFM). "We were missing something—we knew it in our guts."

The governor was tired of across-the-board cuts. He wanted to focus on the big question: What should state government do and what should it stop doing? In the upcoming biennium, he faced an estimated $2.1 billion deficit in the general fund—almost 10 percent—plus another $600 million in the health-services account. "Closing the $2 billion gap we face in the next biennium would require an across-the-board cut of 15 percent—if that's all we did," he announced. "And that is not what we are going to do. I don't want to thin the soup. I want state government to do a great job in fulfilling its highest priorities."

In August 2002, Locke's chief of staff asked our company, the Public Strategies Group (PSG), for help. We made him an "unreasonable" proposal. In the time available, only ten weeks, we were not going to help Washington find cuts equivalent to 10 to 15 percent of its general fund budget—at least not the traditional way. So we shifted the focus from spending cuts and tax increases to helping Governor Locke buy the best possible results for citizens with what remained.

Like most governments, Washington traditionally started with last year's budget and added money to cover inflation, caseload increases, and the like. Then it asked each agency to propose cuts. The agencies traditionally volunteered as little as they thought they could get away with, while padding costs to protect against the cuts they knew were inevitable. Then an army of analysts in the finance office combed through agency submissions looking for savings. As usual, the entire process was based on the assumption that no one could be trusted. More important, it accepted, "with little question, most of the status quo level of spending," says Wolfgang Opitz, deputy director of OFM. "Moreover, it led quickly to discussions about how fairly we've treated each agency's programs in the cut exercise."

In contrast, PSG proposed budgeting for *outcomes:* starting with the results citizens wanted, not the programs the agencies funded. We proposed to start not with last year's spending but with the outcomes that mattered most to the public. We urged the governor and his staff to focus not on how to cut 10 to 15 percent but on how to maximize the results produced with the remaining 85 to 90 percent. Governor Locke decided that this unreasonable approach was the only reasonable thing to do.

PSG helped the governor's budget staff design a process to answer five key questions:

- Is the real problem short or long term?
- How much are citizens willing to spend?
- What results do citizens want for their money?
- How much will the state spend to produce each of these results?
- How best can that money be spent to achieve each of the core results?

These five questions led to five key challenges.

1. Get a grip on the problem.

How you define a problem dictates how you approach its solution. Washington's fiscal staff were clearheaded about their dilemma. They defined the problem as the convergence of three forces: a deep economic recession that slashed revenues; permanent limits on revenue and spending growth imposed by antitax activists through statewide initiatives; and rising costs for the core activities of the state—"education, medication, and incarceration," as Marty Brown describes them. Of the three, only the recession's impact on revenue could be termed cyclical, likely to turn around someday. The other two were more or less permanent. Thus, they decided that solutions had to be more or less permanent.

2. Set the price of government.

This was the purview of a Guidance Team, made of up senior policy people, including Chief of Staff Fred Kiga, and several leaders from business and private think tanks. (Organized labor was invited to participate, but chose not to.) Its first big decision was to build the budget based on expected revenues under existing law, without new taxes. In early November, despite heavy lobbying by Locke, voters soundly defeated a gas tax increase to pay for long-needed transportation projects. This antitax reality—plus a fear that tax increases would further depress the state's economy—led the team to advise the governor against raising taxes.

3. Set the priorities of government.

Here the Guidance Team was assisted by a Staff Team, made up of senior people from the Office of Financial Management. Working together, they defined the key results they believed Washington's citizens most wanted from state government. The Guidance Team refined these into 10 desired outcomes, which the governor called the "Priorities of Government." They included improvements in:

- student achievement in elementary, middle, and high schools;
- the quality and productivity of the workforce;
- the value of a state college or university education;
- the health of Washington's citizens;
- the security of Washington's vulnerable children and adults;
- the vitality of businesses and individuals;
- statewide mobility of people, goods, information, and energy;
- the safety of people and property;
- the quality of Washington's priceless natural resources; and
- cultural and recreational opportunities.

4. Allocate available resources across the priorities.

The next challenge was to decide how to allocate the state's entire budget across the 10 results. The two teams set aside 10 percent for overhead functions, such as pension contributions and internal services, then parceled the rest out among the 10 results, using a citizen's point of view, based on perceived value, rather than an analysis of past practice. In some areas their choices reinforced past patterns, but in a few they made changes—allocating more resources to economic vitality, for example, and fewer to public safety.

5. Develop a purchasing plan for each result.

The Staff Team then put together 10 "Results Teams"—one for each outcome—made up of knowledgeable people from agencies involved in that policy area. "We asked them to forget the loyalties they have to the agencies they represent," said Governor Locke. "'Be like citizens,' we said. 'Tell us where to put the money, so we get the best results. Tell us what similar programs can be consolidated. Tell us what programs don't make a large enough difference in getting the results we want.'"

Each team started by choosing three indicators they would use to measure progress toward their outcome. Then they developed a strategy map, which used available evidence about "what really matters" to create an explicit cause-and-effect diagram showing the best ways to achieve the desired outcome. With a cause-and-effect theory in hand, they developed a general purchasing plan: the five or six key strategies they would use to produce that outcome.

This process stimulated a kind of creativity that is absent from traditional budget development. For example, the team dealing with K–12 education said they needed to purchase more early childhood education, start the shift to a "pay for skills" compensation system for teachers, and move away from across-the-board school funding toward targeted funding for those schools and kids most in need. The health team decided that the highest-impact strategies focused on *prevention:* mitigating environmental hazards, improving food sanitation, providing public health clinics, and the like. They proposed spending more on these strategies and less on health insurance for childless adults.

Next, the process turned to existing state activities—the place traditional budget processes start. Each Result Team was given a subset of the 1,300 state activities funded by the traditional budget. "Their mission," the governor explained, "was to get more yield on less acreage." To do so they had to put together a detailed purchasing plan, indicating four things:

- what they would buy—both new and existing activities;
- what else they would buy if they had more money;
- what they would eliminate first if they had less money;
- and what they would not buy.

Finally, the 10 Results Team leaders met together to talk about what they needed to purchase from one another. The higher-education team decided to use some of its funds to pay for better K–12 education, to better prepare its incoming students. Two teams jointly bought increased efforts to protect water quality, to improve both health and natural resource outcomes. Several teams decided to use some of their money to fund prisons, to reduce the number of low-risk prisoners who would have to be released early. This cross-team buying was necessary because the work of state government is so interconnected: Spending in one area contributes to outcomes in others.

Following this meeting, the Results Teams finalized their purchase plans.

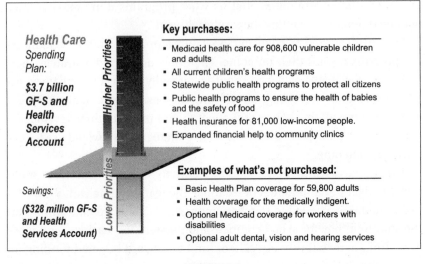

Health Care Spending Plan:

$3.7 billion GF-S and Health Services Account

Higher Priorities

Key purchases:

- Medicaid health care for 908,600 vulnerable children and adults
- All current children's health programs
- Statewide public health programs to protect all citizens
- Public health programs to ensure the health of babies and the safety of food
- Health insurance for 81,000 low-income people.
- Expanded financial help to community clinics

Savings:

($328 million GF-S and Health Services Account)

Lower Priorities

Examples of what's not purchased:

- Basic Health Plan coverage for 59,800 adults
- Health coverage for the medically indigent.
- Optional Medicaid coverage for workers with disabilities
- Optional adult dental, vision and hearing services

FIGURE I.1

These plans gave the Staff Team and Guidance Team a prioritized ranking of all existing activities of state government. Using these and similar rankings provided by the agencies, they made final recommendations to the governor. The result was, in effect, ten strategic programs for state government— linking results, indicators, strategies, and purchase plans.

The governor embraced the product and generally followed the purchase plans in finalizing his budget proposal. Under each of his 10 priority results, his budget showed those activities that would be purchased and those that would not. It was clear, easy to understand, and it explained in simple terms why some activities continued and others were eliminated. (See Figure I.1 for an example of that clarity.)

Governor Locke had warned that the budget would be painful, and it was. It proposed to eliminate health insurance for nearly 60,000 of the working poor; dental, hearing, and optometric coverage for poor adults on Medicaid; and 2,500 state jobs. If passed, it would eliminate cost-of-living increases for state employees, and suspend teacher pay increases and a $221 million class-size-reduction effort both mandated by citizen initiatives. University tuition would rise by 9 percent a year for two years; 1,200 low-risk felons would leave prison early; and a series of smaller programs would shut down.

Yet the response from the state's newspapers was overwhelmingly positive. As former chief of staff Joe Dear put it, "Never has such bad news been received so well."

"Gov. Gary Locke's budget is a big step forward for Washington," declared the *Seattle Times*.

"Few Washingtonians will find much to like about the brutal state spending plan Gov. Gary Locke recommended Tuesday," added the Tacoma *News Tribune*. "But as ugly as the result was, there's a lot to like about the way Locke and his staff arrived at it, using a new process that forced hard choices about the core priorities of state government."

After six years in office, Locke was widely seen as a status quo manager. But by setting clear priorities and making tough choices—while refusing to raise taxes or make across-the-board cuts—he transformed his image. When Republican John Carlson ran against him in 2000, his central message was that Locke had failed to show any leadership. Soon after the budget was released, Carlson wrote a column indicating that he had changed his mind. Locke's "budget for the next two years is a work of bold, impressive statecraft," he wrote. He told the *Seattle Times*, "He is willing to face down the most powerful interest groups in his own party to bring this budget in without a major tax increase. Genuine leadership is doing what must be done when you don't want to do it. And I think the governor is doing that."

In a late January survey, voters agreed. Sixty-four percent endorsed the following statement: "Whether or not I agree with all of the governor's budget recommendations, I respect his leadership and vision to solve the current problem and get the state's economy back on track." Only 29 percent disagreed.

The legislature also liked the new budget format. "It was astounding," says Finance Director Brown. "I've never been to a set of hearings where the reception was so positive, despite the amount of bad news we had to deliver." With the budget framed around 10 desired results and all activities listed in order of importance—including those that would survive and those that would be eliminated—legislators found the documents very clear.

One committee chair asked what would happen if a proposed revenue change in health were not approved, Opitz recalls. "I said, 'Just move the line up $389 million. That shows you what's still on the list and what's off.' There was no hemming and hawing. It made it very clear that our choice was probably better than cutting deeper into the Medicaid program."

In early April, when the Republican majority in the Senate presented its own budget, the first slide was titled, "Following the Governor's Lead." Despite deep differences between the parties over taxes and budget cuts, the legislature ultimately passed a budget that was remarkably close to Governor Locke's original proposal. Legislators approved Locke's major sentencing reform in criminal justice and his proposed delay in initiatives that would have reduced class sizes in K–12 and guaranteed automatic pay increases for teachers. They also agreed to amend another public-initiative-backed plan to expand coverage in the state basic health plan in order to allow its revenue to go toward current programs. And they required that the next biennial budget be structured around the 10 Priorities of Government, with outcome measures for each one and for each activity proposed.

Public reaction was similar. "When we've taken this public, no matter what the setting—business, labor, social services advocates, health care, the classroom, the Rotary meeting—people understand what we're doing and not doing in a much more fundamental way than ever before," according to Opitz. "When they say, 'Well, I don't like that cut,' I say, 'Okay, then what from above this line do you not want to do?' And the response is usually 'Oh. . . . Well, I'm learning to like the cut a little more now.' It seems to be helping resubscribe everyone to the basic business of state government."

Perhaps most important, Budgeting for Outcomes can help public leaders win back some of the support government has lost in recent decades. The Everett *Daily Herald* put it well:

> *The public is not in a forgiving mood. It still holds a grudge for a government it sees as wasteful and unresponsive. Locke's plan, or one like it, might be a good step toward proving otherwise. The more thrifty government becomes, the more generous voters might be at the ballot box.*

Washington State has not finished its work. It has much more to do to maximize the results citizens get for the $24 billion they still spend every two years. Because time was so short, the governor held back some of the more far-reaching reform proposals for further work. He proposed a joint legislative–executive study of the K–12 financing system, for instance, to examine the options more carefully and build the political support necessary for reform. The finance office and Results Teams plan to deepen their reexamination of other strategies to produce the 10 results, in preparation for the next budget cycle. And the agencies will develop outcome and output measures for each activity, so the next budget can include performance targets for every activity funded.

But the Outcome Budget has opened a door, and Governor Locke fully intends to drag his state through it. The goal is not just to save money, but to foster strategic thinking and big reforms that will help government produce better outcomes for less money. And that is precisely what the American people want.

SMARTER GOVERNMENT

As Washington State demonstrates, new ways of doing the public's business already exist. This book will describe them, showing not only how vital services can survive the permanent fiscal crisis, but how leaders can turn that crisis into an opportunity to reinvent the way their bureaucracies work.

Our prescription begins with the five critical decisions Washington State made:

1. **Getting a Grip on the Problem:** Is it short or long term? Is it driven by revenue or expenses, or both?
2. **Setting the Price of Government:** Determining how much citizens are willing to pay.
3. **Setting the Priorities of Government:** Deciding which results citizens value most.
4. **Setting the Price of Each Priority:** Deciding how much the government will spend to produce each of these outcomes.
5. **Purchasing the Priorities:** Deciding how best to produce the desired results at the price citizens are willing to pay.

Once these decisions have focused attention squarely on buying better results for citizens, the 10 approaches described below provide the means. Through smarter sizing, spending, management, and work processes, they make it possible to produce the desired results at the set price, by increasing the value created for every dollar spent.

1. Strategic Reviews: Divesting to Invest.

Because time is short during budget season, smart leaders create ongoing review processes—outside the budget process—to develop new strategies and eliminate programs that are not central to their core purposes or are no longer valuable to citizens. There are many tools they can use to comb through every organization, from top to bottom, including program reviews, sunset reviews, special commissions, and subsidy reviews.

2. Consolidation.

Politicians love to merge organizations, because it looks like they're taking action to save money. But simply moving boxes on an organization chart can actually make matters worse, increasing costs while sowing confusion that hampers performance. A much more powerful alternative is to consolidate funding streams and "steering" authority, so steering (policy) organizations can purchase results from any "rowing" organizations—public or private—that can best produce them. Consider the Pinellas County Juvenile Welfare Board, in the Tampa–St. Petersburg area. As we will describe in Chapter 5, the board uses $46 million a year from a dedicated property tax to contract with some 60 different not-for-profit organizations to improve outcomes for poor children. It does no rowing itself, but these 60 providers offer a wide array of services, from child-care centers to parenting skills to teen centers to residential treatment services. The Juvenile Welfare Board measures their performance, weeds out the least effective, and moves money to strategies and organizations that demonstrate the greatest impact.

3. Rightsizing.

Some organizations work better when reduced in size, but others are crippled. The keys to success are to find the right size, then to make sure your organization has the right mix of skills to maximize the value delivered. Eliminating management layers and closing regional offices can help your organization find the right size, while human-capital planning can help it develop the right skills. Consider the Iowa Department of Transportation, which eliminated 7 construction offices, 5 maintenance offices, and 27 maintenance garages during the recent fiscal crisis. It cut 403 positions (11 percent of its workforce), increasing the average span of control from one manager for every 9 employees to one for every 14. To protect services like snow plowing and highway maintenance, the department bought new technology and cross-trained employees, so the same workers now handle both construction and maintenance. The bottom line: $35 million in annual savings.

4. Buying Services Competitively.

The fastest way to save money and increase value is to force public institutions to compete. Nobody who doesn't own one thinks monopoly is good for business. Why should it be any different in the public sector? When Steve Goldsmith was elected mayor of Indianapolis during the last fiscal crisis, he decided to make public agencies bid against private firms for the right to continue delivering public services. Over the next four years he bid out more than 30 services, from garbage pickup to operation of the city's wastewater treatment system. The average amount saved the first time a service was bid competitively was *25 percent*. Over seven years, competition saved Indianapolis more than $120 million.

5. Rewarding Performance, Not Good Intentions.

If public-sector managers don't know what they're getting for their money, chances are they aren't getting it. The solution is to set performance targets at all levels, measure performance against them, and reward those who improve. In a time of fiscal crisis, however, positive outcomes aren't enough. The new imperative is improving outcomes for less money: value for dollars. One simple tool is "gainsharing," for instance. The public-sector equivalent of profit sharing, it gives teams that cut costs while maintaining or improving quality a portion of the savings they generate, as financial bonuses. In the late 1990s, when managers at the Seattle area's wastewater treatment operation agreed to let employees keep half the savings they generated, total savings over four years amounted to $2.5 million, with no reduction in service levels or effluent quality.

6. Smarter Customer Service: Putting Customers in the Driver's Seat.

When public organizations let their customers choose between providers, rather than imposing services on them, they can achieve much greater customer satisfaction at less cost. With some services, the Internet even makes self-service possible, at enormous savings. But consider a low-tech service like care for developmentally disabled children. During the 1990s, Minnesota's Dakota County stopped paying agencies for services and instead provided grants directly to families. The families chose the services they wanted, subject to certain controls, to make sure they used the money responsibly. This dramatically improved customer satisfaction, because families could now make decisions that made sense for them—like having one parent quit work to care for a child, rather than using a caregiver paid by the county. Everyone was better off, and the county saved money. The innovation was so successful that it was adopted statewide.

7. Don't Buy Mistrust—Eliminate It.

The sad truth of bureaucracy is that 20 percent of government spending is designed merely to control the other 80 percent. The ruling assumption is that most of us, given the opportunity, will lie, cheat, and steal. Not only does this approach undermine performance, it is incredibly expensive. The smarter move is to first win voluntary compliance by simplifying the rules, working in partnership with compliers, making the process of compliance easier, and creating incentives that reward compliance while keeping stiff penalties for those who still refuse to comply.

Ten years ago, for example, Occupational Safety and Health Administration (OSHA) officials in Maine were intensely frustrated by the failure of their traditional inspect-and-fine approach. While they won gold medals from Washington for issuing the most citations and fines, Maine's workplace safety records were the worst in the nation. So they decided to try something different: They asked the 200 employers with the highest volume of injury claims—45 percent of the state's total—to create employee teams that would survey hazards in their plants and correct most of them within 12 months. As long as the company was making a good-faith effort, OSHA would forgo its traditional inspections and fines. Over the previous eight years, OSHA inspectors had identified 37,000 hazards at 1,316 work sites. In the new program's first two years, employee teams identified 174,331 workplace hazards and corrected 118,671 of them. Two of every three companies decreased their injury and illness rates, and payable workers' compensation claims by the 200 firms dropped by 47.3 percent—far outpacing declines in other companies.

8. Using Flexibility to Get Accountability.

From the governments of New Zealand and the United Kingdom to the U.S. Education Department's Office of Federal Student Aid (FSA), examples abound of "performance-based organizations" that have willingly accepted greater accountability in return for freedom from rules and regulations that impede performance. Charter schools use the same formula, with even more independence and accountability: They are free from many state and district rules, and most operate independently of any district, but they can be closed down if they don't perform. The state of Iowa is even working on a "freedom communities" initiative, in which the state would give groups of local cities and/or counties new flexibilities if they modernized their structures and created mechanisms to measure performance and report it to the public.

9. Making Administrative Systems Allies, Not Enemies.

All organizations are creatures—or prisoners—of their internal systems. Traditional budget, accounting, personnel, procurement, and audit systems are nests of red tape that tie employees up in knots. The messages these systems send about following bureaucratic rules are much more powerful than any leadership exhortations to perform better. To get lasting improvements in performance, public leaders have to modernize and streamline these systems. The payoff is dramatic savings: Two major procurement reform bills passed by Congress, in 1994 and 1996, had already saved $12 billion by the end of 1997. Milwaukee's Purchasing Department was able to cut its staff by nearly two-thirds and its budget by more than 55 percent by simplifying processes, investing in technology, and giving more authority to departments. Montgomery County, Maryland, managed to shrink its accounts payable staff by more than half simply by giving departments authority to pay invoices in amounts up to $5,000 rather than sending them to central accounts payable.

10. Smarter Work Processes: Tools from Industry.

To do more with less, organizations must ultimately change the way they work. Some of this involves wholesale substitution of new methods and strategies. But much of it requires that existing work processes of all kinds— from street repair to eligibility determination to tax collection—be streamlined. There are many ways to do this, but we will describe three of the most powerful, all of them tools first developed in industry. Total Quality Management trains and empowers small teams of employees to make continual improvements in their work processes. WorkOuts, invented at General Electric, bring people together for three to five days to solve problems; leaders set a time limit for finding answers, approve or reject recommendations on the spot, and keep everyone on the job until it is done. And Business Process Reengineering is radical, "clean sheet" redesign of complex, large-scale business processes, to increase their efficiency and quality in dramatic ways.

The rest of this book explores these 5 key questions and 10 approaches in depth, then concludes by discussing the kind of leadership necessary to implement them.

The stakes are huge. There are certain basic results that our society demands if it is to remain viable. If we fail—if we continue to lose the battle for public support—the consequences will be all too real.

Nothing is more important in the global marketplace than the skill level of a nation's or region's workforce, yet in our public schools, roughly 30 percent of all students have not achieved even the basic level of proficiency in reading and math.

Public safety is fundamental to a civilized society, and threats of terrorism add frightening new challenges. Yet America's cities and states are laying off policemen and slashing spending for teams that respond to hazardous materials and chemical or biological weapons.

Mobility of people and goods is essential to any region's economic health, yet congestion is endemic in many metropolitan areas.

Higher education is now a necessary ticket to middle-class life, but it is increasingly being priced out of the reach of average Americans.

Forty-four million Americans are without health insurance, yet the American people don't trust government to intervene without making a mess of things.

The 10 warmest years in the twentieth century all occurred during the last 15 years of the century, yet our environmental programs do little to offset global warming.

Spending on Social Security, public pensions, and health care is devouring our public dollars at a frightening pace. Yet our businesses and citizens will tolerate few tax increases, because skyrocketing health-care costs are squeezing them harder every year. The collision between these realities—the heart of the fiscal storm—is already forcing us to strip away valuable public programs.

Given fierce public resistance to tax increases, we can't solve all these problems by raising taxes. Nor can we continue to borrow without undermining our economic well-being and mortgaging our children's future. Yet doing nothing will mean educational decline, impaired public safety, crumbling highways and bridges, polluted air and water, and millions of people defenseless against disease.

Doing nothing will also undermine the sense of community that binds us together. Those who can afford it will take care of themselves, retreating to private schools and gated communities with private security, and everyone else will be left to fend for themselves.

This does not seem to bother many on the right, who still appear to be fighting King George III over the inherent "tyranny" of government. It does bother most on the left, but their only solutions seem to be more spending on dysfunctional public systems that cry out for reform. For too long, both left and right have given us false dichotomies and dead-end choices.

A majority of the American people want a third way. Given the option, they would often vote for "none of the above." In fact, by removing themselves from the political process through low turnouts, that is exactly what they have done. Many are in a "commonsense majority" of independent voters, moderate Republicans, and New Democrats. They don't want to cut spending so far that they destroy our public institutions, but they don't want government benefits at any price. They want government to provide what only the public sector can provide, such as security, national defense, infrastructure, equal-opportunity education, regulation of the marketplace, and social insurance for the poor, aged, and disabled. But they want their money's worth. They want value for dollars. When they can't get it, they often opt for tax cuts and private services. When they do get value from public institutions, however, they are often willing to invest in them.

That citizens want value for their money is no mystery. We all want as much value as we can get from each dollar we spend—including what we spend on government. The price and value of government are up against the price and value of housing, food, clothing, health care, and countless other goods and services that meet people's needs. The price of government is limited, therefore, by the value that citizens want—and get—from government, compared with the value they want and get elsewhere. Government can win this competition for public support only by delivering more value per dollar.

The rising costs of health care, Social Security, public pensions, prisons, and interest on the public debt have put the price of government under immense upward pressure. Yet that pressure has met enormous resistance to broad-based tax increases. President Bush and the Republican Congress have pushed the federal price of government down to its lowest level in 50 years (see Chapter 2), by cutting taxes and borrowing the difference. Spending borrowed money may create the illusion that we're getting more for our money, but it is virtually impossible at the state and local levels, because such massive borrowing is nominally illegal. Yet resistance to tax increases remains strong, because too many voters feel they aren't getting value for their tax dollars.

This fiscal collision is undermining vital state and local services, while generating massive federal deficits. These circumstances suggest that some tax increases are inevitable. But given the political realities, we believe that our governments and school districts must dramatically improve the services they offer, if citizens are to willingly pay a higher price. *Any significant change in the price of government is impossible until the majority of Americans feel they are getting real value for their tax dollars.* And the only way to accomplish that is to reinvent the way we do the public's business. Our public institutions must learn to work harder, but more important, they must learn to work smarter.

Native Americans have many sayings, and one of the wisest is this: When you're riding a dead horse, the best strategy is to dismount.

You don't change riders.

You don't reorganize the herd.

You don't put together a blue-ribbon commission of veterinarians.

And you don't spend more money on feed.

You get off and find yourself a new horse.

Too many public leaders, from school districts to cities, from counties and states to the federal government, have been getting by for the past two decades with "dead horse" solutions. But getting by is not good enough. Getting by has crippled our public services and withered the public's confidence.

During these same two decades, pioneering leaders at all levels of government have been inventing solutions that work. They have been finding new horses. Today, as the permanent fiscal storm batters us, we no longer have the luxury of ignoring them. It is time for the rest of America's leaders to saddle up and ride.

PART ONE

SMARTER BUDGETING

The Five Decisions
That Matter Most

ONE

Getting a Grip
on the Problem

The Minnesota budget debate of 2002–2003 was a classic tale of modern government in action. The story begins in late 2001, when Governor Jesse Ventura got the bad news: The forecast showed a looming budget shortfall of $1.95 billion for the years 2002–2003. For the 2004–2005 biennium, the shortfall would grow to $2.5 billion.

In January 2002, Ventura proposed his solution: a combination of cuts and new taxes that he called "The Big Fix." The plan would trim state government spending by $700 million over 17 months, raise taxes by $400 million, and draw on $667 million in budget reserves. Included in this tough medicine were cuts in state and local services, layoffs of state workers, and sales tax increases on gasoline, tobacco, and some services.

But Ventura did not stop there. He also proposed a four-year plan to address the recurring deficits that were projected for 2004 and beyond, deficits he said would occur even if the state's economy turned around almost immediately. The remedy included additional cuts of $1.35 billion in 2004–2005, along with tax increases of a comparable size.

Unfortunately, Ventura's call fell on the ears of politicians deafened by the sound of upcoming elections. Legislative leaders from both parties said that action on the 2004–2005 problem should await a second economic forecast to be released in late February 2002. As for the immediate shortfall, Democrats and Republicans joined forces to pass their own budget, one filled with dodges and gimmicks designed to create the illusion of a fix. The sleights of hand included draining reserves, masking future costs by stipulating that inflation would no longer be factored into projections of state spending, and using other accounting tricks that changed nothing but made the numbers *look* better.

Despite the fiscal illusions, leaders from both the House and Senate contended that their plan was the only responsible, centrist alternative, and they united in condemning the governor's more draconian measures. With a straight face, one Republican legislator asserted that "politics had nothing to do with this," even though both the Senate majority leader, Democrat Roger Moe, and the House majority leader, Republican Tim Pawlenty, were running for governor. Both men sought to use their quick agreement as evidence that they were not just unifiers, but decisive leaders.

"We are proud of the fact that in almost record time, historic time, we were able to reach an agreement of this magnitude," Pawlenty said.

Moe agreed, adding sagely, "One of the responsibilities of leadership is to solve problems and help chart a course. The sooner we act, the sooner our state can begin its economic recovery."

But at least one would-be gubernatorial candidate, Democratic senator Becky Lourey, took a different perspective. "This is Enron economics," she said, flatly. "They're using every hidden shift that can be found, pretending there is no inflation, robbing from tomorrow."

The governor vetoed the legislature's budget. Then, despite a new forecast showing even greater shortfalls, the legislature overrode the veto.

Moody's Investor Service changed its advisory on the state's financial outlook from "stable" to "negative." Estimating that the 2004–2005 deficit would approach $3 billion, Moody's warned that the situation demanded "dramatic changes in both the state's revenue structure and expenditure levels."

Then the campaign for governor began in earnest, and any hope of grappling with the fiscal crisis was put on hold. Governor Ventura announced that he would not seek reelection, leaving the field to Moe and Pawlenty. Tim Penny, a former Democratic congressman, stepped forward as the candidate of Ventura's Independence Party.

Penny insisted that Ventura's tough medicine had been right all along, and that the state's financial woes would only get bigger because of what the legislature had done. But Moe and Pawlenty stuck to their game plan, waiting for yet another "next" forecast—one that, conveniently, would take place just *after* the November election. Until that all-important budget projection was in, Pawlenty said, it made no sense to suggest cuts that might not be necessary if the economy were to improve.

After a campaign in many ways overshadowed by the sudden death of Minnesota's Senator Paul Wellstone, Pawlenty won the governorship with 43 percent of the vote.

Three weeks later, the much anticipated new forecast was released. The Minneapolis *Star Tribune* described the situation this way:

> *State budget officials unveiled news Wednesday that was worse than anyone had expected: Minnesota faces a staggering $4.56 billion projected deficit over the next two and a half years—nearly 14 percent of its budget, or about $1,000 for every man, woman, and child in the state.*
>
> *That figure includes, despite Herculean efforts last year to balance the state budget for 2002–03, a new shortfall of $356 million for 2003. That immediate gap must be met before the fiscal year ends June 30.*
>
> *And unlike last year, when state officials raided reserves to cushion Minnesotans against the blow of impending deficits, this time the state must weather the crisis with virtually nothing in the bank.*

The illusion of a solution was dispelled. Grim reality hit home, the fiscal storm that Ventura had warned about one year before began its deluge.

DEADLY DECEPTIONS

Unfortunately, Minnesota is the norm, not the exception. For the past few years, politicians in far too many cities, states, and counties—not to speak of Washington, D.C.—have followed the same shortsighted "clap-if-you-believe-in-Tinker Bell" approach. The creative chicanery of public leaders is boundless, but they tend to rely particularly on seven deadly deceptions:

1. Rob Peter to pay Paul.

Most budgets are made up of multiple accounts. The account that gets the most attention is called the general fund. When that general fund gets in trouble, politicians start eyeing "off budget" funds as resources to be mined. New York helped balance its budget in 1992 by transferring the cost of running the Erie Canal from the general fund ("on budget") to the Thruway Authority ("off budget"). Similarly, in 2003, Massachusetts transferred management of Boston's Hynes Convention Center and the Boston Common Parking Garage to the state pension fund, to lower its cash contribution from the general fund. Technically, this allowed the state to show a savings of $175 million.

Sometimes money saved in a special account, such as building funds targeted for future construction, can be transferred into the general fund as well. Robbing Peter to pay Paul can make the budget look better this year, but the same hole will reappear next year, when Peter and Paul will both be worse off.

2. Use accounting tricks to lie about spending or revenue.

As the Enron debacle showed, accounting presents many dangerous choices to leaders who are all too human. Quick-fix accounting gimmicks include pretending (or even requiring) that money you expect to receive early next year will actually come in late this year. The opposite side of the coin is to pretend (or even require) that expenses planned for this year will be made, technically, next year. For example, states tell districts that are expecting a school-aid payment in May (this fiscal year) that they will get it in July (next fiscal year), thus making this year's expenses look smaller. At the same time, they tell retailers who normally submit their June sales tax receipts in July (next fiscal year) to do so in June, thus making this year's revenue look larger. It's all legal and properly accounted for, but it's a lie.

3. Borrow.

Even when the general fund is legally prohibited from being in debt, governments find ways to borrow. New York City mastered this dubious art in the 1970s, when it piled up so much debt that it landed in receivership. Both the city and state of New York are still trying to figure out when and how to pay off all the bonds issued back when New York truly was, in former mayor John Lindsay's famous phrase, "Fun City."

Facing a $5 billion deficit for fiscal year 2004, Illinois recently turned to pension bonding to help "fix" its operating budget. The plan: The state would borrow $10 billion, use part of the proceeds to cover its general fund contribution to the pension systems (taking a nearly $2 billion bite out of its budget deficit), and use the rest to finance a portion of the state's $36 billion unfunded pension liability. The pension funds put the bond proceeds into higher-risk investments, hoping that they would provide a higher return than the cost of the bonds. Writing in *Government Finance Review,* Professor James Burnham described this practice as "risk arbitrage." Others might call it just plain foolish.

A *Chicago Tribune* columnist put it this way: "Without so much as a drum roll, the state doubled its long-term debt in the hope that future investment returns on the borrowing will exceed future interest payments. Do not try that, fellow citizens, with a home equity loan."

California has proven that the "what, me worry?" politics of borrowing works for both parties. In 2003, after months of stalemate, the legislature finally passed a $99 billion budget with *$10.7 billion* of borrowing—all of which appeared to be unconstitutional. Following Democratic governor Gray Davis's recall, the new Republican governor, Arnold Schwarzenegger, immediately endorsed borrowing $15 billion more as part of his "budget balancing" plan. The rating agencies reduced California's rating to junk-bond status.

In 1996, the city of Pittsburgh faced an annual deficit somewhere between $30 and $40 million. City leaders had already dug themselves a big hole, using as a shovel their funding of the municipal pension plan. In response to a 1984 state mandate that set minimal funding standards for pensions, the city opted for a lighter funding burden in the short term, in exchange for payments that increased each year over the 40-year term of the plan. By 1996, their fund had a mere $118 million in assets, compared to its unfunded liability of $519 million. This was bad enough for a city with an operating budget of only $290 million, but the real kicker was that by 2024, the last of the graduated payments to the fund would be $115 million.

In 1998, as that nightmare drew ever closer, city leaders chose to bet the farm: They floated a $256 million pension bond and invested 60 percent of the proceeds in the stock market. James Burnham, writing in *Government Finance Review,* likened this to a poker player who is already in the hole borrowing so he can double his bets on the next hand. When the stock market collapsed, they lost their shirts. By 2003, the city was flirting with bankruptcy. The mayor restructured the city's debt, laid off 700 workers, and asked the state for "distressed municipality status," which would entitle it to special aid. Standard and Poor's lowered Pittsburgh's rating to junk-bond status.

4. Sell off assets.

When times are tight, it is popular to sell surplus buildings, land, or other assets, then use the proceeds to plug a hole in the operating budget by treating the real estate money as though it were "normal" revenue. The problem is that it's a onetime plug and the same hole shows up again next year. Wisconsin, which had been set to collect $5.9 billion in tobacco settlement money over 25 years, sold this asset to produce immediate income of only $1.275 billion to plug an operating deficit. By April 2003, 34 states and counties had followed suit, raising $15.7 billion.

In 1995, rather than solve the city's structural problems, Pittsburgh's leaders sold their water and sewer works to the off-balance-sheet entity that operated it, the Pittsburgh Water and Sewer Authority. Then in 1996, they sold $51.2 million in tax and sewage liens—money due that they had not yet been able to collect—for $32.2 million. Every year since, they have relied on one-shot revenue sources to balance the budget. Each of these onetime gimmicks only put off the crisis for one more year. Meanwhile, says Rowan Miranda, a former Pittsburgh budget officer, they "delayed the realization that the ship is sinking."

5. Make something up.

A budget is really just a forecast, a statement of expected revenues and expenses. If done right it can be a serviceable estimate. But in the end, every budget is based on assumptions, and you can make it look better or worse simply by changing those assumptions. If you expect 1,000 new students to enroll in your schools but you assume (for budget purposes) only 900, you have reduced the basis for your estimate of new expenses by 10 percent. If you believe the economy will grow by 4 percent and revenues along with it but you budget for 5 percent, you have increased your expected new revenue by 25 percent.

Ronald Reagan's approach in 1982 was a classic example of making the budget "work" by working the assumptions. To justify massive tax cuts, his budget director, David Stockman, forecast 5 percent growth for 1982. According to "supply side" theory, this would help create a $28 billion surplus by 1986. As it turned out, the gross domestic product (GDP) *fell* by 2 percent that year—and the largest deficits since World War II soon followed. In his memoirs, Stockman admitted that the entire effort, sardonically nicknamed "Rosy Scenario" by White House insiders, was a fraud.

6. Nickel and dime employees.

Too often, the political response to budget problems is symbolic. Leaders order coffee pots unplugged, travel budgets slashed, and consultants banned. To save energy, they force workers to endure hotter offices in summer and colder offices in winter. Some even outlaw potted plants. In Missouri last year, the governor ordered that every other light bulb in government buildings be unscrewed. While such actions may send a message, they have two critical consequences: They don't save much money, and they kill morale. If a job truly demands travel but travel is ruled out, employees become frustrated and cynical. In Portland, Oregon, where police were denied overtime pay, some undercover officers showed their displeasure by dropping whatever they were doing at the moment their shift ended—even while tailing suspects or executing warrants.

7. Delay maintenance and replacement of assets (and rely on hope).

When our own budgets get tight, we sometimes don't take our car in for its regular oil change, or we don't fix the crack in the driveway. We can save a little money now, but if a missed oil change leads to overheating, we can crack the engine block. The people who make Fram oil filters said it well: "You can pay me now or pay me later." Add your imagination to the dry language of an Alaska Department of Administration budget proposal, and you can see how serious the consequences of waiting until later can be:

> Currently one of the highest priority projects on the deferred maintenance list is the Juneau State Office Building (JSOB) elevator systems replacement and upgrade. For the last ten years these elevator systems have experienced serious problems and significant down time. Over the last five years the problems have significantly worsened. In the last year the majority of the elevators have been inoperable. These elevators need to be upgraded for fire and life-safety and code compliance, to ensure they are operational, and to ensure that users are not injured.

BUDGET BASICS

Using accounting tricks and onetime money in the face of long-term deficits is a recipe for disaster. Quick fixes plug budget gaps without actually solving deeper structural problems. They allow politicians to avoid painful measures such as raising taxes or cutting popular government services. But avoidance becomes addictive, and the real problems fester and grow, ultimately requiring even more painful solutions.

As every recovering addict knows, the first step on the road to recovery is to get beyond denial and deception. If we are to master our fiscal problems, our leaders must get a grip on the real problems they face. They must understand—and communicate to the rest of us—how much of the problem is short-term, due to a recession or other temporary problem, and how much is long-term, due to the permanent fiscal crisis.

For many of us, these budget crises are, as Minnesota's Governor Pawlenty put it, "a brain buster." The numbers are huge, and the complexities multiply like our worst nightmare of a "word problem" back in seventh grade. But there is nothing inherently mystifying about a budget. In fact, we can get to the heart of the matter by paying attention to only five numbers:

1. Starting balance: How much we have in our accounts at the beginning of the fiscal year.
2. Revenues: How much we think we will take in.
3. Expenses: How much we think we will spend.

4. Surplus or deficit: The difference between revenues and expenses.

5. Ending balance: How much we think we will have in our accounts at the end of the fiscal year.

To be clear about our fiscal reality, however, we have to project these five numbers over at least five years, as shown in Table 1.1.

TABLE 1.1   Five by Five Basic Budget

	This Year	*Next Year*	*Year 3*	*Year 4*	*Year 5*
1. Starting Balance					
2. Revenues					
3. Expenses					
4. Surplus/(*Deficit*)					
5. Ending Balance					

Why five years? Because short-term budgeting is an invitation to long-term deception. The last year in a budget estimate is a corner we can't see around. The most popular budget deceptions involve making everything up to that corner look good, while just around the corner, hidden from public scrutiny, the bottom drops out. That was Governor Ventura's argument during the 2002 election in Minnesota. Everyone else wanted to pretend the trap door wasn't there.

Using a "five-by-five" budget extends that blind corner far enough out so that most of the worst surprises are brought into view. But five years is, in fact, a minimum. If lawmakers have planted a time bomb in the budget six years out, it will take a seven-year projection to see the effects. Some of the best-managed governments project every budget line out 10 years.

Of course, no one can make perfectly accurate five- or ten-year economic predictions. Estimates are just that, *estimates*—economic models that allow us to reality-test budget assumptions. The numbers may not pan out, but they *will* alert us to future problems we are creating through decisions we make today.

Is It Structural or Cyclical or Both?

The five-by-five budget tool can reduce any 300-page budget to some very simple arithmetic. But its main virtue is the way it helps people get a grip on fiscal realities.

To begin with, it helps clarify what people mean when they talk about a budget that is "balanced." The commonsense assumption is that a balanced budget means that revenues will at least equal expenses, but politicians often mean something quite different. To them, a "balanced budget" is often any budget that has an ending balance greater than zero. This definition still allows them to spend more than they take in, provided they have enough in their starting balance to make up the difference. That kind of balance—spending more than annual revenues but making up the difference with reserves—can work. But if spending continues to run ahead of revenues once the reserves are gone, disaster lies around the corner.

The five-by-five budget also helps politicians, public managers, and taxpayers understand the nature of their problems: whether they are cyclical, meaning short-term, or structural, meaning long-term; and whether they are caused by revenue shortfalls, spending increases, or both.

A cyclical problem is one that goes away over time, usually because the economy improves and tax revenues increase. In the example shown in Table 1.2, a short-term pause in revenue growth plunges the budget into deficit. (The numbers in parentheses are negative.) By Year 4, the budget is back in balance, with revenues equal to expenses, but not before it has accumulated significant debt. The remedies are temporary revenue or expense measures to avoid digging this kind of hole. As the budget comes back into balance, these temporary measures can "blink off."

TABLE 1.2 Cyclical Budget Problem

	This Year	*Next Year*	*Year 3*	*Year 4*	*Year 5*
Starting Balance	$100 million	$100 million	*($1.9 billion)*	*($3.2 billion)*	*($3.2 billion)*
Revenues	$18 billion	$18 billion	$20.7 billion	$24 billion	$27 billion
Expenses	$18 billion	$20 billion	$22 billion	$24 billion	$26 billion
Surplus/(*Deficit*)	$0	*($2 billion)*	*($1.3 billion)*	$0	$1 billion
Ending Balance	$100 million	*($1.9 billion)*	*($3.2 billion)*	*($3.2 billion)*	*($2.2 billion)*

A structural problem is one that persists—and may even get worse—despite economic recovery. In the example shown in Table 1.3, revenues grow at a moderate rate, but expenditures spike upward, leading to a growth in annual deficits. Here, the problem demands permanent changes in revenue or spending, or both, if the budget is to be brought back into balance.

Most budget problems are a combination of cyclical and structural elements; most will require a combination of measures to resolve them.

TABLE 1.3 Structural Budget Problem

	This Year	*Next Year*	*Year 3*	*Year 4*	*Year 5*
Starting Balance	$100 million	$100 million	($1.1 billion)	($2.8 billion)	($6.4 billion)
Revenues	$18 billion	$19.8 billion	$21.8 billion	$23.9 billion	$26.2 billion
Expenses	$18 billion	$21 billion	$23.5 billion	$27.5 billion	$31 billion
Surplus/(Deficit)	$0	($1.2 billion)	($1.7 billion)	($3.6 billion)	($4.8 billion)
Ending Balance	$100 million	($1.1 billion)	($2.8 billion)	($6.4 billion)	($11.2 billion)

FISCAL FIRST AID

In a fiscal crisis leaders must act—and soon. Here are a dozen examples of fiscal first aid that can be applied immediately, to slow the bleeding, and that do not involve deception or denial and thus do not create even greater problems down the road.

1. Delay program expansions to a date certain—actual delays, not accounting delays.
2. Suspend tax credits and deductions until a date certain.
3. Transfer money from the state's clearinghouse for unclaimed property.
4. Require employees to take unpaid days off, otherwise known as a furlough.
5. Close tax loopholes.
6. Institute amnesty programs to collect overdue taxes. Those who participate pay past-due taxes and fees but do not have to pay fines or interest. Moreover, the state, city, or county promises not to file charges against anyone who pays up during a grace period. In 1983, Massachusetts Governor Michael Dukakis used a 90-day amnesty to bring in $84 million.
7. Hire tax auditors, crack down on tax scofflaws, and enhance penalties on nonfilers and those who underpay taxes. Dukakis turned misdemeanors into felonies, increased audits, brought in private collection agencies, and revoked the licenses and public contracts of any businesses owing back taxes. The commissioner of revenue confiscated yachts and padlocked businesses, including some of Boston's most popular restaurants. Voluntary compliance shot up, and Massachusetts's permanent revenue base increased by roughly 5 percent. By 1986, 17 states had copied the Massachusetts program.

8. Change tax laws to avoid losing revenue due to congressional action. When President Bush cut income tax rates, for example, Governor Howard Dean of Vermont convinced his legislature to uncouple its system from federal tax rates, so the state would lose no revenue.

9. Free up cash for the general fund by issuing general obligation and/or revenue bonds to finance capital projects that were previously financed with general fund money. (There is nothing wrong with prudent borrowing for capital projects that will provide jobs and stimulate the economy, particularly during a recession.)

10. Refinance existing bonds at lower interest rates.

11. Step up fundraising for public institutions. In 2002, while forced to raise tuition and fees by 22 percent, the University of Massachusetts raised $98 million from private sources. In New York City, Mayor Michael Bloomberg raised $14 million for city projects during his first 13 months in office and reactivated Public Private Initiatives, which enlists wealthy individuals to sponsor civic projects.

12. Encourage early retirement. Many governments have reduced their payrolls by providing incentives—one-time bonuses, allowing employees to start collecting at least a portion of their pensions at age 55, and so on.

GETTING A GRIP ON FORECASTING

You can't get a grip on your fiscal problem if you can't get a grip on the five-by-five budget described above. And the utility of the five-by-five budget depends upon the quality of your forecasts for revenue and spending. Forecasting is *not* easy: Forecasts are filled with uncertainty and are subject to challenges to their credibility.

To begin with, forecasters need to get a grip on volatility in revenues and spending. On the revenue side, three things affect volatility: the mix of revenue sources, the breadth of the revenue base, and the economy.

Government revenues generally come from:

- Taxes paid by individuals and businesses based on property value, sales, income, or payroll.
- Charges and fees collected for things such as tuition, licenses, fines, parking fees, and customs duties.

- Transfers from other governments—from the federal government to states and localities, and from state governments to schools, cities, and counties.

The interdependence created by transfers from one level to the next means that volatility in revenue at one level will be felt at the others. When the federal government sneezes, the states catch a cold, and when the states get sick, local governments take to their beds.

Huge variations exist in government revenue sources across the country. For example, New Hampshire has no state sales or income tax but relies heavily on both statewide and local property taxes, plus a host of other taxes and charges. South Dakota, Florida, Tennessee, Nevada, and Washington have no income tax but are very reliant on their sales taxes. Oregon has no sales tax but depends heavily on its income tax. Texas, Alaska, Wyoming, and Montana rely on revenue from oil, gas and coal extraction, while Nevada depends on revenue from gambling.

While most cites and counties lean heavily on property taxes, some have the option of imposing sales taxes. A few, such as New York City, even levy a local income tax. The sources of revenue at each level of government are summarized in Table 1.4.

TABLE 1.4 Sources of Revenue: Federal, State (U.S. average), Local (U.S. average)

	Federal	*State*	*Local*
Personal Income Tax	48 %	20 %	2 %
Payroll Tax—Social Security and Medicare	34 %		
Sales Tax		18 %	5 %
Property Tax		1 %	27 %
Corporate Income Tax	10 %	3 %	
Fees and Charges		9 %	15 %
Transfers from Other Governments		28 %	39 %
All Other Revenue	8 %	21 %	12 %

SOURCES: Federal—*A Citizen's Guide to the Federal Budget, Budget of the United States FY 2001*, Executive Office of the President, Chart 2-3; State and Local—U.S. Bureau of the Census, *Federal, State, and Local Governments: State and Local Government Finances.*

The mix of revenue sources a government chooses has a direct impact on the volatility and predictability of its revenue. By and large, property taxes are the most stable, as are sales taxes on "necessities" such as food, clothing, and medicine. The least stable are corporate income taxes and taxes on oil, gas, and coal.

Every time a government chooses a revenue source, it chooses to live with the risks inherent in that source. When Oregon chooses to rely heavily on the income tax and avoid a sales tax, it chooses to live with greater volatility than most states: Its revenues rise faster than those of most states and plummet faster as well. Similarly, when Alaska and Texas bet on revenue from oil and gas wells, they are choosing to live with the vagaries of the oil and gas markets.

Even after governments choose their revenue sources, they can affect their volatility by how they choose to structure the system. Taxes, fees, and charges that cover a broad base are, in general, more stable revenue generators than those that exclude significant parts of the revenue base. Since the advent of the Worldwide Web, for example, the exclusion of most Internet sales from taxation has made the sales tax less reliable.

Similarly, an income tax with numerous exemptions and exclusions will be more volatile than one that treats all income equally. Progressive rate or fee structures can also increase volatility. An income tax system that taxes rising incomes at progressively higher rates will produce extraordinary increases in revenue—faster than the growth in income overall—when times are good, but also spectacular decreases when income declines.

The point is not that one choice is better than another, but that all choices have consequences, in terms of both volatility and predictability.

The last variable—the economy—is something governments can't choose, at least in the short run. But they can *anticipate* the effects of their economies. Revenues will be more stable and predictable if the economy generating them is not overly dependent on one industry. States and communities that lack economic diversity must anticipate more volatility in their revenues.

As governments consider their revenue choices, they must also consider three major changes that have conspired to make the traditional approaches to revenue less reliable. The first is the growth in Internet commerce. Factories and stores are subject to property taxes, but intangible information assets in cyberspace are not. Similarly, the products sold in brick and mortar stores are taxed at sale, while most sold on the Internet are not. Economists from the Center for Business and Economic Research at the University of Tennessee estimated that $13 billion of sales taxes were lost in 2001 because of transactions over the Internet, and that losses would balloon to $45 billion a year by 2006.

The second factor making revenue systems less reliable is the fact that most states tax few or no services. Yet services have increased from 40 to 60 percent of consumer spending since 1959.

Finally, the move to performance-based compensation and stock options has made income-tax revenues much more volatile. That volatility showed up as surprise surpluses when the economy boomed in the late 1990s and as spectacular deficits when the economy went into recession. While governments cannot choose their economies—or the ways in which they are changing—they can structure their revenues and rainy day funds to compensate for those realities.

On the spending side, the primary factors affecting volatility include demographics, the ups and downs of the economy, spending "by proxy" of one government through another, and the spending "autopilots" that governments write into law.

An old adage says that "demography is destiny." A change in the number of school-age young people affects the demand for schools. A growing elderly population affects the demand for health care, nursing homes, and Social Security. The number of teenagers affects the need for police, courts, and drug-prevention services. A key to managing spending is anticipating changes in these key demographic variables.

Anticipating the impact of economic changes also allows for more reliable predictions. In a good economy, with growing jobs and incomes, demands for safety-net services decline. In a bad economy, spending on unemployment insurance, welfare, food stamps, and the like automatically rises.

Some spending is actually controlled "by proxy" by another level of government. Most of the revenue flowing to states and localities from other governments comes with strings attached, directing how it should be spent. In addition, both the federal government and the states are fond of passing laws requiring states and localities to perform certain functions, in specified ways, without providing any money to do the job. These are known as unfunded mandates. The Americans with Disabilities Act is a prime example. The federal government mandated that all public buildings be wheelchair accessible, yet left it to the states and localities to pay for remodeling their schools, town halls, and other civic buildings. When you are the proxy—or patsy, as many feel—it is hard to predict what spending those in control will demand.

Finally, governments make much of their spending automatic—that is, nondiscretionary. These spending autopilots include cost-of-living adjustments (COLAS) in labor contracts, which automatically increase the costs of salaries and benefits to keep up with inflation; "rate inflators" built into health care, social service, and other appropriations, which operate like COLAS; "formula funding" that bases spending on the number of people who enroll or are eligible for a program; and bond covenants that require annual debt-service payments.

Choices made when spending autopilots are enacted limit choices when the bills have to be paid. Thus a funding formula with a built-in inflation adjustment will automatically ramp up spending if inflation suddenly takes off, regardless of whether the revenue comes in to support it or other spending is a higher priority.

The utility of any forecast or estimate also depends on its credibility, and the credibility of forecasts depends not only on their quality but on their transparency. Any cause for skepticism makes projections easier to ignore, and in a political situation, skepticism will always persist if the party in power controls the forecasting process. That is why Florida law requires that budget staff from both legislative houses and the governor's office agree on all projections. Some governments hire private economic forecasting firms to prepare their projections. In New Zealand, the Treasury Department uses an independent panel of prominent economists to review all forecasts.

In 1987, when the state was reeling from the collapse of the oil boom, Louisiana instituted a process to discipline forecasting and rein in competing projections. A conference consisting of the governor, the speaker of the House, the president of the Senate, and an economist from a university within the state meets at least four times a year. The law requires that they come up with a unanimous forecast, and the legislature cannot exceed that amount when it appropriates money from the general or special funds.

Leaders who want to enhance the credibility of their budgets should publish their projections, in user-friendly form, to encourage public scrutiny. To make sure that legislators pay attention to forecasts as they make budget decisions, long-term projections should be provided to the media and to interest groups, who will, in turn, make sure that legislators hear about any glaring contradictions.

Even the most credible forecasts are of little use unless executives and legislators actually confront the information as they make budget decisions. The U.S. federal government keeps its forecasting separate from the one-year budgets approved by Congress, so dire deficit forecasts have little impact on individual budget votes in committee or even on the floor. Other governments put their forecasts right into the budget documents, so every budget item is projected out five or ten years. Every time the executive proposes, or the legislature votes for, new spending or revenue, the long-term implications are hard to ignore.

"This is one of the things that allows us to keep our problems at arm's length," Rich Napier, a former City Council member from Sunnyvale, California, told us. "We don't make decisions in a crisis. We're in a panic when there's a problem five years out, not five minutes out. We take it very seriously if we have a deficit showing in the sixth year—and it's a lot easier to change that."

Napier went on to describe how, in good times:

The elected official's natural reaction is, "I want a swimming pool in my district—there's money there, why don't we build it?" One of the things this 10-year budget does is allows you to say, "Well, the money's there, yes, but we need it to balance the budget in year three, or to deal with the liability of a case that's in the courts. Or to deal with the Americans with Disabilities Act." It protects your reserves. It gives the politicians an out.

Since 1994, New Zealand has required the government to submit a fiscal strategy report, with forecasts, when it submits its budget to Parliament. This means that the government exposes itself to ridicule if it makes a budget that ignores independent and credible economic forecasts. "Too often in the past a short-term focus has been to our long term cost," said former finance minister Ruth Richardson when she pushed the 1994 Fiscal Responsibility Act through Parliament. "Experience shows that the future needs a voice. In this bill we are giving the future that voice."

Parliament also extended the requirement for accrual accounting and generally accepted accounting practices to all government spending, to ensure that all government losses and liabilities show up on the balance sheet. As a subsequent minister of finance said, "The Parliament and public of New Zealand now have more financial information about the position of the government, and the risks surrounding that position, than shareholders of most publicly listed companies."

BUSINESS AS USUAL

When reality hit after the 2003 election in Minnesota, newly elected Governor Tim Pawlenty finally admitted, "We're in the midst of a financial crisis the likes of which this state has never seen." In relatively short order he had his proposal on the table: another traditional stew of cuts, shifts, and accounting tricks. Of the $4.2 billion shortfall, only $2.5 billion would be absorbed by spending cuts. The rest would be conjured away by accounting gimmicks and onetime transfers. While he proposed no new state taxes, tuition and other fees would rise significantly. Eventually, local taxes would follow suit as the cuts ate into the budgets of cities and towns.

The party-line battle over the budget raged on for the five months of the regular 2003 legislative session, forcing the governor to call a special session. Then, suddenly, the Democrats capitulated. In the face of Republican intransigence, and with no better idea of their own, they essentially said, "You wanted this budget, you've got it, you live with it."

John Gunyou, who had served as finance commissioner for former Republican governor Arne Carlson, provided the following assessment in the Minneapolis *Star Tribune* after the budget was passed and signed:

Ten Things You Should Know About the State Budget

Now that the legislative session is finally over and our leaders are taking their traditional bipartisan bows, here's ten things you should know about the budget they adopted:

1. The governor and legislature didn't inherit the problem, they created it. Ignoring the looming recession, they enacted unaffordable school funding takeover and property tax reform that created over one-half of the deficit. Then last year, they doubled the problem by using one-time fixes, instead of long-term solutions.

2. It's not a spending problem, it's a management problem. They keep making politically popular promises they can't afford to sustain. Minnesota led the nation in tax cuts that cost the 2004–05 budget $5.5 billion, about the size of the real deficit.

3. They're not really spending another $1 billion. The two-year budget confuses the fact that annual spending grew by $1.3 billion from 2002 to 2003, largely due to the school funding takeover and property tax reform. In truth, there's no budget growth from 2003 through 2005.

4. Only K–12 education and health care get any more money. Everyone else gets $1.3 billion less. That's not lower growth, that's absolute cuts. Local aid for police, fire, and streets is cut 22 percent, colleges are cut 9 percent, and economic development, the environment, agriculture, and the rest of state government are collectively cut 14 percent.

5. K–12 education funding goes up in 2004, but declines the next three years. Because they can't afford to pay for last year's school funding takeover with the existing tax structure, they're requiring school districts to replace the lack of future state funding with higher local property taxes.

6. Their health and human services cuts will cost more in the long run. Seniors and uninsured families will be forced into more expensive care facilities. Cuts to early childhood programs are particularly short-sighted, since these programs boast cost saving returns that business executives would envy.

7. There's no reform to control the real cost drivers. K–12 education and health care are two-thirds of the budget, and account for all of the spending growth. Health care costs are projected to grow 22 percent in 2006–07, and K–12 state funding cuts without any cost reform will just further reduce quality.

8. You're going to pay a lot more for worse local service. They're raising school and transit taxes and phasing out value caps. That and local aid cuts will increase property taxes by at least 10 percent to 15 percent. Since public safety and streets represent three-fourths of city budgets, unreasonable levy limits will force service reductions.

9. The transportation system will continue to deteriorate. Rather than dealing honestly with road and transit needs by raising the gas tax, they're borrowing money for one year of improvements, and paying off the debt by cutting rest areas and road maintenance over the next decade or more.

10. They patched things up for one more year, but didn't fix the problem. Up to one-half of the solution relies on one-time fixes, so the state will still spend $1.5 billion more than it will take in during 2004–05. That means we're looking at even more cuts next year.

You don't have to get a solid grip to make a budget balance, you just have to solve the math problem—and the seven deadly deceptions offer seductive assistance. That's politics and budgeting as usual. But governments that accept this easy out are on a slippery slope. When they are put off, fiscal problems snowball. And while leaders are focused on solving the math problem (and re-solving it each year), no one will be focused on the more important problem of buying the best outcomes for citizens at the price they're willing to pay. That's not a math problem; it's a leadership problem.

TWO

Setting the Price
of Government

*In the fierce debate over tax cuts between Gore and Bush, one fact has
gone unnoticed: Both men would allocate roughly the same amount of
money—$500 billion over nine years—to people making less than
$100,000 a year.*

—Glenn Kessler, *Washington Post*, October 17, 2000

In the early 1990s, federal deficits haunted the economy, as they had since
Ronald Reagan's tax cuts and military buildup drove the deficit to 6 percent
of GDP in the early 1980s. By 1992, we were all deficit hawks—afraid of the
impact of red ink on the economy.

President Clinton pushed a tax increase through Congress. Along with
spending restraint from the administration and Congress and inflation restraint from the Federal Reserve Board, it yielded the longest economic expansion in history. By 1998 the deficits were gone.

As surpluses replaced deficits, both major party candidates advocated
tax cuts. Both George Bush and Al Gore recognized that the price of government had risen higher than citizens were willing to sustain.

By the "price of government," we mean the amount of purchasing power
a community is willing to commit to its governments. There is no "right"
price of government, any more than there is a "right" price for Cheerios.
There is, however, an acceptable price, which may vary from one jurisdiction to the next depending on its wealth, history, culture, and values.

Finding that acceptable price is the job of elected officials. It is just as
challenging for them as it is for General Mills. Price your Cheerios too high

FIGURE 2.1   Federal Revenues as a Percent of GDP

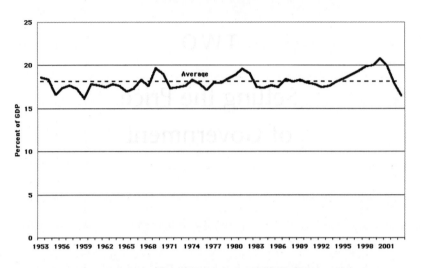

SOURCE: Office of Management and Budget.

and consumers will tell you you're out of line by buying Corn Flakes or Rice Krispies instead. Price your Cheerios too low and your business falls apart.

Similarly, when the price of government gets too high, citizens let government know: They oust incumbents, elect antitax candidates, and/or embrace antitax initiatives. When the price of government gets too low, critical public services like schools, roads, and police forces begin to fray. Allow this decline to reach a breaking point and citizens push the price of government back up, by electing representatives committed to improving services or by voting in referenda to pay more for services they care about.

The graph in Figure 2.1 tracks the federal government's revenue as a percentage of GDP. Note how it fluctuates within a relatively narrow band. When the price gets too high or too low it regresses back to the norm—almost as if there were a thermostat keeping it at an acceptable level. When the temperature drops to the bottom of the comfort zone, the democratic process signals the burner to kick in. When the temperature reaches the upper limit, the democratic process tells the burner to knock off.

Looked at this way, some tax cuts after the 1990s were a foregone conclusion. (Their size and the distribution of the benefits were other matters entirely.) They were necessary to bring the price of the federal government back in line with what people were willing to pay. But the multiple rounds of cuts enacted since Bush's election have in fact gone much further. By 2003,

FIGURE 2.2 Price of Government in U.S.
Cents/Dollar of Personal Income

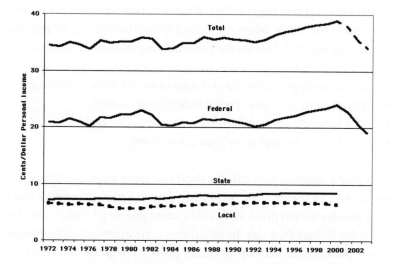

SOURCES: U.S. Bureau of the Census, U.S. Bureau of Economic Analysis,
Office of Management and Budget.

the price of the federal government was at its lowest point since the 1950s—
well below its long-term average.

Our precise definition of the price of government is the sum of all taxes,
fees, and charges collected directly by a given locality, state, or nation, divided by that jurisdiction's total economic resources. The measure we use
most often to represent total economic resources is aggregate personal income. Gross domestic product—as used in Figure 2.1—would be a better
measure, but there is no timely information on GDP for states and localities. Aggregate personal income is the sum of all income that individuals in
the community derive from work, dividends, interest, rent, and transfer
payments, such as Social Security. It is a good proxy, because it constitutes
about 85 percent of GDP and thus approximates a community's "purchasing power." (Aggregate personal income data is available for states, regions,
and counties from the U.S. Bureau of Economic Analysis. For cities, we rely
on the Census Bureau's measure of "money income.")

In Figure 2.2, which uses aggregate personal income, we again can see
the self-regulating nature of the price of government. (Note the similarity to
the federal graph calculated using GDP.) Because the most recent data
available for state and local governments is from 2000, we have extended
the "total" line to 2003 based on the significant drop in the federal price of
government.

While the most dramatic "ups and downs" occur at the federal level, it is important to note that, at every level, the price of government for the past three decades has remained within a fairly narrow comfort zone—except for the end of the 1990s, when the federal government ran a surplus. Starting at the top, Figure 2.2 shows the price holding relatively steady at:

- 35 to 37 cents per dollar for all forms of government combined;
- 20 to 22 cents per dollar for the federal government;
- 7.3 to 8.3 cents per dollar for state governments; and
- 6 to 6.6 cents per dollar for local governments.

This graph suggests that citizens don't just want lower taxes and "cheap government." In reality, they constantly demand more from government, but at a relatively fixed price. They are in effect pressing for more value each year for the dollars they pay. In this respect, government is challenged by the same forces that constrain any other provider of goods and services.

Unfortunately, most politicians and budget managers today don't recognize that a self-regulating price of government exists. For them, budgeting is a scramble to see how much of what they want they can get. Everyone involved has their sacred cows and bêtes noires: Conservatives push for lower taxes, while liberals seek to protect spending for education, the poor, the environment, and other key constituencies. In the legislative sausage factory, the balance of power and the process of political horse trading lead to last minute, ad hoc adjustments. The end result is often a spending plan that has no direct correlation with the priorities of citizens and no explicit recognition that there are limits on the price they are willing to pay.

There is another way: the much more intentional process adopted by Washington State, which we described in the Introduction. This process, which we call Budgeting for Outcomes, turns the traditional approach on its head. It begins not with last year's costs or with demands from interest groups, but with a judgment, made by elected officials, about how much citizens are willing to pay for the government they want. In making this judgment, data on the price of government is the starting point.

GOVERNMENT IN COMPETITION

Leaders need to realize that citizens continually, albeit unconsciously, assess the relationship between value and price in everything they buy, including public services. When price gets out of line with value, they buy less.

FIGURE 2.3 The Price of . . .
Percent Use of Personal Income

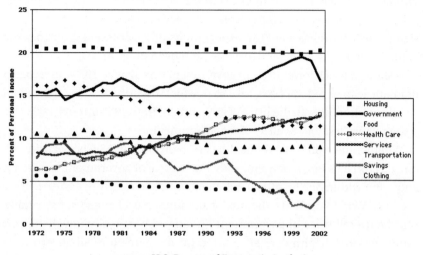

SOURCE: U.S. Bureau of Economic Analysis.

The graph in Figure 2.3 tracks the competition for consumers' dollars over the last 30 years. It differs from the previous graph in that it tracks only those government revenues paid directly by individuals—other than tuition. (Most of the rest is paid by businesses: corporate taxes, the business half of Social Security taxes, sales and gas taxes, which are remitted by retailers, and so on.) Nevertheless, the results are comparable. It shows that, since 1972, the share of personal income going to food, clothing, transportation, and savings has declined to make room for increases in health care, which doubled, and "other services," which increased by half, mostly because of the rapid increase in spending for financial services. (Because the graph is already overcrowded, we have omitted "recreation," which increased from 1.8 to 3.2 percent.)

During this time period, the share of citizen dollars going to government remained fairly constant—until the mid 1990s, when it began a steady run up to its high of 19.6 percent in 2000. Since then it has dropped precipitously as the thermostat kicked in and Congress passed Bush's tax cuts.

The price of government works as a thermostat because citizens have a limited amount of money. When health care is gobbling up ever greater shares of our income, there is little room for the price of government to rise. Industries in which competition is fierce and global, like food, clothing, and automobiles, have been able to deliver dramatically more value for the dollar. With its own rising costs, government is under pressure to do the same.

THE PRICE OF GOVERNMENT OVER TIME

Though the price of government (POG) has been relatively stable for the past 50 years, it has not always been at this level. Before World War II, it was significantly lower, as were the expectations of government. Consider the graph in Figure 2.4, of federal revenues as a percentage of GDP.

It shows a much lower price of government through the 1930s, and then a dramatic leap as federal taxes rose to pay for World War II. Once things had stabilized after the war, the price of government from 1953 through 2003 was again relatively stable, at all levels of government.

Whether the rising costs of health care, pensions, and Social Security will one day force us into a new era, with a new price of government, we do not know. But within one historical era, the thermostat clearly operates. During the post–World War II era the mix of spending has changed substantially, but the overall price of government has stayed within a relatively narrow range. In 1970, health care accounted for 8.5 percent of all government spending, at all levels, and income security (mostly Social Security, welfare, disability payments, and unemployment insurance) accounted for 20.3 percent. By 2001, health care was up to 19 percent and income security was at 23.3 percent. All of this increase and more was offset by a decline in national defense, from 27.4 to 11.7 percent of total government spending.

FIGURE 2.4   Federal Revenues as a Percent of GDP

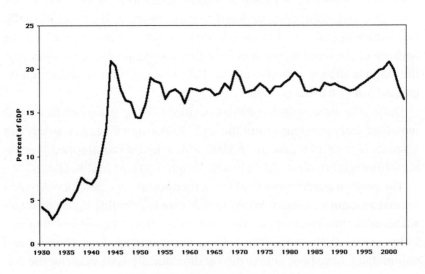

SOURCE: Office of Management and Budget.

Look again at the POG for all years since 1972, as shown in Figure 2.5. The thermostatic effect is clear. On the federal line we can see the effect of a tax cut during the recession of 1974–1975, which increased the deficit, and a social security tax increase in 1977. Then the hyper-inflation of the late 1970s and early 1980s drove taxpayers into higher brackets and rapidly increased federal revenue. Taxpayers fought back first at the local level, the easiest for them to reach through the initiative process. On the local line, we see the impact of the property tax revolt that started in California with Proposition 13, in June 1978, and spread rapidly across the country. Then the voters elected Ronald Reagan, who had pledged a 30 percent cut in income taxes.

In the early 1980s, a deep recession reversed the downward trend for state and local governments, as demand for services rose and the lingering effects of inflation pushed revenues up faster than personal income. This shift was more than offset by the Reagan tax cuts, however. Determined to lower the price of government, the Reagan administration kept taxes down by borrowing 3 to 6 percent of GDP every year.

In 1990, another recession reduced federal tax receipts. The federal POG declined through 1992, while the deficit soared. Meanwhile state and local governments were raising taxes and fees to deal with their revenue shortfalls and pay for health care, pensions, education, and prisons.

FIGURE 2.5   Price of Government in U.S.
Cents/Dollar of Personal Income

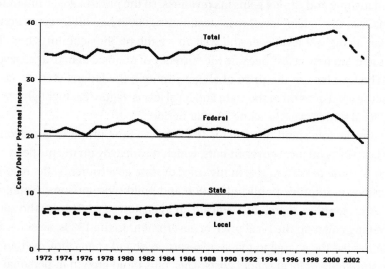

SOURCES: U.S. Bureau of the Census, U.S. Bureau of Economic Analysis,
Office of Management and Budget.

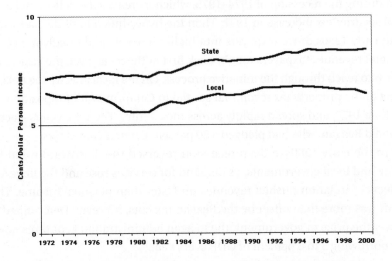

FIGURE 2.6   U.S. State and Local Price of Government
Cents/Dollar of Personal Income

SOURCES: U.S. Bureau of the Census, U.S. Bureau of Economic Analysis.

Matters changed again during the extended period of economic growth in the 1990s. Frightened by the economic damage done by the Reagan-Bush deficits, voters sent a clear message in the 1992 election. President Clinton and Congress raised taxes and held down spending. The resulting boom lifted income and capital gains tax revenues, so the price of government (especially at the federal level) rose steadily. By 2000 it had hit 39 cents on the dollar, its highest level ever and well above the public's comfort zone. Tax cuts and "no new taxes" became the currency of political debate at all levels.

When we look at the price of all government, the federal story tends to obscure what goes on at the state and local levels. Figure 2.6 highlights state and local trends over the same 30-year period.

Three factors stand out. First is the impact of the property tax revolt of the late 1970s on local governments, which rely heavily on the property tax. Second is the persistent rise in the price of state government—the result of decisions to improve public education and build more prisons, combined with the relentless march of Medicaid and pension costs. Third is the countervailing effect on the local price of government in the 1990s, as cities and counties led the charge to reinvent government and states took over an increasing share of local school costs. This, plus rapid growth in personal incomes, allowed the sum of state and local POGs to remain essentially flat after 1993.

FIGURE 2.7   California's Price of State and Local Government
Cents/Dollar of Personal Income

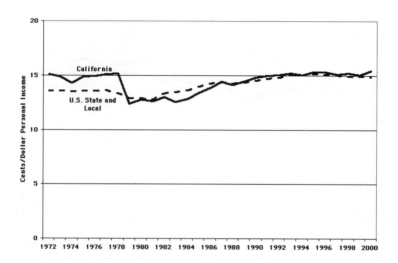

SOURCES: U.S. Bureau of the Census, U.S. Bureau of Economic Analysis.

The correlation between specific events and the POG is even tighter when we look at individual states. Figure 2.7 tracks the price of state and local government in California, the home of Proposition 13. As the chart makes very clear, California's POG was well above the national average through most of the 1970s. Beginning about 1975, as rapid inflation in housing drove up property values, homeowners were hit with whopping tax increases when their homes were reassessed. Meanwhile, inflation drove income tax payers into higher brackets, and the state began to pile up a surplus. Governor Jerry Brown urged the legislature to spend the surplus on property tax relief, but his bill stalled. When two relatively unknown conservatives, Howard Jarvis and Paul Gann, circulated their tax-cutting initiative, the tax revolt ignited. Proposition 13 reduced local government revenue by 23 percent overnight. The state used its surplus to soften the blow, but dire fiscal straits still spawned dramatic increases in efficiency at the local level. (In fact, this crisis prompted the first rumblings of reinvention, in cities such as Visalia and Fairfield.) Even so, with California's price of government dramatically reduced, services deteriorated. Then, 20 years ago, the public began to demand improvements, paying for them by gradually raising the price back up to the national average.

When we look at the graph for Washington State (Figure 2.8), we can see the effect of the late 1970s tax revolt, but also of a second one, in 1993. For

FIGURE 2.8   Washington's Price of State and Local Government
Cents/Dollar of Personal Income

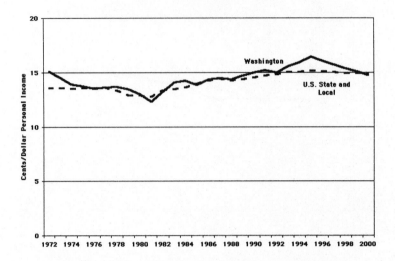

SOURCES: U.S. Bureau of the Census, U.S. Bureau of Economic Analysis.

most of the past 30 years, Washington's price of government has matched
the national average. But in the spring of 1993, Boeing laid off 19,000 employees in the Seattle area, and government revenues began to fall. Facing a
projected $1.5 billion shortfall, the legislature cut spending and raised taxes
by almost $1 billion. Coming in the midst of a severe recession and driving
the price of government well above its norm, the tax increase ignited a
firestorm. In November of 1993 voters passed Initiative 601, which severely
limited state spending. By the time the initiative took effect, in 1995, the
POG was at an unprecedented level. Shortly after Initiative 601 kicked in, a
series of related initiatives passed as well. The price of government began to
fall, and it has not stopped since. Today it is below the national average.

The graph for New York State (Figure 2.9) tells the tale of a high-priced
state. In the Lindsay and Rockefeller years of the early 1970s, New York City
and State went on a spending binge. In 1973 alone, revenues increased by
nearly 14 percent, but it was not enough to match expenditures. The result
was near bankruptcy for both city and state in 1976–1977, when the price of
government peaked. The state imposed a Fiscal Control Board on the city,
which led to drastic cuts in services. Quality of life suffered terribly: The
streets and parks grew dirtier, crime rose, and streets and bridges literally
fell apart. Meanwhile, Governor Hugh Carey (1977–1981) and the legisla-

FIGURE 2.9   New York State's Price of State and Local Government
Cents/Dollar of Personal Income

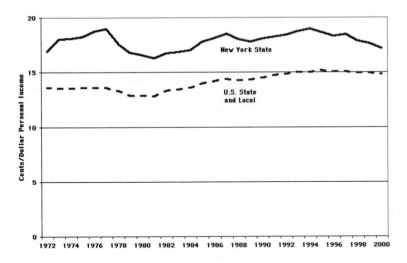

SOURCES: U.S. Bureau of the Census, U.S. Bureau of Economic Analysis.

ture cut taxes and reined in spending, driving down the state's price of government.

Disciplined by memories of the 1970s, Governor Mario Cuomo and the legislature, and Mayor Ed Koch and the City Council, held spending in check through 1984. Then, with the economy booming and citizens demanding better services, they began to rebuild roads and highways, build new prisons, and improve the schools. The POG crept back up to 18 cents on the dollar. In response, Cuomo and the legislature cut income taxes in three phases—1987, 1988, and 1989—and the POG came down a bit. When the recession of the early 1990s hit, elected leaders hiked taxes and fees while personal income stagnated, so the price of government rose again. By 1994 it was back up to 1977 levels, almost 19 cents on the dollar. In 1993 Republican Rudy Giuliani unseated an incumbent Democratic mayor in New York City, and the next year Republican George Pataki defeated Cuomo. The graph makes it obvious why New Yorkers suddenly turned to Republican executives. They and their legislative bodies pushed the price of government steadily back down to about 17 cents on the dollar by 2000—close to 1972 levels.

Texas, which has always been a state with a low POG, provides an interesting counterpoint to New York. Throughout the 1970s and early 1980s its price was about two cents below the national average, as Figure 2.10 illus-

FIGURE 2.10   Texas's Price of State and Local Government
Cents/Dollar of Personal Income

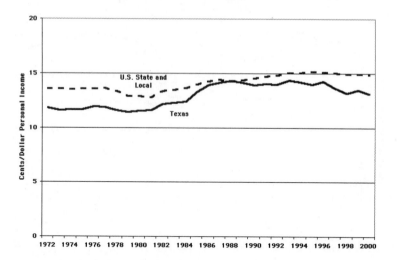

SOURCES: U.S. Bureau of the Census, U.S. Bureau of Economic Analysis.

trates. Then the oil bust and subsequent real estate bust hit, forcing personal income down and the POG to an unprecedented high. By 1989, it
matched the national average. Since then, oil and gas prices have recovered
and Texans have reasserted their preference for a low price of government.

The price of government can be tracked for local governments as well,
though doing so is more difficult. Population and per capita income data for
local governments are available from the census only once a decade. The
Bureau of the Census does provide population estimates more frequently,
however. And the Bureau of Economic Analysis publishes estimates of
county, metro area and state aggregate personal income annually, though
they lag by a year or two. These figures can be used to estimate aggregate
money income for many if not most local jurisdictions. Local government
and school budgets provide annual figures for taxes, fees, and charges.
Taken together, these data allow us to estimate the price of government over
time, using state trends and census information as a reality check. The result
is not perfect, but it is enough to give leaders a good sense of the trends.

Figure 2.11 shows the price of government for the city and county of
Denver, as well as the state of Colorado. Note the relative steadiness and the
downward trend since the mid 1990s, reflecting the effects of a statewide
initiative known as the Taxpayers Bill of Rights, which places a strict limit on
government expenditures.

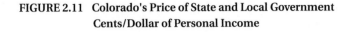

FIGURE 2.11 Colorado's Price of State and Local Government
Cents/Dollar of Personal Income

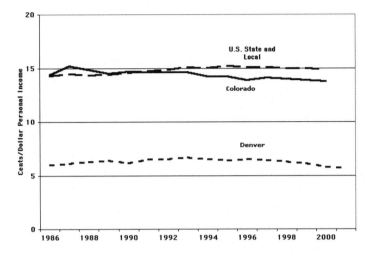

SOURCES: U.S. Bureau of the Census, U.S. Bureau of Economic Analysis,
City of Denver.

The message in all these graphs is that the price of government is not something that elected leaders can set anywhere they choose. Citizen tolerance, both for taxation and for an acceptable level of service, acts as a constraint. That tolerance, of course, is affected by the health of the economy at any given time. But in the long run, the price of government is regulated by the will of the people. It must be acceptable to those who pay it and adequate to deliver the results that citizens demand. The choices that citizens make over time about the price of their governments reflect their unique judgments about the value of public services. Citizens in Texas value their government services differently than do citizens in New York, who in turn value theirs differently than citizens in Washington or California.

COMPARING JURISDICTIONS

Every day, citizens are bombarded with studies purporting to show that their state or local taxes are "out of control" compared with taxes elsewhere. Such studies often bring to mind the old adage about "lies, damn lies, and statistics." Too often, they focus on only one part of the total price of government.

Perhaps the most common comparison is taxes paid per capita. In Massachusetts, this figure is used by conservatives to paint the commonwealth as a high-tax state. This seems perfectly fair, until one realizes two things: Taxes are only part of what we pay to governments (fees and other charges complete the picture), and per capita comparisons leave out the relative wealth of different states. Historically, citizens have demanded more and better public services as they have grown wealthier. As we discussed earlier, citizens have raised the price of government from one era to the next, choosing to fund a social security system, then the world's largest defense force. And within any one era, taxes and fees have remained a fairly steady percentage of personal income, *even as personal income has risen.*

When personal income goes up, personal spending goes up. And like it or not, increased spending by individuals creates increased demands on government. The more citizens drive, the more they need good roads, in good repair. The more they travel by air, the more they need bigger and better airports. And the more affluent they become, the more they demand better schools, safer streets, and cleaner water and air. Hence, rising personal income drives rising service expectations. This is why the price of government rarely falls as communities prosper.

It is Massachusetts's relative affluence that allows it to have both higher-than-average *per capita* government revenue *and* a below-average price of government, as Figure 2.12 shows. The vertical axis (government revenue raised per person in each state) is a measure of capacity. In general, a government with higher revenue per capita can afford to offer its citizens more and better services, because they are wealthier. The horizontal axis (the percentage of personal income devoted to government) is a measure of effort. It reflects how much of their money citizens are willing to spend for the government they get. Because Massachusetts is affluent, it ranks in the top ten in per capita government revenue even with a price of government among the bottom five. (If you're wondering where Alaska is, it is literally off the chart, with a price of government of nearly 40 cents on the dollar, thanks to oil revenue.) Texas has about the same price of government as Massachusetts, but raises considerably less per capita. California and Wisconsin governments raise about the same per capita as Massachusetts, but require a substantially higher price to do so. Poorer states like Mississippi and West Virginia operate with about the same price of government as Wisconsin, but generate substantially less revenue per capita and can therefore afford less in the way of public services.

Tables 2.1, 2.2, 2.3, and 2.4 show the price of government in 2000 for all 50 states, the 50 largest cities and counties, and 9 large city-county combi-

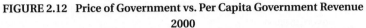

FIGURE 2.12 Price of Government vs. Per Capita Government Revenue
2000

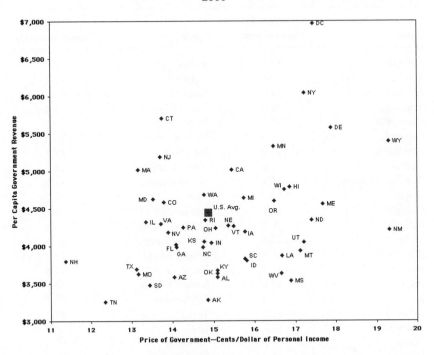

SOURCES: U.S. Bureau of the Census, U.S. Bureau of Economic Analysis.

nations. In looking at these, keep in mind that a higher price is not "better" or "worse" than a lower price; people in different jurisdictions make different choices about what public services they want, at what level of quality, and at what price. In addition, some jurisdictions have access to revenues, such as oil and gas extraction taxes, that are "exportable" to nonresidents. And in looking at city and county budgets, note that several include schools in their budgets and while most do not, because school districts raise their revenues separately.

When it comes to comparing government revenues over time to look at trends, or comparing jurisdictions to look at the choices that people have made, we believe that the price of government is the best measure. First, it accounts for all direct sources of revenue—taxes, fees, and charges. This is important because limits on taxes too often result in higher fees, higher tuitions at state colleges and universities, and higher tolls on roads and bridges. In such cases, "no new taxes" does *not* mean no new revenues. Second, the POG can also account for all levels of government: federal, state,

TABLE 2.1 FY 2000 Price of Government in the 50 States (all state and local governments)

State	Price of Government*	State	Price of Government*
Alabama	15.1	Montana	17.1
Alaska	40.6	Nebraska	15.4
Arizona	14.0	Nevada	13.9
Arkansas	14.9	New Hampshire	11.4
California	15.4	New Jersey	13.7
Colorado	13.8	New Mexico	19.3
Connecticut	13.7	New York	17.2
Delaware	17.9	North Carolina	14.7
District of Columbia	17.4	North Dakota	17.4
Florida	14.1	Ohio	15.0
Georgia	14.1	Oklahoma	15.1
Hawaii	16.9	Oregon	16.5
Idaho	15.8	Pennsylvania	14.3
Illinois	13.3	Rhode Island	14.8
Indiana	14.9	South Carolina	15.8
Iowa	15.8	South Dakota	13.4
Kansas	14.8	Tennessee	12.3
Kentucky	15.1	Texas	13.1
Louisiana	16.7	Utah	17.2
Maine	17.7	Vermont	15.5
Maryland	13.5	Virginia	13.7
Massachusetts	13.2	Washington	14.8
Michigan	15.7	West Virginia	16.6
Minnesota	16.5	Wisconsin	16.7
Mississippi	16.9	Wyoming	19.3
Missouri	13.2	*All States*	14.9

*Cents/$ of Aggregate Personal Income (Own Source General Revenue/Aggregate Personal Income)

SOURCES: U.S. Bureau of the Census, U.S. Bureau of Economic Analysis.

and local governments; school districts; and special districts. This is important because when federal budget cuts hit the states or state cuts hit local governments, those on the receiving end often increase revenues to make up the difference. In such cases, "no new taxes" means no new taxes here—but look what they did there. The POG can help us look at the full price of government in any community. Most of those who pay don't distinguish one unit of government from the rest: It's all government to them.

Finally, the price of government measures government revenues in relation to the economy. This is crucial because it gives government leaders and

TABLE 2.2 FY2000 Price of Government in the 50 Largest Cities

City	Price of Government*	City	Price of Government*
Albuquerque	4.4	Mesa	3.0
Anaheim	4.7	Miami	6.7
Arlington, TX	2.8	Milwaukee	3.6
Atlanta	9.4	Minneapolis	6.1
Austin	4.4	New Orleans[b]	7.2
Baltimore[a,b]	9.1	Oakland	8.7
Boston[a,b]	9.0	Oklahoma City	5.6
Buffalo[a]	4.9	Omaha	3.3
Charlotte	4.6	Phoenix	4.6
Chicago	5.7	Pittsburgh	5.7
Cincinnati	8.6	Portland	5.2
Cleveland	10.3	Sacramento	5.9
Colorado Springs	6.2	Saint Paul	5.2
Columbus	5.3	San Antonio	3.8
Dallas	5.9	San Diego	5.4
Detroit[a]	10.8	San Jose	4.3
El Paso	4.4	Santa Ana, CA	5.0
Fort Worth	4.8	Seattle	5.7
Fresno	4.5	St. Louis[b]	11.6
Houston	4.6	Tampa	5.8
Kansas City, MO	8.4	Toledo	4.9
Las Vegas	2.8	Tucson	4.4
Long Beach	7.9	Tulsa	6.5
Los Angeles	5.9	Virginia Beach[a]	6.8
Memphis	4.0	Wichita	3.1

*Cents/$ of Aggregate Money Income (Own Source General Revenue/Aggregate Money Income)

[a]includes schools

[b]includes county functions

SOURCE: U.S. Bureau of the Census.

citizens alike a common stake in making their economy as robust as possible. As we suggested above, a healthy economy can sustain a given level of public services at a lower price than a weak one. Conversely, how much governments raise and how they use their revenue affects economic growth. Governments cannot raise their prices to uncompetitive or unacceptable levels without paying an economic price. But they need to use what they do raise to deliver as much value as possible—especially in areas that will sustain the economy. Many people don't realize that just as driving the price of government too high can damage an economy, so driving the price too low

TABLE 2.3 Price of Government in the 50 Largest Counties

County	Price of Government*	County	Price of Government*
Alameda County, CA	1.2	Maricopa, AZ	1.0
Allegheny County, PA	1.1	Miami-Dade County, FL	6.1
Baltimore, MD[a]	5.2	Milwaukee County, WI	1.7
Bergen County, NJ	0.9	Montgomery County, MD[a]	6.2
Bexar County, TX	1.6	Nassau County, NY	3.0
Broward County, FL	2.7	Oakland County, MI	0.5
Clark County, NV	4.1	Orange County, CA	1.2
Contra Costa County, CA	1.8	Orange County, FL	3.6
Cook County, IL	1.0	Palm Beach County, FL	2.1
Cuyahoga County, OH	1.9	Pima County, AZ	2.0
Dallas County, TX	1.2	Pinellas County, FL	2.1
DuPage County, IL	0.7	Prince Georges, MD[a]	5.5
Erie County, NY	3.9	Riverside County, CA	0.7
Essex, NJ	1.2	Sacramento County, CA	2.4
Fairfax County, VA[a]	4.3	Salt Lake City, UT	1.6
Franklin County, OH	1.3	San Bernadino County, CA	1.9
Fresno, CA	1.7	San Diego, CA	0.7
Fulton, GA	2.6	Santa Clara County, CA	1.0
Hamilton, OH	2.1	Shelby County, TN[a]	3.9
Harris County, TX	1.3	St. Louis County, MO	1.1
Hennepin County, MN	1.6	Suffolk County, NY	2.7
Hillsborough County, FL	3.6	Tarrant County, TX	1.2
King County, WA	1.6	Travis, TX	1.0
Los Angeles, CA	1.8	Wayne County, MI	1.5
Macomb, MI	0.8	Westchester County, NY	2.8

*Cents/$ of Aggregate Personal Income (Own Source General Revenue/Aggregate Personal Income)

[a]includes schools

SOURCES: U.S. Bureau of the Census, U.S. Bureau of Economic Analysis.

can undermine its viability. In the Information Age, the keys to economic success are education levels, quality of life, and connectivity (the ability to reliably move information, goods, and people)—and these things cost money.

Beginning in Colorado and Washington State in the early 1990s, citizens have passed initiatives that set spending limits tied to growth in population and the rate of inflation. These sound perfectly reasonable, but they are intended not just to limit spending or taxes but actually to reduce the price of government every year—without regard to acceptability, affordability, or competitiveness.

TABLE 2.4 FY2000 Price of Government in the Largest Combined City/County Governments

City/County	Price of Government*	City/County	Price of Government*
Anchorage	5.3	Nashville/Davidson	5.9
Denver	6.7	New York	9.8
Honolulu	3.2	Philadelphia	6.8
Indianapolis	4.4	San Francisco	6.5
Jacksonville/Duval	4.1		

*Cents/$ of Aggregate Personal Income (Own Source General Revenue/Aggregate Personal Income)

SOURCES: U.S. Bureau of the Census, U.S. Bureau of Economic Analysis.

How? Total personal income grows with population, inflation, *and* growth in productivity. As a result, total personal income generally grows faster than the combination of population and inflation alone. Limits that ignore this fact relentlessly lower the price of government. Taxpayer Bill of Rights initiatives sound like common sense, and they are spreading, but they are in fact disingenuous. They are designed to cut the price of government—to "starve the beast"—not to get as much value as possible for the price citizens are willing to pay.

We believe that citizens should know and debate their price of government. They should consciously decide what level is acceptable, affordable, and competitive. When they feel the need to limit taxes or spending, however, they would be much wiser to tie these limits to the price of government—capping all taxes, fees and other charges at a set percentage of personal income.

FINDING THE "RIGHT" PRICE

With this understanding, how should public leaders go about setting their overall levels of revenue as they prepare their budgets?

They should start by determining their historic price of government. Under current budget practices, what citizens pay for government services emerges almost randomly, at the end of a long and indirect process of horse-trading. Our message is that leaders should begin by securing agreement on total revenue from all sources, then focus their energies on how best to use that money to purchase results (our topic in Chapter 3). The price of government is an excellent tool with which to forge that agreement. It captures the thermostatic feedback citizens have been giving elected officials for years, in response to changes in taxes, fees, charges, and the quality of services.

First, assemble and graph the data, over time, on the taxes, fees, and charges paid to all governments serving citizens in your area, expressed as a percentage of the aggregate income of that area. Show both the overall POG that citizens pay and the share paid to each governmental unit.

Second, chart the up ticks and downturns to see what price levels have triggered resistance and what levels (and commensurate reductions in service) have prompted a willingness to pay more.

Third, evaluate this historical information, combined with knowledge of trends in your local economy (particularly trends in personal income) and knowledge of the POG in competing jurisdictions, to arrive at a price appropriate for the area. (Leaders may want a public education and consultation process to help them arrive at that decision.) We are *not* recommending that government leaders passively accept the status quo. They may decide that their citizens will embrace a reasonable tax increase to restore services, or that they are already at the point of rebellion and need the burden of taxes reduced. The trend analysis used in understanding the current price of government provides the best basis for making these decisions.

Next, consider the share of the POG paid to each government—state, local, and federal. In the best of all worlds, do this jointly with other governments. Demonstrate to citizens that you and your colleagues recognize that there is in fact a limit to the price of government, and that together, their governments strive to provide the best value for their money. For several years, the major jurisdictions in Ramsey County, Minnesota—the county, the city of Saint Paul, and the Saint Paul Public Schools—have met annually to jointly set their property tax limit. When this has worked as it should, it has raised public confidence that these governments are accountable for their annual tax bills. In 2003, Multnomah County, Oregon, joined with the city of Portland and with its school district to sponsor a tax referendum that would allow the county to raise taxes to support the schools, public safety, and human services. The voters saw the value in this proposition and passed the measure.

If you can't do this jointly, then at least demonstrate that you know there is a limit to the collective price of government. Tell citizens what you think that number is, out loud, and announce that you will set your share of that price at what appears to be an acceptable portion of the total.

Next year's price of government is, ultimately, a choice. Once it is made, it can and should drive all other decisions throughout the budget process. Deciding on revenue levels from all sources up front turns the traditional budget process on its head. If done first, it liberates time to focus on an even more important step, to which we turn next: buying results that citizens value.

THREE

Setting the Priorities
of Government

Buying Results That Citizens Value
(at the Price They Are Willing to Pay)

If you ever have a flat tire on the freeways around Minneapolis and St. Paul, or you run out of gas or have engine trouble, chances are that within minutes, a green truck from the Minnesota Department of Transportation will stop and give you a hand. These trucks are part of the state's Highway Helper program, a service that helped Minnesota's newly elected Governor Tim Pawlenty learn the harsh realities of traditional budgeting.

When Pawlenty entered office in January 2003, the state was forecast to spend $31 billion in the biennium, but the revenue estimate showed a shortfall of $4.2 billion—"the Mount Everest of budget deficits," as the new governor put it. Bound by a "no new taxes pledge," he saw no alternative but to slash the budget by 14 percent.

The Highway Helper program costs the state about $1 million every year. Pawlenty saw it as a low-priority item, easily sacrificed. His ally, the House speaker, said that people should simply go back to changing their own tires. Almost immediately, drivers and their advocates began to howl, and their outrage became front-page news. Reporters interviewed citizens who told heartwarming stories of Highway Helper pulling them back from the brink of disaster. How could the governor cut a program that did so much good for so many people? The publicity and pressure continued to build, until, finally, Pawlenty relented and announced that the program would be spared.

Highway Helper would have been a $1 million cut. Pawlenty needed the equivalent of 4,200 such cuts to have any hope of reaching a balanced budget, yet he had been defeated on his opening move.

This is the first lesson of traditional budgeting: When it comes to cutting, there are no volunteers.

Pawlenty's Highway Helper hiccup also illustrates the second lesson: Budget debates focus on programs, not results. The typical budget is not organized by results, but by who spends the money. Allocations are made to agencies, departments, and divisions, and any discussion of priorities—usually addressed in terms of the fairness of who got how much—is carried out within the context of the organization chart. Thus, who spends the money trumps the question of the results it produces. Furthermore, advocacy groups have organized themselves in a way that parallels the organization chart, custom fitting their efforts to ensure that money flows to the organizations they care most about. But citizens don't care about the career aspirations of government employees, the needs of their organizations, or the interest groups that support them; they care about results. They should not have to decode an organization chart before they can discuss the issues they want addressed.

Nor should the only people who care about making sense of the budget as a whole be the chief executive and the chairs of the Finance and Appropriations Committees. But the way traditional budgeting works, virtually everyone else is out to protect his or her piece of the pie—not to worry about the condition of the pie itself.

That's because the rules of the old budget-balancing game focus entirely on cuts. As we saw through the example of Washington State in the Introduction, however, there is a better way—a new game that focuses not on cuts but on "keeps." It shifts the debate away from *how best to trim* 10 or 15 percent to *how best to spend* the 85 or 90 percent that remains. This conceptual shift changes the game from defense to offense and the politics from appeasing advocacy groups to delivering results that citizens value.

NEW RULES FOR A NEW GAME

Under the traditional system, the game begins when the budget office receives proposals from department heads. Virtually *every* budget submission starts by proposing to spend what was spent last year. This amount is called the "base" or the "current services" amount. The concept of the base is at the heart of the old system—and at the heart of its defects. The base represents the "minimum necessary" for agencies and departments to keep doing what they've been doing in the way they've been doing it. Getting money into the base and having it thought of as the "minimum necessary"—a nondiscretionary spending item—gives it cover from the scythes of budget cutters.

But last year's spending is only the starting point in defining the base. Invariably, departments propose additions that they consider essential to preserving their minimum necessary programs. Departments use three justifications to increase their base: (1) Inflation makes everything cost more; (2) an expanding caseload means they have to cover new units (be it students or hospital patients or homeless people); and (3) a new law has created a new mandate. The K–12 education base, for instance, goes up with rising enrollment and new requirements for bilingual or special-needs education. Likewise, the health-care base expands with the growth of the client population and the rising price of medical care.

Declining enrollment or client populations can also push the base downward. When that happens, however, department heads often ask to be "held harmless." Knowing there will be cuts somewhere down the road, they try to get as much money as possible into the base, where it can be protected.

On top of the base, managers ask for more money to serve new needs or to serve old needs in new ways. They know they should ask for more, because they understand that the budget office or elected officials will invariably trim their requests. After all, that's what a budget office is for.

Here's how Jeff Zlonis, former deputy commissioner of the Minnesota Department of Administration, describes his approach to winning this game:

> One trick in the legislative budget hearing was to make sure that you had one or two items that cost about $25,000 that would attract the legislators' attention—maybe even get them a little angry. They could understand the value of $25,000. It was small enough for them to relate to. I really liked bringing one of these up right before the $60 million for technology operations.
>
> My favorite item was uniforms for the state band, for $30,000. I used it for a number of years. I would insert it right in front of something large and controversial I was concerned about. I could always get them to spend at least a half hour haggling over the state band uniforms; then they would only spend two or three minutes on my $60 million item.

To compensate for the likelihood of cuts, departments build in enough extra to ensure that after the trimming, they end up with what they feel they really need to operate effectively. When the budget office trims too much, clever managers fight back by threatening to shut down their most popular programs. Among federal administrators, this is known as "closing the Washington Monument." It is the most flagrant of the many tactics used to make any cut frustrating—if not excruciatingly painful.

To get the budget in balance, budget staff and elected officials have to pare away at all these layers of justification, while simultaneously fending off vocal, entrenched defenders. Unable to tell fat from fundamentals, they often resort to across-the-board cuts, which penalize any administrator who filed an honest budget (and underscore the message that such foolish honesty should never be repeated). When the trimming starts, officials are excoriated for what they cut but rarely thanked for what they spare. It takes hand-to-hand combat to justify each dollar pared away, while the "keeps" are taken for granted.

In today's political climate, elected officials are always looking for ways to demonstrate their fiscal prudence while also supporting their favorite programs. The insidious alchemy of a base that has many built-in increases allows them to simultaneously cut a budget *and* spend more than they did last year. As long as the "cut" from the new base is less than the amount by which the old base was inflated, an agency can get more money and claim a cut at the same time.

At its worst, the old budget game can lead to egregious policy mistakes. At its best, it burns up hundreds of thousands of nonproductive hours. Few people win, many lose, and there is plenty of blame to go around.

The new game, which we call Budgeting for Outcomes, has no concept of "base." Last year's number is not an entitlement, and there is no argument about adding to or subtracting from it. Instead, the starting point is an agreed-upon price of government, and the objective is to buy results. Accordingly, the department head's job shifts from padding the base to proving that his or her programs will produce the desired outcomes for the best price.

The job of the budget office is no longer to play "Truth or Dare" with department heads; it is to compare competing strategies to determine which ones offer the most bang for the citizen's buck. Budget officers cease being mere watchdogs and bean counters and become essential players in steering the organization toward results. For everyone involved, from elected officials to budget analysts to department heads, being a public servant suddenly focuses on delivering results that citizens value at a price they are willing to pay.

Although this is a challenging task, it wastes significantly less time than the old budget game. Agencies and budget offices need to invest more in measuring results and evaluating competing strategies and programs, but

The Old Budget Game vs. the New Game

	Cost/Agency Based Budget	Budgeting for Outcomes
Starting Point:	Last year as the base "entitlement"	Price of government: how much citizens are willing to spend for services
Focus:	Add/subtract from base entitlement	Buying results that matter to citizens from competing offers
Addition:	Autopilot increase = new base	Since there is no base, there is no adding and subtracting
Subtraction:	"Cut" from new base	
Submission:	Justification for needs and costs, plus extra	Offer to deliver results at the set price
Incentives:	Build up costs and make cuts hard	Produce the most results that matter, at the set price
Analyst's job:	Find hidden/unnecessary costs	Validate offers or find better choices
Elected official's job:	Choose to cut services or raise taxes, and get blamed (or blame someone else)	Choose the best offers, to get the most results for citizens at the price they will pay
Debate:	What to cut, what to tax	How to get even better results

more than enough time is freed up by no longer having to play "hide and seek" with the numbers.

The table above sums up the fundamental differences between traditional budgeting and Budgeting for Outcomes.

BUDGETING FOR OUTCOMES

In government, as in most realms of life, we find it safer and easier to do what we've always done, simply because we've always done it. Only on rare occasions—usually at times of crisis—do we step back to gain a broader perspective, erase all our preconceived ideas and routine behaviors, and take a fresh look at how to make the most of our limited time and resources.

Budgeting for Outcomes allows public leaders to do some of this big-picture, creative thinking *each time* they prepare a budget. In fact, the process demands it.

The results-based approach clears away all the games and the preoccupations with departmental needs by employing a very simple progression:

Step 1: Determine the priorities of government: the outcomes that matter most to citizens.

Step 2: Decide the price for each outcome.

Step 3: Decide how best to deliver each outcome at the set price.

"The temptation is to make budgeting a math problem," explains Washington State's Wolfgang Opitz:

It's not. When you focus on it as a math problem all you get is a mathematical solution. People don't care about the difference between $16 million and $16 billion. They care about whether or not they can renew their driver's license without having to spend six hours waiting in a line.

Step 1: Determine the Priorities of Government

The process starts with deciding what outcomes are of most value to the public. This is not a matter of compiling some whimsical wish list. Elected officials need to find out and articulate what matters most to their constituents, using many of the same methods they use to get themselves elected:

- Polling: random sampling of public opinion.
- Focus groups: multiple discussions with randomly selected participants.
- Town hall sessions: multiple public discussions with whoever shows up (facilitated by experienced staff).
- Civic journalism: news media initiatives to engage readers, listeners, and viewers in interactive discussions, debates, and feedback about priorities.
- Web sites: Web-based feedback collected in response to efforts to heighten awareness.

In the Introduction, we presented the list of priorities that Washington State came up with. When the same question has been put to the leaders of other states and localities, their lists have been similar but not identical. The power of these priorities is not in their novelty or counterintuitive insight, however. It lies in the way they redirect and focus public spending.

Multnomah County, Oregon, which includes Portland and some of its inner-ring suburbs, is the state's largest county, with 20 percent of the population. In 1994, the County Board of Commissioners developed a performance budgeting system with 85 outcome goals, called "benchmarks." "We adopted a philosophy that every division should have a benchmark, because some of them were feeling left out," says Beverly Stein, who chaired the Board of Commissioners and served as county executive. Realizing that this list was far too long to provide any focus, the board later selected 12 of the 85 as "urgent benchmarks":

- Reduce teen pregnancy.
- Increase the percentage of drug-free babies.
- Reduce domestic abuse.
- Reduce student alcohol and drug use.
- Reduce violent crime.
- Increase success of diversion programs.
- Reduce recidivism.
- Increase drug-treatment services.
- Increase health-care services.
- Increase mental-health services.
- Increase county work-force and contractor diversity.
- Increase county government accountability and responsiveness.

Eventually, Stein and her colleagues decided that even a dozen goals was too many. In 1996, they isolated three high-priority "long-term benchmarks":

- To increase high school completion rates.
- To reduce the percentage of children living in poverty.
- To reduce crime.

Then they developed a hierarchy, with all the other benchmarks feeding into those big three. "I came to this reluctantly," Stein told us. "But I found it very useful, because I could now actually remember the list. Whenever I spoke I said, 'We have three long-term benchmarks, and we need the community to help with this.' I think it's hard to remember more than three or four benchmarks."

In 2002, the mayor and city council of Oakland, California, used seven goals as a starting point to develop a performance-based budget:

- Make Oakland a safe city.
- Develop a sustainable city.
- Improve Oakland's neighborhoods.

- Ensure that all Oakland youth and seniors have the opportunity to be successful.
- Model best practices to improve customer service and to be a fiscally sound and efficiently run city.
- Maintain and advance Oakland's physical assets.
- Inspire creativity and civic engagement.

Some school districts also set outcome goals. The Broward County School District, in Florida, adopted the following set in 2002:

Goal 1: All students will achieve at their highest potential.
- Objective 1: By June 2005, all students will read by the 4th grade and 80% of all students tested will score Level 2 and above on FCAT Reading.
- Objective 2: By August 2004, all classes K–1 will have an average class size of 18 students; all classes 2–3 will have an average class size of 20 students, to enhance the teaching and learning environment.
- Objective 3: By June 2004, all schools will receive a grade of C or better on the Florida School Performance Grade Category Designations.

Goal 2: All schools will have equitable resources.
- Objective 4: By August 2004, all students will attend a school that is safe, secure, and conducive to student health and well-being.
- Objective 5: By August 2004, reorganize and align the essential student support systems, school operations, and technology to maximize student achievement.
- Objective 6: By August 2003, every student will have a competent, qualified teacher.

Goal 3: All operations of the school system will align with student achievement and needs.
- Objective 7: By August 2004, reorganize and align all resources from all administrative divisions, including personnel, budget, facilities, etc., to support student achievement.

Goal 4: All stakeholders will work together to build a better school system.
- Objective 8: By Spring 2005, customer satisfaction with Broward County Public Schools will have increased to an average of 90 percent as measured by surveys of students, parents, teachers, and community groups.

- Objective 9: By September 2001, there will be a fully developed and implemented communication infrastructure to enhance effective and positive internal and external communication.

San Diego has a traditional budget, but the mayor has established 10 goals for his four-year term. Not all are expressed as outcomes, but San Diego does consult with its citizens to determine their priorities. A Citywide Service Priority Ranking Survey asks the people of San Diego to rate 40 city services in terms of where the city should spend its money. The survey is not ideal—it asks about services rather than results—but it certainly shows that San Diego is different from most cities. Citizens' number-one priority in 1999 was protecting recreational water resources from pollution. The second was relieving traffic congestion. Third was the paramedic service. Seventh was life guarding at city beaches. Obviously, beaches are very important to the quality of life in San Diego, and the traffic is bad.

Prince William County, Virginia, adopted its first strategic plan in 1992, setting forth the county's mission statement, its strategic goals, its desired community outcomes, and its strategies and objectives. County leaders involved more than 1,300 citizens in establishing a set of five broad goals for economic development, education, human services, public safety, and transportation, with five or six specific outcomes sought within each. They repeated the process in 1997 and again in 2001. Each spring, the county also sponsors a survey conducted by the University of Virginia, in which citizens rate their overall satisfaction with county government and with a variety of specific services and facilities. In 2000, 80 percent of citizens expressed satisfaction with the value of dollars spent by county government, up from 65.5 percent in 1992.

From these examples and other experiences over the years, we have derived certain general rules for turning priorities into targeted goals, the first step in Budgeting for Outcomes. Leaders should:

- Create a short, focused list. Ten goals is good; five is better; fifteen is too many. List the outcomes that matter most to the citizens you serve.
- Involve citizens and important stakeholder groups, such as business, labor, and community organizations, in the process of goal setting.
- Focus on outcomes, not outputs or activities. For instance, what matters is a reduction in the incidence of child abuse, not an increase in the number of family visits by social workers.
- Be realistic. Don't adopt "pie in the sky" goals. Setting a goal of cutting the rate of teen pregnancy in half in five years, as Oregon did, makes

people feel good, but falling short then leads to a sense of defeat. Oregon overreached in setting its goals, whereas Washington chose to focus on "improving" each of its ten priority outcomes.

- Get a politically neutral body to publish annual scorecards showing how the government is doing in relation to its goals.
- Make sure the executive (president, governor, mayor, executive, or superintendent) owns the goals. If he or she doesn't, the goals won't change anything, because the executive staff and cabinet won't use them in decisionmaking.
- Get bipartisan buy-in from both the executive and legislative branches, as well as buy-in from key stakeholders.

Choosing Indicators

A list of outcome goals makes priorities clear, but to measure progress you will need to define specific indicators of success. Without measuring, how can you really know whether student achievement has increased, or whether the health of citizens has improved?

We recommend choosing a maximum of three indicators for each outcome goal, to make sure everyone is focused on what is *most* important. This is not easy, because it will leave out big chunks of government. But the point is to force everyone in the budget process to focus on the most important results. Though participants will find it extremely difficult, it needs to be done well, because, as we all know, what gets measured gets managed. If you measure the wrong things, people will manage the wrong things. During the Vietnam War, for example, the Defense Department began to use "body count"—the raw number of Viet Cong killed—as a measure of progress. This distorted strategy, leading to pointless "search and destroy" missions that cost thousands of U.S. and Vietnamese lives.

In choosing indicators, our experience suggests several lessons:

Balance subjective and objective measures. An objective measure of public safety is the crime rate. A subjective measure is how "safe" people perceive themselves to be. If the crime rate goes down, but people don't feel safe, government has not delivered. If people are somehow made to feel safe but the actual crime rate remains the same, the promise likewise remains unfulfilled. In this and many other cases, success means passing both the objective and subjective tests.

Don't settle for data that are readily available; include "coming attractions." It is tempting to use indicators for which you already have data. Often, however, most of those measure activities or outputs, not outcomes. It is easy, for example, to get information about the number of violations and fines that result from environmental inspections. But delivering clean air and water to citizens is not the same as carrying out enforcement activities. The only indicator that really counts is a direct measurement of air and water quality.

Leaders need to hang tough until they can measure what matters, even when those indicators have to be listed as coming attractions. When direct indicators will not be available for some time, your best choice is to develop proxies. For example, many jurisdictions set goals related to the quality of the work force, but there is no obvious measure of workforce skills. Some use as a proxy the percentage of workers with a high school diploma.

Use indicators that will make sense to citizens. This is the acid test. Many school districts report average test scores for their schools, for example, but it is hard for citizens to tell what these numbers really mean. A measure that told them the percentage of students who made at least a year's worth of progress during a year in school would have more value. In the environmental arena, reports about parts per million or billion of pollutants or decibels of noise are meaningless unless they are converted into scales (such as a smog alert scale) that tell citizens what they *want* to know: am I facing health hazards or not? In each case the same or similar data are used, but a little extra effort makes them meaningful to citizens.

If capturing a particular outcome with three indicators is impossible, develop an index. Where a single measure can capture the result that citizens want, use it.

But no single statistic—or even three statistics—can capture all the issues related to certain complex areas, such as health. In such cases, develop an index. Everyone is familiar with indexes, from the Consumer Price Index to the Index of Leading Indicators. Charlotte, North Carolina, worked with the University of North Carolina at Charlotte's Department of Geography and Earth Sciences to develop a neighborhood quality of life index. It includes 19 variables, measuring crime levels and social, physical, and economic quality of life. Once established, such broad indices can serve as benchmarks of progress in relatively complex areas.

Governor Locke and his advisors chose the indicators displayed in the table opposite for the results they targeted in Washington State.

This list, like any, can be praised or criticized. In preparation for the next budget cycle, the finance office has already refined it. But the important point is that Washington has made improving performance on these indicators the driving force behind its budget.

Washington State's Indicators

Outcome Goal	Indicators of Success
1. Increase student achievement in elementary, middle, and high schools	• Reduced gaps in student achievement • Improved test scores • Increased high school graduation rates
2. Improve the quality and productivity of the workforce	• Increased possession of skills and abilities required by employers • Increased employment rate • Increased earnings levels
3. Deliver increased value from postsecondary learning	• Increased percentage of adults completing certificates/degrees • Increased graduate and student satisfaction • Increased number of students prepared to meet workforce needs
4. Improve the health of Washingtonians	• Improved index of epidemiological measures (Washington Report Card on Health) • Improved self-assessment of health • Improved access
5. Improve the condition of vulnerable children and adults	• Increased percentage living above poverty line • Increased percentage living in permanent, safe home or community settings • Increased percentage who make progress toward self-sufficiency
6. Improve economic vitality of businesses and individuals throughout the state	• Increased percentage of people employed • Increased percentage of prosperous individuals • Increased percentage of profitable businesses
7. Improve the mobility of people, goods, information, and energy	• Sufficient capacity to meet demand • Minimized delay and downtime • Fair and reasonable pricing
8. Improve the safety of people and property	• Reduced preventable injury and loss • Increased emergency response • Increased citizen confidence of their safety in community
9. Improve the quality of Washington's natural resources	• Improved percentage of days with healthy air • Improved percentage of water bodies/sources that meet quality standards • Reduced rate of land converted to urban areas • Improved trends in fish stocks and wildlife populations
10. Improve cultural and recreational opportunities throughout the state	• Increased availability and access • Increased participation • Increased satisfaction

Step 2: Decide the Price for Each Priority Outcome

Setting outcome goals answers the question, What are we here to accomplish for the citizens we serve? A joint executive–legislative resolution setting these goals can be a powerful precursor to the budget process itself, because it tells departments what elected officials want to deliver to citizens. Many budget debates are implicitly about this very question. Having the debate up front clarifies priorities and allows everyone to move to the next questions: how much to spend to produce each outcome, and how best to spend it.

If the price of government establishes what citizens are willing to pay for all government results and the priorities of government establish the results that matter most to citizens, the "price of the priorities" establishes how much citizens will pay for each outcome. There is no "right" price, just as there is no "right" price for a pair of shoes. It is a judgment to be made by policy-makers based on the realities and values of their jurisdiction at the time they begin the budget process.

Since Budgeting for Outcomes dispenses with the base, it dispenses with precedent as a guide. Even when history might appear to offer some guidance, results are never neatly arranged according to the traditional organization of the budget (or the organization chart). For example, increases in student achievement might be due not only to the state Education Department, but also to the actions of human service agencies, the Health Department, recreation programs, and criminal justice agencies. Most traditional budgets would not reveal these connections or track their impacts on the result.

Leaders should keep in mind that the initial price they choose may not be the final price. As with any other purchasing plan, the initial price and the results expected may change once all the choices are presented. But determining the price at the outset is essential to get the process started and to send a clear signal that you are no longer simply paying costs—you are buying results.

Setting the initial price for each result can be based on as much input as time will allow. Elected officials can use the kinds of meetings and surveys employed in San Diego and Prince William County, to ask citizens and stakeholders to divide 100 percent of the pie among the identified priority results. If you don't have time for that much involvement, the budget staff or a core group of advisors can do the same thing.

In Washington State, the Guidance Team assembled to develop the Priorities of Government worked with the Staff Team to allocate resources to the priorities, in a process that took two hours. The Staff Team did one iteration, then shared the result with the Guidance Team, which had done its own iteration. The two groups came up with remarkably similar results. The percentages were calculated initially by averaging the rankings from each member of the team. Further discussion moved things only a half point here or there. The percentages were then converted into dollars, using the previously determined price of government as the total. The Guidance Team then debated the allocation, relying on the Staff Team to answer questions.

It sounds easier than it was. Before offering their own instinctive assessment or judgment, the Washington State teams wanted to know how much was being spent for each of these results in the current budget. Public Strategies Group (PSG) consultants told them they would simply have to dive in, because that information did not exist in the old budget, organized as it was by agencies, not results. The new process needed to begin with judgments based on an intuitive sense of relative value, followed by closer analysis, debate, and bartering as the agencies and budget staff pursued the challenge of delivering the intended results at the specified prices.

Deputy Finance Director Wolfgang Opitz agreed: "The 'power of rough numbers' gives us more insight than do the precise dollar figures that we're used to," he concluded. "It's okay for us to lower our standards a bit. The choices we make are much more important than precision in the numbers."

The table on the following page lists the percentage of resources the Guidance Team decided to use to "buy" each desired result from state and local governments during the biennium. It excludes 10 percent taken off the top for overhead and governance functions, but it includes all state funds, not just the general fund. (For the actual budget, these numbers had to be broken apart to distinguish between the various funds.)

(Overhead functions are a special case, since they are rarely, if ever, a priority for anyone. For overhead functions, such as human resources, accounting, purchasing, and information technology, there are three choices: Take them off the top and budget for them separately; allocate them back to the results and expect the Results Teams or the agencies to budget for them; or turn them into public enterprises and make them earn their money by selling their services directly to the agencies. The third option, which we call enterprise management, is described in Chapter 8. Governance functions like the legislature and the elected executive should be taken off the top and budgeted separately. These functions provide the organization with the direction and policy guidance needed to achieve the results that citizens value.)

It was obvious to the Guidance and Staff Teams in Washington that 8.5 percent for safety and 11 percent for health did not even come close to what

The Price of the Priorities in Washington State

Priority of Government	Allocation of General and Other Funds (percentage)	Allocation of General and Other Funds ($ billion)
1. Increase student achievement in elementary, middle, and high schools	29%	$15.6
2. Improve the quality and productivity of the workforce	6.5%	$3.5
3. Deliver increased value from postsecondary learning	9%	$4.8
4. Improve the health of Washingtonians	11%	$5.9
5. Improve the condition of vulnerable children and adults	10%	$5.4
6. Improve economic vitality of businesses and individuals throughout the state	5.5%	$3.0
7. Improve the mobility of people, goods, information, and energy	12%	$6.5
8. Improve the safety of people and property	8.5%	$4.6
9. Improve the quality of Washington's natural resources	5%	$2.7
10. Improve cultural and recreational opportunities throughout the state	3.5%	$1.9
Total	100%	$53.9

had been spent in the past. They still went along, because there was consensus that the new allocations corresponded to the relative value citizens put on each outcome. It simply meant that the Results Teams were going to have to stretch to achieve their goals.

Step Three: Decide How Best to Deliver Each Priority Outcome at the Set Price

As we explained in the Introduction, the Guidance Team created Results Teams for each of the 10 priorities and asked them to define what the state should purchase to achieve the desired outcome at the set price. Each team had a leader from the Office of Financial Management, either a budget analyst or someone from the policy staff. These people were accustomed to doing research and analysis and pulling together recommendations. They were not accustomed to leading teams, or, for that matter, driving policy. They also knew that they had only six weeks to deliver a purchasing strategy. But they dived into the job—one even bringing in a placard that said, "Suspend Disbelief."

Whether you use this mechanism or some other mechanism, getting to a final purchasing decision—also known as a budget—requires the following steps:

1. Designate a purchaser for each outcome goal.

Those charged with creating a budget need to see themselves as buyers, or purchasing agents, for the citizens. This was the job of the Results Teams in Washington: to look at the choices through citizens' eyes and make the best decisions they could. As such, these buyers cannot be tied to any potential supplier—whether an agency, a department, or a private contractor. Instead, they must be impartial figures who can take a government-wide perspective. Candidates for these purchasing agents include the governor's staff, budget office staff, leaders of policy groups and think tanks, citizen panels, and combinations of these four alternatives. Whether you draw upon one source or several in combination, their charge is to develop a purchasing plan that will give citizens the best results for their money.

2. Develop a cause-and-effect "map."

The first job of these buyers is to articulate their "theory of what matters most"—how different activities contribute to the desired outcome. This means answering questions such as, "When it comes to student achievement (or the health of citizens, or decreasing congestion), which strategies have the most impact, and how do different strategies interact?" The resulting cause-and-effect maps provide the basis for deciding which routes to follow.

In Washington, the leader of the student achievement team asked for clarification about what PSG meant by "causal factors." And then it sank in: "Oh," he said, "you mean you want us to list the things we know actually work?" As teams realized that their purchase plans would not be recitations of past budget practice but opportunities to allocate money where it would do the most good, their enthusiasm picked up. The student achievement team decided that the state should target more of its resources on interventions that had proven they worked in schools where achievement was lagging.

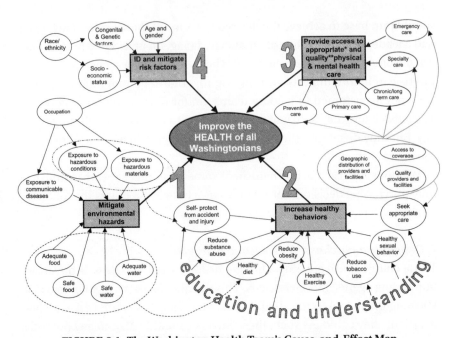

FIGURE 3.1 The Washington Health Team's Cause-and-Effect Map
SOURCE: Guidance Team Report to the Governor, Results Team Summaries.

The mobility team had the hardest time with its strategy map. Its assigned result was to improve the mobility of people, goods, information, and energy. But its members came with backgrounds in highways and public works, so they were accustomed to focusing on roads and cement. As they wrestled with the outcome, they identified potential trade-offs between moving someone to an office as a commuter and moving that same intelligence over the Worldwide Web. Both types of mobility involved corridors, infrastructure, and possible congestion, but each demanded different resources. Ultimately, the team came to understand the fundamental distinction between the pouring of cement and asphalt and the efficient movement of people, ideas, goods, and energy. There is no one right way to create cause-and-effect maps. Figure 3.1, the health team's map, provides one example. Creating such a map requires those involved to be clear about how they think activities add up to results. Doing so subjects each "theory of what matters most" to a challenge from every competing theory—exactly the kind of debate the budgetary process should stimulate.

3. Develop a purchasing strategy.
Cause-and-effect maps allow purchasers to choose from among many possible strategies and to assign a relative priority to each. Washington State's

health team identified four possible strategies: increasing healthy behaviors among citizens (getting them to eat better, to drive more safely, to quit smoking, and to get more exercise); mitigating environmental hazards (ensuring cleaner water, air, and food); identifying and mitigating risk factors related to gender, socioeconomic hardships, and genetic predispositions; and providing access to appropriate high-quality physical and mental health treatment. These four strategies appear on their map.

When the team ranked these strategies in terms of their contributions to the end result, it decided that mitigating environmental hazards was most important, increasing healthy behaviors was second, providing access to health care was third, and mitigating risk factors was fourth. With limited resources, it decided to increase the state's emphasis on the first two. Research data had convinced team members that this was the way to get the most bang for their buck, even though it meant reducing spending on more traditional—and highly expensive—patient care. In fact, their analysis showed that these two strategies would yield a 16-to-1 return on investment.

The old budget game would have led the health team to focus on the strategies with the greatest costs. The new approach asked them to ignore last year's numbers and figure out where the best results could be obtained for the money available. The "aha!" moment came when PSG consultants asked why they weren't emphasizing personal choice and behavior by focusing on drugs, alcohol, and obesity. "Oh, we could never say that out loud," the leader responded. But the consultant pushed them to go ahead: If they truly thought that such investments in prevention would produce more health for Washingtonians than would comparable investments in treatment, they should say it.

4. Solicit offers.

With their outcome goals and strategies clearly in mind, buyers solicit offers to see who can deliver the most results for the money. This step departs most radically from the old budget game. Instead of asking agencies or departments to add or subtract from last year's numbers, the purchasing agents incorporate the results, price, and purchasing strategy they have settled on into something like a "request for proposals"—let's call it a "request for results" (RFR). This solicitation replaces traditional budget instructions. The RFR can be sent to all agencies and departments, to other governments, even nonprofit and for-profit organizations. It asks potential suppliers to identify how they would deliver the expected results, and at what price.

In developing their responses sellers need not, indeed cannot, take anything for granted. They must assume that for each result there will be many proposals from many potential sellers: public and private. If they expect to get funded, they have to offer up proposals that deliver the needed results at a competitive price. Since an individual bidder may choose to submit multiple proposals (for its various programs and activities), it will in a sense be competing against itself. This will force it to challenge its own practices, to examine whether they are the most cost-effective means to the end. While it will be challenging to bidders, it will also liberate them. They need not be limited by their pasts; the process will encourage them to be innovative, to come up with new approaches and creative twists. Some will forge partnerships with other departments or agencies, with other governments, and with nongovernmental organizations. The bidding process will also encourage them to consider ways they could contribute to more than one of the priority outcomes.

(To compare different bids on a level playing field, governments need to adopt "full cost accounting," which assigns all direct and indirect, or overhead, costs to a program or activity. This way, decisionmakers can compare apples to apples. If a public program excludes overhead costs such as pension obligations and other employee benefits from its bid price, it will have an unfair advantage over nongovernmental bidders.)

This application of competitive pressure to prompt innovative solutions is not entirely new. It is the essence of how charter schools work, for example. Under a charter school system, some steering organization—a school board, or state board of education, or in some states even a university or city government—has the authority to offer performance contracts, based on proposals, to run schools for a set period, usually four or five years. Many charter schools are run by churches, colleges, community organizations, or groups of teachers, while others are run by for-profit organizations. By providing more choices to purchasers, charter schools offer alternative ways to achieve educational results. The authorizing authority doesn't give them a budget as such. Instead, they get a certain dollar amount per student enrolled, most of which typically comes from the school district the student left.

The same principle applies when governments use steering or purchasing organizations (see Chapter 5), such as state and local children and family commissions. These entities have control over some pot of money, large or small, with a mandate to articulate results they want to achieve and the strategies they will fund to achieve them. They then solicit bids from many different organizations, public and private. They might fund work to decrease the crime rate among youths, or to help abused mothers and their children, or to run after-school programs, or to provide effective alternatives to incarceration, such as supervised community service. They might accept bids from a broad array of potential suppliers—local government agencies, state agencies, nonprofits, community groups, even religious organizations. (See pages 118–121 for a good example, the Pinellas County Juvenile Welfare Board.)

In a traditional budget framework, a department of public works would get a budget allocation (starting with its base) for maintaining the public infrastructure. With Budgeting for Outcomes, the jurisdiction would develop an outcome goal related to its infrastructure and a strategy related to maintenance of the infrastructure. It might divide that strategy into sub-strategies, one of which might relate to cleanliness. Then its department of public works, similar departments in other jurisdictions, and private companies would bid for the opportunity to deliver those strategies. Their bids would almost certainly involve street-sweeping, but they might also involve advertising campaigns to fight litter, "adopt a street" programs with community groups, cooperation with the police department to tow cars for street sweeping, and so on. The key is to stimulate new thinking about how to deliver better results for less money.

Because of time constraints, the step of soliciting bids was truncated in Washington. Traditional budget instructions had already gone out and submissions had already been received when the new process got under way. Fortunately, Washington had also asked its agencies to submit inventories of their activities and the costs for each. This inventory was intended to serve as a basis for priority setting in a traditional "focus-on-the-cuts" process. The same inventory was instead used as a set of "offers" in the process that each of the Results Teams went through. Each team was given a subset of the inventory, but they had access to the entire list if they wanted it. For them it was, in effect, a catalogue of possibilities from which they could shop.

5. Review the offers and choose what to buy.

After the offers are in, the first task is to rank them in terms of results delivered per dollar, then move down the list, buying according to priority until available funds have been exhausted. This buying plan becomes the budget. It is a list of keeps, not cuts: positive choices for spending the citizens' resources to buy the citizens' results.

Those items ranked too far down the list to be purchased don't make the budget. For defenders of these programs, the challenge is clear: Improve your ranking. Either demonstrate that your program will deliver better results (or the same results at a better price) than the others being offered, or demonstrate that there are more efficient ways for those at the top of the list to deliver their results, thereby making "room" to add more purchases. Here again, the incentives are as they should be: better results for citizens, at a better price.

Washington added one more step before the Results Teams developed their final purchasing plans. The 10 team leaders met together to talk about what they were purchasing, what they weren't purchasing, and what they needed to purchase *from* one another. As we explained in the Introduction, the higher-education team decided to use some of its funds to improve K–12 education; the health and natural resources teams jointly bought more efforts to protect water quality; and several teams funded prisons, to reduce the number of low-risk prisoners who would be released early. PSG consultants began by calling this process the "swap meet," but the participants labeled it the "bizarre bazaar." It was necessary because the work of state government is so interconnected: Programs in one policy area contribute to outcomes in others.

Ultimately, the Results Teams put together detailed purchasing plans, indicating new and existing activities they would definitely purchase, ranked by priority; activities they would *not* purchase; activities they would purchase if they had more money; and activities they would give up if they had less money. The result was a clear set of priorities designed to get the most value for the money.

They presented their purchasing plans to the Guidance Team at a four-hour meeting. This was the first time any of them had heard a rationale for the entire state budget, rather than for one department or program at a time. Under the old rules, it was almost impossible to see the whole budget at one time. There were simply too many trees—more than 1,150 individual budget activities—to allow a good view of the forest. Participants found the experience of hearing all the hard choices laid out—all rooted in 10 core purposes of state government—quite powerful. "This is unbelievable," said one of the business leaders on the Guidance Team. "In four hours, we have heard the whole budget presented. I understand the trade-offs considered and the strategies chosen."

At this four-hour meeting, the Guidance Team developed its recommendations to the governor, most of which he followed as he finalized his budget proposal.

Going the Full Monty

As of this writing, Washington's new budget process has been something akin to emergency triage, ultimately making do with the ready-made solutions that its own agencies could offer. The state has implemented only the first three steps in what we call Budgeting for Outcomes. The fourth and fifth steps—soliciting offers from all comers and choosing what to buy from a broad array of responses—are tasks that remain for future budget cycles.

Washington will have to transform its Results Teams into permanent purchasing or "steering organizations"—bodies that operate as buying agents, purchasing programs and outcomes on behalf of citizens every time they prepare a budget. The complexity of this role, and the time required to do it well, make biennial budgets highly desirable.

Steering organizations are a well-established tradition in a few governments, but as a general phenomenon they have emerged only within the past two decades. They set outcome goals, choose strategies, fund providers to carry out those strategies, and measure their performance in delivering the desired outcomes. In addition, they can:

- Convene community leaders to do visioning, strategy development, and goal setting.
- Do research and analysis on current strategies, potential strategies, and best practices elsewhere.
- Keep the outcome goals visible to the entire community—for example, by publishing or getting another group to publish annual scorecards measuring progress.
- Educate elected officials and other policymakers about strategic issues, goals, and strategies—in particular the executive and his or her staff, the budget staff, and the legislature and its staff.
- Evaluate why strategies are succeeding or failing. Often data show that the expected results are not forthcoming, but they do not explain why. In such cases, steering organizations need to buy strategic evaluation, which examines why the expected cause-and-effect relationships between strategies and outcomes are not occurring. (See *The Reinventor's Fieldbook*, pp. 56–59, for more on strategic evaluation.)
- Develop new strategies and modify strategies that are not proving effective enough, and recommend these policy changes to elected officials.

The second major element Washington will need to add is definition and measurement of outcomes and outputs for every strategy, every public program, and every private provider. This way, as they develop budgets, each purchasing organization can look at the data for each strategy, program, and provider and make more informed decisions—dropping some programs and providers, giving more funding to others, and soliciting new providers.

To provide a concrete example, envision a steering organization whose goal is to improve the quality of the workforce. It would fund a series of strategies, one of which might be job training for low-income people. The organization would make sure the outputs and outcomes of that strategy were measured: results such as the percentage of job trainees who graduated; the percentage of job trainees who found jobs in the field; the average wage of those jobs; the trainees' average level of satisfaction with the program; and their employers' assessment of the quality of their preparation.

Within the strategy, there might be a number of different programs—one operated by community colleges, one run by a state agency, a third run by community organizations. Each program might have multiple providers. The first could involve multiple community colleges; the state agency program might include agency units as well as private, contracted organizations; and dozens of community organizations might provide the third. The steering organization would need data on the performance of each of these providers, to see which were most cost-effective.

With "steering" firmly in place, Washington will also need its "rowing" organizations, or sellers (public and private agencies that actually deliver results), to drive measurement down through the ranks, so that every division, unit, and work team is focused on its own handful of key performance targets. In this step, the cause-effect connections between inputs, processes, outputs, and outcomes must be made explicit and used to improve performance.

The key breakthrough is to focus on results rather than activities. But there are two kinds of results: outputs (the actual work produced, such as courses taught or miles of asphalt laid) and outcomes (the affects of that work). It is important to connect the work processes through the outputs to the ultimate outcomes so that the entire organization can see the links between the work people do and the results they deliver. (For more on performance measurement and management, see *The Reinventor's Fieldbook*, Chapter 6 and 7.)

THE DIFFERENCE BETWEEN OUTCOME BUDGETING AND PERFORMANCE-BASED BUDGETING

Only a few governments have used Outcome Budgeting. Washington State pioneered it, and as we write, Los Angeles and Asuza, California, are following suit. But many jurisdictions have begun transforming their budgets from the other direction, engaging in a process known as performance-based budgeting, or performance-based program budgeting (or, for short, simply performance budgeting).

Just as in Budgeting for Outcomes, in performance-based budgeting those who create the budget (staff, executives, and legislators) examine performance data as they make their decisions about where to move money. But most performance budgets are traditional agency-based and cost-based budgets, with performance measures added for information. Adding measures is a good thing, but in the end they are a decoration on a process rooted in "base" spending by organizational units. To move from redecorating the cake to a whole new recipe requires that outcomes and price be the starting point for delivering results to citizens.

Nor does performance budgeting use steering organizations to reconsider the current set of strategies for delivering the results, or to solicit bids. Performance budgeting takes the existing set of programs for granted, measures their performance, and uses that information to make incremental changes in shaping the budget.

Budgeting for Outcomes starts with the results most important to citizens, then purchases programs and activities from all comers to achieve those results. It takes no existing programs as givens; it asks all programs to compete with other public and private organizations to deliver results at the best price. It combines program budgeting's focus on programs rather than organizations, performance budgeting's focus on the results of those programs, zero-based budgeting's habit of reexamining priorities every budget cycle, and managed competition's method of letting all kinds of organizations, public and private, compete to deliver programs. (See Chapter 7 for more on managed competition.)

Sunnyvale, California, pioneered performance-based budgeting in the early 1980s, and numerous cities and counties have since followed. Texas was the first state to succeed in institutionalizing performance budgeting, in 1991; since then, Louisiana, Florida, Maine, and others have followed. New Zealand, Australia, Sweden, and a few other countries also use performance budgets. (For a full discussion of performance budgeting, see *The Reinventor's Fieldbook*, pp. 43–53.)

Performance budgeting is a huge improvement over traditional budgeting. Merely by calling attention to outcomes, it can drive serious rethinking of strategies. Sunnyvale offers a good example. During the 1980s, its budget focused mainly on outputs, but in the mid-1990s, its leaders decided to shift to outcomes. "That has a much stronger and more powerful capability to raise questions about policy setting, about strategies and tactics you use to achieve outcomes, and about fundamental organizational structure," former city manager Tom Lewcock told us. He cited police services as an example. Sunnyvale set nine outcome goals for the police, each given a weight of one to five to indicate how important it was. When the police began measuring these outcomes and adding the weights, they realized that domestic violence accounted for 50 percent of the weighted crime. The Public Safety Department then reorganized internally to attack domestic violence more effectively, and it convinced the City Council to spend more on combating domestic violence. "That wouldn't have happened with the old system," said Lewcock.

The new focus on outcomes motivated managers to think very hard about whether they were using the right strategies and producing the right outputs to achieve their outcome goals. This in turn forced them to look at whether their organizations were structured correctly and whether their internal rules were barriers to improvement. "It just forces people to take on those kind of issues," said Lewcock. "It has stimulated much more creative thinking by staff about strategic and tactical options—ways to do things differently to enhance the outcomes."

But even as practiced by Sunnyvale, performance budgeting takes for granted that the current public departments and agencies will continue to be monopoly providers of most strategies and services. It also sets outcome goals and measures progress for departments and programs, but not for the entire community. In contrast, Budgeting for Outcomes starts by defining the most important outcomes for the entire community (or state or nation), then asks budget makers to decide how much to spend to produce each one. In this way, it pushes them to rethink their fundamental allocation of resources every time they prepare a budget.

In places like Texas, performance budgeting has led to incremental changes, but politics still trumps logic most of the time. "All these strategies have their own constituencies, which fight like heck to keep their money coming for their particular strategy," former House Appropriations Committee chair Robert Junell told us. Once in a great while a program is eliminated because of poor performance, or funds are moved to a better-performing alternative. And sometimes directors of public agencies are forced to rethink their mix of services and outputs. But rarely are big changes made in the mix of strategies and services funded by governments that use performance budgeting.

In contrast, Budgeting for Outcomes gives us a tool to make big changes, at a time when they are absolutely necessary. It roots those decisions in results, helping public leaders deliver the outcomes citizens value even as they slash budgets.

ACCOUNTABILITY:
THE DIFFERENCE BETWEEN
CONTROL AND INFLUENCE

How does accountability work in a system of Budgeting for Outcomes? Very directly: If providers perform poorly, they can find their funds rerouted to competitors.

This process should not be automatic, however. If a program is failing to achieve its goals, it might need a change in leadership, it might need to rethink its theory of cause and effect, it might need to adopt more successful practices, or it might need more money. Each case needs to be analyzed to understand why performance is suffering and what the most effective remedy might be.

Even when budget makers and elected officials act with such care, however, many top managers fear the accountability of Outcome Budgeting. "How can I be accountable for outcomes when I don't control them?" they ask. It is true that no one agency or steering organization has complete control over broad policy outcomes. They are the results of many, many factors, some of which—like the health of the national economy—are far beyond the control of government. But governments do *influence* those outcomes. And their leaders should be expected to use that influence as effectively as possible.

Take, for example, mobility and the reliability of our roads. Half of all traffic congestion is caused not by roads that are too small but by traffic accidents. Most traffic accidents are a result of inappropriate driver behavior (drunkenness, inattentiveness, or distractions, such as cell phones). Highway departments spend billions building new roads, millions on incident response to clear the roads after accidents, but only pennies on trying to alter driver behavior to reduce the number of accidents. In fact, most highway departments take the view that altering behavior is the job of law enforcement. If they are going to deliver the mobility and reliability that citizens want, however, they need to demand more from drivers. They need to partner with law enforcement, education, motor vehicle departments, and everyone else who can help cut the accident rate. Sure, they can't drive the car, but highway departments can influence those who do—if they choose to.

So high-level officials can and should be expected to influence out-comes. But how do we hold them accountable for doing so?

This is the trickiest issue we have run into.

Let's start with steering organizations. The policy outcomes they are try-ing to improve often take years to change, and they are deeply affected by trends outside the control of governments. So it is not easy to hold steering organizations accountable for improving policy outcomes, particularly in the short term. We believe they should be held accountable for outcomes *and* for probing, challenging, asking the right questions, and actively refin-ing their strategies. If they are not working to create and refine fundamental strategies for improvement, they should be fired. If they are showing signs of developing the right answers and improving outcomes at a reasonable pace, however, they should be rewarded.

Steering organizations can hold rowing organizations accountable through performance agreements, which should spell out not only the budget provided but the program outcomes and outputs expected and the rewards and consequences for performance. Think of charter schools: Their charters should spell out the results they expect to produce and the conse-quences. Rewards for success include the ability to attract more students and hence more income. Consequences for failure include the possibility of losing their charter.

Employees within rowing organizations are another matter. If their orga-nization's future is at risk, they obviously share in its accountability for per-formance. Beyond that, it is usually unfair to hold most front-line workers and managers accountable for outcomes, because they have so little direct control—or even influence—over those outcomes. But they can and should be held accountable for delivering outputs: for example, processing a cer-tain number of environmental permits per month, within set deadlines, with high service ratings; or sweeping X lane-miles of streets per week, with high cleanliness ratings after sweeping. They can be rewarded for improve-ment or penalized for repeated poor performance. This is properly done through a performance management system, not the budget system.

Performance management, the subject of Chapter 8, creates an incentive system to get every employee working to achieve the results citizens value at the price they are willing to pay. Performance management systems es-tablish performance standards or targets, measure results (outputs and outcomes), reward good performance (financially, psychologically, or both), and penalize poor performance.

Budgeting for Outcomes and performance management are different systems, which serve different purposes. Budgeting for Outcomes is designed primarily to improve steering: Those who steer choose from among the strategies and "rowers" available to produce the results citizens want. Performance management is designed to improve rowing: Those who "row" are held accountable for effectively delivering their assigned results with their assigned resources.

The two systems should support one another: The program outputs and outcomes rewarded through performance management should help achieve the policy outcome goals in the budget. But one should not be pressed into service to do the other's job. A county government might choose as an outcome goal reducing the rate of child abuse, for example. Many factors influence the rate of child abuse, including economic conditions, the rate of alcohol and drug abuse, and the effectiveness of interventions when abuse is suspected or reported. So it would be unfair to reward or punish child welfare agency managers based on the rate of child abuse. It would be more effective to evaluate their performance and assign consequences based on other goals, such as a reduction in the number of *repeat* incidents of child abuse.

But someone in the government has to be accountable for policy outcomes—for actually reducing the rate of abuse. That is largely the province of Outcome Budgeting: The executive and legislature should be accountable to the voters for such outcomes, and the executive's steering organizations should be accountable for their contributions. If they are not, no one in the entire system will really care whether outcomes improve. New Zealand, whose budget and performance management systems have focused largely on outputs in the past, experienced this problem. Everyone concentrated hard on improving the current outputs—both their efficiency and their quality. But few leaders focused on whether those outputs were actually improving the outcomes citizens cared about. To deal with this problem, New Zealand is now shifting its focus to outcomes.

THE LEGISLATIVE BRANCH

Legislative and budget committees are normally linked tightly to the structure of the budget, which is linked to the structure of the government. Often there is a committee, in essence, for every department. To institutionalize Budgeting for Outcomes, legislatures need to change these committee structures. They need to shift from committees focused on *organizations* to committees focused on *outcomes*. The Washington legislature, for instance, needs a committee focused on each of the state's 10 priority outcome goals.

These committees would parallel the governor's Results Teams. This would help the legislative body steer toward results that matter to citizens, rather than just responding to the needs of organizations and interest groups. It would also help separate governance and policy functions from management of the departments and agencies.

A second challenge is getting lawmakers to use performance information to shift funding from strategies that are less cost-effective to those that are more cost-effective. This has succeeded in Sunnyvale, California, in Multnomah County, Oregon, and in Washington State, where the legislature approved most of Governor Locke's budget. Texas has done a bit of it. But more often, performance budgeting has led to very little shifting of resources. Even where legislators find the information useful, they don't use it to steer. Politics continues to crowd out performance, as legislators continue to craft budgets that deviate from previous years only in ways that respond to powerful constituencies or political imperatives. Most of the strategic changes driven by performance budgeting are made by executives and managers, not legislators.

Performance data will never crowd out politics in a democratic legislature, but it can enter the mix. One way to make that happen is to involve legislators in the process of creating outcome goals, so they develop some sense of ownership. Another is to demonstrate that improving outcomes matters to their constituents. Publish scorecards, for example, showing annual progress. But keep them simple and short: The point is to engage citizens in the process of grappling with how to improve outcomes.

You will need key champions in the legislature to lead the adoption and use of Outcome Budgeting. Performance budgeting worked in Texas largely because two key legislators, Ric Williamson and Henry Cuellar, led the charge. They in turn converted House Appropriations chair Robert Junell to their cause.

"You've got to have advocates," says Beverly Stein, the former Multnomah County commissioner and Oregon state legislator, "some peer who has the ability to persuade, to be the one with the rallying cry—and hope you have one in each party, and one in each house, at least." Where you don't have this kind of legislative leadership, she says, you have to recruit it.

Finally, educate and train both legislators and their staffs. "You've got to have continual education and training in order to maintain momentum," says former Texas representative Henry Cuellar. "Legislators leave, and new ones come in. You've got to educate them and keep doing it."

THE ISSUE OF REORGANIZATION

Many policy outcomes cannot be achieved unless multiple organizations work on them, so Budgeting for Outcomes always raises issues of organizational structure. Consider something as simple as street sweeping: If the police department doesn't enforce parking regulations that prohibit parking on one side of the street on sweeping days, the public works department can't sweep the streets. Or ponder something as complex as lowering infant mortality rates. How many state and local organizations own a piece of that goal?

Some outcomes can be achieved only through cross-agency—or even cross-jurisdictional—efforts. Because reorganization can be so difficult and time-consuming, however, Budgeting for Outcomes is the best way to deal with this challenge. Steering organizations can define a comprehensive set of strategies to achieve their outcome goal or goals, then buy pieces from many different organizations. Most of the coordination can be done at the steering organization level. (See Chapter 5 for more on this topic.)

When most participants have come to the conclusion that some reorganization would help improve outcomes, go ahead and merge and/or uncouple organizations that need it. But understand that your external environment will continue to change, and your organization chart may need to be redrawn again in a few years.

In any case, make sure your information infrastructure is cross-agency, because this will enable your cross-agency steering organizations to be effective. If information stays bottled up within each agency, boundary-spanning steering will be difficult. You want an information system that is systemwide, so you can span any boundary at any time.

BUDGETING FOR OUTCOMES IN 12 EASY— AND NOT-SO-EASY—STEPS

To summarize what we have argued in these first three chapters, leaders who are serious about kicking the habit of fiscal overindulgence and delivering the results citizens want at a price they are willing to pay should follow this 12-step program:

1. Set the price of government: how much citizens are willing to spend.
2. Determine the priorities of government: the outcomes that matter most to citizens, along with indicators to measure progress.

3. Decide the price for each priority outcome.
4. Decide how best to deliver each priority outcome at the set price: Create steering organizations to act as purchasing agents and have them develop "cause-and-effect" strategy maps and purchasing strategies.
5. Set outcome goals and indicators for each of the strategies and programs, and make sure the results are measured.
6. Solicit offers, then choose which programs and activities to purchase.
7. Negotiate performance agreements with those providers, spelling out the key outputs and outcomes to be produced, the indicators to be used to measure progress, the consequences for performance, and the flexibilities granted to help the organization maximize performance (see Chapter 11).
8. Eliminate line items in your budget below the program or strategy level; appropriate lump sums for the results of each strategy and program.
9. Develop full-cost accounting, which attributes all direct and indirect costs to a program or strategy, so you know the real cost of each program and strategy.
10. Create a process to review performance against the targets, in both the executive and legislative branches. Ideally, this should take place in executive-branch steering organizations and legislative committees organized to focus on the same outcomes.
11. Use data on results and performance management to drive improvement in programs, strategies, outputs, and work processes.
12. When performance dictates it, make changes in the organization chart, in both the executive and legislative branches.

These 12 steps are obviously not for the faint of heart. When you embark on this journey, you are embracing a fundamental paradigm shift. Such a transformation has the potential to yield tremendous results, but it will not take place within one or two years. It is a huge amount of work. Because of this, we recommend unrolling the process step by step, over a period of years. But we do *not* recommend dipping in a toe with pilot programs. From the beginning, you should commit to converting your entire system, rather than a few pilot agencies. Don't try to take all the steps at once, but when you take a step, commit the entire organization.

"If you're going to institute a culture change, it happens best all at once, where everybody's in the same boat," says former Texas budget director

Albert Hawkins, who helped pioneer performance budgeting while he was with the Legislative Budget Office. "The greatest risk is that you will never get the rest of the system in place; [pilots] allow resistance to change to get a foothold."

But take heart, adds former Texas representative Henry Cuellar. "If you screw it up, it can't be any worse than what you're doing now."

PART TWO

SMARTER SIZING

It Does Matter

FOUR

Strategic Reviews
Divesting to Invest

Governor Locke's Results Teams in Washington State proposed some fundamental shifts in state strategy. Among the boldest was the K–12 education team, which proposed that the state suspend two initiatives passed by the voters that would have increased teacher pay and reduced class sizes, in order to spend more on early childhood education, shift to a "pay for skills" compensation system for teachers, and move away from across-the-board funding toward a formula that put more money into schools and kids that were struggling.

Governor Locke is an experienced politician, however, a veteran of both the legislature and the governor's office. He understood that such radical changes in something as critical to the public as education would trigger months—if not years—of heated debate. A realist, he decided he needed more time to prepare both the public and the legislature. He proposed suspension of the voter initiatives in his budget, but he asked the legislature to create a joint legislative–executive study of the K–12 financing system, to examine the options and build the necessary political support. (The legislature suspended the initiatives but declined to go along with his plan for the study.)

Locke's decision illustrates an important lesson. In budget season, there is often not enough time to handle the politics of deep strategic change. Smart leaders create forums outside the budget cycle in which to do the strategic work of eliminating obsolete functions and ineffective strategies, developing new strategies, refining strategies to make them more effective, and moving funds from less effective to more effective strategies.

Leaders call these forums by many different names: program reviews (Canada), performance reviews (the Clinton administration), performance audits (North Carolina), strategic program area reviews (Arizona), zero-based management reviews (San Diego), prior options reviews and now quinquennial reviews (the United Kingdom). We'll call them strategic reviews, to emphasize that their purpose is to improve the strategies used to create results citizens value at a price they are willing to pay.

Typically, newly elected executives have the impulse to clean house all at once. Legislatures get the same impulse in times of fiscal crisis. Both often set up special commissions and try to sweep clean the Augean stables of government in six months or a year. President Clinton's National Performance Review was originally conceived as a six-month exercise; in reality, it lasted eight years. The first Texas Performance Review was originally seen as a one-time exercise, as was Canada's Program Review in the mid 1990s. But it is impossible to rethink so much government in such a short time. It is far wiser to institutionalize the effort as a recurring process, focusing on one policy arena at a time.

The state of Arizona has learned this lesson. Each biennium the Joint Legislative Budget Committee chooses a few policy areas to examine in detail, through a Strategic Program Area Review. In recent biennia these reviews have focused on domestic violence, special education, children's services, and state financial assistance to counties, among other topics. They examine all programs within the policy domain, across multiple agencies. Both the governor's Office of State Planning and Budgeting and the Joint Legislative Budget Committee staff perform reviews. They then submit a joint report to the governor and to the state legislature. This adds weight to the system, because it requires that staff members of both branches come to agreement on the issues and their recommendations—whether to retain, eliminate, or modify programs. (Most often, they suggest modifications.)

One of the most common forms of strategic review is the sunset review. "When a man knows he is to be hanged in a fortnight," wrote Samuel Johnson in the eighteenth century, "it concentrates his mind wonderfully." A sunset law is the administrative equivalent of a scheduled hanging: It requires that a program be reauthorized periodically by elected officials to survive.

Evidence from 25 years of experience with sunset laws suggests that the threat of a necktie party can indeed concentrate the minds of elected officials, government managers, and special interests—if the sunset commission takes its job seriously. Too often, however, sunset reviews produce little more than superficial analysis, and elected officials routinely grant the condemned function a reprieve. Sunsets have proven most useful when analysts recommend ways to improve performance and legislatures adopt them. "The beauty of sunset is not so much that you can get rid of something," explains Brad Mallon, a former government regulator in Colorado. "The beauty is the chance to take an objective look at an agency and make needed changes."

Texas has one of the best sunset programs. There, says Dale Craymer, once a budget director for Governor Ann Richards, sunsets usually result in fine-tuning, rather than elimination, of agencies. Joe Walraven, review director for the Texas commission and a 15-year veteran of the process, told us, "Most commonly we find that functions don't need to be abolished. You don't go in and flat out get rid of something. It really becomes a question of how to make improvements for efficiency and effectiveness."

Occasionally, though, an execution does take place. By 2003, the Texas Sunset Advisory Commission had killed off 44 agencies and folded 11 more into other agencies. Most of those that were shut down were fairly small or inactive, Walraven says.

Sunset laws have several shortcomings, by their nature. First, they are limited in scope, focusing on a singular program or regulation or organization. They don't consider broader strategies to achieve outcomes, or alternative programs or providers. Second, many governments passed sunset laws without creating good performance measurement systems, so sunset commissions lack the data they need about results to decide whether to eliminate or change programs. And third, legislators often aren't involved in sunset commissions, so they don't get personally involved in the decision to terminate. When faced with constituencies defending the program, they are loath to carry out the order.

Another common approach, "blue-ribbon commissions," often provides little more than the illusion that action is being taken. Typically such commissions are made up primarily of outsiders who have neither the in-depth knowledge of government to produce real strategic change, nor the credibility with elected officials to make their recommendations stick. Exhibit A was President Reagan's famous Grace Commission, chaired by business mogul Peter R. Grace. Established primarily to root out waste and fraud, it was composed of businesspeople who were contemptuous—or at best patronizing—toward government. So, naturally enough, Congress ignored most of its recommendations.

While commission members may be distinguished in their fields of accomplishment, too often they don't know government well enough to get at the fundamental changes that need to take place. They can see waste, but they can't see the structural roots of the problem. So they recommend that some programs be eliminated and others be contracted out, but they do nothing to transform the systems—such as procurement, budgeting, and personnel—that create the waste. They may understand that certain special education laws need to be repealed, but they don't understand how the very organization of public education into centralized districts with quasi-monopolies creates low-performing institutions in which fundamental change is almost impossible.

Commissions can be effective, however, if their members are well chosen, if they are given real authority, and if the rules are set up to circumvent the political obstacles that have frustrated the normal processes of government.

In the mid 1980s, to overcome parochial resistance to military base closings, Republican congressman Richard Armey devised a plan that called for eight-member Base Closing Commissions, nominated by the president and approved by the Senate. The commissions had their own staffs, which reviewed the Pentagon's suggestions for bases to close. The commissions held hearings, then issued recommendations, which often were at odds with the Pentagon's choices.

In the past, efforts to close bases had usually failed, because they triggered fierce resistance from communities chosen to make the economic sacrifice. The president always objected to closings in politically important battleground states, and no congressman would ever allow a closing in his own district without a fight. Yet the General Accounting Office reports that the Base Closing Commissions have been a great success: They have saved taxpayers $2 to 3 billion a year, while most affected communities have recovered within two years. Hence this model is an excellent example of how to overcome parochial interests to make difficult decisions. It succeeded because its rules contained the following provisions:

The president and Congress had to take it or leave it. They could accept or reject the commission's list of bases, but they could not amend it. This meant that anyone trying to protect his own military base would have to assemble a majority vote in both houses of Congress to block the entire package—highly unlikely when so many congressmen did not have bases under the gun in their districts.

The decision was bundled into one vote. Rather than consider many bills to close many bases, Congress had to face the issue all at once. This made the vote highly visible. Base closings could not be killed in subcommittee, far from the glare of publicity. This didn't prevent politicking, but it kept it to a minimum.

Inaction and delay were impossible. If Congress did not pass legislation rejecting the entire plan within 45 days after receiving it from the president, it would automatically become law.

OTHER FORMS OF STRATEGIC REVIEW

There is no one, right way to perform a strategic review. In smaller organizations, if the leaders are behind the review process, it can be quite simple.

In December 1993, when Peter Hutchinson and his Public Strategies Group (PSG) colleagues signed a contract to act as superintendent of schools in Minneapolis, the district faced a $5 million budget shortfall. At the same time, it was embroiled in a complex and difficult negotiation with its teachers union. Three months later, Hutchinson and the school board had cut the budget, but the labor negotiations had completely broken down. When the district and the union took their dispute to arbitration, the arbitrator decided in favor of the teachers. Suddenly, the district had to come up with another $7 million to pay for the contract.

According to the long-established rules of the game, balancing the budget was the superintendent's problem. None of the other participants, other than the school board, saw the budget as their responsibility. Quite the contrary: Each department head, school, advocacy group, and union felt an obligation to fight for everything they could get, then to hang on for dear life to every dime allocated.

Adding to PSG's dilemma was the fact that they had taken the district to arbitration in the labor dispute—and lost. In people's eyes, they had driven the school system into this new, $7 million hole. PSG had to solve the problem, and most stakeholders were poised to play defense and lay blame.

Peter Hutchinson, who sat in the superintendent's chair, recognized this as a crossroads. Though a balanced budget was necessary, he and his PSG colleagues were more worried about the impact of the budget debate on the organization's central mission—ensuring that all children learn. They knew that accomplishing that mission would require the engagement of every stakeholder. But the usual budget debate would likely bring disengagement, even open conflict. They could see that business us usual was not going to work.

So Hutchinson invited representatives from all the stakeholder groups—from parents to teachers to custodians—to a set of budget meetings. And for two long evenings he kept them there, all 52 of them, sitting in a huge circle. "The mission of the Minneapolis Public Schools," he reminded them, "is to ensure that all students learn.

> *We need to balance this budget. But we need to do it in a way that will make us* better *able to achieve our mission. If we don't balance this budget, not only will we fail at teaching these kids, but we will end up fighting with each other so much that we'll convince the citizens that we care more about our own little empires than about the kids we are here to serve.*
>
> *It's my responsibility to submit a budget to the school board. If we can build a budget together that supports our mission and is balanced, I promise I will submit it. If we fail, I will still submit a balanced budget, but I will make no commitments about what will be in or out.*
>
> *I also don't think that the best way to get at this is to start by talking about what to cut. Instead, let's begin by making a list of things we would do—if we had the money—to improve student achievement. For every item on the list there will be a price tag, because dreams don't come free.*

People started making suggestions, some of them very innovative. Ultimately, they added up to $7 million. "Now," Hutchinson told them, "for every dollar we collectively can manage to save, I will allocate fifty cents to the shortfall, and fifty cents to the wish list. We will keep going, offering savings ideas, until we have completely funded both pots."

With the incentive of matching funds to support their best ideas, everyone was able to get beyond playing defense. Knowing that they might get as well as give, virtually everyone in the room volunteered line items for cutting. Inspired by the thought of spending on creative new programs, the participants became just as creative in finding ways to save money. And they found the $14 million they needed—$7 million for the deficit and $7 million for the wish list. They divested, because they wanted to invest in better outcomes.

This worked, in part, because there is no separation of powers in an American school district. The executive, the superintendent, works for the legislative body, the school board. This "unitarian" simplicity also exists in many locales where the city council or county board hires and fires the city manager or county executive. It is also true in parliamentary systems, in which the prime minister is simply the leader of the majority party in the legislative branch.

But when the executive is elected separately from the legislature—as is the case with the U.S. president, all governors, and most mayors—the politics of divesting to invest are much more difficult. Important changes must be put into legislation, and interest groups can usually protect their favorite programs by getting the legislators they support to block change in legislative committees. In a bicameral legislature, which the U.S. government and 49 states have (Nebraska being the exception), opponents only have to block the change in one house. A crisis can help drive reform, but strategic shifts in direction are never easy.

For governments with separate executive and legislative branches, an ideal approach might take this form:

1. An annual strategic review of, say, two of ten key policy outcome arenas. (In Washington State, this would mean reviewing two of the 10 Priorities of Government.)
2. A special commission to conduct the review, consisting of members of the executive (in Washington this would include members of the Results Team responsible for that outcome); members of both houses of the legislature; staff from an independent auditor's or comptroller's office; and outside experts (not stakeholders with an interest), such as consultants, academics, businesspeople, or members of think tanks.
3. Rules similar to those the federal government used to overcome parochial objections to closing military bases. (For more, see Lesson 7, p. 106.)

Whatever method you use, the important step is to make strategic reviews a permanent element of your steering process. By making them regular and permanent, you can:

- do them in a sequence, which will cover the entire government over time, rather than all at once;
- keep the pressure on agencies, programs, and private providers to improve their performance in order to justify their continued existence;
- have time to make changes for the sake of improving results, not just to cut budgets;
- maintain a permanent capacity to perform strategic reviews, rather than trying to build it from scratch in a crisis; and
- create real opportunities for public dialogue about the proper role of government. Because the reviews would occur regularly—and everyone would know the schedule—they would create an expected forum for sustained examination of fundamental issues.

LESSONS LEARNED ABOUT STRATEGIC REVIEWS

From our study of strategic reviews, as well as our participation in several of them, we have drawn a baker's dozen lessons:

1. Make sure high-level leadership is visibly driving the process.

It takes heavy lifting to eliminate government functions, change government's strategies, and reform government's spending patterns. Because there are so many demands on his or her time, the leader must delegate the bulk of this work. But in the words of John Kost, a former deputy budget director in Michigan, "Delegating decision making to a part-time citizen commission or to staff who are not empowered and who lack the explicit support of the chief executive is a sure recipe for failure." The political leader must visibly demonstrate deep personal interest in the success of the initiative, get his or her political appointees and allies on board, and stick with the agenda. If not, everyone involved and affected—managers, employees, legislators, lobbyists, reporters—will see the lack of personal involvement and draw the same conclusion: This is something he/she thinks would be nice, but it is not a priority. Then they will act accordingly.

2. Involve both the legislative and executive branches.

Typically, one branch (usually the executive) decides to go it alone, and once its recommendations are complete, it tries to bring the other branch along. This seldom works. There are substantial benefits to establishing joint ownership at the outset. It is very hard to move legislation through a bicameral legislature if no one in that legislature feels personal ownership of the measure. And the best way to get that personal ownership is by involving legislators in the process.

In 1993, half a dozen members of the Senate Governmental Affairs Committee filed bills to create a joint commission to lead some kind of strategic review of the federal government. Unwilling to share the credit, President Clinton decided to go it alone with his National Performance Review. This turned out to be a major tactical error. When Clinton and Vice President Gore released their recommendations in September 1993, Congress displayed polite interest and then moved on. The only major legislation that passed within the next year was a procurement reform bill that Senator John Glenn was already sponsoring, to which he attached the National Performance Review recommendations. Because he already owned procurement reform, the effort moved. Clinton and Gore later put many recommendations into their budgets, and over the years, some of these passed.

But much of the most important legislation called for in the 1993 report, such as civil service reform and budget reform, dropped from sight. "If the first year (of the Clinton effort) proved anything," wrote public administration expert Donald Kettl of the University of Wisconsin and the Brookings Institution, "it is that truly important reform. . . is impossible without building congressional support (or avoiding congressional opposition)."

As we noted above, Arizona's strategic program area reviews are done by both executive and legislative staff, who must then submit a joint report to the governor and legislature. The legislative staff work for the Joint Legislative Budget Committee, so they represent both houses. Since all must come to agreement, their recommendations carry real weight.

3. Get the political stars aligned if you want to make fundamental change.

You can't propose major changes, as the education team did in Washington, and just expect legislatures to pass them. Big changes create winners and losers, and the losers will mobilize to defeat you. You need fertile ground— such as a permanent fiscal crisis—to even try for fundamental change. You have to do the advance work necessary to convince key interest groups and convert key legislators. And you have to make a compelling argument to the media and the public.

If the stars are not aligned, don't tackle that particular problem. Canada's two program reviews in the mid 1990s were very successful, for instance (see *The Reinventor's Fieldbook*, pp. 78–81), but Canada's leaders put several very contentious issues off limits, including federal transfer payments to the provinces and major entitlement programs such as unemployment insurance.

4. Make sure you have clarity of purpose.

Confusion will kill you. Those doing the review need to know the exact scope of the review, how deep leaders want to go in proposing changes, what the expected product is, and how long they have to produce it. In 1993, President Clinton's mandate to the National Performance Review (NPR) was fuzzy. Clinton's State of the Union address called for the elimination of 100 programs, but he never told the NPR's leaders that this was their job. Different leaders involved in the process gave different advice, and there was always uncertainty about how far to go. Some teams thought they could get fundamental reforms passed; others felt that politics would defeat anything big and were more incremental in their recommendations. Vice President Gore, who led the review, wanted bold thinking, but there was no clear signal from the president. And Clinton's aides were nervous about some proposals, afraid of alienating members of Congress whose votes they needed on the budget. This confusion led to time being wasted generating ideas that went nowhere.

5. Review by policy arena, not program.

A strategic review should be more than a sunset review, looking at one program at a time. It should not just eliminate ineffective programs and refine existing strategies; it should create new strategies. Washington State's Results Teams, for instance, each reviewed one "Priority of Government." Thus the team that focused on improving the health of Washingtonians examined all aspects of achieving that outcome. As we have said repeatedly, the most important question is not whether program X or Y should exist, but how best to produce the results citizens value at a price they are willing to pay. To answer this you must look at all the strategies being used to contribute to that outcome—and alternative strategies that might work better. Strategic reviews should scan the country and globe for best practices. Standing alone, a program might look effective. But when compared with three other programs that produce double the results at lower prices, it might look very different.

6. Create a powerful, independent board or commission that can act in the general interest.

The biggest obstacles to fundamental change are interest groups bent on protecting their pieces of the pie. To combat them, you need a powerful group that represents the public interest: a sunset commission, a special task force or ministry, a commission such as the federal Base Closing Commission, an independent office such as an auditor, or even a special cabinet member. (In Canada, in 1994, the prime minister appointed a special "minister for public renewal.") Give them the staff, expertise, and time they need to carry out a thorough review, and ensure that they are protected from lobbying pressure from special interests.

7. Create a process that reduces the power of special interests to block change.

Recommendations accepted by the executive should become law unless one or both houses voted against them within a set amount of time. In this way, change could be blocked only by an active, public vote—not by the normal inertia of the legislative process, nor by decisions made out of public view, in committees and subcommittees. (One could also require that the entire package be voted up or down as a whole, with no amendments, but this might be going too far for most legislators.)

8. Use the expertise of both insiders and outsiders.

Those who work within government know best how it functions and how to improve it, but are often blind to alternative strategies that do not use government employees, such as tax credits, vouchers, and contracts with nonprofits. In addition, their knowledge of alternative practices from other jurisdictions is often limited. Combining knowledgeable outsiders, such as consultants, think-tank experts, and academics, with knowledgeable insiders yields the best of both worlds.

If the leaders of the strategic review are able to think outside the box and are committed to deep, fundamental change, they can get by without outsiders. Canada did so in its program reviews. But in general, knowledgeable voices from outside government provide a much broader perspective, because they are not attached to existing ways of doing business and existing organizational turf.

9. Make sure you have performance data—particularly data on effectiveness.

Sorting out which of government's current strategies and programs contribute the most to the outcomes citizens care about is impossible without data about the actual results of these programs and strategies. Strategic reviews without performance data have been fairly ineffective, because they offer little basis on which to make decisions. If you don't have the data, spend time building a performance measurement system before you initiate strategic reviews.

10. Build into the process consultation with customers and other stakeholders.

Customers can give you great insight into what works and what does not. Using surveys and focus groups, ask a set of knowledgeable customers to rank the value of all the activities they are familiar with in a certain policy arena, such as health care or K–12 education, or in a city or county government. Stakeholders such as business groups, teachers, and those who are regulated by government agencies can also provide fundamental insights into what needs fixing and why.

Final decisions, however, should not be determined by the views of customers and stakeholders. A strategic review is designed to act in the interests of the general public—the "owners"—not individual customers. Customers often don't know that much about a policy area, other than their own preferences. And they may like a particular service (such as having school gyms, rinks, and other athletic facilities available and free to the public during non-school hours) that may not contribute significantly to any key outcome goal. In the eyes of those who represent the general interest, the money might be better spent elsewhere.

11. *Don't forget to include subsidies and tax breaks in the review process.*
Most strategic reviews focus on government programs. But government does its work through many other mechanisms, including tax breaks and subsidies. These are rarely examined, but they provide rich opportunities for savings. Consider state subsidies for colleges and universities. Rather than maintain the relatively low tuition at most state universities—which acts as a subsidy for every student, wealthy or poor—perhaps it would be better to let tuition rise but give subsidies directly to those who need help the most. The University of Virginia follows this strategy to some degree, charging more than $25,000 a year to out-of-state students who, given the school's quality, compete fiercely to get in.

Similarly, tax breaks offer ripe territory for savings. "Tax expenditure budgets," as they are known, are huge. Tax breaks are often given for economic development purposes, but they should be reexamined periodically to see if they are the best strategies to achieve the state's goals. Many of them are ineffective; others just move jobs around within the state, rather than creating new jobs. Often, the money would be better spent elsewhere: on education, training, or infrastructure, for example. Strategic reviews should reexamine all subsidies and tax breaks, to see if they are the least costly ways to achieve the desired outcomes.

12. *Make sure most observers perceive the process as being fair and sensible.*
In Washington State, every program was subjected to the same process and the same logical test: Could it deliver better results than other alternatives? Because the media saw this approach as sensible and evenhanded, they gave the result a warm reception. The process created many losers, but sometimes it's easier to make big changes when you take on many interests at once than when you take them on one by one. When many groups have to sacrifice, it is harder for any one group to convince legislators that it should be spared.

In Washington, so many oxen were gored—and the basis for decision-making was so transparent—that the entire package had real credibility. And with the budgets showing so clearly what was cut and what was kept, everyone knew that if they succeeded in restoring funding for their program, the lowest one on the "keeps" list would be cut. If they helped themselves, in other words, everyone could see whom they would be hurting. "We made it clear to everyone what the trade-offs would be," says Deputy Finance Director Wolfgang Opitz, "and that clarity greased the skids."

13. Ease the pain by creating humane transitions.
Sometimes you can mitigate both the pain and the political opposition to change by phasing out programs gradually and treating employees humanely. No lay-off policies—so all downsizing comes through attrition and early retirement incentives—are one of the most obvious ways to achieve this. As we discuss in Chapter 6, there are many other tools available as well.

ACROSS THE POND

Though few Americans realize it, we are not world leaders in reinventing government. Since the early 1980s, it is the British who have been showing the way. (For the British story, see *Banishing Bureaucracy,* Chapter 1.) Under Margaret Thatcher and John Major, the Conservative government focused primarily on making government smaller and more efficient. Then, under Tony Blair, the Labor Party shifted the focus to effectiveness. Both parties have relied heavily on strategic review processes.

Beginning in 1987, the Conservatives restructured their giant, centralized government departments, by creating smaller, mission-focused "executive agencies" within them, each with a five-year agreement called a "framework document." At least theoretically, the department steers and the agencies row. Each agency has a clear mission and performance goals, with targets specified every year, and a great deal of management flexibility.

Every five years each agency undergoes a strategic review—formerly called a "prior options review," now a "quinquennial review." The department examines the agency's role and performance to see whether it should be abolished, sold, contracted out to private contractors, merged, split, or otherwise restructured. If the agency survives the scrutiny, the department negotiates a framework document with the agency that specifies its role for the next five years. Reviews are publicized, and outside comment is solicited. Two central organizations, the Treasury Department and the Cabinet Office, which promote reform government-wide, monitor the review process to make sure it is thorough and to provide the reviewers with advice.

The Blair government added what it calls a comprehensive spending review, which examines all spending across the government, sets priorities, projects spending limits for the next three years, and defines the results it wants for the money spent. As the Treasury Department Web site puts it, "Spending Reviews set firm and fixed three-year Departmental Expenditure Limits and, through Public Service Agreements, define the key improvements that the public can expect from these resources."

Public service agreements (PSAs) are three-year agreements negotiated with each department. In addition, there are a handful of crosscutting PSAs, such as one for the criminal justice system, one for childcare and the early years, and formerly one on welfare to work (before the government reorganized, creating a new Department for Work and Pensions). These agreements include what we could call the department's mission, outcome goals, indicators of success, and efficiency goals. The Treasury Department describes the basic elements this way:

- *Aim: a high-level statement of the role of the department.*
- *Objectives: in broad terms, what the department is looking to achieve.*
- *Performance targets: under most objectives, outcome focused performance targets.*
- *Value for money: each department is required to have a target for improving the efficiency or value for money of a key element of its work.*
- *A statement of who is responsible for the delivery of these targets. Where targets are jointly held this is identified and accountability arrangements clearly specified.*

In its 2000 Spending Review the national government also negotiated a local government PSA with the Local Government Association, setting out "key national targets that rely on local government for delivery." It has since negotiated PSAs with at least 60 local governments, linking national targets with local priorities. These PSAs also give the local government a range of "freedoms and flexibilities" they will need to achieve the goals. As an incentive, local governments earn extra funding when they hit their targets.

In 2002, to boost their ability to do this kind of strategic thinking, the British created a new "Strategy Unit" within the Cabinet Office, reporting to the prime minister through the cabinet secretary. Its stated purpose is "to improve government's capacity to address strategic, crosscutting issues and promote innovation in the development of policy and the delivery of the government's objectives."

The new unit has four main roles:

- *undertaking long-term strategic reviews of major areas of policy;*
- *undertaking studies of crosscutting policy issues;*

- *strategic audit (occasional assessments of how well the UK and UK government are doing); and*
- *working with departments to promote strategic thinking and improve policy making across Whitehall.*

From American shores, it is difficult to tell how well this new focus on steering works. But it is clearly a major step forward—light years beyond anything in the United States. We would be wise to keep an eye on our friends across the pond.

FIVE

Consolidation
Smart Mergers

In the 1970s, a group of young reformers in the Florida legislature were upset about services for poor, at-risk children. "We had all these independent fiefdoms," remembers Buddy MacKay, a Young Turk who was later elected to Congress, and, in 1990, as lieutenant governor. "We had a Department of Juvenile Affairs, and Child Protective Services, and Health and Rehabilitative Services, and more, and none of them spoke to each other. You'd have a troubled juvenile who would be in two or three of these systems, and they wouldn't even know he was in the other systems. So we jammed them all together and made them divisions of one department."

The new Department of Health and Rehabilitative Services (HRS) was soon the largest state government department in all of America. By 1990 it had 45,000 employees—nearly 4,500 of them in central headquarters in Tallahassee—and eight layers of management.

"In the '70s," MacKay says ruefully, "we were like East Germany or the Soviet Union. Everything we did was to centralize power, and we did it with a vengeance."

The problem was, the old departments continued to operate as separate divisions, each its own stovepipe. The same old bureaucracy remained, only much, much bigger. "The fundamental mistake was that we never got the system so the people in charge of operations [in the regional districts] were in control," says MacKay.

We never took the heads of the old agencies out. The operations people were theoretically in charge of everything that happened, but in fact the decisions were still being made by the program managers in Tallahassee. In each dis-

*trict you would have a sub-program director who was answering to someone
in Tallahassee rather than to the operations guy or gal. And everybody of
course said, "Well you can't hold me responsible."*

When Lawton Chiles won the governorship in 1990, with McKay beside
him on the ticket, HRS was one of their first targets for reform. In their first
year they could convince the legislature only to spin off a few functions and
decentralize a bit of authority to the department's 15 regional districts. But
in 1992 a crisis erupted. In the late 1980s a Republican secretary of HRS had
contracted with EDS to install a massive, centralized, mainframe computer
system to handle case management of 1.5 million Medicaid, welfare, food
stamp, and other clients. As it came online in 1992, problems erupted.
Overwhelmed by the volume, it slowed to a crawl. Employees had to wait 30
minutes for it to process their entries, so their waiting rooms began to fill up
and spill out into the street. And when caseworkers deleted people who
were no longer eligible for Medicaid, the computer kept sending them Medicaid cards—which quickly blew a hole in the state budget. When all this hit
the newspapers, Chiles had the opportunity he needed to begin breaking
up this monolithic bureaucracy.

He and MacKay proposed to do two things. First, they would spin off
more HRS functions—public health, health care, workforce training, and
juvenile justice—into separate departments or agencies. Second, they
would decentralize what was left of HRS down to the 15 districts, each with
its own community board. The legislature approved the new model, and
when implementation proceeded too slowly for Chiles, he fired his director
and installed MacKay.

MacKay did away with three layers of management, eliminated 25 of the
38 senior management positions, cut headquarters staff by 25 percent, reduced middle management by 20 percent, and eliminated 2,300 positions
in Tallahassee. His objectives, he says, were to "wipe out anybody in headquarters who is duplicating what's going on in districts," and then to "give
authority to the districts."

MacKay's successor pushed HRS back toward centralization, however.
There have been innumerable restructurings since. Today, the organization
is called the Department of Children and Families (DCF). It has 23,000 employees and a $4 billion budget, and it primarily handles mental health
services and protection of abused children. "After a series of reorganiza-
tions, there is now a separate Department of Health, an Agency for Health
Care Administration, a Department of Juvenile Justice, a Department of
Aging, and God only knows how many others," says MacKay. "Each now has

its own legislative committee, plus an appropriations subcommittee in each house. It was probably inevitable, and the unintended consequence is that we are right back where we were in the late '60s, with no single coordinating body and policy being set in a kind of annual Lobbying Olympics between the various interest groups."

In October 2003, DCF announced plans for yet another major restructuring—the twenty-third in 33 years—because the current administrative system was "unmanageable and inefficient."

Unfortunately, this wasteful merry-go-round of failed reorganization is all too common. When money is tight or a crisis erupts—when a child dies in a foster home, for example—elected officials feel a powerful need to "do something." Too often, their knee-jerk response is consolidation: merging separate organizations into one big agency or department, with promises that the merger will do away with duplication and overlap, save money, and result in integrated services for the citizens.

Consider the federal government's new Department of Homeland Security, born of the need to "do something" after the September 11, 2001, terrorist attacks. It merges at least 170,000 federal employees from 22 agencies, working in areas ranging from agricultural research to port security to disaster assistance. It brings together the Transportation Security Administration (TSA), Customs Service, Immigration and Naturalization Service (INS), Secret Service, Coast Guard, and Federal Emergency Management Agency (FEMA).

Within Homeland Security, the Information Analysis and Infrastructure Protection Directorate absorbs the FBI's National Infrastructure Protection Center, the Defense Department's National Communications System, the Commerce Department's Critical Infrastructure Assurance Office, the Energy Department's National Infrastructure Simulation and Analysis Center, and the General Services Administration's Federal Computer Incident Response Center.

The Border and Transportation Security Directorate oversees the Coast Guard, TSA, much of the Customs Service, the Border Patrol, the Federal Protective Service and Federal Law Enforcement Training Center, the INS, the Animal and Plant Health Inspection Service (formerly in the Agriculture Department), the Office of Domestic Preparedness (formerly at Justice), and FEMA's former Office of National Preparedness.

The Science and Technology Directorate, focused on developing countermeasures to chemical, biological, radiological, and nuclear weapons, includes what was formerly Agriculture's Plum Island Animal Disease Center,

Energy's Lawrence Livermore National Laboratory, and Defense's National Bioweapons Defense Analysis Center.

The Emergency Preparedness Division hosts most of FEMA; the FBI's National Domestic Preparedness Office; the Health and Human Services Department's National Disaster Medical System, Metropolitan Medical Response System, and Office of Emergency Preparedness; the Justice Department's Domestic Emergency Support Teams; and the National Oceanic and Atmospheric Administration's Integrated Hazard Information System.

Few management experts expect the new department to succeed any time soon. Like Florida's HRS before it, Homeland Security is a classic example of the knee-jerk impulse to consolidate. This impulse promises greater efficiency through elimination of duplication and overlap, but too often it delivers huge bureaucracies with so many layers that authority is fragmented, communication is difficult, and decisions take forever. Those who sponsor such mergers remind us of troubled young couples who decide that getting married is the cure. No wedding ever solved the underlying problems in a relationship, and after the honeymoon the headaches remain.

Even in the private sector, the payoff from consolidation has often proven chimerical. "In the short term, the experience of major private sector mergers and acquisitions is that productivity and effectiveness actually *decline* in the period immediately following a merger and acquisition," reports Comptroller General David Walker, who runs the U.S. General Accounting Office. "This happens for a number of reasons. For example, attention is concentrated on critical and immediate integration issues and diverted from longer-term mission issues. In addition, employees and managers inevitably worry about their place in the new organization."

Slamming multiple organizations together often results in organizations with so many different missions that top leaders have no expertise in most of what the organization does. They have trouble agreeing on what is most important, and they can't decide what to focus on. Large organizations with multiple missions are notoriously poor performers.

Lower down, employees spend their time worrying about their futures and defending their turf, rather than doing their jobs. "Employees often have existing loyalties to the old chain of command, and it's hard to get people to switch over," says Princeton University sociologist Frank Dobbin. Creating a truly integrated corporate culture, he adds, "can take 10–15 years—enough time for a large portion of the workforce to turn over."

Sometimes the cultural differences are inherent in the work itself. The new Homeland Security Department brought together border inspectors

from the Customs Service and agents from the Immigration and Naturalization Service—a logical move, since both did roughly the same thing and
some had already been cross-trained. But integrating agents of the Plant
Health Inspection Service—college science majors with a different mission
and culture—was another matter. As their union president told *Government
Executive*, "We're food people. We're not gun people." Many worried that
within the consolidated Bureau of Customs and Border Protection, the
work of plant inspectors would be considered of secondary importance,
leading to poor decisions by management.

Even Customs and INS agents complained about pay and benefits issues
and the fact that the new law allows managers to make personnel changes
without the unions' consent. In the first year, turnover among agents was
about 20 percent. Immigration people worried that top management,
which is filled with Customs people, was not attuned to the intricacies of
immigration law. "Customs law is different than immigration law," one attorney told *Government Executive* magazine. "And my direct chain of command doesn't have the same experience in the area that I practice in."

No matter how you draw the overlapping circles to create a new organization, the boundaries will be messy. Total perfection simply is not possible
in trying to fit people and functions into any logical scheme. There will be
reporting relationships, employee classifications, and space issues that refuse to conform. Different financial, administrative, and technology systems will require an enormous amount of time and energy to unify. And different field office structures will have to be integrated. Before and during
the period of transition, consolidations demand vast amounts of energy,
most of which is directed at the bureaucratic structure and the people inside. They divert energy *from the work to the workplace.* "It's going to take
three to five years when all is said and done to get everything organized in
the way that will be its final form," the Coast Guard's Rear Admiral Harvey
Johnson said of the Homeland Security consolidation.

Jesse Rasmussen, former director of human services in both Iowa and
Nebraska, helped drive a massive consolidation of human service agencies
in Nebraska. "I was arguing for this, because I thought it was the only way
we'd get a different system," she says. But she learned a sad truth:

> I learned . . . that if you do that massive a restructuring, the restructuring itself
> is so distracting that people lose sight of why it's a good idea. You ought to just
> change business practices and business relationships, and then change struc-
> ture when it's in the way. The same thing might have happened if the gover-
> nor had said to the director of Human Services and director of Public Works,

"I want your departments to do one plan for each child in your systems. Change the business practices and relationships, as opposed to rearranging the rooms in your house." It got down to people saying, "I paid for that wall, and I'm taking it with me." It was bizarre. And emotionally, people couldn't do the work.

THE BEST SOLUTION: CONSOLIDATE STEERING AND SEPARATE IT FROM ROWING

We need to learn to think differently about consolidation. Fragmentation is a big problem in government, and overlap and duplication do exist. But there are better ways to consolidate than to create Soviet-style megabureaucracies.

In any jurisdiction, the first step is for elected leaders to figure out the results they want to achieve, which should be the outcomes citizens value most (see Chapter 3). The next step is to determine the most effective strategies to achieve those results. Only then should public leaders consider the best organizational structure to carry out those strategies.

Often, their best option will be to consolidate funding streams and steering authority, but not the organizations that do the actual rowing. As we discussed in Chapter 3, steering—setting policy and direction—focuses on doing the right things. Rowing—service delivery and compliance operations—focuses on doing things right. Housed in separate organizations, each can concentrate on its mission.

Steering well is almost impossible if an organization's leaders also have to focus on rowing. Peter Drucker captured this point emphatically 35 years ago, in his book *The Age of Discontinuity:*

> *Any attempt to combine governing with "doing" on a large scale paralyzes the decision-making capacity. Any attempt to have decision-making organs actually "do," also means very poor "doing." They are not focused on "doing." They are not equipped for it. They are not fundamentally concerned with it.*

Once the steering function has been separated out, it can be consolidated to ensure that policies are integrated and mutually reinforcing across a government. To use the Florida HRS example, policy work related to at-risk children could be brought into one relatively small steering organization, which could design a service delivery system that would offer high-quality, integrated services. All funding streams for at-risk children could be put under the control of that organization, which would use them to purchase results from service organizations—public, private, and not-for-profit.

In the United States, many government funding streams are highly fragmented, because Congress has created hundreds of separate grant programs that are carried out by state and local governments. The states have done smaller versions of the same thing. San Diego County, for example, has more than 100 separate funding streams for health and human services alone—and this is the norm, not the exception. Such fragmentation creates service delivery systems shaped by the requirements and restrictions of federal and state laws, not by the needs of customers.

Using consolidated funding streams, steering organizations can purchase results from any rowing organization they consider best equipped to produce them. Consolidated funding gives citizens the benefits of more effective steering *and* more competitive service delivery. It is a radical, fundamental change, yielding exponential increases in bang for the buck.

Envision, for a moment, a relatively small steering organization overseeing an area such as human services. It sets outcome goals, chooses the most effective strategies, uses its consolidated budget to purchase results from myriad providers through competitive performance contracts, evaluates their results, and continually shifts resources away from low-yield strategies and providers to high-yield strategies and providers. The steering organization becomes, in effect, an agent for citizens, buying results on their behalf.

To consolidate in this way, elected officials don't have to move many boxes on the organization chart, and the vast majority of employees can remain in their rowing organizations. The essential steps are for elected officials to sharpen their focus on the results they want to produce, then charter a new steering organization to accomplish them. The legislative body can appropriate one lump sum to the steering organization, or if it wants more control it can appropriate a sum for each strategy or program under the steering organization's purview. (It can also give the steering organization control over funding streams from higher levels of government.) The steering organization would prepare its proposed budget; the executive and his or her budget office would review and amend or approve it; and the legislative body would make the final appropriations.

Many models already exist for this fundamental shift. One of the first was created 60 years ago, in Pinellas County, Florida, which comprises the area around Tampa and Saint Petersburg. In 1944, Judge Lincoln C. Bogue of the Pinellas County Juvenile Court confronted a growing problem: children who clearly needed help, showing up in his courtroom time and time again.

The judge's options were meager, and most—such as reform school or the county jail—seemed ill suited to turn around the lives of neglected, abandoned, or abused youths.

When Judge Bogue turned to the county commissioners for help, they appropriated the princely sum of $250. Seeking a solution that was a little more far-sighted, the judge drafted a state law authorizing the formation of "an autonomous board of citizens," with taxing authority, to look after child welfare. Known as the Juvenile Welfare Board, it was, according to its current leaders, "the nation's first countywide agency utilizing dedicated property tax revenue to better the lives of children and families." In 1986, the state legislature passed enabling legislation allowing other counties to create such boards. Called Children's Service Councils, there are now eight of them with the authority to levy taxes.

The Juvenile Welfare Board has 11 members: the superintendent of schools, one county commissioner, one public defender, one state attorney, one juvenile court judge, and six members appointed by the governor. It spends about $46 million a year, mostly from a dedicated property tax voted by the citizens, to improve outcomes for children. Its staff and board identify needs, prioritize them, and develop a budget for each one. The organization does no rowing itself. Instead, it finds the best providers to meet each need, funds them, and measures their success and the county's success in addressing the needs. It funds almost 60 different providers, focusing as much as possible on prevention: neighborhood family centers and teen centers, counseling, domestic violence shelters, residential treatment services, after-school activities, child-care centers, home monitoring, recruitment and training of substitute child-care workers, and a 24-hour resource and referral service.

Every provider working for the JWB is assigned to a contract manager, who works with the program's staff to help it achieve its goals. The board also has a Web-based system for monitoring performance. "What makes it unique is it has a measurable objective component that can be tailored to each program," long-time JWB executive director James E. Mills told us. "This can be negotiated in the contract. That system has been picked up, and we ended up in the hosting business." Counties now making use of the Pinellas system include Jacksonville, Martin, Palm Beach, and Broward, and Dade County is considering the model for its new children's trust.

Performance measurement leads to consequences: The best providers grow and the worst lose funding. "Last spring [2003] the board defunded 16 programs," Mills explains. "We cleaned out some marginal performers and some duplication of effort. . . I think we went from about 80 to 60." Elimi-nating contracts allows the board to expand high-performing programs and strategies and add new providers.

One of their most effective strategies is the Healthy Families Program, Mills says. Serving roughly 1,500 households, it aims to reduce child abuse among high-risk families. "We use paraprofessionals recruited from the neighborhoods these people come from, targeted on high-risk census tracts," Mills explains. They go into hospital maternity wards in poor areas of the county, try to identify high-risk families, and offer them services. "You're hitting people at the time when they really want in the worst way to be good parents. They don't set out to be bad parents; they don't set out to abuse their kids." About 90 percent accept and commit to the program until their child is five years old. "The family sets goals for themselves, which makes it very much asset based: What are your strengths; where do you want to go? We help mobilize resources to help you get there."

Through a contract with a university, the board carefully measures and evaluates outcomes. "We found tremendous progress in many areas—jobs, stability in adult relationships, and so on," says Mills. He has also noticed that deaths among young children are now significantly lower in Pinellas County than in Hillsborough County, whose demographics related to at-risk children are otherwise quite similar—an improvement he attributes to the program.

"We made a major new commitment to that program last summer," he says. "We're probably up to $3 to $4 million a year, and we're now covering about 70 percent of the high-risk births in the county."

The staff also measures several dozen key indicators of the status of chil-dren, including dropout rates, drug and alcohol use rates, and rates of do-mestic violence. They compile this information into an annual "Pinellas Profile," which analyzes trends over time.

If the Juvenile Welfare Board were both a steering and operating body, Mills says, "It would change what we are and what we do incredibly:

I know from a staff standpoint we would all recommend against it, and the board would vigorously resist. We have as a policy that we're not a service provider. Once you start delivering direct service you lose your credibility as a planner, and you lose your credibility and objectivity as an evaluator, because you're just like everybody else. You simply do not mess around with mixing those two up, if you can help it.

In an era of declining resources, you also would spend all your time man-aging cutbacks, rather than figuring out new ways of doing things. It's easier if you have hands off, so you don't have to deal with, "Where's old Bill going to find a job at age 53?" We can focus on the best way to use these resources in a declining fiscal environment.

The state of Iowa took a slightly different approach with its at-risk and abused children. Like other states, Iowa's human service efforts were already hindered by fragmented funding streams when, in the 1980s, demand for services exploded. The farm crisis and the loss of manufacturing jobs at places such as John Deere contributed to a sharp increase in the incidence of substance abuse and family violence.

As a result, the number of children placed in care outside their homes leapt by 40 percent between 1982 and 1987. This was a very expensive proposition, especially given that some of the care had to be provided out of state. By the mid 1980s, the skyrocketing cost of providing these services was eating up 90 percent of the child welfare budget, leaving very little to invest in prevention of child abuse and neglect.

As in most states, Iowa's systems for dealing with at-risk kids—child welfare, mental health, and juvenile justice—were highly centralized, and they did not communicate well with one another. The state had few solutions for family problems other than foster care or institutionalization within the juvenile corrections system. And the fact that out-of-home care was effectively an entitlement, with no cap, while services such as family counseling and therapy had fixed budgets, drove caseworkers to remove more and more kids from their homes.

To attack these problems, the Iowa legislature created "decategorization boards": steering boards at the county level whose job was to develop more comprehensive, creative, preventive strategies. Each board had to include a member of the elected county board, the county court, and the county department of human services; some also included representatives of the schools and even faith-based community organizations.

"Decat" boards, as they came to be known, helped county agencies figure out how to spend their categorical funding streams. But the magic of "decat" was a policy that allowed the boards to roll over any money that was left over at the end of the fiscal year and use it for creative new efforts such as prevention and treatment. "It really promoted a local decision-making process around child welfare, all of child welfare," says former DHS director Jesse Rasmussen. "Because if you did better in your intervention strategies, you would have this money left over that would be decategorized. When you rolled it over, it lost its strings; they could use it however they wanted to. That was the beauty of it; it launched a lot of creative efforts."

Dubuque County offers a good example. "We start with the premise, What would this family need for the child to live at home and be treated there?" says DHS administrator Gary Lippe. The family, social workers, neighbors, educators, and other interested parties meet together regularly in a process called "case facilitation," to develop a case plan specific to the family. The Human Services Research Institute reports that:

> *Families have become more equal partners in the planning and decision making over services, new services were created out of the needs of individual families, agencies were forced to address turf issues and work more coopera- tively on the team, new service providers have been brought into the fold, front-line workers gained greater understanding and commitment to the philosophies associated with decategorization, and out-of-county placements were reduced while in-home services were dramatically increased.*

Statewide, the percentage of child welfare money being spent on out-of- home care declined from 87 percent in 1991 to 57 percent in 1998, while the number of out-of-state placements fell 21 percent between 1994 and 1998.

THE ADVANTAGES OF CONSOLIDATING STEERING AND UNCOUPLING IT FROM ROWING

More and more, we see public leaders struggling toward this kind of solu- tion. Typically, they create steering organizations, such as state workforce development boards and children and family councils, to develop new pol- icy approaches and coordinate multiple agencies. (Unfortunately, public leaders rarely give these organizations control over consolidated funding streams, so many steering bodies remain weak.)

Consolidating steering and funding streams and separating them from rowing has many advantages:

It keeps policymakers from getting sucked into the minutiae of opera- tions. They can focus on the big picture: setting goals, contracting with ex- cellent programs to deliver on those goals, and monitoring progress. In public education, where districts own all the schools and employ everyone, the attention of the school board and superintendent is constantly diverted away from student achievement to day-to-day problems of personnel, food, buses, books, and buildings. When Peter Hutchison and PSG served as su- perintendent in Minneapolis, they and the school board faced constant di- versions. One year, the buses did not run at the beginning of the school year. One winter, it got so cold that the pipes froze. Another year, two students were killed in accidents. Once, several high school basketball players were declared academically ineligible for the final game of the state tournament. All of these incidents—and thousands more—demanded their attention and interfered with their focus on achievement.

It minimizes micromanagement. Contracting with independent organizations to operate programs hands genuine management control to those programs. The steering organization sets overall policy, vision, and goals and chooses which mix of operators can best meet those goals, but it is not authorized to meddle in day-to-day management. As a result, program managers feel they are in control of their own institutions, and their morale and commitment rise. This environment also helps them attract the best leaders and staff.

It frees leaders from much of their political captivity to service providers. In traditional systems, employees with a vested interest too often have the power to block changes that could help customers. In public education, for example, school boards and administrators have trouble removing incompetent teachers, moving to more computer-based instruction, or shutting down failing schools and starting new ones in their place. Why? Because teachers and other staff have unions that organize at election time, and they vote in school board elections at much higher levels than the rest of the population.

The school board members and superintendents usually want to do what is best for the children. But too often, that creates problems for the adults in the system. And when children's educational interests collide with adults' economic interests, the children usually lose.

Ted Kolderie, a Minnesota education reformer who was one the inventors of charter schools, explains the dynamic well:

> As they consider proposals for change, the superintendent, board, principal, union, and teachers weigh the potential benefits to the kids against the risk of creating "internal stress." They want to help the kids. But upsetting people might create controversy. It might produce a grievance. It might lose an election. It might cause a strike. It might damage a career.

When purchasing organizations contract with independent organizations, the battle of self-interest is different. Rowing organizations still push for their own interests, but they no longer act as a unified block. For every service provider that opposes a particular change, another might support it. Every time a contract is terminated for poor performance, other operators line up to take its place. This liberates steering organizations to do what is best for their customers.

It makes accountability for performance real. Steering organizations can shut down programs that perform poorly, and everyone knows it. Consider what would happen if this were the case in public education. It would give teachers and principals little choice but to overcome all the very real obstacles that stand in the way of improvement. For the first time, virtually every adult's most urgent priority would be student achievement.

It gives leaders much more flexibility to meet customers' very different needs. When new needs emerge, steering organizations can simply contract with new operators to meet them. Traditional school districts have been slow to create schools that use information technology in a meaningful way, for example. But if every public school were independent, operating on a performance contract (in effect, a charter school), technology-intensive schools would spring up quickly, and students would flock to them.

Consolidating steering and funding, but not rowing, creates a fundamental—radical—shift in governance. It abandons the failed strategy of jamming together already large bureaucracies on the theory that they will somehow be less bureaucratic, more efficient, and more effective. Instead, it gives leaders the power to steer more effectively while forcing service providers (and compliance agencies) to continually improve their efficiency and effectiveness. In an era of permanent fiscal crisis, the payoff is huge.

CONSOLIDATING ROWING FUNCTIONS

Other, less radical forms of consolidation can also produce savings and improve results. The most common is consolidation of specific operating units that do similar kinds of work. This brings efficiencies without creating as much fear and negativity as when whole agencies consolidate. For example, it makes sense to combine a public works unit that collects water and/or sewer fees with a similar unit in finance or revenue that collects taxes, or to combine a unit that cuts grass for the highway department with a unit that cuts grass for the parks department. (You can also consolidate discrete services by outsourcing them to a private provider on a contract shared by multiple agencies or jurisdictions.)

In a handful of districts, the Federal Bureau of Land Management and the U.S. Forest Service have experimented with this kind of ad hoc "consolidation from below." In southeast-central Oregon, for instance, employees of the Fremont–Winema National Forest and those of the Lakeview Bureau of Land Management District carry out very similar missions on two different kinds of lands. The BLM land is high desert; the Forest Service land is mountainous. Consolidation made sense because both agencies protect the land, fight forest fires, manage watersheds, protect rare and endangered fish, and support recreational and commercial use, such as logging and grazing.

Back in 1986, simply as a matter of logistics, the two agencies integrated their firefighting efforts. As budget cuts came down in the 1990s, they made a more concerted effort to merge resources. When the BLM office lease came up for renewal, the district manager and forest supervisor decided it was an opportunity to find a joint location. About the same time, each agency's administrative officer retired, so the two leaders decided to combine the jobs and hire just one person. Since then, the agencies have consolidated human resources, training, their fleets of trucks and automobiles, road maintenance, property management, the front desk information center, the mail room, telecommunications, the supply room, and their geographic information systems. The district manager and forest supervisor work as a two-person team, making all significant decisions together. "We think conservatively we've saved probably about $3.2 million, total," says Dede Domingos, the interagency administrative officer.

Though employees were initially nervous about the threat of losing their jobs, no one was laid off. "Only when there were vacancies did we look for ways to consolidate," says Domingos. "So that put aside most of the fear." Interviews with staff reveal a great deal of satisfaction with the approach. "One of the fun things about it," Domingos adds, "is your options for solving problems just multiply when you have the two agencies together. It's like playing cards and having extra aces and face cards to win with."

Consolidating Internal Support Services

Units that serve other public organizations, such as printing, fleet maintenance, telecommunications, and information technology (IT), are also ideal candidates for consolidation, preferably using an enterprise management model (see Chapter 7). For example, Cincinnati does not maintain its own IT services, but uses a government agency called the Regional Computer Center (RCC), funded by direct appropriations and by fees paid by its customers. Those customers include the city of Cincinnati itself, Hamilton County, a regional law enforcement data service, and a regional geographic information consortium. Each customer shares the cost of standard services such as e-mail, but each also receives customized services for which they pay individually. Because they don't have to employ redundant staff, they each see substantial savings.

Washington State began consolidating much of its IT function in the late 1980s, creating a single public entity to handle service centers and consolidation of the network. Paul Taylor, former chief information officer of Washington State, describes it this way:

> They picked the spots where they thought there were efficiencies, leaving other parts of it in a very federated environment. Agencies were still responsible for their own applications, but the data centers were consolidated with a view to becoming a shared hosting network. All state traffic became consolidated on a single network, creating more robustness, more cost-effectiveness, more efficiency.

In 2002, the agency returned $15 million to the general fund to help with the deficit.

Consolidating Access

As we have argued, government services are highly fragmented, often because funding streams are so fragmented. Many citizens or businesspeople have to visit multiple offices to get services or permits, an immensely frustrating process. Much of what government does involves the collection and processing of information, but accessing that information can also be cumbersome and expensive, both for internal users and for the public.

To solve these problems, governments have been busy co-locating related services or, better yet, creating "one-stop shopping" offices where customers can take care of all their business. Today they are taking the next step: creating Web portals where citizens can access multiple sources of information and many different services with just a few clicks. This offers enormous convenience for citizens and enormous savings for their governments.

By late 2003, 18 states and eight cities had contracted with a company called the National Information Consortium (NIC) to provide customized Web portals built on the same technology platform. In Utah, a business can now go to one portal and do everything that once required contacting a half dozen agencies. The portal also includes handoffs to the IRS, to other federal agencies, and to local governments. Indiana, which had the first NIC portal, has worked hard to make its portal the first choice for everyone in the state. In 2003, instead of sending out license renewal forms to nurses, the state sent postcards that suggested renewing online. In small print, the card provided a telephone number people could call if they preferred. Some 72 percent of nurses used the portal, at enormous savings for the state. (See Chapter 9 for data on savings.)

Maine's NIC portal, called InforME, operates without a single dollar from the general fund. The legislature required that consumers pay no transaction fee beyond those they would pay for off-line transactions. Instead, InforME charges $75 for an annual subscription fee. By 2003, InforMe offered more than 300 online transaction services, including license renewals for more than 130 professions. More than 50 cities also used InforME to offer a common registration renewal service for vehicles. The secretary of state predicts that by 2006, 20 percent of all state revenues will be collected online.

Multiple jurisdictions can consolidate their Web-based services to save even more money. For example, the National Association of State Insurance Commissioners hosts insurance filings for all 50 states. In Iowa, the County Treasurers Association is working to move all 99 counties toward online service delivery. It negotiated a contract with Iowa Interactive, a NIC subsidiary, to launch a statewide online property tax payment service. (The company receives a fee of $1.50 per transaction.) When it succeeded, the Treasurers Association moved on to driver's license renewals.

Consolidating "Back-Room" Activities

Another area ripe for consolidation is back-room functions, such as phone answering, purchasing, and data storage. In 2000, the city of Portland, Oregon, had operated a successful three-person Information and Referral Call Center for three years. The center's telephone number appeared on all the city's trucks, and it was promoted as the one number citizens could call to get the information they needed from the person who actually did the work. Multnomah County, which includes Portland, had its own two-person call center. Diane Linn, then director of Portland's Office of Neighborhood Involvement, proposed merging the two systems. Dr. David Lane, who succeeded Linn, says, "We got a lot of county calls, because our trucks were everywhere. And I'm sure the county got city calls . . . Realistically, wouldn't it be better if the citizens in the county had one number to call, instead of two?"

The consolidated program went into operation in the fall of 2001, with the same staff of five taking 15,000 to 18,000 calls a month. Spending remains constant, adjusted for inflation, while call volume has increased substantially.

The Bush administration has made the consolidation of back-office functions through technology a high priority. Its "E-Payroll" initiative, which is consolidating 22 federal payroll centers down to two, while simplifying and standardizing payroll procedures, aims to save $1.2 billion over 10 years. The E-Travel initiative will provide a government-wide, Web-based travel service to handle everything from travel planning to authorization to reimbursement. The goal is to replace all existing agency end-to-end travel services with these online services by the end of 2006. Advocates of the new system say that E-travel will provide far greater speed and efficiency at a huge cost savings—as much as 50 percent. For the 93,000 federal employees who travel each day on official business, there will also be advantages: no more waiting for a supervisor's approval; no need to use commercial travel agents to find hotels and flights at the government rate; no filing for reimbursement and wondering whether it will arrive in time to pay the government travel card bill before late fees kick in. Two separate contractors—Northrop Grumman Corp. and CW Government Travel Inc.—will operate systems, to ensure competition and give federal managers a choice. Online services will be backed up by telephone call centers for travelers who need help.

THINKING BIG: SEPARATING STEERING AND ROWING IN PUBLIC EDUCATION

As we have argued, consolidation comes in many forms—only some of which will yield better results or lower costs. Of the many options, the biggest payoff comes from consolidating steering and funding while separating them from rowing. Why? Because this change alters the incentives and dynamics for everyone in the system, both steerers and rowers. It is time we learned to do this with our most important public institutions.

Consider public education. A school board is a steering organization, but in the consolidated model we developed in the twentieth century, the board and district own virtually all the schools and employ virtually all the employees, from teachers and aides to custodians and bus drivers. The same organization—the school district—is responsible for both steering and rowing.

We have already discussed some of the problems this creates. Employees with a vested interest have the power to block changes that could help children. With all their employment contracts, regulations, sunk costs, and infrastructure, districts find it impossible to change their offerings fast enough to keep up with what their customers want and need. And those who should steer—board members and superintendents—find their energies sucked into the job of employing people and managing buildings, rather than ensuring student achievement.

A new survey of 100 public school superintendents in large urban districts illustrates these problems. Most of these superintendents, it reports, feel "the job is well-nigh impossible." Their role as employers continually overwhelms their role as purchasers of results. In large cities, school districts are among the largest employers, and as the report makes clear:

> Control of the jobs is highly coveted and is never ceded lightly; the jobs themselves become central battlegrounds for unions, community groups, and local politicians. No politician can afford to ignore them. And very few do. . . . pressures for districts to respond to adults' financial demands rather than the children's education needs [are] a frustrating reality for many superintendents.

One superintendent was even more candid:

> The real problem is that the district is a big pot of money over which adults in and out of the system fight to advance their own interests and careers. Better jobs, higher status, bigger contracts, and career advancement are what's at stake. All the public talk about teaching and learning has to be understood as secondary to that economic dynamic.

Does it have to be this way? Of course not. In the late 1990s, the Education Commission of the States—made up of governors, state legislators, state superintendents of education, and other education leaders—created a National Commission on Governing America's Schools. Its members studied the governance system of public education and issued a report recommending that states and districts make big changes in the consolidated model. The first option proposed was to introduce full public school choice, decentralization, and competition, within the consolidated paradigm. But the second was a more radical break. It said, in essence, that those in charge of education should separate steering and rowing. School boards should stop being owners and operators of schools and become purchasers of education programs on behalf of the communities they served. The board should grant charters—five-year performance contracts—to independent groups (teachers, colleges and universities, nonprofits, businesses, community organizations) to operate schools. The commission said, in effect, that every public school should become a charter school.

If this were done, the commission pointed out, school boards could close down schools in which students were not learning, replace them with schools more tailored to the needs of those students, and quickly contract for innovative new schools that embraced technology, used particular learning methods (from Montessori to computer-based learning), and/or offered specific content themes, from performing arts to math and science to community service. When the board closed a school, it would not face the united opposition of every teacher, aide, clerk, and principal; indeed, competitors would line up eagerly to replace it. The board would no longer be a political captive of its employees because it would have so few; schools would be the primary employers.

Teachers in every public school would know that their jobs were safe only as long as students were making academic progress and parents were satisfied. The door to innovation would suddenly swing open, and the size, shape, and pedagogical methods of public schools would change rapidly.

Many superintendents appear intrigued by the idea. In the survey of superintendents of large urban districts, two-thirds agreed that the "district should be able to charter all schools or enter into contracts with schools governed by accountability for education results."

Even more surprising, some districts are already moving in this direction. Milwaukee parents now have access to charter schools, contract schools, vouchers, and traditional public schools. Houston has charters, contract schools, and placement in a private school by contract, as well as traditional public schools. Minneapolis has traditional schools, charter schools, and contract schools; 30 percent of high school students graduate from alternative schools, many of which are operated by nonprofits on contract. Washington, D.C., has a separate school board for charter schools, created by Congressional legislation, which has chartered 25 schools.

Philadelphia's school district has authorized 43 charter schools and contracted with seven for-profit and nonprofit organizations to run 45 more schools. Pennsylvania has assumed control of the Chester Upland School District, under legislation empowering the state to take over struggling districts. The state-appointed board has contracted with for-profit organizations to run 9 of the district's 13 schools; 3 others were already charters, so the district operates only one school itself.

Barnstable, Massachusetts, has begun to convert each of its public schools to charter status. In California, three small districts have already done much the same. San Carlos has made six of its seven public schools charters. The Hickman Community Charter District has only three schools, but all are charters. And the Twin Ridges Elementary School District has two traditional schools and two charter schools within its boundaries, but has sponsored ten charter schools outside its boundaries.

Uncoupling steering from rowing by turning all public schools into charter or contract schools may sound radical, but the basic model is now common in other governmental contexts—as we explain further in Chapter 7. This change, more than any other, will break the logjam that holds back innovation in public schools.

If we want better results at a price citizens are willing to pay, we need to redefine the word *consolidation*. We need service delivery systems full of competing providers, held accountable for performance by revocable contracts, funded by steering organizations with consolidated funding streams. Government needs to steer more and row less, as *Reinventing Government* argued, but it also needs to steer *differently*—so rowing organizations will perform differently.

SIX

Rightsizing

The Right Work, the Right Way,
with the Right Staff

In the spring of 2001, Iowa governor Tom Vilsack knew that his state was in deep fiscal trouble. Despite its strong agricultural tradition, Iowa today depends far more on factories than on farms, and Iowa was among the manufacturing states that first felt the brunt of the recession. Vilsack decided to do an in-depth, six-month "Improving Government" review of all spending, the first comprehensive assessment of the executive branch in 15 years. He brought in our firm, the Public Strategies Group, to help.

The urgency was not purely economic, however. As the Iowa economy had changed, the demands on state government had changed, and the bureaucracy had not realigned itself to meet the new challenges. Now its leaders had no choice but to realign: to consolidate, streamline, and eliminate programs and offices; to create new partnerships and leverage other funds; to adopt new technologies and reengineer processes; and to make rules and procedures more rational and efficient. The challenge Vilsack issued to his department heads was not just to make government smaller, but to make it smaller in ways that would maintain services. He did not just want to downsize, he wanted to "rightsize."

The Department of Human Services, Iowa's largest agency, closed all five regional offices—thereby eliminating an entire layer of bureaucracy—along with 38 multicounty administrative offices. However, the department dropped no one from Medicaid and eliminated no Medicaid services. And despite the loss of roughly $20 million in federal money for services to abused children, DHS laid off no caseworkers. Department leaders concluded that those working directly with clients provided the most value; therefore, 70 percent of layoffs came from middle and upper management.

Similarly, at the Department of Transportation, with 3,759 positions the state's second-largest agency, restructuring "wasn't just about saving money," says Mary Christy, head of the director's staff division. "It was also about safety issues, customer service, and how to be more efficient in delivering our core services."

The department eliminated 7 construction offices, 5 maintenance offices, and 27 maintenance garages. It sold $4.5 million worth of buildings and downsized its fleet and equipment inventory. Department leaders decided they could get by with 102 fewer snow plow trucks, 23 fewer motor graders, 13 fewer crawler tractors, and 56 fewer mowing tractors. Finding the right size meant cutting 403 positions (11 percent of the workforce), but also restructuring to increase the average span of control from one manager for every nine employees to one for every 14. To protect services such as snow plowing and highway maintenance, the department invested in newer, more efficient technology. Equally important, they cross-trained employees, so that the same workers could handle construction, maintenance, and materials. Overall, the rightsizing saved $35 million a year.

The Department of Natural Resources downsized its central office and radically decentralized its field structure, again moving decisionmaking closer to the ground. Working from the same belief that the most value is added the closer you get to the customer, Vilsack reduced central administrative services by $9 million. To cope with the reductions, he merged five administrative agencies into one and turned internal services such as maintenance and printing into revolving funds with no appropriations, using the enterprise management approach. (See Chapter 7.) To survive, such funds would have to earn their revenues by selling their services to state managers in competition with private firms.

Too often in these days of fiscal distress the measure of a president's, governor's, mayor's, or board chair's "toughness" is how many positions they've eliminated. For them, size does matter. Political leaders think they have to report on the number of bureaucrats they've thrown off the public payroll if they are to get the public's attention and win some measure of trust.

Downsizing can be a potent symbol, but in the long run, what counts even more is value for dollars. If done wrong, downsizing can cripple performance, leading to crises of another sort: failing police departments, rising crime rates, dirtier cities, longer waits for service, and deteriorating roads, rails, and buses. What citizens care most about is the relationship between the taxes they pay and the quality of the services they receive. If it takes an extra employee to produce the results they want at the price they are willing to pay, that's usually fine with them. No one, for example, argues that public education would improve if we had fewer teachers. What people do want is more effective teaching. In education, as in all public services, the challenge is to put the right combination of staff and other resources in the right location, at the right time, doing the right things to produce the desired results within the assigned financial constraints. The challenge isn't downsizing; it is rightsizing.

Like Iowa, Charlotte, North Carolina, offers a good example of successful rightsizing. In the early 1990s, the city was clobbered by the national recession and reduced state funding. In Charlotte's case, helping to offset the effects of the general downturn was the arrival of Bank of America, which instantly made the city the nation's second-largest center for banking and financial services.

The urban center for a 15-county, bi-state region, Charlotte had seen its population double in 25 years. By 1990 it was 395,000. Despite this rapid growth, it had managed to maintain a desirable level of service without raising taxes. It also had earned a reputation as a "corporate town." More than 290 Fortune 500 companies have offices in the city, and approximately two-thirds of Charlotte's employed citizens work for "corporate America." This strong corporate presence has had a compelling influence on Charlotte's overall mindset, including its approach to city government.

In 1991, North Carolina withheld from Charlotte $4.5 million that had already been budgeted. In 1992, it cut another $9.4 million. Meanwhile, the recession was slowing the city's own revenue growth. City leaders responded in traditional fashion: They froze hiring, invited general-fund employees to take unpaid leave or five unpaid holidays, raided funds that were still in surplus, froze operating expenses (they forbade out-of-town travel, cut back on subscriptions and membership fees, and so on), and reduced services, including garbage pickup and transit.

Then in January 1992, at its annual retreat, the City Council decided to launch a "rightsizing" initiative. In March they adopted a "Blueprint for Rightsizing," which laid out a goal of transforming Charlotte's government within a year into an organization that was:

- *customer-focused,*
- *decentralized,*

- *competitive with private services,*
- *with many decisions made by self-managed work teams,*
- *able to respond quickly to innovation and technology,*
- *results-oriented and innovative at solving problems,*
- *flexible in dealing with citizens, and*
- *with more emphasis on leadership as opposed to supervision and management.*

In 1993 Mayor Richard Vinroot led city managers in a visioning exercise, called "A Picture of Our Future." It was meant to define what the city's services and workforce would look like in four years—what the "right size" would be. The city's managers conducted an environmental scan, in which they looked at trends and the expectations of political leaders, citizens, and city employees. The rightsized Charlotte they envisioned would have fewer employees, with a greater proportion of police and firefighters relative to the city payroll. Some services would be cut in order to save for higher-priority items. The city would consolidate functions and work through partnerships and brokered services more than through new programs. City services would be put up for competitive bidding. There would be no increase in property taxes. And in staffing, they would increase the use of temporary workers without benefits, promote nontraditional work routines, and focus on workforce preparedness, specifically through exposure to technology and through cross-training.

From these exercises emerged a rightsizing process that proceeded on two tracks, one for policy and the other for management. On the policy track, the City Council debated what services to provide and how they should be financed. On the management track, City Manager Wendell White and his staff evaluated alternative ways to organize for effective and efficient service delivery.

With these two tracks, the city's leaders asked four fundamental questions, and the answers helped reshape all city departments and services:

- *What services should city government provide?*
- *How should services be financed?*
- *How should resources be organized to deliver services effectively?*
- *What is the most efficient method of providing city services?*

The first question, which we addressed in Chapters 3 and 4, asks, "Are we doing the right work?" The rest ask, "Are we doing the work right?"

DO THE RIGHT WORK

In Charlotte, the city approached the first question through a "services assessment" process involving the City Council, a 44-member citizens' panel, and city staff. The leaders gave each participant information about 41 different services and asked them to rank them, using paired comparisons ("In your opinion, which of the following two services is of more importance and value to Charlotte?"). The results were hardly surprising: Police and fire ranked highest. But the results reinforced the theme that customer service was the city's highest priority.

The assessment led city leaders to rethink their bureaucratic structure. They had become accustomed to a department for every type of service provided. But they decided that achieving the right size meant moving from 26 departments to 9 "key business units" (Aviation, Planning, Engineering & Property Management, Fire, Neighborhood Development, Police, Solid Waste Services, Transportation, and Utilities) and 4 "key support business units" (Business Support Services, Budget and Evaluation, Finance, and Human Resources). In some departments this involved major restructuring; in others, such as Police and Fire, there was less change. Meanwhile, the bureaucracy's hierarchical layers were reduced throughout city government, in an effort to empower employees to make more of their own decisions.

In assessing the value of any function, there are two key questions: Does this work contribute in some way to producing one of our desired outcomes? And who is the customer for this work? By "customer" we mean the *principal intended beneficiary* of the work, whether that is the public at large (as with a police department), a group of citizens (such as a school's student body and their parents), specific individuals (clients of a job training agency, for instance), or other government agencies (which use the services of an internal maintenance shop or information technology office, for example). Everything should be done for a customer, or it should not be done at all.

If work no longer has value, the next step is simple—stop doing it. If the work is connected to a priority outcome and has a customer, there are several questions that follow:

- Does the customer still want this work?
- What aspects or attributes of the work are the most valuable?
- What aspects can be eliminated?

For Iowa's Department of Human Services (DHS), rightsizing meant eliminating functions that added the least value. In the course of helping DHS redesign its approach to child-protection services, the Public Strategies Group (PSG) learned that caseworkers were spending 50 to 80 percent of their time doing paperwork, much of which they considered nonessential. PSG recommended a design that eliminated 50 percent of the paperwork and reallocated the time to serving more clients, more intensively. Even if paperwork consumed only 50 percent of caseworkers' time, a 50 percent reduction is the equivalent of a 25 percent increase in staff available to serve people. And it can be achieved without adding a single employee.

DO THE WORK RIGHT

Ensuring that the work is done right often involves the techniques of Business Process Analysis and Business Process Reengineering that we discuss in detail in Chapter 13. But before getting into business processes, there are a number of organizational steps you can take to make sure you are delivering the most value for the taxpayer's dollar.

1. Substitute technology for people and paper in processes that are repetitive, routine, and require only limited adaptation to changing circumstances.

Computers and the Internet have redefined license renewal, routine permitting, tax filing, fulfilling information requests, submitting reports, purchasing, accounting, and payroll. (See Chapter 9, pp. 202–207.) In Iowa, the Department of Education has cut back 40 percent on paper and postage by posting all newsletters on its Web site or sending the information electronically. By using electronic funds transfer to disburse state and federal monies, it has eliminated staff time required to mail checks. And by eliminating or reducing some phone services, it has saved 10 percent of those costs. The Department of Cultural Affairs launched a model electronic granting system that allows constituents to make applications online, standardizes application procedures, and streamlines workflow within the agency. The Department of Personnel allows applicants to apply for state jobs over the Internet.

In Charlotte, technologies such as a citywide local area network, voice mail, and pagers and cellular phones helped the city eliminate 60 clerical and administrative positions.

2. Eliminate layers and units that don't add more value than they cost.

Hierarchy was invented to provide large organizations (armies, churches, corporations, and governments) with the information, direction, and control they needed to succeed. But information technology has rendered much hierarchy obsolete. So why do so many layers persist? Largely because the personnel system uses layers as the justification for pay levels. This too is inherited from the bureaucratic past. When these systems were created, a difference in competence and responsibility among layers actually justified their existence. People at the top, with college educations, really did know significantly more than people at the bottom, who had not finished grade school. But those days are gone. The level of education in the workforce has never been greater, and information technology now makes direct communication throughout an organization the norm. The result is that organizations no longer have to consist of a "top" and a "bottom," with layers in between. Instead, people working together toward a common purpose can be nodes in a web of information, each with a direct link to all the others.

In 1991, during another time of great fiscal distress, the Minneapolis Foundation asked the Public Strategies Group to assess the finances of Hennepin County, the state's largest. One of our most surprising discoveries was the existence of as many as eight layers between front-line workers and the county administrator. In 2003, while working with the New York State Department of Transportation, we again discovered eight layers between the front line and the commissioner.

In Charlotte, street maintenance workers once had to deal with eight levels of management. Today, using self-managed teams, the city operates with a guideline that no business unit should have more than five layers of supervision. Layers are further capped based upon the size of the unit: Units with 50 to 125 employees are capped at three layers, and those with fewer than 50 employees are capped at two layers.

Regional offices offer another layer that can be eliminated. Often a service system will have front-line offices where the public is actually served, regional offices that supervise, and a headquarters that makes policy. Regional offices are usually holdovers from the days when travel was slow and communication was limited to the telephone. In today's world, many are completely unnecessary.

In Iowa's DHS, the five regional offices and 38 multicounty supervisory–administrative offices were eliminated and replaced by eight new area offices, some of which are now open less than full time. To offset this reduction in customer service, the agency let Iowans seek DHS services in a place other than their home county, call for an appointment (rather than having to set up the appointment in person), and pick up various application forms at locations other than DHS offices.

3. Build up your strengths; offload your weaknesses.
No individual or organization can be good at everything. Rightsized organizations devote their own energies to what they do best and outsource the competencies they lack. For example, organizations typically contract for:

- Unique, specialized, seldom-used competencies, such as designing a complex computer program or appraising the value of a nuclear power plant for tax purposes.
- Peaks in workload, such as increased security for special events.
- An independent or objective point of view, as in a financial or performance audit.
- Routine, highly automated activities, such as payroll processing.

Through contracting, a government can rightsize by funding a service without producing that service itself. Many cities in Los Angeles County contract with the L.A. County Sheriff's Department for policing. The city ensures that the service is provided and that it meets certain standards; the county produces the service by actually hiring, training, equipping, and deploying police officers.

4. Abandon "one size fits all," and rightsize services to suit the customer.
Within the city of Los Angeles itself, there is a single police department. However, some neighborhoods need more officers on the beat than others. In some, squad cars are used; in others, it makes more sense to have officers on bicycles. In a paper presented at the University of Southern California School of Policy, Planning and Development, Professors Ronald Oakerson and Shirley Svorny put it this way:

> In rightsizing Los Angeles, the issue is one of matching the authority to make provision for services to the size and shape of the problems being addressed. One size does not fit all, nor does it have to. The scale at which services are provided—selected, financed, and procured through a governmental mechanism—does not have to coincide with the scale at which services are organized for the purpose of production and delivery to residents. . .

*An extensive series of studies of police departments of varying size con-
cluded that the most efficient systems combine immediate response services at
a relatively small, local level with various support services provided on a
larger scale.*

*Another example would be the provision of routine versus specialized serv-
ices in elementary or secondary school. The local school is the locus for provision and production of "routine" education services in a typical classroom.
But for children with special needs—the school district or even a consortium
of districts may be the producer of services (i.e., specialized teaching and support services) that are provided in the local school but not located there permanently.*

MANAGING THE TRANSITION HUMANELY

Rightsizing disrupts organizations and the people in them, and you can be
sure those people will resist. Not only is a humane approach the kind thing
to do, it will also minimize this resistance. Charlotte's most painful step was
the elimination of more than 250 positions—approximately 8 percent of the
workforce—between 1991 and 1993. To lessen the trauma, Charlotte froze
hiring and "banked" critical job vacancies, setting aside these jobs to be
filled by city employees whose jobs disappeared. It also created early retirement incentives. Although some employees were transferred to different
business units, the city kept its promise that no one would lose their job as a
result of rightsizing. The city redesigned the process of allocating positions
to make sure that workforce reductions did not hurt service levels or quality.
Then it invested in training, technology, and customer service—and under-
scored this by placing the training and customer service functions in the
City Manager's office.

Charlotte's leaders worked hard to communicate their plans so that employees would understand both the reasons for rightsizing and its goals.
They created teams in each department and across the organization to focus on training, technology, customer service, and communication and, in
the process, to begin changing the culture.

Charlotte has continued to eliminate positions where possible and create
positions where necessary. Since 1991, as the city's population and land area
have expanded, the number of police and fire employees has increased from
1,886 to 2,664, while the number of general-fund employees not working in
public safety has fallen from 2,150 to 1,313. The latter number is a reduction
of 40 percent per 1,000 population. By 2000, three of every four general-fund

employees worked in one of four organizations: police (32 percent), fire (21 percent), solid waste (11 percent), and transportation (11 percent).

Following Charlotte's example, you can use a number of simple tools to minimize the trauma of rightsizing:

Use attrition rather than layoffs. The typical government has a 4 to 10 percent annual attrition rate, which fluctuates as economic conditions change. Using this natural attrition, organizations can shift displaced employees into jobs vacated by those retiring or leaving. Using attrition, many governments, from the United Kingdom to Indianapolis, Indiana, have shrunk their civil service payrolls by 25 to 30 percent with no significant layoffs. The challenge, of course, is that you can't choose who will leave through attrition. Organizations that rely on attrition must have retraining and redeployment strategies in place to reposition staff as vacancies occur.

If the personnel system has too many rigid job classifications and rules, the organization may also need to create the flexibility necessary to move people from one job to another. Charlotte shifted to a "broadband" job classification and pay system, to give it the flexibility it needed.

Encourage early retirement. Incentives for early retirement can be a very effective way to get smaller. They work as fast as layoffs but, like attrition, are scattershot in their application. With little control over who leaves and who stays, organizations will need to be able to quickly retrain and redeploy to avoid significant disruption.

Create options for those whose jobs disappear. These include:

- retraining workers and placing them in other government jobs;
- temporarily placing workers in a job bank until a vacancy they can fill turns up;
- requiring public or private contractors who take over production of city services to hire city employees who want to make the shift; and
- providing outplacement services to those who choose to leave their jobs, while keeping them on the public payroll until they find another job.

When you have to resort to layoffs, measure twice but cut once. Use layoffs only when you must stem the flow of red ink immediately, or when an organization's level of denial is so overwhelming that it demands radical surgery. But because layoffs are so traumatic, when you must cut, cut deeply enough to ensure that you do not need to come back later for a second round. At the very least, layoffs should have the virtue of providing certainty and closure, both for those who go and for those who stay.

Eliminate employee "bumping" rights. When public organizations reduce their numbers through layoffs, civil service employees with seniority
normally have the right to bump those with less seniority. This combs out
all the young, eager employees and leaves behind the deadwood, in jobs
they neither know nor want. This is one of the most destructive things a
public organization can do.

HUMAN CAPITAL PLANNING

Every field needs competencies that fit today's challenges. Too often in government we have competencies appropriate for what we used to do. For example, the 25-year-old accounting systems operating in governments
across the country must be fed by an army of accounting clerks doing data
entry. That army was necessary to support the "new" computer technology
that existed 25 years ago, when these systems were last rebuilt—which was
a big step up from ledger sheets and adding machines. But today, data entry
can be built into transactions in real time. Today, rather than clerks, we
need analysts to interpret the information, understand the underlying
trends, report on performance, and help produce better results.

In bureaucratic jargon, the solution is known as "strategic human capital
management." In simple terms, it means making sure you have the right
people, with the right skills, for the work you need done.

For leaders, the first step is to determine the competencies their organizations require, then inventory the competencies that already exist within
the organization. The second step is to apply strategies for retraining, smart
hiring, retention, and contracting in order to acquire the skills that are lack-
ing. The final step is to institute performance management and accountability, which we explore in detail in Chapter 8.

In his testimony before the National Commission on the Public Service,
U.S. comptroller general David Walker itemized the human capital planning done by the General Accounting Office to ensure that it had the right
skills. The GAO:

- Prepared a profile of employees and needs assessment to understand
  their demographics and distribution.
- Conducted employee surveys to understand the agency's status and
  progress and where it needed to improve.
- Completed an inventory of employee knowledge and skills.

- Conducted an employee preference survey so that it could give staff more opportunities to work in their areas of interest, in keeping with institutional needs.
- Created an Executive Candidate Development Program to prepare managers for assignments in the Senior Executive Service.
- Launched a Professional Development Program for newly hired analysts to help them make transitions as they moved through their careers.
- Initiated a redesign of the training curriculum to support core competencies.
- Established an Employee Advisory Council to facilitate open communication between line employees to senior leadership.
- Provided an on-site child-care center and a fitness center and implemented business casual dress, flextime, and public transportation subsidies, to help attract and keep talent.
- Used recruitment bonuses, retention allowances, and help repaying student loans to attract and keep employees with specialized skills.
- Implemented a new performance appraisal system based on the organization's strategic plan and the key competencies it needed.

A more dramatic example of rightsizing and human capital planning comes from Peru, which restructured its revenue agency, the National Tax Administration Superintendency (SUNAT). As the World Bank explains:

Before reform, Peru's tax administration was riddled with corruption and on the verge of collapse. The tax agency neither recruited experienced professionals nor provided training. Salaries were low, yet the wage bill was high due to overstaffing. . . . Tax revenue dropped from 14 percent of GDP in 1978 to 9 percent in 1988.

In 1991, President Alberto Fujimori decided to re-create the agency as a semiautonomous authority, with private-sector personnel rules and a dedicated revenue stream protected from political manipulation. Superintendent Manuel Estela, intent on creating an honest, educated, motivated staff, decided that the first step was to address the human capital issues. He gave all staff members the option of a generous voluntary retirement incentive or applying for a position with the new agency. If they applied, they had to go through a psychological evaluation focused on personality, intelligence, and moral judgment; an exam testing their knowledge, reasoning capacities, and professionalism; and a set of personal interviews.

Though the union fought it, the plan went through. SUNAT lost two-thirds of its staff—down from 3,025 to 991. (More than 1,000 retired, and 430 failed the evaluation process.) Estela then recruited about 1,000 new staff members through a rigorous new process, aimed at attracting graduates of the nation's elite private universities. The entire restaffing effort cost more than $2.3 million, but it yielded a workforce whose talents matched their tasks. Because the reform law allowed him to operate under private-sector labor laws, Estela was able to pay private-sector wages, so he increased the average salary from $50 to $1,000 a month. The investment was well worth it: By 1997, internal tax revenue had risen to 13 percent of GDP, and 90 percent of large corporate taxpayers surveyed said that service had improved.

Results like these demonstrate why it is so important to rightsize rather than downsize. Charlotte tells a similar story: Rightsizing helped it weather a fiscal crisis, maintain its AAA bond rating, and reduce its general-fund budget by one percent through 2000 despite rapid growth in the city, thus avoiding property tax increases. By 1999, citizen surveys indicated very positive feelings about the city, with 84 percent of those surveyed rating Charlotte as a good place to live, 87 percent finding it a good place to work, and 90 percent saying that it provided the right kind of environment in which business could succeed. The 1999 survey gave the city very high scores on garbage collection (83 percent positive), emergency services, including firefighters as first responders (88 percent), fire control and suppression (88 percent), and 911 radio dispatch (79 percent). Ratings on overall road conditions were much lower, suggesting that congestion was one of this rapidly growing city's primary problems.

Four years later, after another recession, scores related to the climate for business and jobs had slipped, and scores on road conditions had gone from bad to worse. But many other city services either held their own or improved, with slight increases for garbage collection, emergency services, fire services, and 911 radio dispatch. Overall, the percentage rating city services in general as "very good" or "good" rose from 68 to 70. When asked whether they preferred that services be provided by city staff or private companies, 70 percent chose city staff, up from 44 percent in 1999.

In Iowa, Governor Vilsack's rightsizing strategies were vindicated on election day. In 2002, moderate Republican Doug Gross, a former chief of staff to Vilsack's predecessor, mounted a serious effort to return the governorship to the Republicans. Vilsack was the first Democratic governor in 30 years, and Gross capitalized on the state's economic difficulties to charge him with fiscal mismanagement. It was a hard-fought, contentious race, and for months the candidates were neck and neck in the polls. But Vilsack pulled away to win by a surprising 53 to 45 percent.

Vilsack succeeded in large part because his rightsizing effort had inoculated him against Republican attacks. "They hit him where he was strongest; they pounded right into his wheelhouse," says Babak Armajani, CEO of the Public Strategies Group.

"Even conservative voters looked at it this way: 'He didn't raise taxes, and by God, he laid off some of those state bureaucrats,'" adds Jesse Rasmussen, Vilsack's former director of human services. Meanwhile, liberals supported him because he had protected most vital services, sparing health care and K–12 education from draconian cuts.

Evidently, cutting costs while preserving the quality of services is the right way to run a government.

PART THREE

SMARTER SPENDING

Buying Value, Squeezing Costs

SEVEN

Buying Services Competitively

In 1994, San Diego embarked on a program to implement competition within city services. It chose a hybrid approach, in which some departments were required to explore whether private businesses could provide their services more cost-effectively. These "optimization studies" were designed to help the agencies learn from business and lower their costs. If they couldn't, the city retained the option of contracting the service out to a private firm.

In 1997, it was the Metropolitan Wastewater Department's (MWWD) turn. Departmental managers had followed the success of Indianapolis, the first large American city to contract out management of its wastewater treatment plants. Indianapolis had experienced enormous success, saving more than $13 million a year (almost 30 percent of its former costs) while maintaining or improving quality. (See *Banishing Bureaucracy*, Chapter 5, for the full story.) Charlotte, North Carolina, and other cities had followed suit, and private wastewater treatment companies were aggressively lobbying San Diego's mayor and city council to join the parade.

The MWWD has four major plants, 1,020 employees, and a budget of $200 million. It serves 2.1 million citizens. Its managers used the optimization study to measure themselves against the best practices of their industry, to look for ways to reduce their operating budget, and to consider the option of "managed competition," in which the department would have to bid against all comers for a contract to operate the system. Deputy Director Joe Harris remembers visiting Indianapolis, Charlotte, and other cities to learn from their experience with managed competition. "My read was that Susan Golding, the mayor, wanted to privatize and wasn't worried about the politics at all," he says. "The marching orders I had were, 'We don't care about the [labor or political] opposition; we just want to say at the end of the day that local labor was given an even break.' I went into it thinking I was going to run a managed competition."

As he examined the experience of other cities, however, Harris began to worry. He saw private firms submitting bids that struck him as too low— quoting prices he was sure they would not be able to honor. He knew that wastewater treatment was complex enough that it was hard for anyone to know whether a bid was realistic until it was too late. Yet wastewater treatment was critical to public health, and he didn't want San Diego to be the city that woke up with a failing system, a bankrupt operator, or a default on a contract.

"Atlanta has proved the point," he told us in November 2003. "Atlanta Water was privatized three or four years ago, and just within the last six months, the company defaulted on its long-term contract. We were saying that defaults can be very painful and are to be avoided, and that's one of the possibilities of these potential lowball bids." Several years into its contract, the contractor in Atlanta asked the city for millions of dollars more than it had bid, and when the city refused, the company defaulted. The mayor and council had to take the system back.

"It was painful," says Harris. "That's American capitalism, but there are certain operations that are so sensitive we may not want to take that risk."

Working with the Office of the City Manager, Harris and his colleagues approached the unions with an alternative. They called it "Bid to Goal." The city would have an independent consultant who knew the industry well prepare a "mock bid," and the department would have to match it or see the service contracted out. This strategy, Harris believed, incorporated the best features of private contracting—competition and a performance contract with detailed goals, incentives for exceptional performance, and penalties for unsatisfactory work—with the best features of the pubic sector: retention of control over publicly funded infrastructure, accounting transparency, tax-exempt financing, and no conflict between the profit motive and public health.

To avoid the potential for strain between labor and management, the department would create a Labor–Management Partnership Committee, consisting of 14 unionized employees and three managers. Their job would be to monitor progress and identify any issues that might be barriers to success. They would also make recommendations regarding new technology, training to increase effectiveness, and the allocation of rewards for exceptional performance.

Step one in the Bid to Goal process was to engage an arm's-length consultant, HDR Consulting Group, which had participated in a number of managed competition efforts in other places. To establish a benchmark, HDR prepared a mock bid. It had to be realistic and competitive, just as if a private contractor had submitted it. It also had to meet or surpass industry standards and existing service levels. Then it had to pass muster with a second industry expert.

In step two, management asked the union to respond to the mock bid and prepare a counteroffer with even greater savings. Management worked with the union to make sure their bid was consistent with standards, safety, and service levels. The union offer promised to reduce the cost of operations by $78 million over six years, while achieving full compliance with environmental standards. The result was a Memorandum of Agreement signed by the city manager, the City Council, union representatives, and MWWD management. Results would be monitored and audited annually by San Diego's Audit Division. If the labor–management partnership failed to deliver the promised savings, the city manager could issue a request for proposals for private bids the next day. Leaders of the effort called this provision the "shark in the tank."

Happily, there has been no need to feed anyone to the shark. Savings are far ahead of schedule—the audit for year six of the program shows cumulative savings in excess of $109 million. Grievances are down by roughly 75 percent. Absenteeism and overtime have been reduced because of the scheduling flexibility workers agreed to as part of the labor–management partnership. And employees appear genuinely motivated by their desire to meet the cost-savings goal.

Another source of motivation is a gainsharing program, which gives employees 50 percent of any savings beyond the goal, up to an annual limit of $4,500 per worker. The other 50 percent goes into a taxpayer/ratepayer fund, to offset future costs or rate increases. So far, employees have received gainsharing checks every year, from a low of $1,500 to the maximum of $4,500. (The Labor–Management Partnership Committee can invest some of their gainsharing money in new technology and other improvements—something it has done repeatedly—or hold onto it if its members are worried about meeting their savings goal in a future year.)

"The Bid to Goal project has forged a solid partnership between the wage-grade labor force and the salaried management of the facility," says Robert Mallet, who investigated the project for the Innovations in American Government program. A former city administrator and deputy mayor in Washington, D.C., and deputy secretary of the U.S. Department of Commerce, Mallet goes on to say:

The two union reps . . . spoke of "how the project empowered the front-line worker to focus on job performance and accountability . . ." and how it "had contributed to a reduction of grievances filed by employees and the fact that employees felt 'listened to.'"

Workers now believe they have a shared responsibility for the operation and maintenance of the plant, and that if they perform at levels beyond base ex-pectations, they will share in some of the financial rewards through gainshar-ing. Not only do they have an opportunity to share in the rewards, they also get to determine, within an established range of acceptable rewards, what those rewards will be and who will get them. This shared responsibility then creates an atmosphere for workers to think beyond merely what they are being paid or how much overtime they can accumulate, but also what they need to perform their jobs, why costs are important, and how to improve their life's skills.

While savings have averaged $18 million a year, service has improved. Through 2003, the department met wastewater quality specifications 100 percent of the time. MWWD was the first public wastewater agency in the United States to receive ISO 14001 certification, an international system to certify that plants are operating according to best practices. It also won a Pro-gram Excellence Award for Innovations in Local Government Management from the International City/County Management Association in 2001, and it was a finalist for a prestigious Innovation in American Government Award.

In 2001, San Diego signed a second Bid to Goal agreement with its the Wastewater Collection Division, the unit that operates and maintains more than 80 pumps and 3,000 miles of pipeline that convey sewage to the treat-ment facilities. No large savings were anticipated, because the optimization study had found that the division's budget was already competitive. Yet in the first year, the operation saved more than $1.5 million, and employees earned gainsharing checks. The real goal was to improve quality, and so far, sanitary-sewer overflows have been dramatically reduced. As we write, the city Water Department is negotiating another Bid to Goal agreement, and cities from Seattle to Boston are considering replicating the model.

MANAGED COMPETITION

Competition is the single fastest route to savings without eliminating serv-ices. When public agencies are required to compete, they unleash the cre-ative potential of their employees, because the incentives for success and penalties for failure are so direct. (Competition should *not* normally be used in policy or regulatory organizations, such as the Environmental Protection Agency. In policy work and regulatory work, competition can lead to turf war, making it harder to develop comprehensive strategies that succeed. But in service and compliance functions, its potential is enormous.)

Perhaps the most common form of competition is competitive contracting, in which public organizations solicit bids to deliver specific services. Governments have used this tool for years in contracting with private firms, but in recent decades, they have begun to let their own agencies compete for contracts.

This approach was first developed in Phoenix, Arizona, where the City Council decided to contract out garbage collection in 1978. After the decision, the mayor asked Public Works Director Ron Jensen whether he was going to compare the bids with his own costs. "Mayor," Jensen replied, "we'll bid [for the job] too."

As *Reinventing Government* reported, Phoenix divided the city into districts, with trash collection in each district bid out on a five-to-seven-year contract. The department instituted a no-layoff policy, requiring private contractors to hire displaced Public Works employees and allowing those who wanted to stay with the city to move to other jobs. To make sure that all costs were taken into consideration, the city auditor's office examined each bid, both public and private.

Jensen and his crew lost the bidding three times in a row, but they didn't give up. Competition did its job, which was to force the department to dig ever deeper for new ideas. In 1984, the contract was open for the city's largest district. By building new technology into their bid, Jensen's group beat its nearest competitor by $6 million. Over the next four years, Public Works went on to win back all five districts, lowering solid waste costs for the city by 4.5 percent a year in real, inflation-adjusted dollars. By 1988, Phoenix's costs to pick up a household's garbage were half what they had been in 1978.

In 1992, Indianapolis's newly elected mayor Steve Goldsmith adopted Phoenix's approach for most city services other than police and fire. (See *Banishing Bureaucracy,* pages 115–130.) Other cities, counties, and states began to follow suit, and private companies, eager to drum up new business, began to lobby cities, counties, and states to privatize, offering deep savings as an inducement.

During the second Clinton administration, the Department of Defense (DOD) launched a major initiative. It contracted out 784 services, roughly half through public–private competitions and half without public competition. The biggest contracts were for operating military bases. By 1999 the initiative had saved $5 billion, and there were three contract employees for every regular civilian employee of the federal government. More recently, President Bush has made managed competition a priority for the entire government.

Other countries embraced competition even earlier. In the late 1980s, New Zealand required local governments to examine every service to see whether private providers might do it better or cheaper. Local governments more than doubled their contracting in five years, from 22 percent of local services in 1989 to 48 percent by 1994. And this was done by a Labor Party government!

During that same era, the British government ordered every local jurisdiction in the country to use managed competition for most of its services. The national government even created "Partnerships UK" to assist its national agencies in the effort. That organization helps agencies become better purchasers by standardizing contracts, offering guidance, sharing best practices, and moving employees into agencies for up to six months. Its employees, drawn from the worlds of investment banking, law, management consulting, and engineering, have extensive business experience.

Not all public functions should be in private hands, of course. In addition to policy and regulatory functions, others that are normally considered off limits are those that involve state-sanctioned violence (police forces, armed forces, high-security prisons), those that must protect due process rights (the courts, permitting agencies), those that handle sensitive security and privacy issues (the CIA, agencies handling nuclear waste), and those that require absolutely fair and equal treatment (citizenship decisions in an immigration service, for example). But even in these cases, competition can be a powerful weapon: Governments can force public agencies to compete with other public agencies. As we noted earlier, many cities in Los Angeles County contract with the county Sheriff's Department or another city police department to provide their services, rebidding the contract every few years to make sure they get the best value possible.

Other organizations use performance scorecards (described in detail in the next chapter). They measure their own performance, compare it to that of similar organizations, and often reward units that outperform their competitors. Still others adopt what we call competitive benchmarking: They look at the best in their business and compare themselves to that standard. The U.S. Air Combat Command benchmarks some of its functions against private firms, for example. San Diego's Bid to Goal model is a kind of hybrid: competitive benchmarking backed up by the threat of managed competition.

The city of East Lansing, Michigan, developed its own hybrid about the same time, though the threat was not as explicit. Familiar with the Indianapolis story and eager for similar savings, City Manager Ted Staton sent his director of public works, Pete Eberz, to attend a conference on contracting out wastewater operations. Eberz came back convinced that public wastewater facilities could run at the same or lower costs as privately managed facilities—provided they adopted the practices used by the private firms.

East Lansing's wastewater treatment facility, with 26 employees, cost about $3 million a year to run. In 1997, the city hired EMA Services to do a study comparing East Lansing's performance with that of 120 other privately and publicly managed wastewater facilities. The consultants came back with good news and bad news. The good news was that while the plant had an excellent record, it could still save 20 percent—$614,000 a year—by adopting best practices. The bad news was that capturing the savings would require the elimination of eight full-time positions.

Knowing that privatization was an option, employees overcame their fears and put together a six-year plan that eliminated the positions through attrition rather than layoffs. They also proposed a gainsharing plan that would give the staff 25 percent of the savings, minus the cost of new equipment. And in just two years they dropped their operating cost by the expected 20 percent.

THE POWER OF COMPETITION

In *Reinventing Government*, we outlined many of the reasons competition is so effective. In brief:

It provides more bang for the buck. The root of government inefficiency is not so much public ownership as it is the cushioning effects of monopoly. Many academics have studied competitive contracting, and virtually all have found savings. Worldwide, the average savings the first time a service is competitively bid appears to be about 20 to 30 percent. The Center for Naval Analysis studied 2,138 DOD competitions between 1978 and 1994 and found an average cost savings of 31 percent. Indianapolis saved 25 percent on average from its first 64 public–private competitions. The British national government saved 21 percent from its first round of public–private competition. The U.S. General Accounting Office reports that American taxpayers now save 30 percent on average from contracting out federal work.

Each time a government rebids a service, it saves even more, because the bidders think anew about how to produce the results for less money. Technology also plays a significant role, because technological advances often drive costs down, and bidders—always looking for the competitive edge—are often the first to adopt new technologies.

Competition forces public (or private) services to respond to the needs of their customers. Before Minnesota's Department of Administration took away Central Stores' monopoly on supplies for state agencies, it never bothered to stock Post It Notes. Why should it? Its buyers could not go elsewhere. Then the commissioner lifted the ceiling on purchases outside the system, raising it from $50 to $1,500. With its monopoly blown apart, Central Stores was shocked back into responsiveness. It quickly stocked Post It Notes.

Competition rewards innovation. The best thing about competition is that it is a continual force for innovation and change, the kind of spur to action that government otherwise lacks. Competition forces organizations to sense and respond, to shed their skins and grow. It is the Darwinian force that leads to "survival of the helpful."

Competition boosts morale. This may sound counterintuitive, but we have repeatedly found it to be true. People fear competition, but if the threat of job loss can be taken away through a no-layoff policy, they eventually get past their fear. And most people want to do good work. Competition may make them work harder, but it usually gives them more control over their work, because managers realize they have to rely on their employees' knowledge to drive costs down. In San Diego, in Indianapolis, in Phoenix, and in every other example we have investigated, employees in competitive enterprises no longer have to check their brains at the door. Their work becomes more rewarding, and when they win a competitive bid or meet a benchmarking target, they have objective proof that they're doing a good job. Morale and pride soar, because they have proven that they are not lazy bureaucrats. They shed the ubiquitous image that drags down so many public employees.

Competition helps boost public faith in government. Again, former deputy secretary of the U.S. Department of Commerce Robert Mallet: "Citizens want their governments to work, and they are more amenable to change when they have confidence that their tax dollars are not being wasted. By educating the members of the [citizen] Advisory Commission on the impacts and potential of Bid to Goal, the program increases the respect and confidence of the public for public employees and the work they do."

Competition improves quality. Use competition correctly and you can not only lower costs but produce much higher quality. Performance contracts can include increased quality standards, which contractors must meet to receive their full pay. In 1995, Robert J. Dilger and other academics did a survey of managed competition in 66 of the largest U.S. cities. They found that 82 percent of the cities' managers said they were satisfied or very satisfied with the resulting performance, while the other 18 percent were neutral. On average, managers reported a 25 percent improvement in service—on top of savings of up to 60 percent.

But competition can improve quality in other ways as well. Consider the Tacoma–Pierce County Health Department, which took the bold step of contracting out all clinical services. Under Dr. Federico Cruz-Uribe, the department redefined its mission from "providing clinical services" to "improving the health of the citizens of Pierce County." Dr. Cruz-Uribe defined four objectives: expanding access to health care, increasing the number of providers available to Health Department patients, providing comprehensive primary care, and providing effective care regardless of the ability to pay. He then closed the department's one clinic and contracted with 13 private clinics for care—thus escaping the treadmill of routine service delivery and freeing the department to focus on its larger mission. By stepping back from applying Band-Aids, he and his staff could now devote their energy to prevention, particularly in three areas: controlling communicable diseases such as tuberculosis; reducing consumption of drugs, alcohol, and tobacco; and enhancing the safety of the water supply.

During the first year, the department eliminated 109 positions at its clinic and saved $650,000. But with 13 contract clinics, its system could care for nearly twice as many patients, while providing service around the clock. The number of tuberculosis cases dropped dramatically, and the cost of treatment for tuberculosis dropped by $200,000.

ENTERPRISE MANAGEMENT

For all its benefits, managed competition is demanding and time-consuming work. Those overseeing the process must have the expertise to define what they want done and the results they want to produce. They must write requests for qualifications, requests for proposals, and contracts. They must read bids and negotiate with bidders, then monitor performance and impose consequences: rewards for high performance and penalties for low performance. Public agencies even need to develop backup plans to cover them should a contractor go out of business or fail to perform up to standard.

For some services, there is a simpler alternative. (This is *not* for compliance functions such as police departments or permitting offices.) We call it "enterprise management," and it can be used with any *service* that can *charge its customers*—a maintenance unit, a print shop, a training program, a recreation program, even a telecommunications system. It forces these public organizations to function like businesses, with financial bottom lines. They remain publicly owned, but they are no longer fully supported by budget allocations. They must sustain themselves by selling services in an open market, usually in competition with other providers, public and private.

Enterprise management removes the monopoly held by certain public-sector organizations, takes away their budget appropriation, and forces them into competition with private providers. Suddenly, survival for these organizations depends on how well they please their customers, and at what price. Gerald Turetsky, a former administrator with the Federal Supply Service—the "Staples" that provides office supplies for federal agencies—described the change this way: "It was like being thrown into an ice-cold shower with your clothes on."

Facing the challenge to sink or swim, most public organizations find ways to dramatically lower their prices and improve their performance.

One example of this technique is Sunnyvale, California's approach to "leisure services." In 1991, in a recession, city leaders decided to withdraw full budget support from recreation programs. Rather than cut back the city's offerings, however, they turned the Leisure Services unit into an enterprise fund, which had to charge for most of its services. Leisure Services' leaders did research on what the public wanted for their recreation dollars and began to roll out new offerings: after-school classes in music, art, and the like for school children; exercise classes; yoga classes; and so on. They sent managers to the Disney customer-service training program, then installed these newly minted experts as an internal training team for customer service. They instituted an unconditional money-back guarantee. They created partnerships with the school district, exchanging maintenance services for access to school playing fields and renting unused time in school gyms and auditoriums to the public.

In 1990, 75 percent of the funding for Sunnyvale's Leisure Services came from tax dollars. By 2000, taxpayers provided only 20 percent—a savings for the city of millions of dollars.

Fox Valley Technical College, in Appleton, Wisconsin, plunged deeply into Total Quality Management in the late 1980s. Soon other institutions were making pilgrimages to Appleton to learn from the experts. President Stanley J. Spanbauer saw an opportunity and created a Quality Institute to instruct those outside the college's ordinary enrollment. By the time of Spanbauer's retirement in 1994, the institute had generated $650,000 in training fees and returned a $28,000 profit. Entrepreneurial faculty had gone on to create 16 more "enterprise centers," to increase revenue without costing the taxpayers a cent.

Again, enterprise management works only for those units of government that can sell their services to their customers. These include external services, like water, wastewater treatment, and recreation, and internal services, like maintenance, printing, and training. It excludes units that serve the public at large rather than specific customers, such as public health, national defense, and fire prevention. Enterprise management is in wide use in many places, including the states of Minnesota and Iowa; the cities of Indianapolis, Phoenix, and Milwaukee; the Edmonton, Alberta, school district; and Australia, New Zealand, and the United Kingdom. In our experience, it can save 10 percent of the cost of services a year, for several years.

There are four basic steps to enterprise management, which can be rolled out over one year or several. (For more detailed guidance, see *The Reinventor's Fieldbook*, Chapter 4.)

1. Turn the agency into a public enterprise or enterprise fund (often called a revolving fund), which must earn all or most of its revenues by selling to its customers.
2. Allow it to operate much as a business, free from most of the bureaucratic constraints imposed on public organizations.
3. Take away its budget appropriation and distribute 90 percent of the money to its customers. (Recoup the other 10 percent as savings.)
4. Unless the service is a natural monopoly such as a water or sewer utility, let customers purchase the service wherever they choose. If it is a natural monopoly, give it a customer board and regulate its prices.

Enterprise management is enormously powerful, for a number of reasons:

- It makes agencies directly accountable to their customers. Because its customers can go elsewhere—or buy less, if it is a natural monopoly—a public enterprise must respond to what those customers want.

- It forces continual improvement, because agencies are in competition for customers every day, not just when contract renewal time rolls around every few years.
- It sharpens the consequences of an agency's performance, because the enterprise can either prosper and grow, if its customers are happy, or shrink and die.
- It frees enterprises to make the long-term financial decisions necessary to maximize value for their customers, such as borrowing to invest in technology or train their employees. In contrast, traditional public organizations are limited to annual budgets and cannot usually borrow.
- It saves money, because the competition is constant. And compared to contracting, it is much simpler and cheaper to administer.
- It eliminates much of the internal warfare over rules. The constant battle between a service agency and the central budget and personnel offices—over what it can spend, how many people it can employ, and what investments it can make—virtually disappears.
- It radically simplifies the politics of improving performance, because there is no vote to privatize a service or hold a managed competition. Unions find it less threatening than managed competition, and no one has to choose who wins a contract, defend the contracting process from charges of favoritism, or withstand a lobbying assault from disappointed contractors. Customers decide who offers the best deal, not administrators and politicians.

WHEN JOBS ARE AT RISK

Public employees often do surprisingly well in competitions. Of 320 competitions at the Department of Defense, from 1995 to 2001, employees won 66 percent of the time. In the United Kingdom, in the first four years of managed competition (which the British call "market testing"), public organizations won two-thirds of the contracts. Public enterprises flourish in competition with private companies because they are much closer to their customers, who are typically other public managers. They also have history on their side, because they have been serving those customers for years.

And yet, competition creates anxiety among government employees whose jobs may be at risk. To succeed, it has to be done in a way that is fair and shows respect for everyone involved. We recommend that public leaders adopt a no-layoff policy and create a menu of options for employees whose jobs are eliminated, as we outlined in Chapter 6. Not only is this the right way to treat human beings, it helps remove political obstacles. It allows leaders to use competition more extensively, because it reduces resistance from those who might be affected. With less fear of job loss, it also becomes easier to change organizational culture.

No-layoff policies are much more practical than one might think. A 1997 study by the Center for Naval Analysis found that at large depot maintenance facilities undergoing public–private competitions, after retirements, transfers, and voluntary shifts of workers to the winning contractors, only 3.4 percent of employees were laid off. A 1989 U.S. Department of Labor study that examined dozens of examples of contracting out involving more than 2,000 public employees discovered that on average only 7 percent were laid off. Some 58 percent took jobs with the contractor, 24 percent took other positions within government, and 7 percent retired. A 2001 study by the U.S. General Accounting Office found that in three privatization programs in the Defense Department, only 8 percent of the 1,000 employees affected were laid off. Twenty-six percent were transferred to other positions and 65 percent retired or took buyouts. Of those who left voluntarily, 26 percent took jobs with the successful contractors.

Most organizations can easily absorb 8 percent of employees when a service is contracted out. They simply use their natural rate of attrition from retirements and departures, keeping positions open when competitions approach.

In Chapter 6 we discussed a series of techniques that have been used successfully to protect employees during rightsizing. Several more apply specifically to the use of competition:

Shift public workers into private firms taking over the work. In Phoenix, Philadelphia, and the U.K., virtually all contracts contain a "first hiring preference" clause, which requires that contractors taking on work for the government give preference to displaced government workers.

Require that contractors pay comparable wages and benefits. In the U.K., European Economic Community rules require that in most cases, new hires for contract work enjoy the terms and conditions of their previous government employment.

Help agencies pay for early retirement incentives and outplacement. These extra costs can discourage agencies from using competition if they have to pick up the tab. In the U.K., the government set up a special fund to cover 80 percent of outplacement costs. Sweden created a transition fund for workers to help them retrain for employment elsewhere in their government or in the private sector. The government sets aside half a percent of payroll to finance this Job Security Foundation, which is jointly run with the public-sector unions.

Help managers take their organizations private. Creative leaders sometimes help their employees "spin off" their operations into startup companies. Often, the government provides the fledgling firm with an initial contract for services, to help its employees get on their feet. In return, the new companies have been known to give a discount to the old government authority, while seeking greater growth and profits elsewhere.

In 1994, for example, the Office of Personnel Management's Investigative Services arm performed security clearances and other investigations for the federal government. Operating at a loss of $1 million a month and already $35 million in debt, it was downsized once and was on its way to privatization, in part because the shrinking federal workforce required fewer security checks. Instead, the Clinton administration allowed its senior managers to turn the unit into an employee-owned security firm, now known as U.S. Investigations Services, Inc. (USIS). It offers clients from both government and business a wide range of security services, including rapid-response background screening, drug and alcohol testing, security staffing, and information security. While many employees initially resisted the idea of privatization, all were offered jobs with the new company, and more than 90 percent made the transition. Due to profit sharing and growth of the company, the average employee received bonuses that exceeded 25 percent of salary and stock equal to 43 percent of salary over the first three years of the enterprise.

Who lost in this scenario? Taxpayers saved $20 million a year; the federal government shed more than 700 employees it didn't need; and the employees who chose to join USIS made out handsomely. If it were always this easy, the permanent fiscal crisis would be no crisis at all.

EIGHT

Rewarding Performance, Not Good Intentions

Once every two weeks, each department head in Baltimore is called to the "Big Room." A podium stands at the center of one wall, flanked by two giant six-by-ten-foot viewing screens. Projectors hang from the high ceilings, and a sophisticated control booth sits in back, where staff members project charts, graphs, maps, spreadsheets, and photographs that dissect the performance of the department in question.

Ten times a week, Mayor Martin O'Malley or First Deputy Mayor Michael Enright, their staff members, and other department executives take their places behind a semicircular table, facing the podium. One of 16 department directors takes the "hot seat," at the podium, normally flanked by members of his or her staff, and answers questions from the mayor and his top aides.

The mayor's staff has pored over the latest performance data from the department: for example, the backlog of work orders at the Department of Public Works' Water and Wastewater Division; the number of delinquencies, shutoff notices, and shutoffs; the amount of water produced and consumed; the number of complaints and their topics, what percentage were resolved by the deadline, and what percentage are overdue; and personnel basics such as overtime hours, absenteeism, time off due to disabilities suffered on the job, and disciplinary actions. Data on the last two weeks are compared to those of the three previous two-week periods. The staff has analyzed all the numbers, looking for patterns, and boiled them down into a 10- to 12-page report for the mayor and his assistants.

Sometimes the Big Room projectionists show photographs of dirty parks, of police officers sleeping in their cars, or of other unpleasant realities.

Sometimes they roll video from the local news, stories about problems the media have uncovered.

The mayor and his staff grill the department head. Why has the number of parking citations gone up so rapidly? Will the courts be able to handle them? Why are complaints about mixed refuse so high? Why does one supervisor have 52 errors? And why are so many files missing when you take people to court to enforce sanitation rules?

If there's no file, mayoral aide Matthew Gallagher points out, the case is dismissed. "Look at this," he adds. "One day 11 of the 20 cases had files missing. You can solve this. I have a three-year-old at home that I can bring down to help. If you have double-digit cases dismissed next time, bring the clerks with you to the meeting."

If the subject is property abandonment, or rats, or lead poisoning, maps and data will show which neighborhoods have been hit worst. If it is car theft or breaking and entering, the maps point everyone toward trouble spots where more police should be deployed.

Discussions are blunt, though not without a certain degree of Southern gentility. Participants brainstorm about solutions. Their analysis moves down to the neighborhood and block level, then back up to citywide trends. Other department heads or their subordinates sit nearby in case problems come up requiring their assistance. "They can't pass the buck to another department," says Elliot Schlanger, chief information officer. "Things get resolved in real time. We call during the meeting for additional information if we need to. We've killed that old excuse: 'It's in the Law Department.'"

The mayor and his staff often ask for follow-up reports in two weeks—then press the department head about progress when he next appears. But the Big Room is not all Pepto Bismol moments. Sometimes the mayor and his staff offer congratulations, and the mayor occasionally rewards presenters and their subordinates with Orioles or Ravens tickets, or seats at a concert. Overall, though, "There's not much praise," says Joseph Kolodziejski, director of the Solid Waste Bureau in Public Works. "Last meeting I had a lot of statistics showing improvement, and the deputy mayor said, 'That's fantastic; but we're not here to talk about the good; we're here to solve problems.'" Still, says Kolodzieski, "I would use this to manage even if they stopped it now, because it's good information."

The Big Room grillings are part of a process known as CitiStat, designed to imbue city government with continuous accountability. It began in June 2000, O'Malley's first year in office. The new mayor was just 38 when elected, but he had been on the City Council and he knew how things worked. He was also in a hurry to turn them around. "If we only looked at performance every year at budget time, I'd be old and gray before anything would change," he told *Governing* magazine. "CitiStat brings the sense of urgency that we need around here."

"CitiStat has redefined what our jobs are," added Recreation and Parks chief Marvin Billups. "Collecting all this data has *become* our jobs. We need to constantly evaluate what we're doing and see if it makes a difference."

Baltimore had been a city in decline for decades. In the 1990s, a thousand middle-class residents left the city every month. The population fell from 736,014 in 1990 to 651,154 in 2000. Some 40,000 abandoned houses were left behind, vacant and decaying. Nearly 23 percent of city residents were living in poverty—almost three times the rate of poverty for Maryland overall. Baltimore was one of the only big cities in America in which the crime rate did not fall during the boom years of the 1990s; more than 300 murders were committed every year. To make matters worse, the property tax rate was nearly twice that of any other county in the Baltimore metropolitan area.

Today, conditions in Baltimore are improving, because department managers know there is no place to hide. Since he launched CitiStat, Mayor O'Malley has fired two agency heads for poor performance, replacing them with the CitiStat analyst assigned to their department—a loud message that CitiStat was to be taken seriously. Department heads have in turn cracked the whips in their own bureaucracies. In the first year of CitiStat alone, the Department of Public Works terminated 94 employees who missed work chronically, issued 462 warnings, and meted out 102 suspensions.

CitiStat is also a way of ensuring responsiveness to city problems. The mayor made a big public splash with a guarantee that all potholes reported by citizens would be filled within 48 hours. Some 1,500 reports are phoned in every month, but the Department of Transportation has met the mayor's goal on 95 percent of them. In examining garbage collection, CitiStat uncovered a problem with illegal dumping. Further discussion revealed that the Public Works Department lacked the power to arrest violators, so the Police Department assigned a special unit to respond quickly to dumping complaints. CitiStat also revealed that four different agencies had responsibility for dead animals, depending on the type, location, and time of day. After discussion, city leaders consolidated the responsibility in the Department of Public Health.

Because so many problems cross departmental lines, the mayor created interdepartmental data gathering and CitiStat sessions on drug abuse (DrugStat), homelessness (HomelessStat), project planning (ProjectStat), and juvenile delinquency (KidStat). With homicide the leading cause of death for black teens, KidStat identifies youths with more than one arrest in high-risk neighborhoods and offers them a battery of social services.

O'Malley also formed a LeadStat team to deal with lead poisoning. Not a single enforcement action had been taken on lead abatement in the previous 10 years, but since the team was formed more than 1,000 sites have been cleaned up. The LeadStat team has developed a map of the city with red dots for every case of lead poisoning. It meets twice a month to find solutions, trains health and housing inspectors in tandem to look for lead problems, and works with state environmental officials to abate them. The rate of lead poisoning among children has fallen by 36 percent, serious poisoning by 61 percent.

A general report card for CitiStat's first year shows impressive results:

- Violent crime fell 24 percent, shootings 34 percent.
- Homicides fell from 305 to 262, the lowest number in more than a decade.
- Emergency hospital visits due to drug overdoses fell 25 percent.
- The city saved $13.6 million, $6 million of it in overtime costs, because chronic absenteeism declined dramatically.
- All but 200 of 2,700 illegal dumping grounds were eliminated.

By the end of fiscal year 2003, the city claimed to have saved and/or helped generate more than $43 million, almost half of it from a 40 percent reduction in overtime and absenteeism. Meanwhile, services had improved, and violent crime was down 29 percent. Baltimore was one of only a few major American cities not crippled by budget deficits and not laying off workers, cutting services, or increasing taxes. And cities from Chattanooga to Syracuse to Anchorage were copying CitiStat. O'Malley summed it up this way for the *Toronto Star:*

> *When we arrived, it was basically, "If the mayor really wants to know, we can find out, but we'll have to pull people off their jobs and it'll take weeks," or "We'll get to that as soon as we can, but it'll take a few months because of budget cuts." Or even, "That's the way we've always done it. We're already doing that. We tried that and it didn't work." Now we've replaced all that with accurate and timely intelligence shared by everyone, by rapidly redeploying resources, by applying effective tactics and strategies, and by relentless follow-up.*

In one sentence, O'Malley has captured one of the most important lessons a twenty-first-century leader needs to know: *When managers and em-*

ployees get direct, immediate, personal feedback on their performance, with consequences, they respond by improving it. If our government leaders want to improve their bang for the buck, they need to measure performance, provide feedback, correct low performance, and reward high performance—relentlessly. If that feedback is to be of maximum use, it should be direct, personal, and immediate. "Our budget had performance goals, inputs, outputs, updated every three months," says CitiStat Director Matt Gallagher. "By the time the mayor saw it, it was five months after the fact; there was no time to react. Now the budget is reviewed by CitiStat at least once a month."

Competition may be the fast lane to improvement and savings, but public organizations can't use competition for every service. Where they can't, performance management is imperative. And even when public services have to compete, performance management is an indispensable tool to help them win.

In 1992, when *Reinventing Government* was published, the simple act of *measuring* performance was still rare. Now cities, counties, and states from coast to coast—as well as the federal government—measure performance. Many of them issue a performance report to the public, such as the *Mayor's Management Report* in New York City, or Portland, Oregon's *Service Efforts and Accomplishments Report*. These are important steps forward. But faced with a permanent fiscal crisis, it's time to take the next step: to make public employees *accountable* for their performance.

When people in government hear the word "accountability," what registers in the brain is usually "punishment." That's what politicians often imply when they use the word in campaigns, so public employees hear accountability and think audits, inspections, and the boss coming down on them.

But citizens aren't interested in punishment—they want results. To us, people are accountable when they get direct, immediate, personal feedback on their performance, followed by consequences, both positive and negative. That kind of accountability is at the heart of CitiStat. As Michael Enright says, "What gets watched gets done."

CitiStat actually has its roots in New York City's famous crime-fighting process, Compstat. The Baltimore police hired Jack Maple, who had launched Compstat, as a consultant. Under Maple's tutelage, as Mayor O'Malley explained at Harvard's Kennedy School of Government, "Instead of checking performance every few months, or scheduling an annual review meeting, the leaders of the Police Department [began] meeting every week.

Crime-fighting strategies and resource deployment were being adjusted constantly, and follow-up was never allowed to slip more than a week."

Baltimore's crime rate immediately started to fall. Seeing the results, the mayor drove Jack Maple around the city, grilling him about how to measure other city services. He quickly decided to extend Compstat to all of city government, building on its four key tenets:

- "Accurate and timely intelligence" (performance measurement);
- "Effective tactics and strategies" (with constant discussion);
- "Rapid deployment of resources" (which means freedom for departments to move their resources to areas of need);
- "Relentless follow-up and assessment" (with direct, personal, and immediate feedback for department heads).

"In order to change the outcomes produced by government, you have to change what government does," O'Malley explained at Harvard:

CitiStat changes what government does, by measuring what it produces and creating a mechanism to make timely changes. . . . CitiStat is helping us re-place a culture of delay and avoidance with a culture of accountability and results—monitored by technology—that is penetrating every city agency. It puts information into the hands of many managers, rather than a few. And this shared knowledge allows government to change and adjust more quickly to better serve the public.

In New York City, CompStat began with the realization that the police were measuring the wrong things—the number of arrests—when the result that citizens wanted was less crime. In 1994, police commanders and agency executives began holding weekly, then twice-weekly, Crime Control Strategy Meetings, focused on their computerized statistics—hence the name CompStat. Each of the 77 precincts would supply a daily index of crimes and other data, including civilian complaints.

Mayor Giuliani described the system this way:

The purpose of it is to see if crime is up or down, not just citywide, but neigh-borhood by neighborhood. And if crime is going up, it lets you do something about it now—not a year and a half from now when the FBI puts out crime statistics. After all, when you find out that burglary went up last year, there's nothing a mayor can do about it because time has passed and the ripple of criminal activity has already become a crime wave.

The CompStat meetings bring together all levels of management—something rare in police work. They draw upon the department's collective expertise to develop new strategies and tactics. At early Compstat meetings, writes Iona College professor Paul E. O'Connell, "People . . . were astounded to see the chief of patrol (an administrator who is literally situated at the pinnacle of the organizational chart) engaged in lively and in-depth conversations with precinct anticrime sergeants or detective squad commanders (individuals who rarely had direct access to upper-level managers at headquarters)."

Compstat is therefore far more than an efficient performance monitoring system. It is a knowledge management device that enables the agency's chief decision makers to tap into and use the intellectual capital of the entire organization. This includes not only what is expressly known by the organization and its key administrators ("explicit" knowledge) but also what is known and understood intuitively or instinctually by the individuals who actually perform the work.

Receiving dependable data in close-to-real time allows precinct commanders to learn quickly whether a new strategy is working. Compstat works because the Police Department also gives those precinct commanders unprecedented authority over all aspects of police work in their domain, including personnel. With that authority, of course, comes true accountability.

Public accountability in front of one's peers is highly motivating. Most commanders, knowing the public exposure that lies ahead, do not wait to deal with issues after the fact. They anticipate and ameliorate problems before they appear in precinct statistics. Every time Compstat expanded to include another indicator, such as arrest warrant enforcement, performance in that area improved dramatically. In 1995, for instance, Compstat began to track graffiti arrests. Total "collars" for that year were 475. By 2001, the number was 1,485. As Mayor Giuliani wrote in his book, *Leadership,* "If we could count it, we could Compstat it."

As for getting his huge police force to buy in, the mayor credits the fundamental management strategy known as "consequences." "Anyone above the rank of captain can be demoted," he pointed out. "And those below the management ranks could be reassigned—a police officer who lived in Westchester might find himself stationed in Staten Island." On those explicit terms, individuals either "bought into Compstat or were told to find another line of work."

In time, the system led to open—and healthy—competition among commanders eager to outshine their peers in other precincts. Looking back,
Mayor Giuliani called CompStat "the centerpiece" of his efforts to reduce
crime. "The core of it is the principle of accountability. Holding the people
who run the precincts accountable for achieving what the public wants
them to do, which is to reduce crime."

And reduce it they did. Major felonies declined by 12.3 percent in the
first year of the program. For murder and robbery, the one-year declines—
17.9 percent and 15.5 percent, respectively—were the largest one-year
drops ever. Between 1994 and 2001:

- overall crime fell 57 percent;
- murder plummeted 66 percent;
- police shootings fell from 212 to 73;
- robberies were down from 85,883 to 32,213;
- burglaries dropped from 100,993 to 38,155;
- auto thefts fell from 111, 611 to 35,673; and
- emergency response time declined from 8 minutes and 36 seconds to
  7 minutes and 30 seconds.

When then deputy commissioner of corrections Bernard Kerik decided
to take Compstat into the Department of Corrections, the city's notorious
Riker's Island detention center was out of control. "Correctional officers did
their tour of duty covered in garbage bags to protect themselves from the fe-
ces and trash tossed at them from cells," according to a site visit report by
an investigator for the Innovations in American Government Award. "Ex-
cessive force by correctional officers against inmates was ingrained in the
culture, characterized by 'greeting beatings' for new inmates, and the subject of a class action lawsuit by a group of 15 inmates against the city filed in
1991."

Kerik required all wardens to attend monthly meetings, four wardens at a
time, focused initially on 16 performance indicators related to inmate violence. Previously, malicious and violent behavior perpetrated on one inmate by another had been viewed with a blind eye, but when accountability
entered the picture, wardens got the message that things had to change.
Those wardens then conveyed the message to inmates that crimes committed during incarceration would be prosecuted like any others. Even while
the prison population increased, violent assaults dropped from 1,093 in
1995 to 70 in 2000. Inmate stabbings and slashings dropped from 1,093 incidents in 1995 to 102 incidents in 1999.

With results like that, Commissioner Kerik decided to go a step beyond Compstat and use his "Total Efficiency Accountability Management System" (TEAMS) to manage his entire organization. His staff began to monitor a total of 160 indicators, including the number of inmates reporting for sick call and how long they waited to see a physician; inmate attendance in law libraries and religious services; the number of food service violations and meals served cold; the number and status of maintenance projects; and the number of inmate grievances filed.

With TEAMS, no one has to wait for a monthly report. Instead, managers can observe "spikes" on a daily basis, begin asking questions, and intervene immediately if necessary. Tracking even apparently meaningless statistics can provide unexpected benefits. Under TEAMS, for example, the Department of Corrections tracks sales from prison commissaries. If sales of candy and cigarettes suddenly increase, prison officials know that a riot may be in the offing. (The first response to a riot is a lock-down that confines prisoners to their cells; stocking up is a giveaway that trouble is in the air.) A sudden jump in attendance at Mass helped prison officials break up gang activity. Knowing that he would be asked to explain any unusual statistics, the warden looked into the sudden outbreak of religious observance and discovered that it was being used as a cover for meetings of the Latin Kings.

With less violence, staff can focus on other improvements. As a result, the jails are clean and staff morale is up. By 1999, absenteeism was down 28 percent compared to 1995.

As in the Police Department, TEAMS meetings figure heavily in decisions about promotion and demotion. According to the department's application for the Innovations in American Government Award:

> *The challenge was to demonstrate to middle and senior management that TEAMS would be the means to improve agency performance, and that their future careers were dependent on that performance. Managers who fail to take responsibility or who demonstrate that they are unfamiliar with their operations are readily identified through the TEAMS process. Those managers who embrace the concept of accountability and who demonstrate ambitious and creative problem solving are promoted.*

BEYOND COMPSTAT AND CITISTAT

CitiStat, Compstat, and TEAMS are valuable breakthroughs. But for all their value, these efforts are not complete performance management systems.

One constraint is their limited effect beyond the departmental managers who participate in regular performance review sessions. In its application for the Innovations in Government Award, New York's Department of Corrections acknowledged:

> *The most significant shortcoming has been the inability, thus far, to embrace the entire agency in the TEAMS process. The men and women who now work in the jails every day represent the department's future. They need to know that the reductions in violence and other improvements in their working environment did not happen by accident, but through a process of strategic planning and managerial accountability. For this to occur and become an enduring management philosophy, the TEAMS message must be embraced and understood at all levels of the department. The agency recognizes that involving this untapped potential resource will help ensure that TEAMS will continue to be a dynamic and evolving management system.*

To motivate every employee, leaders need to institute similar meetings at lower levels. Some departments in Baltimore have held "mini" stat meetings in advance of the official meetings, a big step in the right direction.

Equally important, however, is the issue of *what is measured*. Because Compstat measures actual crimes committed, it focuses on the key *outcome* citizens care most about. This focus on outcomes drives precinct captains to keep looking for new strategies and tactics that can lower crime rates. Outside the Police Department, however, Baltimore's CitiStat focuses almost exclusively on *outputs*—on measuring the work that employees do, rather than the results it produces. And there is no link between the outputs it measures and the mayor's five outcome goals for the city: "Make Baltimore a safe, clean city; increase educational, cultural, and recreational opportunities for children; create stable and healthy neighborhoods; strengthen Baltimore's economy by increasing the tax base, jobs, and minority business opportunities; and make city government responsive, accountable, and cost effective." Indeed, progress on those five outcomes is not measured in any systematic way.

CitiStat's managers admit that theirs is a rudimentary measurement system, designed to deal with the basic operational problems they found when they took office. "When we first started, we were so operationally inefficient that the low-hanging fruit was falling off the trees so fast we had to wear helmets," says Schlanger. The initial focus was improving very simple things, like employee absenteeism and abuse of overtime.

The bottom line is this: *CitiStat helps most departments become better at what they do, but it doesn't help them rethink whether the outputs they produce are the most effective way to get the outcomes the mayor wants.* To add that next step, Mayor O'Malley would be wise to visit Charlotte, North Carolina.

Charlotte's leaders have been reinventing their government for more than a decade, as we described in Chapter 6. About five years ago, the City Council defined five focus areas of top priority: community safety, "city-within-a-city" (strengthening individuals, families, and neighborhoods), economic development, transportation, and restructuring government. With the city manager's help, they developed a strategic plan focused on these priorities, then a "corporate scorecard" of 19 objectives for the five areas. Reflecting the city's balanced scorecard approach, the 19 represent four different perspectives: the customer perspective, the financial perspective, the internal business perspective ("can business processes be changed to improve performance?"), and the learning and growth perspective ("is the city maintaining technology and employee training for continuous improvement?"). The 19 objectives include reducing crime, strengthening neighborhoods, enhancing service delivery, growing the tax base, growing the skills base, achieving a positive employee climate, maximizing the city's cost–benefit ratio, and improving productivity.

For each objective, the city has established one critical measure to track progress. "We call them our corporate objectives," says City Manager Pam Syfert. "They are the indicator to the council and the community of how well we're doing in terms of carrying out the strategies and vision the council has. They are one of the factors I use for evaluating how the key business unit executives are doing."

Each key business unit (Charlotte's name for departments) develops a business plan with its own balanced scorecard of key measures, reflecting the four perspectives. Citywide, there are some 250 measures to quantify these business unit objectives. They are chosen with an eye on the corporate scorecard: In theory, achieving each unit's objectives should help the city achieve its corporate objectives. This way, the entire organization aligns its work to achieve the results most valued by citizens.

A quarterly performance report captures progress on the 19 corporate objectives. Twice a year, key business units submit reports on their numbers. Business unit executives hold meetings with their staffs, typically monthly (but weekly in the police department), to review the numbers and spot areas that need attention. And when the city manager and her assistants evaluate each key business executive once a year, that executive's salary increase and onetime bonus depend on the scorecard for his or her unit.

Charlotte is now building the system down through the ranks, with the goal of having every work team adopt its own balanced scorecard. The city also has an incentive pay plan in which employees get bonuses if the city has saved money and their business unit has met some or all of its key performance targets. Full bonuses (for business units that hit all their targets) typically range from $300 to $650. But as Pam Syfert told us:

I used to think that it was only financial rewards that had any meaningful effect. But through some of our programs like the recognition program—taking breakfast to the garbage collectors and telling them what a great job they did and giving them prizes and so forth—I've learned that recognition can be just as motivating as getting a larger paycheck. I really think both financial and nonfinancial rewards are necessary.

Charlotte's approach does not provide as much direct, immediate, personal feedback as Baltimore's. But it is far more sophisticated in what it measures. The business units track the quality, customer satisfaction, and effectiveness of their outputs, and the corporate scorecard tracks the outcomes produced by all those outputs. This helps citywide and business unit leaders detect the need for changes in their spending priorities and strategies—or even the need for new strategies. They can see not only whether they are doing what they do well, but whether they are doing the right things.

Charlotte also adds positive consequences that reach beyond top management—its incentive pay system, its recognition program, and its gain-sharing programs, which we will discuss later in this chapter. If leaders want to ensure that performance feedback permeates their organization—if they want the entire organization to take it seriously and use it to produce better results—they have to build in rewards. They can do this by adding some or all of the following tools.

DIRECT CUSTOMER FEEDBACK

In the Public Strategies Group (PSG), we like to say that "feedback is the breakfast of champions." Such feedback can be particularly powerful when it comes directly from customers. Babak Armajani, PSG's cofounder and CEO, was once deputy commissioner of the Department of Administration in Minnesota. He tells a story that demonstrates the power and simplicity of direct feedback from customers:

> *Back in the 1980s, our state printing department was receiving far too many complaints, and its director was struggling with how to get the people who actually did the hands-on work to grasp the concept of customer satisfaction. His inspired idea was to have the people who actually ran the presses drive the trucks out to their customers and personally deliver the printing jobs. Delivery work was not in the union contract, of course, so there was much resistance, and even a formal grievance. The dispute heated up when the Finance Department complained that this was grossly inefficient. I explained the situation to the finance commissioner and he roared with laughter and said, "Don't worry, I'll take care of it."*
>
> *For these guys with ink on their hands, actually meeting the people on the receiving end of their printing had an incredible effect. They were making a personal connection, and they were getting direct, personal, and immediate feedback. Seeing that they were doing the job for another person, and getting feedback from that person—it was as simple as that. That's all it took to solve the problem; their quality soared. Customer satisfaction and employee satisfaction both rose, and so did their revenues.*

Some agencies use customer comment cards to get immediate feedback; others use customer focus groups and surveys. But nothing is better than face-to-face contact.

PERFORMANCE AWARDS

Recognition is a wonderful motivator. It not only boosts morale, it signals to every employee the kind of performance leaders are looking for. Used fairly and sincerely, to show appreciation for good work, recognition is almost impossible to overdo.

Pam Syfert is absolutely correct when she says that both financial and nonfinancial rewards are important. In the 1960s, Frederick Herzberg did seminal research at Case Western Reserve University to establish the relative importance of the leading factors known to motivate people. In order of importance, they were achievement, recognition, challenge, interest, responsibility, advancement, and—in seventh place—salary and benefits.

Charlotte not only has the City Manager's Employee Recognition Program, it has a Customer Service Award and a Strategic Planning Award. The

Customer Service Award goes to individual employees or teams of employees, such as a solid waste crew, who have provided outstanding customer service. The City Manager's Recognition Program involves one award per month to a division or team for extraordinary performance. And the budget office gives out the Strategic Planning Award to the business unit with the best strategic operating plan.

PERFORMANCE BONUSES

Money may be last on Herzberg's list, but it is there because it matters. The idea of bonuses for government employees was borrowed from the private sector, migrating into government in the late 1970s. By 1995, both the U.S. and Canadian federal governments had adopted bonuses, and ten states tied at least some employees' pay to performance. Schools began to offer merit pay to teachers, and now performance bonuses go to groups of teachers or even entire schools in Denver, Cincinnati, Dallas, Houston, Columbus, Minneapolis, Indianapolis, Rochester, Charlotte–Mecklenberg County, Kentucky, Florida, and North Carolina, among others. Florida state law requires school districts to develop plans that allow teachers and principals to earn at least 5 percent of their salary as a performance bonus—based primarily on the actual learning gains of their students. Performance bonuses for principals are even more common: A 1998 survey found that about 15 percent of grade-school principals had incentive or bonus-pay contracts. In 1995, Cincinnati became the first to link even central office managers' pay to student test scores, dropout rates, and other performance measures.

The reason for this widespread adoption is obvious: Cash incentives work. Diane Smith, principal of Fox Creek Elementary School in Douglas County, Colorado, told the *American School Board Journal*, "You know how people will say, 'Somebody ought to do this or somebody ought to do that.' [With performance pay], some things get accomplished that would not get accomplished otherwise. It gives that little bit of a monetary kick." She recounted how she and her colleagues began a project to boost student achievement. The first year they failed to earn bonuses because writing scores didn't go up—so the next year they focused on how to improve the writing program. "Follow the money" is good advice not only for journalists.

Most people think of using salary increases as rewards for performance, but bonuses—onetime cash awards—are far more effective. Salary increases are expensive, because they are a gift that keeps on giving in subsequent years. Budget officials typically get nervous about escalating personnel costs and soon cap these increases, undermining the value of the tool. Outstanding employees also hit the top of their salary range after several pay increases, at which point the tool becomes useless. When that happens, good employees often begin looking for jobs that pay more—the worst kind of unintended consequence. Salaries should be determined by what it takes in a particular labor market to attract and keep talented employees, and bonuses should be used to reward performance.

The Texas legislature has authorized bonuses of up to 6.8 percent of an employee's annual base pay for classified employees who contributed to performance improvement in agencies that hit at least 80 percent of their performance indicators. In the 2000–2001 biennium, at least 19 Texas state agencies developed performance bonus plans.

In the federal government, a few agencies have made similar efforts. Historically, the federal bonus system has been based on subjective evaluations of employees, which are notoriously ineffective. Several years ago, the Postal Service and the Veterans Benefits Administration (VBA) took the lead in changing their executive appraisal systems to focus on objective performance standards. VBA executives can earn bonuses that by law range from 5 to 20 percent of salary if their stations (regional offices) perform well. But subpar performance also has its consequences: One station director has been reassigned and five others have been put under performance review.

Driving this approach down through the ranks, the VBA established national performance standards for its five dozen stations, then created a three-tier incentive award system. In the first tier, $3 million is divided equally among stations, whose directors can distribute the money to employees to reward performance as they wish. In the second tier, $4.5 million is divided only among stations that meet performance targets—about 20 of the 57 competing stations in 2002 and 2003. Typical employees can earn up to $3,000 in personal bonuses this way. The final tier, at $1.2 million, is reserved for the undersecretary to award. Nominations come in from the stations for groups of employees who have done extraordinary work, and a committee makes the final decisions.

"It's made a real difference," says Mike Walcoff, associate undersecretary for operations:

> There are now a lot of questions from stations about the criteria for level two bonuses, because the word has gotten out that this is real money. And I can't tell you how impressed I am by the results. All of a sudden our backlog numbers are coming down, our quality is going up, and our customer satisfaction is going up.

Due to new legislation, VBA's workload had exploded. It was completing about 30,000 compensation cases a month, according to Walcoff, but roughly twice as many new cases were coming in each month, so the inventory of unresolved cases had risen to 432,000. "The secretary went on record saying he was going to get that inventory down to 250,000 cases by September of 2003," Walcott says. "That seemed like a pretty daunting task. But in fiscal year 2003, we completed 68,000 a month, and we finished September at 253,000."

A leader always takes a risk in creating performance bonuses, because critics will argue that public employees should not be paid extra for just "doing their jobs." This criticism is shortsighted, but not uncommon. Fortunately, there are other tools leaders can use if politics makes bonuses impossible.

GAINSHARING

Gainsharing is profit-sharing for the public sector. It guarantees employees a portion of financial savings achieved by their organization, as long as the organization meets specified levels of service and quality. It is quite common by now: It has worked well in places as diverse as San Diego; Indianapolis; King County, Washington (Seattle and environs); Portland, Maine; Charlotte, North Carolina; Baltimore County; and the New York City Sanitation Department. (See *The Reinventor's Fieldbook*, pp. 215–216 and 237–241.)

Charlotte's leaders like the tool so much they use three types of gainsharing. First, units that have to bid against private firms in managed competition—street maintenance, solid waste, fleet service, utilities, and few smaller units—enjoy normal gainsharing programs. If they win a bid and then deliver the service for less than they bid, employees get to divide up to 50 percent of the difference; the rest goes back to the general fund.

Second, all employees can take advantage of an employee suggestion awards program, in which they can get up to 25 percent of the first-year savings from ideas they come up with, to a maximum of $5,000. Groups are also eligible, and payouts have ranged from $25 to $5,000.

Third is the citywide incentive plan mentioned earlier. All employees can qualify for a share in savings if their business unit hits its performance targets. The city manager sets an annual savings goal for the city, and each business unit picks two to five key performance measures from its business plan, called "incentive targets." If the citywide savings are achieved, business unit employees get a share. If they hit 100 percent of their targets, they get a full share; if 60 percent, a 60 percent share.

Most gainsharing programs reward savings by individual departments, agencies, or divisions. But Charlotte chose to make its incentive payment based on citywide savings, because city leaders felt it was fairer. "We were deliberate in our decision not to do it based on the department," says Lisa Schumacher, the budget and evaluation analyst in charge of performance management, "because some were small and had small budgets, and would feel like they could never meet the target."

However it is structured, gainsharing turns every employee into a budget cutter. "Departments have been willing to hold vacancies longer, to postpone some expenses, to look for alternative solutions that might be less expensive, in order to meet either gainsharing or the employee incentive award," says Schumacher.

City manager Pam Syfert adds:

Back when we first introduced the incentive payout, we were having a real problem with sick leave. In my office specifically, we'd had some problems with what we thought was sick leave abuse, and it was a challenge in some of the field operations, too. When that incentive went in and we said, "We have to reduce our sick leave abuse by this much to be eligible for the full payout," I saw behavior change in this office. And folks out in the departments said behavior changed there, too.

Most places that take gainsharing seriously have similar experiences. Joe Harris, deputy director of San Diego's Metropolitan Wastewater Department, told us:

This program forced attention to financial reports and fiscal performance much more than we ever had. Our labor–management committee is not just one more committee. This committee, literally on a monthly basis, looks at financial reports, looks at them from facility to facility, and recommends and makes moves to address any negative variances. Now, that was always done at the management level, of course, and attempted to be transferred to our employees, but it's day and night between before this program and after it.

Gainsharing offers a win for everyone. It provides a huge incentive for better performance without costing the taxpayers a dime; in fact, the taxpayers save money. In an era of permanent fiscal crisis, every public organization should adopt it.

SHARED SAVINGS

Shared savings is gainsharing for organizations: It creates a departmental incentive to save money by allowing each administrative unit to keep a portion of the funds it has saved during the fiscal year. (See p. 249 for more.) It is not as powerful as gainsharing, because no money goes into employees' pockets. But it eliminates the universal end-of-the-year spending rush, because organizations no longer lose all the money they don't spend. The greatest challenge is to convince financially strapped budget offices and appropriations committees to keep their hands off the dollars saved. Allowing organizations to keep 50 percent may be as far as they are willing to go, and they may need a pilot project—one or two agencies being allowed to keep their savings—to demonstrate the benefits. But half a loaf is better than none.

PSYCHIC PAY

When it is impossible to use financial rewards, for political or other reasons, psychic pay offers an alternative. It offers benefits of real value to individuals—such as paid time off, payment for courses or conferences they want to attend, new equipment, or refurbished facilities—to reward them for outstanding performance. For decades the U.S. Air Combat Command has given squadrons that meet their monthly performance targets a three-day weekend at the end of the month.

PERFORMANCE AGREEMENTS WITH MANAGERS

Many jurisdictions negotiate performance agreements between the executive (mayor, city manager, county executive, superintendent, governor, or president) and department heads or principals. They spell out the key outputs and outcomes they are expected to produce, other priorities, and any rewards they can earn. Many department heads turn around and negotiate such agreements with their top managers. For our favorite version of performance agreements, see Chapter 11.

PERFORMANCE CONTRACTS WITH PROVIDERS

Chapter 7 discussed the value of forcing public and private organizations to compete for contracts. Such contracts should always be based on performance: They should include objective performance standards, clear incentives to reward high performance, and clear penalties for poor performance.

In 1999, Vermont created the nation's first statewide "energy efficiency utility" to foster conservation of electricity. For almost a decade the state had required its 22 electric utilities, as most states did, to offer efficiency programs to help households and businesses consume less. But because the utilities' underlying financial incentives were to sell more electricity, their conservation programs were never very serious, and their investment in energy efficiency declined with each passing year.

The Vermont Public Service Board (PSB) decided to create one comprehensive utility, known popularly as Efficiency Vermont, and fund it with a small charge on customers' bills—about 1.5 percent. The state decided not to operate Efficiency Vermont itself, but to farm it out on a performance contract. Six organizations responded to the request for proposals, and the not-for-profit Vermont Energy Investment Corporation won the contract.

The key desired outcome in the performance contract was 83,766 megawatt hours of energy savings. In addition, the contract called for "total resource benefits" (TRB) of $36,162,000, in lifetime net resource savings in electricity, fossil fuels, and water. It also set 21 other specific performance targets, such as the number of lighting retailers participating in conservation programs; the number of large retrofit projects completed in one year; the number of committed projects in the pipeline at the end of the three years, to make sure the provider didn't neglect investments that would pay off after the contract ended; and the equitable provision of services in all geographic regions of the state, to make sure the utility didn't just concentrate on urban areas. If it met all performance targets, Efficiency Vermont could earn an extra 2.9 percent of the contract value. The state Department of Public Service would formally evaluate its performance, annually verifying energy savings and total resource benefits.

The conservation utility uses every trick it can find to reduce consumption: advertising; coupons and rebates for those who buy energy-efficient appliances, lights, motors, and air conditioners; weatherization of low-income single-family housing; work with architects to help them design energy-efficient buildings; special help for residential customers with the highest electrical use; and financial incentives and technical assistance for the 200 largest commercial and industrial electricity consumers in the state. In its first three years, Efficiency Vermont:

- exceeded its goal for electricity savings, producing 99,217 megawatt hours;
- almost doubled its total resource benefits goal;

- met or exceeded all but one of its other 21 performance targets;
- provided services to more than 67,000 customers, compared to 17,000 in the eight years prior to its existence by all the electric utilities;
- did projects with more than 28 percent of the state's largest business consumers; and
- reduced 632,037 tons of carbon dioxide emissions, 973 tons of nitrogen oxide, 2,578 tons of sulfur dioxide, and 218 tons of particulates—the equivalent of taking 7,400 cars off the road for a year.

Not surprisingly, in January 2003, Vermont signed a second three-year contract with the same provider.

PERFORMANCE-BASED GRANTS

Financial incentives also work to spur performance in state and federal grant programs. In 1996, President Clinton directed the Department of Health and Human Services to find a way to move children in temporary foster care or public institutions more quickly into permanent homes, either by returning them to their families or through adoption. The Children's Bureau of HHS developed legislation, and in 1997 Congress passed the Adoption and Safe Families Act.

This bill redesigned the federal grant program for state child-welfare services, to require outcome measures on foster care, adoption, child safety, reunification of children with their parents, reducing the overrepresentation of minorities and older children in foster care, and decreasing inappropriate use of institutional and group care. In addition to measurement of state child-welfare programs, it created financial incentives for improved performance.

At least partially as a result of this change, adoptions from foster care rose from 26,000 in 1995 to 46,000 in 1999.

This kind of model has also cropped up at the state level. Twenty years ago, Pennsylvania's highly regarded Ben Franklin Partnership invented what it calls "challenge grants" to fund local economic development centers. As originally designed, the size of the grant to each of four competing centers depended in part on past performance: how many jobs they had created, the amount of private money they had attracted, the amount of private venture capital invested in companies they had funded, and so on.

PERFORMANCE SCORECARDS

Using scorecards, public leaders make performance a matter of public record. They issue "report cards" or "performance tables" to compare the results produced by similar public organizations—fostering competition between organizations and appealing to their members' pride. At the same time, the scorecards can be used as the basis for financial rewards.

In Great Britain, the competitive performance of local government services, hospitals, and schools won't push Manchester United's football exploits off the front pages, but the British Audit Commission's scoring of public services receives an enormous amount of press. Each year, the commission compares rural areas against rural areas, cities against cities, and London boroughs against London boroughs, and the newspapers devote many column inches to the results, with elaborate charts and graphs. Appropriating a term from the sports pages, the media have dubbed these comparative statistics "league tables"—the British expression for league standings. Citizens as well as elected officials and managers get caught up in the findings—arguing, complaining, and analyzing—and the resulting debate creates real pressure for improvement. The exercise is triply powerful. The potential for humiliation is a great motivating force for those near the bottom; those who score well earn significant credit; and the competitive analysis forces politicians to deal in results rather than mere rhetoric.

To be effective, a performance scorecard must do more than throw data at the public. It must organize that data in a form that will lead people to action. Many states post data on test scores, attendance rates, dropout rates, and the like on their Web pages, but it never leads to any comparison or pressure to improve. In contrast, the visual presentation of bar graphs in the British tabloids—which make it very clear how one's own city or school compares with others—creates a stir. Parents of school children scour the charts for comparisons; citizens look to see how well their local government is performing; and public leaders push hard for improvement.

In the United States, some states now publish comparisons of test scores and other school data. Florida, which does one of the best jobs, presents school data on a wide variety of measures: test scores in reading, math, and writing; average class size; the number of high school students who took the ACT and SAT tests and their average scores; dropout rates; incidents of school violence; the number of suspensions; the percentage of students absent more than 21 days; the percentage of students qualifying for a free or reduced-price lunch; the percentage who have limited English proficiency; the percentage in gifted programs; the four-year high school graduation rate; the stability rate (the percentage of students from the October count who are still in school in February); the percentage of teachers with advanced degrees; the average years of experience of teachers; and per pupil expenditures.

On the Worldwide Web, interested citizens can make use of the data in many ways. They can look at data on one school or compare a series of schools or districts, on one indicator or many.

But what really puts the spotlight on school performance is Florida's grading system. The state grades schools exactly as schools grade students: A, B, C, D, and F. As the Department of Education's Web site explains, "School grades are calculated by measuring student achievement, learning gains, and the improvement of the lowest-performing students at each school." The calculation involves six numbers: the percentage of students meeting high standards in reading, math, and writing; the percentage making expected annual gains in reading and math; and the percentage of the lowest 25 percent making expected learning gains in reading. The state adds up these six percentages and comes up with a number. If the number is above 410 the school gets an A; 380 to 409 yields a B; and so on.

The simple grading scheme, which is perfect for media consumption, puts intense pressure on schools that receive C's, D's, and F's. On top of that, the state has added real consequences. Schools that improve their performance by one or more letter grades from one year to the next, or maintain a grade of A, receive "school recognition funds." Those with F's go on the "Assistance Plus" plan, which gives them roughly $1,000 more per student, school improvement facilitators, reading coaches, technical assistance, and assessments to monitor student progress. But students attending schools that receive a grade of F twice in four years are eligible to move to a higher-performing public school or take a voucher to a private school that participates in the Opportunity Scholarship Program.

This system has had a remarkable impact on low-performing schools. In four years, between 1999 and 2003, the number of schools receiving F's fell by more than half, from 76 to 35. The number receiving D's fell from 601 to 141; C's from 1,230 to 527. In 1999 there were 1,230 C's, 51 percent of the total; by 2003 there were 1,230 A's, 47 percent of the total.

A few local governments also publish reports comparing their performance in selected areas to that of similar-size counties or cities. Prince William County, Virginia, publishes a *Service Efforts and Accomplishments Report*, for example. It tabulates performance in 16 service areas, including fire and rescue, police, jails, real estate assessments, welfare, tax administration, the vehicle fleet, and building permits. The county publishes comparisons between itself and Fairfax, Henrico, and Chesterfield Counties, all major suburban counties with similar demographics and respected public services. It also lets each department head pick one other jurisdiction for comparison, as long as it is within Virginia or the Washington metropolitan area. Craig Gerhart, county executive, describes the impact this way:

> *It wasn't but a year or two when we started to report this data, and we learned that our libraries were getting great citizen satisfaction, but they were also spending more per capita than anyone else we were comparing to. We almost immediately squeezed the libraries a little bit to see if we could maintain that level of service, but bring our costs down a bit. We delayed some new library projects until we could get our cost per capita into a range we thought was acceptable.*
>
> *Similarly, the Police Department had a lower case closure rate than those jurisdictions. Some of it was different counting methods, but we also found that they were doing some things we could bring back to our detectives. Our rate of delinquent taxes as a percent of the total levy seemed to be significantly higher than other jurisdictions, so we made some changes in Treasury and convinced our county board to approve hiring of some more auditors. We brought our rate down from 10.9 percent to 5.6 percent in only three years. Now we're closer to the middle. So that SEA report is something that brings a lot of attention and a lot of focus on how well we're doing, in comparison to some other very highly ranked counties.*

MAKING PERFORMANCE CONSEQUENTIAL: SOME LESSONS LEARNED

Use the performance data. The beauty of CitiStat, Compstat, and TEAMS is that regular discussion of results with the top brass ensures that managers will actually *use* the data to improve operations. But there is no one formula for success. In Charlotte, as we said, key business-unit executives hold monthly or weekly staff meetings to go over the numbers. In Florida, the secretary of environmental protection uses performance data to designate areas as "good," "watch," or "focus." In the focus areas, the secretary creates a team to investigate and fix the problem—perhaps to work with industry to improve cleanup technology, or to beef up state regulations if necessary. By 1999, the secretary had designated 28 focus areas, and within one year 25 were already showing measurable improvement.

Collecting performance data takes a great deal of time and effort. If you're not going to use it to manage, don't bother.

Magnify the power of incentives by applying them to groups as well as individuals. Most results are produced by teams, not by individuals. In such cases, use collective rewards for performance. Unless individual work leads directly to outputs you can measure, you are better off rewarding teams. Individual rewards can spark jealousy and resentment, whereas group rewards bind employees to a collective purpose.

Team-based rewards are most effective if the teams have real control over their work. Can they get rid of bad apples? Can they change their work processes? Can they hold their internal suppliers accountable for their performance? Can they buy what they need elsewhere if support agencies let them down? If they can do these things, they can usually improve their performance dramatically.

Be careful what you target, you might get it. Because performance incentives can be so powerful, leaders must carefully select the results they intend to reward. If goals are all short-term, that's what people will focus on—to the detriment of the long-term health of the organization. If they emphasize productivity but not effectiveness, the organization may generate incredible numbers of "units" (be they widgets, reports, or cases handled) while sandbagging the larger mission. At the IRS, before Charles Rossotti took over and instituted a balanced scorecard approach, dollars collected was the all-important, all-consuming performance target. Individual employees and managers, as well as the agency's 33 district offices, were measured and evaluated almost exclusively on how well they met collection targets. This single-minded drive led to violations of taxpayers' rights, critics charged, and Congress held a series of highly publicized hearings and decried the policy as a scandal.

A balanced approach, measuring a combination of efficiency, effectiveness, quality, customer satisfaction, and employee satisfaction, helps maintain perspective and avoid such problems.

Avoid arbitrary targets. Among the famous 14 points of W. Edwards Deming, the pioneer of Total Quality Management, is "Eliminate slogans, exhortations, and numerical targets." Deming argued that all targets are arbitrary, because you can't know how much performance can increase until *after* you have improved your work processes. Arbitrary targets create cynicism, he added: When workers fail to hit targets set too high, they feel unfairly blamed. If they exceed targets, they are praised and rewarded, even if the sights have been set unreasonably low.

We agree with Deming about eliminating *arbitrary* targets, but not about removing all performance goals. After all, the businesses he worked with continued to measure profit and loss, market share, return on investment, net worth, and customer satisfaction, and they continued to reward managers based on whether or not they reached their numbers.

Sunnyvale, California, the city that pioneered performance management in the early 1980s, has what we feel is the best solution. They simply measure current performance and create rewards for continual improvement. Managers in Sunnyvale whose units demonstrate significant improvement are eligible for raises and bonuses of up to 10 percent of their salaries, but each year the bar goes higher. To get this year's bonus, managers must exceed last year's performance level.

Tie rewards to objective measures of performance, not subjective appraisals. In a 2002 survey, the Office of Personnel Management found that only two in five federal employees thought that strong performers were appropriately recognized, and only three in ten thought their organization's awards programs gave them incentives to do their best. The traditional federal evaluation and rewards approach, based on subjective ratings by supervisors, is an utter failure.

When rewards are based on subjective ratings, employees distrust and resent the process. Several years ago, when *GovExec.com*, the Web publication of *Government Executive* magazine, invited e-mail messages on the ratings system, responses flooded in. A comment by Joe Chandler, of the Marine Corps Logistics Base in Albany, Georgia, was typical:

> *I can't believe that there can ever be a fair performance rating system. There are always going to be personalities involved, be they good, bad, or indifferent, and there will always be a supervisor, and no matter how good or bad they are, or no matter how hard they try, there will always be favorites, and there will most certainly always be a whipping boy.*

Managers find the process equally troubling. Few want to give employees poor ratings and take on the unwelcome job of documenting this low performance. Nor do they want to anger or demoralize most of their employees by singling out a few for superior ratings. So most simply bless all but the absolutely deadest of the dead wood, giving virtually everyone else positive ratings. Any financial rewards get so diluted as to be almost meaningless.

By rewarding marginal and superior employees equally, the traditional system promotes mediocrity. Superior performers become demoralized and cynical and either reduce their efforts or leave their jobs.

The solution: Base rewards heavily on objective performance measures of the individual, unit, or organization in question and lightly on subjective evaluations.

Make performance bonuses big enough to get people's attention. People with experience in performance management recommend bonuses that are at least double the size of a regular pay increase. The old Performance Management and Recognition System for federal managers failed in the 1980s in part because the bonuses and merit increases were simply too small. Few managers felt it was worth all the time and effort for an extra $1,000 or $1,500. A good minimum threshold for onetime bonuses is five percent of salary.

Involve employees, owners, and customers in negotiating performance goals. Setting performance goals should involve at least three parties: the organization, including both its leaders and employees; a neutral executive agency committed to performance improvement; and something like a customer council. In New York City, for example, the nonprofit Fund for the City of New York has pulled together focus groups from neighborhoods to help several departments develop better performance measures. If possible, those involved in creating performance targets should have information about the performance of comparable organizations.

Don't make reward formulas too complex. Many agencies at all levels of government have made this mistake. In an effort to create the fairest formula, they include so many goals and such complex weighting formulas that few employees can understand the process. And what people can't understand, they often fear.

You don't have to include everything you measure in the reward formula. You might use some data for feedback and learning, not for rewards. For example, a 360-degree evaluation, in which everyone is rated by their supervisors, peers, and subordinates, provides wonderful feedback. But if you attach financial consequences to it, you may find that employees won't respond honestly, and that it triggers serious trust and morale problems.

Create a culture of learning, not fear. Performance management can create anxiety, which is not all bad. A certain level of dread can motivate people to perform. But too much concern for negative consequences can lead employees to do almost anything to meet their numbers—even fudging them. In the manufacturing world, this sometimes leads to meeting quotas by shipping defective merchandise. Among the solutions: Reward experimentation, innovation, and learning as part of your performance management system; and focus on rewards far more than penalties. The best performance management systems ask not only what happened, but why and what people are going to do about it. They build learning into the process and make both actual performance and learning from it consequential.

Verify the accuracy of measurement. Most elected officials won't trust performance data unless they know it is audited for accuracy. The city of Baltimore, in addition to CitiStat staff audits, requires each department to maintain its own audit functions. It even assigns a CitiStat analyst to the field with a digital camera to make surprise visits to city facilities. In New York, a Compstat team assembles, analyzes, and sometimes audits the data brought to each meeting. Among their tools is a computer program that flags unrealistically positive results—similar to those used to monitor the performance of stock portfolios to detect insider trading. Chattanooga, Tennessee, which has a program modeled on CitiStat, created an independent Audit Advisory Board to examine the accuracy of the data.

Texas, which has a two-year budget cycle, maintains an annual review of sample indicators. The Legislative Budget Board recommends agencies and indicators for scrutiny, but the State Auditor's Office makes the final selection. It then examines a combination of key outcomes, outputs, and efficiency indicators and rates agencies as "certified" (meaning that reported performance has been verified accurate within 5 percent), "certified with qualification" (meaning that performance data appeared accurate but controls over data collection were inadequate), "inaccurate" (meaning that there was a discrepancy of more than 5 percent), or "factors prevented certification" (meaning that necessary documentation was not available).

This kind of spot check of agencies chosen at random keeps everyone on their toes.

THE POWER OF INCENTIVES

In traditional bureaucracies, the incentives are clear: Keep your head down, do what you did last year ("stay low and go slow"), and you can keep your job and get an annual pay increase. Performance management is designed to turn those incentives on their head.

Even one simple change in an incentive system can often have a dramatic impact, if it is the right change. Consider Illinois's child welfare system. In 1996, Illinois had 17.1 foster children for every 1,000 children under age 18, the highest rate in the nation and 2.5 times the national median. Workloads of 50 to 60 children per caseworker were common. The goal was to move kids into permanent homes, through adoption, guardianship by a relative, or other means, and Illinois was doing a very poor job of it.

When the Department of Children and Family Services (DCFS) removed a child from the home of abusive or neglectful parents, it paid a basic rate for temporary foster care. It contracted with private not-for-profit agencies for this service, and the more children in foster care, the more it paid the agencies. When the child returned to his or her family or found a permanent home, the agency lost the income stream. "This dynamic leads to the predictable practice of maintaining constant caseloads rather than discharging children," the department concluded.

Prodded in part by the federal Adoption and Safe Families Act, DCFS decided to change the incentive. Starting July 1, 1997, in Cook County, home to more than 75 percent of the state's foster care children, DCFS began to pay for achievement of its desired outcome: the placement of foster-care children in permanent homes. It would pay each agency to care for a predetermined number of children, say 100. In addition, the contract would call for each agency to receive a set number of new children into its care, say 25, each year. In essence, that established a quota for maintaining equilibrium. If the agency placed 25 children into permanent homes while receiving 25 new children, it would break even. If it placed 30 children in homes while receiving 25 new children into its care, it would have a caseload of only 95 children—but it would still get paid for 100. Conversely, if it placed only 20 children in homes, it would have a caseload of 105 children but be paid only for 100.

"People didn't think they could increase adoptions by 10 percent," said Jess McDonald, then DCFS director. But adoptions almost doubled, from 2,229 in 1997 to 4,293 in 1998, then almost doubled again to 7,315 in 1999. The number of children placed in permanent guardianship with relatives— a new option—zoomed from 1,276 in 1998 to 2,199 in 1999. In two years, the department doubled the percentage of kids in foster care who were moved to permanent homes within one fiscal year, from 16.1 percent in 1997 to 32.4 percent in 1999. The overall caseload dropped from 46,000 to 28,500. It was simply a matter of creating a financial incentive to produce the desired result.

In the competition for public support, good intentions are not good enough. The public wants results for their money. They expect leaders to make performance matter. When they do, those leaders—and their employees and the citizens—win.

NINE

Smarter Customer Service
Putting Customers in the Driver's Seat

Citizens expect as good or better service quality from governments as from the private sector. Expectations of public sector service quality have increased steadily since 1998.

—**Citizens First 3,**
Institute for Citizen Centered Service
and Institute of Public Administration of Canada

Historically, government has defined the time, place, and means of contact with citizens and business. Time and distance is disappearing, and interactive technologies are putting citizens in charge of the conversation. They are accustomed to self-service—they like it, and they are using it in increasing numbers.

—**Citizen 2010,**
Center for Digital Government

In 1981, registering a car in Minneapolis was an all paper, all in-person process executed at the Hennepin County government center. The public service floor in the huge 24-story building was a collection of counters around an otherwise open space design. Each counter was designated for a particular kind of service and was surrounded by a sea of chairs. The message was clear: If you come here for service, be prepared to wait.

The first step in the registration process was a visit to the "triage" desk, where customers made sure they had the right collection of documents, picked up forms to fill out, then took a number from a dispenser as they would at the deli counter of a supermarket.

Step two was to sit and wait . . . and wait. Meanwhile, other customers would be called up to the counter to present their paperwork. Often there were mistakes on the forms they had filled out, which the customer and the clerk worked to correct while those in the chairs waited. Then the clerk would go to the files in the back to look up related information, return to the desk to ask for payment, then go to the storeroom to get new license plates, or to a file to get the license tabs to apply to existing plates. Finally, the clerk would go to the cashier's desk to present the check and get a receipt, then return to the main counter to deliver the registration and say good-bye.

The busiest times at the counter were at lunch hour and at the end of the day, as harried people found a moment to work in this tiresome chore. Because people procrastinated, the end of the month was much busier than any other time. But none of this influenced staffing. The same number of people were on the desk every day. They took their lunch breaks at noon and closed up at 4:30, the busiest times of the day. Their behavior almost shouted, "Come at your convenience and you may be out of luck, but come when it is convenient for us and we will have plenty of staff to take care of you."

In 1995, when Peter Hutchinson arrived at the government center for this annual ritual, both the citizen and the consultant within him were overjoyed to find a dramatic innovation—an express line for those who had to renew only their license tabs.

At last, he thought, they get the message: Don't waste people's time! No number. No sitting and waiting. Just stand in a line that moves quickly through these relatively simple transactions. Admittedly, by 1995 he could do all his banking at a machine with a card, and he had heard that Internet commerce was right around the corner. But still, an express line was progress.

So there on the vast public service floor of the Hennepin County government center he took his place in line behind four other people. Then there were three, then two, then only one. He doubled-checked his form in anticipation. The customer at the desk picked up her tabs and began to move away, and Hutchinson moved in. But two steps from the counter he was stunned to hear the clerk announce, "It's 3:30. The Express Line is closed. Please get a number and wait in one of the chairs." He was dumbfounded. Closing the express lane at 3:30 was ridiculous. He knew from experience that the "I'll-do-it-on-my-way-home rush" was about to begin. Nonetheless, he took a seat and waited 25 minutes until his number was called.

When he finally completed his transaction, steam was still coming out of his ears. This, he thought, is why people hate dealing with government. Even when they try to do the right thing, they screw it up!

Happily, by 2002, the business of license tab renewal had been completely transformed. When Hutchinson received his usual renewal letter, it now included three options. He could still show up and wait; he could mail in the renewal; or he could complete the entire transaction online. And he could pay by check or credit card. Finally, he thought to himself, after 21 years of doing this, I can do it when I want, how I want, where I want.

Twenty-first-century citizens are more demanding than ever. We have said repeatedly that citizens want value for dollars—but we have yet to discuss how the meaning of "value" has changed. People no longer take waiting in line and filling out forms for granted. With the private sector and the Internet revolutionizing customer service, citizens' expectations have risen—and will continue to rise dramatically. Today's citizens expect to be in the driver's seat. Increasingly, they are delivering a very clear message:

- I want choice.
- I want control.
- Don't waste my time.
- And personalize the experience for a market of one—me.

For governments drowning in the permanent fiscal storm, there is every reason to listen. When citizens are placed in the driver's seat, they will actually take far more responsibility for the driving. In the same way that ATMs made customers into their own bank tellers, citizens will, when given the opportunity, fill out forms, do the data entry, arrange for payment, and do the scheduling connected with services. In the end, they will get better service, feel more satisfied with the experience, and save their governments both time and money.

I WANT CHOICE

Choice matters to anyone who wants a service. Choice gives customers a sense of control, and it allows them to maximize those aspects of the service they value the most. In education, for example, "Choice makes a difference in parent satisfaction," according to the National Center for Education Statistics. "Parents whose children attended either public, chosen schools or private schools were more likely to say they were very satisfied with their children's schools, teachers, academic standards, and order and discipline than were parents whose children attended public, assigned schools."

But choice also matters to those who provide the service. If they lose a slice of their revenue when a customer chooses a competing provider, it matters a great deal. Customer choice is almost always a good thing, but when married to consequences for providers, it is powerful indeed.

For generations, choice in public education was limited to students who could pass entrance exams into a few elite institutions, such as the Bronx High School of Science or the Boston Latin School. For most American kids, public education meant attending the school to which you were assigned. Beginning in the 1970s, though, alternative schools sprouted up. Families demanded and school boards permitted more experimentation with edu- cational formats—hands-on learning, open classrooms, arts academies, Montessori programs. Families who chose such options were often engaged and passionate about their choices.

As these experimental public schools prospered, others in the commu- nity began to take notice. Why couldn't they have similar opportunities—or their own opportunities? Why were they limited to the one-size-fits-all pro- gram in the local school?

The drive for more diversity in school offerings was accelerated by deseg- regation. To attract children of all races, school boards created magnet schools that emphasized unique offerings. Others went even further and adopted "controlled choice" as a tool to integrate all district schools. By the late 1980s, a few urban districts found themselves operating large-scale choice programs within their boundaries. And once families got a taste of choice, they wanted even more.

During this same period, school reformers identified choice as a prime strategy for improving educational outcomes. They realized that with choice came comparisons—and with comparisons, competition. The fear of losing students and income would motivate teachers and administrators to improve their schools, they believed.

Between 1985 and 1988, Minnesota Governor Rudy Perpich led a drive to create the first statewide public school choice system in the United States. (For more on this story, see *Reinventing Government*, pp. 96–101, and *Ban- ishing Bureaucracy*, pp. 157–173.) Youngsters could choose to attend any school district in the state (the Open Enrollment Program); take courses at colleges and universities during the 11th and 12th grades (the Post-Sec- ondary Options Program); and if they were at risk of failing or dropping out, they could select alternative programs tailored to their needs (the High

School Graduation Incentives Program, known informally as the "second chance" program). In each case, the state's education dollars followed the student—a blow to schools that lost students and a reward to schools that gained them.

In short order, public high schools doubled their number of advanced placement courses (in two years) and their world language offerings (in four years). Both expansions were accomplished without any substantial increase in appropriations. By 1996, almost two of every three secondary schools offered at least one course for college credit, and almost four of every 10 high schools offered courses under contract with colleges. The percentage of students who took an advanced placement exam had tripled.

In 1991, Minnesota took another step and invented charter schools: public schools that operate independently of most state and district rules, but negotiate four- or five-year performance contracts ("charters") that can be revoked if they fail to deliver the results they promise. Almost 40 states have followed suit. Other cities and states have created limited voucher programs, mostly for poor urban students. Overall, public school choice has exploded.

Jay Greene, at the Manhattan Institute, has examined the impact of all this on student achievement by creating an "education freedom index" (EFI) for each state. The index is based on:

- "Charter school choice": the percentage of all public schools that are charter schools and the extent to which the state charter school law facilitates charter schools.
- "Subsidized private school choice": the availability of vouchers, tax credits, and direct subsidies for certain expenses that support private schools.
- "Home-schooling choice": the percentage of pupils being home schooled and the degree to which home schooling is regulated.
- And "public school choice": the availability and feasibility of interdistrict transfers.

Greene then examined the relationship between the level of educational freedom and student achievement. He looked at scores on the National Assessment of Education Progress (NEAP) in mathematics at 8th grade—controlling for income, racial makeup, and per-pupil spending. His conclusion: ". . . the observable relationship between education freedom and student achievement remains strong. Where families have more options in the education of their children, the average student tends to demonstrate higher levels of academic achievement."

Greene also found that choice is extremely cost effective: ". . . a one point increase in the EFI score would produce the same expected improvement in NAEP math results as increasing per pupil spending by $2,490, about a 36 percent increase in spending over the current national average. It is certainly cheaper to adopt policies that permit greater education freedom . . . than to try to realize similar test score gains simply by increasing per pupil spending."

The bottom line: "Parental choice leads to more efficient educational outcomes."

Other studies have proven that if schools and/or districts lose enough money when parents choose to send their children elsewhere, administrators start paying close attention to what their customers want. The Minneapolis school district has lost more than 5,000 students in the last five years. The Minneapolis *Star Tribune* recently reported the reaction of district leaders:

> More Minneapolis families are choosing not to send their children to the city's public school system, opting instead for charter schools and suburban schools, according to a new Minneapolis school district report. . . .
>
> If the trend continues, the state's largest school system could shrink from 41,004 students enrolled this fall to 32,504 in 2008.
>
> And with state funding doled out to districts on a per-pupil basis, that trend could hurt the district's long-term financial health.
>
> "This doesn't say this is what the future will be," interim Superintendent David Jennings said of the report, based on five-year projections. "This does say this is what the future will be if the status quo remains . . . if we don't change our method of doing business."
>
> In Minneapolis, city schools are competing not only with charter schools but also with open enrollment programs that allow students to enroll in suburban public schools. Minneapolis loses more students than it gains through open enrollment, according to the report.
>
> District leaders say they hope to recapture more of the student market by reassessing what parents want in a school. . . .
>
> In determining the district's future, school leaders will try to figure out what's driving parents' choices. "What is it that parents, collectively, want? What part of it are we willing to compete for, and what part of it aren't we willing to compete for?" Jennings said. For example, some parents might want a religious component to their children's education, but the district is not going to offer catechism classes, he said.

Choice has the same kind of impact in any service system. Sometimes the customers lack the capacity to choose: those with severe retardation or mental illness, for example. But even in such cases, a representative of their interests can choose for them. A few years back, Minnesota consolidated funding sources for alcohol and drug treatment that had normally gone to hospitals. They gave the money to the counties and Indian reservations, then let their staffs pick the best treatment providers. Many clients received treatment more appropriate to their needs, much of it less expensive than hospital care. And because providers now had to compete, the state saved enough to serve 33 percent more people.

Choice matters. It increases citizens' satisfaction, and when money follows customers to their providers of choice, it imposes consequences on public organizations. Choice puts citizens in the driver's seat.

I WANT CONTROL

Citizen ballot initiatives and recall campaigns are extreme examples of citizens' desire to control their governments. In a democracy, naturally enough, citizens expect to be in charge. When they have a complaint or want information, they want a response—and increasingly, they want it now. They don't want to be put on hold or transferred into oblivion.

One of the most profound advances in this arena has been the development of "311" call centers, which take citizen complaints and questions and provide rapid action or answers. Under former mayor Kurt Schmoke, Baltimore invented the first 311 number, to take nonemergency calls off of its 911 system. But Chicago's Mayor Richard Daley and his staff made the real breakthrough. They developed a 311 system that puts citizens in control by actually reshaping the way services are delivered.

In January 1999, Chicago eliminated a number of smaller call centers and implemented 311 as their "one-stop shopping" point of access for all city services, including nonemergency police services. Chicagoans can dial it 24 hours a day, seven days a week, to complain, report problems (such as potholes), request service, obtain information about city programs or events, or file police reports. (They can do the same on the Internet, through an alderman's office, at a community policing office, or at city offices.)

Millions of calls come into 311 every year. Trained operators and enterprise-wide software route them to the proper department. The software allows managers to set deadlines for response times and measure the percentage of overdue requests. Citizens can call back to track progress on their requests. When a service request is fulfilled, the system generates a letter to the person, which gives them a phone number to call if they are not satisfied.

The data on overdue requests are compiled into real-time reports, much like those of Compstat and Citistat, which we discussed in Chapter 8. These reports help department heads manage staff, track trends, improve work processes, recognize outstanding performance, and squeeze the most bang out of every buck. For example, city managers used reports of dead animals to track the spread of West Nile virus. The Sewer Department used "water in basement" reports to pinpoint areas of flooding during heavy storms, so its staff could make adjustments to the sewer system. It reduced average response time to requests for service from 17.2 days in 1999 to 7 days in 2001, and it learned enough about how much time each assignment took to cut the time allowed for work assignments in half.

The city's Graffiti Blasters program reduced its response time to complaints from 7.7 to 3.5 days. By analyzing patterns, the Graffiti Removal Group figured out how to remove 85 percent of graffiti before a complaint had been registered. The Department of Streets and the Sanitation Department's Bureau of Electricity used the 311 system to identify duplicate requests to replace street lights that had gone out. This saved hundreds of worker hours by eliminating the assignment of multiple crews to the same problem, and it has cut the number of open service requests from 6,000 to 300.

When fire hydrants were being repeatedly opened in the summer of 2001, wasting hundreds of millions of gallons of water, the 311 system generated a report pinpointing the most frequently opened hydrants, and the Water Department installed locking caps. Water consumption dropped by as much as 150 million gallons a day, a considerable savings. The Sanitation Department used 311 data to identify landlords with a history of complaints about lack of heat, then contacted them before the winter to warn them that their buildings would be closely watched.

Chicago won an Innovation in American Government Award for its 311 system. Steve Miller, the expert who examined the system and wrote the site report, put it this way:

> What makes Chicago special is that from the beginning, Chicago 311 was intimately tied to a transparent work assignment and progress tracking system, and the key people in city government quickly exploited that system for improving city operations. . . . One of the most exciting aspects of Chicago 311 is the way the mayor's office and other oversight units have seized on the newly available data to successfully push their agenda for improving responsiveness

to citizen requests, increasing workforce productivity, allocating resources to
emphasize preventive action, and generally "doing more with less."

Chicago created a Customer Advocacy Unit to help department managers use the information derived from 311 reports to improve performance. These internal consultants evaluate business processes and help redesign them, help set customer service goals and review performance against them, and help make other improvements in efficiency and effectiveness. Miller summed up 311's impact this way:

The service request system tracks the progress of the assigned task through its
various steps, which allows citizens—and city managers—to measure task
duration and output levels, leading to increased accountability and output.
The patterns of service requests turn out to be exactly the kind of data depart-
ment managers need for proactive work assignments that catch problems be-
fore they become crises. Incoming calls also give city officials advance warning
of quickly flaring problems, from street flooding to crowd control. Putting all
the data together gives oversight agencies new tools to push for increased effi-
ciency and more managerial creativity during tight fiscal times. In the future,
the city hopes to combine 311 data with financial information to reveal unit
pricing and use that data for better budgeting.

Baltimore and New York have both adopted Chicago's 311 model, as have other cities. "It's not just a citizen service hot line, it is the most powerful management tool ever developed for New York City government," Mayor Michael Bloomberg told the *New York Times*.

New York's 311 lines received 3.69 million calls during the system's first nine months, as many as 30,000 on a day of heavy service. As the one number to call, 311 draws together all the complaints, questions, and commentary that formerly came through on hundreds of different phone lines in hundreds of agencies. Here, too, the information is analyzed to provide a real-time picture of how well the city is doing.

After a tough winter in 2003, Transportation Commissioner Iris Weinshall saw a surge in pothole complaints and deployed an extra 150 workers to the asphalt and gravel brigades. The backlog of complaints dropped from 3,000 to 975. Police used 311 to track resident complaints about noise, double-parking, and public urination back to their source—illegal social clubs.

"[The 311 system] allows us to do more with less because we can see exactly how agencies are performing and manage our existing assets better and smarter," Gino P. Menchini, the city's commissioner for information technology and telecommunications, told the *Times*. "It allows us to be able to do what we need to do without having to add additional resources. It's cost avoidance, more than anything else."

The telephone number, plastered across everything from city buses to trash baskets, is also a ubiquitous symbol of Mayor Bloomberg's administration.

Weinshall told the *Times* about being quizzed by the mayor at a social event: "You don't want to say, 'I don't know,' and have him say, 'Well, I know, you have 975 pothole complaints.' It keeps you on your toes."

The 311 data, monitored and analyzed, have allowed city agencies to create standards for response time to each type of complaint and track their records on meeting them. Customer service standards like this can be powerful tools if the departments take them seriously. (For more on customer service standards, see *The Reinventor's Fieldbook*, Chapter 9.)

"311 really has changed the way we do business," says Thomas R. Frieden, the health commissioner.

Adds the mayor: "I can't imagine running the city without it."

A 311 system may not put real control in the hands of the customer, but when an agency has to respond to customer complaints and set deadlines for solving their problems—and when those who complained can track the agency's progress—citizens do get the feeling that what they says matters.

DON'T WASTE MY TIME

In a world of two-career couples, heavily scheduled kids, and work that follows us home by way of cell phones, laptops and PDAs, time has become a precious commodity. According to *American Demographics*, today's average married couple works 717 hours more each year than a working couple did in 1969. A study from the Department of Labor finds 84 percent of respondents saying they would trade future income for free time, with nearly half willing to trade a 10 percent raise for more free time.

In the face of this reality, wasting people's time is a serious offense. "Customers are time-starved, they're stressed. They want what they want when they want it, and it's our job to give it to them," says Mary Jean Raab, head of new business development for Borders Books.

The National Governors Association sums up the challenge this way:

State agencies will continually be challenged to adapt to constituents' (customers, business partners, and employees) demands for anytime access to in-

formation and services they desire. In the new consumer society everything is becoming a service, and service value is dependent on information quality. Customers are determining business hours and increasingly seeking customized products and services. State governments will be expected to be flexible and responsive as a service business that has increased value.

Public organizations can start by making basic transactions accessible and convenient. They can change hours, staffing, and locations to reflect citizen preferences. They can create service centers and call centers, like 311 systems, to handle large volumes. They can separate complex from simple transactions, by creating express services for the simple transactions and providing appointments or other special handling for those that are more complex. And they can provide options for completing transactions: in person, by mail, by phone, or on the Internet.

Travis County, Texas, eliminated the huge amount of time wasted in the jury-selection process. Typically, prospective jurors are selected at random and told to report to the courthouse. They wait to see whether they are selected for a jury, then wait to see whether they are to be impaneled or excused. The experience is frustrating, inconvenient, and, given that time is money, extremely expensive. Travis County alone, home to the city of Austin, selects more than 150,000 prospective jurors every year. That is a tremendous number of unnecessary trips to the courthouse.

So county leaders created I-Jury, which allows prospective jurors to respond to the summons from their home computer or a terminal at the public library. The online questionnaire identifies disqualified jurors, lets people list schedule conflicts that would pose difficulty in fulfilling their jury duty, resolves predictable excuses, and gives jurors an opportunity to present other excuses for consideration. It also allows them to request postponement. Novell software analyzes all the data, then e-mails a reply, telling prospective jurors their status, giving specific information about the court assignment, and telling them when and where to report.

I-Jury puts a premium on citizen time. It redesigns the process around the convenience of the citizens, rather than the convenience of the courts.

The New York State Council on the Arts, which makes grants to arts organizations large and small, took a similar approach in revamping its application process. Historically, NYSCA's process was all paper, and it required that every applicant—even long-term recipients—file anew each year. In 2002, the council processed about 3,000 requests. For each of the arts organizations, this meant an annual cycle starting from scratch: filling out the same forms, photocopying pages and pages of repeated documentation, then sending them in and waiting, often for months. The entire process was extremely wasteful, since most organizations got essentially the same grant every year.

When NYSCA staff stepped back and took a hard look at the process, they challenged themselves to eliminate virtually all the wasted time and paper. They created a system that allows organizations to register once online. Then, each year, a returning organization can simply update the material already on file. These changes have reduced the workload on those who apply, simplified the review process. They will allow agency staff to commit nearly 50 percent more time to actually working with their client organizations.

THE WONDERFUL WORLDWIDE WEB

Increasingly, today's world operates 24 hours a day and seven days a week. And that is a huge difference: A 24/7 organization is available four times as often as a conventional eight-to-five organization. Yet 24/7 operations are an expensive proposition in an age of permanent fiscal crisis.

The solution is the Internet. The Worldwide Web is always open; it is accessible from any location the user desires; it provides multiple services; and it can handle transactions both simple and complex. In fact, the Internet takes the best of what a service center or call center can provide and delivers it to the citizen's desktop. *Pay IT Forward*, a report published by the Center for Digital Government, tells the tale:

> *By 2003, fully 72 percent of all American households were online—including 46 percent of African American households and 42 percent of Hispanic households. Couple that with the coming of age of the first generation of Americans for whom a network-connected computer is just another household appliance, 73 percent of whom use the Internet as part of their daily lives. The online population in the United States now totals at least 169 million. Importantly, this new digital majority is demonstrating a growing appetite for self-service, with some 30 percent reporting they have done business with government online. Their activity translates to adoption rates for digital government services in excess of the conventional 33 percent benchmark for designation as a mass medium. Even a 33 percent online adoption rate takes one in three people out of line. This allows public employees to focus their energies on people who cannot or choose not to use online services, whose needs may require personalized attention, while volumes of routine transactions are handled through automated means.*

Citizens appear eager to do business online. According to *Citizen 2010*, also published by the center, "Fully 77 percent of Internet users believe digital government is a high priority, as do 73 percent of all adults. Remarkably, even two-thirds (67 percent) of non-Internet users put a high priority on digital government."

The Bush administration's strategy document on e-government adds:

A survey released in April 2003 by the Council for Excellence in Government noted that 75 percent of E-Government users think E-Government has made it easier to get information, and 67 percent like doing transactions with government online. Nielsen/NetRatings, the global standard for Internet audience measurement and analysis, reports that more than one-third of all Internet users visited a federal government Web site in February 2003, and about half of all businesses went online in January 2003 to interact with the federal government.

FirstGov.gov, the federal mega-portal, provides three-click access to federal, state, and local services; Yahoo named it one of its 50 "most incredibly useful" Web sites. GovBenefits.gov, which provides a single point of access to more than 400 government benefits programs, had more than four million hits in its first year; *USA Today* listed it as one of its "Hot Sites." GoLearn.gov, which provides inexpensive training, at pennies per course; it has more than 45,000 registered users and had more than 60 million hits in its first nine months. Free File (www.irs.gov/efile/) allows taxpayers to prepare and file their taxes electronically for free; by April 2003, 2.4 million taxpayers used the service. In 2003, the American Customer Satisfaction Index, a sophisticated survey used widely in business, found that taxpayers filing electronically were significantly more satisfied (score of 77) than those filing the conventional way (score of 53).

Cities, counties, school districts, and states also use the Web to provide services. The Center for Digital Government identified the 10 most common online services offered by state governments as online job searches (98 percent of which are now online), unclaimed property searches (96 percent), legislation tracking (94 percent), state college admissions (94 percent), looking up court decisions (70 percent), looking up sex offenders (68 percent), vital records (68 percent), looking up professional licenses (62 percent), and business tax filing (58 percent).

The public is adopting these Web-based services more rapidly than one might expect, because they are quicker and more convenient. According to *Pay IT Forward*, by 2003 the leading adoption rates by customers were for impounded vehicle service (98 percent), uniform commercial code filings (83 percent), vital statistics (75 percent), business registration renewal (75 percent), accident reports (73 percent), initial business registration (70 percent), business licensing (67 percent), patient eligibility verification (59 percent), professional license renewals (38 percent), campsite registration (38 percent), parking ticket payments (13 percent), driver's license renewals (12 percent), income tax payments (11 percent), and vehicle registration renewals (11 percent).

The savings are huge: Utah saves 75 percent on each online license lookup and verification; Maine saves 50 percent on every online vehicle registration; Tennessee saves 36 percent on every driver's license renewal; and Kansas saves 66 percent on online uniform commercial code (UCC) filings. Paul Taylor, who now runs the Center for Digital Government, says, "Just 11 examples out of eight states—out of the dozens of examples we cite—put about $1.7 billion back into the state treasuries last year."

These savings occur because citizens and computers are now doing much of the work public employees once did. And citizens like it.

But since citizens don't experience the savings personally, they care more about other things. They want Web sites that:

- are organized around what they want to do, not how the government is organized;
- use plain language;
- provide easy navigation and searching;
- allow online payment options;
- allow scheduling of appointments; and
- provide opportunities for customization.

The state of California's Web portal (Figure 9.1), Singapore's eCitizen portal (Figure 9.2), and the U.S. government's FirstGov portal (Figure 9.3) all offer good examples. Each is built around the needs of citizens—and it shows. They focus on frequent transactions. They use plain language. They emphasize simplicity and ease of access. And they can be customized.

Unfortunately, a great many government Web sites are not up to this standard. Too often, citizens find their time online as confusing, frustrating, and wasteful as their dealings with government in person. In a 2003 survey done by Darrell West, of Brown University, only 21 percent of 1,663 state and federal government Web sites offered three or more services.

But the potential of Web-based services is enormous. Consider the nation's first multichannel electronic service delivery system for motor vehicle

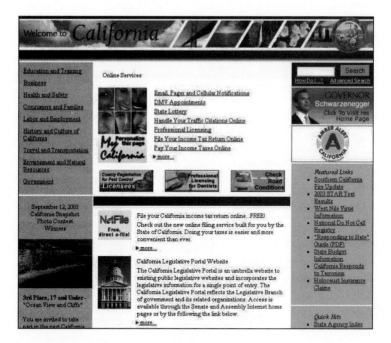

FIGURE 9.1

California's Web portal, http://my.ca.gov/state/portal/myca_homepage.jsp

FIGURE 9.2

Singapore's eCitizen portal, http://ecitizen.gov.sg/

FIGURE 9.3

U.S. government's FirstGov portal, http://firstgov.gov/

transactions, ServiceArizona. Developed in 1997 in partnership with IBM, this Internet and phone system allows citizens to complete transactions with the Motor Vehicle Division (MVD) at any time, day or night, without leaving their homes or offices. License renewals can be completed in less than three minutes by connecting to a dedicated Internet Web page or by dialing a toll-free number. IBM funded startup costs and receives $1 per registration fee, as well as 2 percent of each vehicle license tax.

A traditional license renewal costs $6.60 to process; online, the cost is $1.60—a savings of 76 percent. With 250,000 transactions a year, this translates into an annual savings for Arizona of $1.25 million. Another advantage is that instant data entry makes up-to-date information available to law enforcement officials in real time. And even for those who continue to visit the DMV, shorter lines mean shorter waits.

In 1996, the Kansas Department of Human Resources established three call centers to handle an average of 2,100 new unemployment claims per week. But when more than 7,500 claims were filed in December 2000, the system began to crash. The state projected that claims would increase 85 percent by 2002, while the budget would grow by only 10 percent and the staff would shrink by 5 percent. Departmental leaders replaced their claims-taking network with an integrated Internet and phone system, doubling productivity and dramatically improving speed, customer access, and reliability. The average time required to process a claim fell from 47 minutes to 11 minutes. With the online option available, the overloaded call centers saw their workloads drop by 35 percent.

PERSONALIZE THE EXPERIENCE

There are probably very few customers who go to a restaurant or a hardware or clothing store who are not favorably impressed when they are greeted by name. Personalization makes the customer feel valued. Not only that, it enhances expectations that the service will be exceptional.

If you've ever purchased something from Amazon.com, you know that each time you log back in you receive a series of personalized recommendations. Amazon uses collaborative filtering software to get to know your preferences and to anticipate products that might be of interest. When you buy a book, CD, or DVD, you are given a list of similar items that purchasers of your book, CD, or DVD also bought—opening a window to products you often didn't even know existed. You can then read a few pages of any book that strikes your curiosity, or listen to short cuts from a CD.

Government Web sites are not quite as "personal" as Amazon.com, but some can be customized, allowing users to shape what they see and how they interact. For example, California's MyCalifornia Web site, http://my.ca.gov/, can be customized so that the content of the Web page reflects the interests of the individual users. In addition, users can register to receive up-to-the-minute commuter information, lottery results, press releases, and official notifications.

The federal student aid Web site, http://studentaid.ed.gov/, goes one step further by allowing individuals, once they have a PIN, to apply for and manage their student loans online.

The Internet creates huge opportunities to customize services and relationships, but not all customization or personalization is high tech. States let you customize your license plates—converting a compliance requirement into a personal service—and charge a higher fee for the privilege.

In the early 1990s, Minnesota's Revenue Department fundamentally rebuilt its sales tax system. (See Chapter 13 for the whole story.) The sales tax is relatively complex, because it treats different kinds of sales and businesses differently. This meant that the tax form was very complicated, with each business using only the parts that applied to its circumstances. As a result, sales tax filings contained a high rate of errors, which required notification, investigation, and resubmission.

One goal of Minnesota's effort was to simplify the process for businesses. By the time they were done, the reengineering team had developed an elegant solution: personalized tax forms. Following an initial business registration or filing that included the required information, the department would create a customized form. From that point on, unless something about the business changed, businesses got customized sales tax forms every year. They made many fewer errors and were more satisfied, while the department enjoyed lower administrative costs and higher collections.

Done properly, personalization reduces errors, increases compliance, and helps citizens and businesses get what they want in the way they want.

THE ULTIMATE PAYOFF

The American Customer Satisfaction Index (ACSI) calls itself "a uniform and independent measure of household consumption experience." Produced through a partnership of the University of Michigan Business School, the American Society for Quality (ASQ), and the CFI Group, an international consulting firm, it provides valuable benchmarks for companies, industry trade associations, and government agencies.

According to ACSI, customer satisfaction with public services, while valuable in itself, also contributes to increased public trust. Lack of trust is not the same as dissatisfaction with specific public services. Nor does lack of trust lead to dissatisfaction with services. But satisfaction with services *does* lead to higher levels of trust.

The Canadian Institute for Citizen Centered Service and Institute of Public Administration discovered the same thing. Their researchers tested a model connecting people's satisfaction with services to their confidence in government. Service quality for hospitals, public schools, the Customs & Revenue Agency, and Canada Pension Plan/Old Age Security, as well as ratings of federal, provincial, and territorial services in general, were correlated with the number of respondents who agreed with statements such as:

- "Governments in this country conduct their business in an open and accountable manner,"
- "I believe governments do a good job,"
- "I get good value for my tax dollars," and
- "Governments are responsive to the needs of citizens."

The study found "a strong quantitative relationship between government services and confidence in governments. Services, broadly defined, account for 67 percent of the variance in citizens' overall ratings of government." Their conclusion: "This new empirical analysis reveals that service quality has a significant impact on citizens' confidence in governments. Since measures of confidence in government have been falling for several decades, this link establishes service quality as an important influence on civic health."

But the authors added this warning:

The good news is that service quality scores are increasing, but this does not mean that the public sector can relax its efforts to improve. Citizens' expectations of public sector services are also increasing. . . . Because service is critical in shaping citizens' confidence in government, it is vital that the focus on the service agenda increase, not diminish. The challenge for the public sector may be bigger now than ever before.

Customer satisfaction is a moving target, in other words. Consider your own experience—or Peter Hutchinson's. As we described at the opening of this chapter, when the Minnesota Department of Motor Vehicles brought its renewal process into the twenty-first century, Hutchinson was delighted . . . for about 20 minutes. By the time he reached his office, he was already wondering when the DMV would embed the necessary information on a chip in the license plate itself, so he could complete the registration process wirelessly.

The rate of change drives rising customer expectations, which then drive the rate of change. It is a relentless cycle, and—like the fiscal crisis—it is a permanent feature of twenty-first-century government.

TEN

Don't Buy Mistrust—
Eliminate It

Symbols of distrust are everywhere: time sheets, multiple approvals of
travel requests, systems to track people's activities, checks and limits on
people getting the tools they need—like Internet access.
> —President Bill Clinton and Vice President Al Gore,
> *The Blair House Papers*

In 1990, when Peter Hutchinson became commissioner of finance in Minnesota, his name began to appear on each of the state's 46,000 payroll
checks. Fortunately, he didn't have to sign each check—a machine did that
for him. But he did have to sign 50 to 100 time sheets every month, each
serving to document the work record of a Department of Finance employee. His signature affirmed the accuracy of the record and authorized
one of those machine-generated payroll checks.

After signing these time sheets for several months, Hutchinson came to a
startling realization. In virtually every case, he had no actual knowledge of
the work hours he was vouching for. He did not take attendance or supervise most of the people whose time cards he was signing. He relied on the
signatures of those who signed before him: the employee, the employee's
boss, the boss's boss, the boss's boss's boss, and in some cases, the boss's
boss's boss's boss.

Each time he signed, he was, in effect, lying. Given the customs and culture of his agency, he had to assume that everyone else in this chain of signatures was lying as well. In fact, the only people who actually had the
knowledge they were claiming were the employee and his or her immediate
supervisor. The rest were just piling on—and in so doing, wasting an enor-

mous amount of energy. Most employees assumed that time sheets and time reporting were an inevitable part of working life. But when Hutchinson began to consider the scope of this routine behavior, he asked his staff to find out two things: how time reporting started and how much it cost. What he learned was alarming.

In Minnesota, "positive time reporting"—accounting for every hour in the day, week, or month—had been instituted 20 years before, when two employees were paid a couple of thousand dollars each but never showed up for work. This was the kind of scandal that could energize the local television station's crack "I-Team" investigative unit, so to protect the state's image—and make sure this kind of graft never happened again—management adopted time reporting. With its advent, the problem caused by a couple of bad apples who stole several thousand dollars went away.

The catch is that the state is still paying. The system of filling out, signing, and processing time sheets cost Minnesota $13 million a year to administer. But that was just the financial loss. The more profound cost was the message these time sheets sent out every two weeks: that the state didn't trust its employees to work an honest day, or its supervisors to supervise.

Of course, the Gopher State was not alone. When David Osborne helped run Vice President Gore's National Performance Review, he and his colleagues discovered that one of every three federal employees was there to control, oversee, audit, or investigate the other two. In town meetings Gore held in every department, the vice president heard tale after tale about the cost of mistrust. As his 1993 report recounted:

> *The district managers of Oregon's million-acre Ochoco National Forest have 53 separate budgets—one for fence maintenance, one for fence construction, one for brush burning—divided into 557 management codes and 1,769 accounting lines. To transfer money between accounts, they need approval from headquarters. They estimate the task of tracking spending in each account consumes at least 30 days of their time every year, days they could spend doing their real jobs. It also sends a message: You are not trusted with even the simplest responsibilities.*

> *A supervisor at the Centers for Disease Control complained that it can take six to eight months and as many as 15 revisions to a job description in order to get approval for a position he needs to fill. . . .*

> *One of the Labor Department's regional directors for unemployment insurance complained that even though he is charged with running a multimillion-dollar-a-year program, he isn't allowed to hire a $45,000-a-year program specialist without getting approval from Washington. . . .*

As we noted in the Introduction, traditional public bureaucracies are built on the assumption that most of us, if given the opportunity, will lie, cheat, and steal. Consider special education, where teachers spend up to 50 percent of their time filling out forms to demonstrate compliance with federal and state regulations. Or child welfare, where caseworkers report spending up to 80 percent of their time on paperwork and documentation.

All these rules were inspired by specific problems and instituted to keep them from recurring. But the cost of this mistrust is enormous. Finding less expensive ways to win compliance would improve both morale and performance, while giving our schools and child-welfare workers a massive infusion of what they need most to serve our kids: time.

There is a better way. By simplifying the rules, working in partnership with compliers, making the process of compliance easier, and creating incentives to reward compliance, leaders can often win voluntary compliance at a fraction of what they now spend, while achieving equal or higher compliance rates.

WINNING COMPLIANCE

When we talk with public leaders about compliance, we usually begin with three questions:

Do you regularly attempt to follow the rules and pay what you owe when you file your income taxes? Typically, everyone says yes. Most say they do so because it is required. They acknowledge the chastening effect of the threat of being audited, and the desire to avoid unpleasant consequences. But others say they pay their fair share simply because it's the right thing for citizens to do.

Do you recycle your garbage at home? Roughly 85 to 90 percent say yes, even though it is not actually required, and there are no consequences for noncompliance.

Then we add the third question:

Do you regularly obey the posted speed limit on the interstate? Ninety percent of people say no, even though compliance *is* required, and people *do* regularly get caught and penalized.

What accounts for the difference? The fact is, people generally adhere to community norms and expectations, not all of which are written into law. Most of us want to be good citizens. We know we need to pay taxes, and as long as everyone else appears to be doing it, most of us follow suit. More or less the same thing happens on our highways. There is a speed limit that people follow—it's just not the one that's posted by government officials. It's the speed that the traffic is flowing at any given time.

The lesson for reinventors is that compliance is best achieved by establishing and promoting community norms, a method that is much less expensive than massive enforcement efforts.

The compliance functions of government include tax collection, enforcement of environmental protection laws, policing, food and drug enforcement, and of course enforcement of the ubiquitous internal rules that hamstring public employees and waste so much money. The results vary wildly. More than 90 percent of us comply with the tax laws. At best, 60 to 70 percent of us comply with mandatory seat belt laws, and only about half of all liquor stores comply with prohibitions on the sale of alcohol to minors.

To achieve compliance, most public organizations rely on detecting and punishing violations in order to deter inappropriate behavior. This approach can be effective, but it is almost always expensive, squandering both taxpayers' dollars and public support for government. Witness the early enforcement regimes at the federal Occupational Safety and Health Administration (OSHA), which drove businesspeople up the wall until the agency changed its approach in the 1990s. Or consider the "scandal" brought on by overzealous Internal Revenue Service (IRS) collection agents in the late 1990s, which brought on congressional hearings, severe tongue-lashings from outraged members of Congress, and a reform bill.

Enforcement agencies often assume the worst—and produce the worst—from the public they are trying to regulate. This is because their methods are based on a set of assumptions that are not generally valid. They assume we have to *force* people to do things, when in fact, most people want to comply with what is expected of them. When citizens don't comply, it's often because they don't know what compliance in a given situation means, or how to go about it. In the early 1990s, for instance, the Minnesota Department of Revenue discovered that 50 percent of noncompliance on individual tax returns was a result of people not understanding the instructions or making simple mistakes on the forms.

Enforcement also relies on fear as the primary motivator. While this may be necessary in some cases, people are motivated more often by pride, peer pressure, rewards, and recognition.

All of this makes enforcement a blunt instrument. As public leaders recognize its limitations, governments around the world are shifting to cheaper, more effective options. They are winning voluntary compliance, with enforcement kept in the holster as a last resort.

Nine Steps to Boost Voluntary Compliance

Every other Wednesday, just as the sun comes up, thousands of people in Peter Hutchinson's Minneapolis neighborhood stumble to the end of their driveways with bins full of old cans, bottles, and newspapers. In the small town of Essex, Massachusetts, where David Osborne lives, they haul these items to the dump every Saturday.

These citizens are participating in what has become a community ritual—recycling. It wasn't always this way. Not so long ago, we blithely threw our bottles, cans, and newspapers in the garbage, en route to overloaded landfills. Now we treat these discarded items with great reverence. We separate and wash the bottles and cans, bag the newspapers, and put them all in the appropriate containers.

Garbage just isn't what it used to be. Somehow, our governments have convinced us to comply with a new set of expectations and norms. They did so without resorting to the usual set of compliance tools. There are no recycling inspectors. There are no recycling police or recycling tickets. You can't be hauled off to a recycling court, and there is no 12-step program for recovering nonrecyclers. Yet a majority of American households recycle regularly. It's a dirty, filthy habit, but most people do it.

Recycling succeeded because public leaders advertised and educated (especially in schools). Then they made it relatively easy, by distributing recycling bins, establishing regular collection cycles, and so on. The bins had the powerful side effect of mobilizing peer pressure: Everyone in your neighborhood can see whether you're doing your civic duty. Finally, some governments rewarded recyclers with a small credit on their solid waste bills, or provided an incentive by charging for garbage but not for recycled materials. By using these and other tools, many governments have achieved a high rate of voluntary compliance, without resorting to enforcement approaches that are expensive, antagonistic, and often ineffective. We call this new strategy, which is spreading rapidly, "winning compliance." It has nine steps that your governments and school districts can use to boost voluntary compliance. They work equally well with internal government rules and with those designed to regulate the behavior of citizens and businesses.

1. Build support for standards by working in partnership with compliers and other stakeholders.

To convince people and businesses to comply with society's rules, give them a voice in setting those rules and designing the compliance process. Community policing is built on the notion, among others, that law enforcement should work hand in hand with neighborhood leaders to design strategies and fight crime. When Madison, Wisconsin, reformed its purchasing system, it urged purchasing agents to involve police officers, firemen, and other city employees in the process of drawing up product specifications and testing equipment the city might buy.

At the Environmental Protection Agency, the Common Sense Initiative brought together business, environmental, community, and EPA leaders in committees that each focused on one industry, such as metal finishing, iron and steel, or computers and electronics. The committees developed methods to streamline compliance processes and eliminate barriers to compliance. EPA's Project XL did the same thing with individual companies, as then EPA administrator Christine Todd Whitman explained at the National Environmental Policy Institute:

> *The ground has shifted. We are ready for a new approach, finding common ground to achieve shared goals. Project XL:*
>
> * *Is a model of how EPA should work with all environmental stakeholders.*
> * *Focuses on results and builds partnerships that help achieve those results.*
> * *Provides positive incentives and produces positive results.*
> * *Proves EPA is ready to move from command and control to cooperation and accomplishment.*

Leaders at OSHA tried to launch a similar national partnership, and their frustration illustrates the importance of building support among compliers. In the Introduction, we described a remarkably successful initiative called the Maine Top 200 Program. OSHA officials there had experienced the failure of their traditional inspect-and-fine approach: They won gold medals for issuing citations and fines, but the state's workplace safety and health records were the worst in the country. So they changed strategies. They invited the 200 employers with the highest volume of injury claims to create employee teams focused on improving safety. The teams would draw up action plans, conduct comprehensive surveys of hazards in their own plants, and correct most of them within 12 months. As long as the company was making a good-faith effort, OSHA would forgo its traditional inspections and fines. But each quarter, the employers had to file a report outlining their progress. Occasionally, OSHA would visit to verify those reports. Employers who failed to fulfill their obligations would be subject to comprehensive inspections.

Faced with the alternative of increased OSHA inspections, all but a handful of firms chose the self-inspection model. In the program's first two years, participating employers identified and fixed *14 times* as many hazards as OSHA had on its own. Their payable workers' compensation claims dropped by 47 percent—far outpacing declines in other companies. The businesses saved money, and the taxpayers got exponentially greater value for their dollars.

In Maine, OSHA had consulted extensively with the 200 firms before rolling out its experiment. But when the agency implemented the program nationally, the U.S. Chamber of Commerce filed suit to block it, claiming that it was in fact coercive, not voluntary, and therefore required a formal rule-making process in which business could comment. The lesson: building partnerships requires extensive discussion with compliers ahead of time to get their buy-in. "Even when an agency has the solution, you can't just impose it on people," former OSHA head Joe Dear told *Government Executive* magazine. "We got in a big rush to replicate the program and we skipped some of the preparatory work."

2. Make regulations results-based.

Many regulations prescribe exactly how compliers have to toe the line, particularly in the environmental arena. They tell businesses what technology they must use, how it must be installed, and how often it must be inspected. Often compliers know that a better way exists, but the law won't allow it. Reinventors have begun to substitute regulations that define the outcome required but leave it up to compliers to figure out how to produce it. If a new technology will meet the goal at a lower price, they are free to use it. This not only makes it easier for them to comply, it stimulates innovation to find better and cheaper methods.

Both EPA's and OSHA's reinvention efforts during the 1990s exemplify this principle. For example, EPA's metal finishing committee adopted performance goals that would cut toxic emissions by as much as 75 percent, while giving companies more flexibility in how they reached them. OSHA shifted its performance goals for area offices from maximizing citations to reducing work-related injuries, illnesses, and deaths. After a survey of 80,000 employees around the nation, it gave field offices data on injury and illness rates in high-hazard industries, company by company, so they could target workplaces with the highest rates.

The Massachusetts Environmental Results Program (ERP) originated in 1995 when two stakeholders got together to talk about substituting performance standards for permitting as a way to get much more pollution prevention without spending more money. Few small businesses were captured by the permitting system (only 10 percent of dry cleaners were even identified by the state), and it would have been very expensive to force them all to apply for permits. Instead, ERP required that a senior company official in all dry cleaners, photo processors, and printing shops annually certify that the facility was and would continue to be in compliance with all state air, water, and hazardous waste performance standards. The Massachusetts Department of Environmental Protection (DEP) helped with this self-certification by providing assistance, including sector-specific workbooks and workshops that were developed with the help of businesspeople. DEP evaluated compliance with random sampling and statistical analysis. Staff could then focus their limited resources by concentrating on sector-wide problems and targeting inspections and assistance to facilities that fell short.

3. Educate compliers about what is expected of them.

In a paper summarizing its reinvention efforts, the EPA concluded that "For some, the failure to comply comes down to a simple lack of understanding about what's required." Anyone who has ever filled out a government document such as the IRS's long form knows this problem firsthand. The EPA added, "We need to do a better job of providing information in timely, helpful ways so people can fulfill their environmental responsibilities."

In the mid-1990s the U.S. Customs Service developed an education strategy called "Informed Compliance." It shifted part of its staff from inspecting goods brought into ports and airports to helping importers improve their internal control processes. "Those out to break the law will continue to be apprehended," explained Dennis Murphy, director of public affairs, "but we're moving from what you might call a 'gotcha' focus, in which we just try to catch somebody, to one of trying to make sure that the people we deal with understand what's required of them so they don't make mistakes based on ignorance, sloppy work, or poor communications." Overall compliance rates, measured through statistical sampling of imports, improved.

When the Minnesota Department of Revenue realized that half of its noncompliance was the result of taxpayer errors, it decided to invest in more taxpayer assistance rather than more auditors. The result was greater compliance and a $20 million increase in tax receipts.

Similarly, the IRS set up an education program to help small businesses, and the EPA created virtual compliance assistance centers on the Web, developed in partnership with industry, environmental, and academic organizations. They give businesses quick access to regulatory requirements, information on how to prevent pollution, and a summary of best practices in other firms.

4. Make the process of complying easy.

Most compliance processes can be made easier without lowering standards at all. The best way is to simplify the rules and streamline the process. If government can make it a snap to pay our taxes, ensure a safe workplace, and meet our legal obligations when we employ nannies and after-school babysitters, more of us will comply with the law. The Minnesota Department of Revenue radically simplified its short form, down from some 50 lines to nine, and rewrote each line in plain language. Then it ran television ads encouraging people to use the short form. The ads showed a husband and wife: While she did their taxes, he looked over her shoulder and asked why she was drawing on the form. She showed him a picture of a bunny and explained that there was so much space left over that she thought she'd draw a little picture for their friends at the Revenue Department. The ads were a big hit. Not only did they increase the level of compliance (and tax receipts), thousands of people used the two-thirds of the page that was blank to send messages to their state government.

OSHA, EPA, the IRS, and other federal agencies—as well as similar agencies in states, cities and counties—have begun creating one-stop permitting processes, consolidating related processes into single applications, and waiving rules for businesses that are already performing well.

Public organizations can also save money by simplifying their own internal rules and processes. We will discuss this in depth in the next two chapters, so for now, one example will suffice. In Winnipeg, Manitoba, the City Council was concerned a decade ago that employees were spending too much on travel, so they demanded that the finance director do something about it. When he investigated, he discovered that any request to travel had to be signed by seven people, including the employee making the request, his or her supervisor, the division manager, the department head, the city attorney, and someone from the finance office. Yet not one of them took the procedure seriously, because everyone assumed that someone else was providing real oversight. So the finance director cut back to one approval, that of the employee's supervisor. It saved everyone's time, and the supervisors began looking closely at travel requests. In the first six months, spending on travel fell by 50 percent!

Another way to make compliance easy is to offer services that facilitate it. For example, OSHA has developed a series of Web-based "expert systems"—computer programs that answer questions and guide people through compliance processes. Each is focused on a separate problem or substance, such as asbestos, lead, or cadmium.

After Congress hauled them on the carpet in 1998, IRS leaders struggled to make it easier to file your taxes, even in the face of increased complexities imposed by new tax laws. The agency simplified forms and notices; created a 24-hour-a-day, seven-day-a-week telephone hotline; expanded its electronic and telephone filing options; opened 250 IRS offices on Saturday mornings during tax filing season; and added temporary locations in banks, libraries, and shopping malls (and even a mobile facility on a bus serving rural areas), to distribute forms and publications. It also implemented "problem solving days" in every district, during which employees listened to and resolved taxpayer problems.

5. Make the quality of agency service to compliers consequential.

If compliance agencies face consequences when they provide poor service to compliers—and rewards when they provide excellent service—they will hasten to improve. The 1998 IRS reform law dipped a toe in this water by listing 10 actions for which employees could be fired. It also created a new taxpayer advocate, who can determine compensation for taxpayers who suffer significant hardship because of poor performance at the IRS.

But these are relatively blunt instruments, and the listing of firing offenses backfired, causing IRS employees to proceed with such caution that disputed tax collections plummeted. Several state governments have been far more creative, setting service standards and offering compliers some form of compensation when the agency fails to meet those standards.

A decade ago, for example, the Massachusetts Department of Environmental Protection set strict time limits for processing each permit and issued a money-back guarantee: If the department missed the deadline, it had to return the permit fee. "It was the single best thing we did," recalls former commissioner Dan Greenbaum.

> *The dynamic it created was like a business trying to collect a fee for a service. It provided impetus for management reforms, like a real tracking system so you would know what was happening with each permit.*
>
> *Staff told us they'd need lots more people to meet the time lines. But we met the deadlines the first year; it turned out there was a lot of slack in the system. Part of it was poor management: for example, no tracking system to tell you how many permits were in the pipeline, how many got permits, and so on.*
>
> *And part of it was that the department had people who were environmentalists and believed that by delaying things they were protecting the environment.*

Over the first four years the department missed only 75 deadlines out of 14,000. Word got around about which regional and program offices were refunding the most fees. Thomas Powers, Greenbaum's successor, noted, "There's a certain pride in not being the one to show up as doing the worst."

6. Report compliance information.

Most people respond to feedback. If taxpayers are told that they have filed incorrectly, or businesses discover that they have violated environmental rules, most (but not all) will correct their errors. Think of how you respond when you drive by one of those flashing signs the police set up to clock your speed. According to a U.S. Department of Justice report, these "speed display boards have been shown to reduce speed and crashes."

When citizens care about compliance and organize to demand it—as the environmental movement does—reports to the public are also powerful, because citizen groups use them to keep the heat on public officials and polluters. The EPA has seized on this tool to give the public an extraordinary amount of data. Its "Envirofacts" Web page, www.epa.gov/enviro/index_java.html, provides access to information from a dozen EPA databases. Users can see drinking water and air quality, toxic and hazardous waste sites, water discharge permits, and Superfund sites in any zip code, city, county, state, watershed, or basin in the country. The site includes an application called EnviroMapper, which can present that data on a national, state, or county map. EPA's Enforcement and Compliance History Online (ECHO) site, www.epa.gov/echo/, provides compliance and enforcement information for approximately 800,000 regulated facilities nationwide. The site allows users to find information about inspections, violations, enforcement action, and penalties at facilities for the past two years. ECHO reports provide a snapshot of a facility's environmental record, showing dates and types of violations, as well as the state or federal government's response.

7. Treat different compliers differently.

There is little sense in treating law-abiding citizens or businesses that have made an honest mistake the same as you might treat habitual scofflaws. The police don't do it, the courts don't do it, but unfortunately, many compliance agencies do.

Before its late-1990s reforms, the IRS went after everyone who owed them money. If it was a significant amount, they brought down the hammer—often going after the equity in people's homes—regardless of the taxpayer's past record, current situation, or ability to pay. Thanks to the 1998 reform bill, the agency now is allowed to use discretion and common sense. If the payment problem is chronic, the IRS still brings down the hammer. But otherwise, its agents can offer taxpayers several options, including compromise payments and installment payments. If a taxpayer is ill or has lost a job and has no history of avoiding payments, the agent can design a special "hardship" installment plan.

The Kansas Department of Revenue instituted a database that stores each taxpayer's payment history. If a business misses a due date, the agency can tailor its automated schedule of responses accordingly. Those with a good record of payment receive a notice. If they fail to respond, the options escalate to more notices, telephone calls, and, ultimately, collection efforts. For those with a more questionable payment history, the schedule is greatly accelerated.

Many school districts demand accreditation visits on a rigid, five-year cycle. Iowa changed the rules so that if a district has had a sterling record and no issues arise suggesting the need for on-site inspection, accreditation visits can be on an as-needed basis.

The Consumer Product Safety Commission won an Innovations in American Government Award in 1998 for its decision to create two different tracks for product recalls. Traditionally, recalls had dragged on for months while the CPSC staff investigated, then negotiated with the manufacturer's attorneys. Meanwhile, the dangerous product stayed on the market. In 1995, the agency announced what it called "fast track product recall," in which companies that acknowledged the defect could reach agreement with the agency and launch corrective action within 20 days. Speed was critical, because recalls missed most products once they had moved from the retail shelves into people's homes. According to Harvard professor John Donohue, who reviewed the innovation for the award program, "Fast track recalls take less than half as long as the traditional process and reach three times the proportion of affected products."

8. Create a continuum of public consequences and rewards.
Governments usually use sticks to ensure compliance: They create stiff penalties for failure, including fines and jail time. Those who adopt the winning compliance approach don't abandon the sticks, but they add carrots.

The Interior Department's Fish and Wildlife Service (FWS) has the ultimate stick: By invoking the Endangered Species Act, it can shut down commercial operations such as logging or development on vast swaths of land.

However, that kind of action is so draconian—and politically explosive—that it is rarely used.

In the 1990s, FWS turned to a carrot called a habitat conservation plan. Businesses and local governments can apply for permits to work or develop land important to endangered species, but the plan must promote the long-term conservation of the species. For example, a plan negotiated with local governments and developers in Orange County, California, set aside 38,000 acres of land as nature reserves to protect more than 40 species. A similar plan set aside 172,000 acres in San Diego. The carrot: Those who donate the land get to develop other parcels free from restrictions. They also get a promise that as long as they abide by the plan, they will not be required to take or pay for further conservation measures in the area, even if the species continue to decline. Instead, the government will foot the bill.

The EPA has developed a series of incentives for businesses that reduce pollution, from waivers and flexible permits to reduced reporting requirements and inspections. Oregon's Green Environmental Management Systems Permit Program provides three tiers of incentives for facilities meeting increasingly higher standards. It allows "modifications to regulatory requirements for facilities that achieve performance significantly better than otherwise required by law," the state explains. The first tier—the Participant Permit—is for facilities beginning to implement a program. Participants are eligible for technical assistance, a single point of contact at the agency, and public recognition. The second tier—the Achiever Permit—is for facilities with a more comprehensive program addressing a wide range of issues, including environmental impacts that are not covered by regulation. Added incentives include streamlined reporting, regulatory flexibility, and expedited permit review. The third tier—the Leader Permit—is for facilities that demonstrate industry leadership in considering impacts, including those outside of the immediate facility, over the life cycle of products and services. Added incentives include a tailored regulatory relationship that can allow for permit applications for multiple facilities, including those of partnerships between the company, its customers, and its suppliers.

West Virginia has instituted a similar program. It offers expedited permitting, less-frequent inspections, tax incentives, interest rate reductions, reduced rates on insurance premiums, and other incentives requested by complying businesses.

Despite the effectiveness of rewards, the continuum still needs to include stiff penalties. In Maine's Top 200 initiative, for instance, when one of the 200 companies subjected its employees to unsafe, unsanitary conditions, OSHA stepped back in quickly with inspections and fines.

9. Create market incentives to encourage compliance.

Perhaps the most powerful way to win voluntary compliance is to reward it financially. When some states required five-cent deposits on bottles and cans—to be returned when the empty bottle or can was turned in for recycling—they were using a classic market incentive. Without a single public program or employee, these "bottle bills" significantly reduced litter and broken glass in streets and parks.

Any form of tax on pollution encourages voluntary compliance. Perhaps the granddaddy of winning compliance initiatives is emissions trading, in which the government gives credits to companies that reduce pollution below the amount required by law and allows them to sell those credits to other firms. The idea is to reward companies for reducing pollution but let the companies figure out for themselves how to do it. If they can reduce one source of pollution economically, they can use the credits they generate to offset areas where reduction is too costly. The federal government has used this mechanism for 25 years, to clean up the air, get lead out of gasoline, and reduce acid rain. It has saved American businesses tens of billions of dollars, while meeting the government's environmental goals.

These nine steps can work in virtually any compliance activity. Used as a checklist, they can help leaders come up with alternatives to enforcement strategies they can no longer afford. When an agency such as OSHA can afford to inspect the average workplace only once every 80 years, cheaper alternatives are imperative.

The winning compliance toolkit offers enormous bang for the buck, in all corners of the public sector. It can cut costs—for government, business, and citizens—at the same time that it improves outcomes. Compliance is a crucial foundation of any society, but not at any price. With limited resources and the demand to produce more with them every year, winning compliance is no longer simply a nice idea. It is a necessity.

PART FOUR

SMARTER MANAGEMENT

Reforming How Government
Works on the Inside
to Improve Its Performance
on the Outside

ELEVEN

Using Flexibility
to Get Accountability

In every public school, there are one or two teachers who everyone knows should not be teaching. You remember them. If you have kids in public school today, you can probably name them. Once they get tenure—after just two or three years of teaching—they are virtually impossible to fire. Most principals simply put up with them; aggressive principals transfer them elsewhere. In Houston it's called "passing the trash."

Why can't principals fire teachers who clearly aren't up to the job? In his compelling book on 10 years of education reform in Houston, former school board member Donald McAdams explains why. When he joined the board, any principal who tried to fire a teacher bought himself a long guerrilla war. The teacher often filed a grievance, tying up enormous amounts of the principal's time, and the union often set to work spreading rumors and making life difficult. If the principal persisted and succeeded, the school board had to approve the termination. The teacher could then appeal to a committee of teachers and administrators—then appeal their decision back to the board. At that point, board members had to spend two to three days holding a formal hearing—something they, as unpaid volunteers, found extremely difficult. "On more than one occasion [the president of the Houston Federation of Teachers] threatened openly that if the superintendent and board did not work with her on teacher termination issues, she would simply appeal every case to the board and tie it up in endless termination hearings," McAdams reports.

Once the hearing was over, five of the nine members had to deny the appeal. "If the teacher accused the principal of racism, and this happened, holding the five votes for termination was very difficult." If five members did vote to terminate, the teacher could still appeal to the state commissioner of education. And if the teacher lost there, he or she could sue for wrongful termination.

Needless to say, firings were scarcer than snow days in Houston. According to McAdams, the district spent up to $6 million a year "on employees who had been parked in nonjobs" in the early 1990s—and untold millions more on those who had been transferred to jobs they could not perform effectively.

Our colleague Jeff Zlonis tells this story from his days in the Minnesota Department of Administration:

> One day I was leaving work and I passed the copying room, where Barbara, an assistant from our personnel department, was using the machine. I stuck my head in to say good night and asked what she was doing. "Copying time sheets," she told me. All 1,000 of them. Now, I was opposed to having salaried employees filling out time sheets in the first place. Why not just fill something out when there's an exception? But for now, I was curious to know why we were making copies of a document I didn't think we needed in its original form. So I asked Barbara, but all she knew was that copying time sheets was in her job description. So I asked what she did with the copies. "I file them," she told me.
>
> Barbara had worked at the agency for six years, and she had done this every week. Now that the task had come to my attention, I asked her to talk to her boss and find out what it was all about. But Barbara's boss had no idea why they were doing this either. In fact, she was surprised to discover that they had whole filing cabinets full of these things. The time sheet was a four-part form. One copy went to payroll for processing checks, one went to the departmental HR office, one went to the department of employee relations, and one went to the manager. So at various places in the building we had five versions of this document, which, according to further inquiries by Barbara's supervisor, no one ever looked at.
>
> The supervisor probed a little more and discovered that eight years before, the legislative auditor had come in to audit time sheets and wanted photocopies. It was during this time that the office had written a job description for the HR clerk position, with copying time sheets as a responsibility. The auditor went away with his month's worth of copied sheets, and Barbara's predecessor, and then Barbara, continued doing the work. For eight years they had perpetuated a pointless activity that served no one, except, perhaps, our friends at the Xerox Corporation.

The federal government sends hundreds of billions of dollars in categorical grant programs to state and local governments every year. The money comes with strings attached. In the mid 1990s, when Sue Cameron was director of the health department in Tillamook County, Oregon, she and her colleagues were working hard to improve Oregon's dismal pediatric immunization rate. Unfortunately, federal rules said that federally funded shots had to be given in public or private health clinics—not in the hospital. Hence nurses on the maternity ward could not immunize the infants before they went home.

On top of that, there were six different streams of federal immunization money: one for diphtheria, two for hepatitis-B, and so on. "With each different kind of money for each different kind of thing—not just the different kinds of immunization, but nutrition programs, mental health, teen pregnancy, and so on—we have to keep separate records," Cameron explained. "That means that everybody who works here—from the receptionist to the doctor—is keeping track of which federal program they work on each minute to fill out time sheets for Washington."

Three stories; three examples of massive waste. Yet this is not the kind of waste politicians normally rail about. It is not waste found in unnecessary spending programs, but waste found in unnecessary work. And it is the single largest source of waste in government. The busywork persists because employees have little recourse but to follow unnecessary rules and inherited practices. The solution is to give public managers and employees the freedom to waive or eliminate silly rules and simply use their common sense. This is one of the most powerful things our leaders can do to squeeze more value out of the tax dollars we entrust to them.

Consider Florida's Division of Worker's Compensation. When Governor Lawton Chiles was elected in 1990, this agency had a huge backlog of cases. This was a problem that compounded itself, because when claims lay dormant, workers often sued to collect, and the suits ate up the division's time and money.

Governor Chiles's appointment as labor secretary, a well-connected African-American lawyer named Frank Scruggs, was widely respected in the state legislature. Scruggs and Chiles worked together to convince legislators to give the Worker's Compensation Division some new freedoms. They succeeded in exempting Worker's Comp from the civil service system, which controlled hiring, firing, promotion, job classifications, and the like. They also gained an exemption from the normal rules of line-item budgeting,

which made it possible for Scruggs to move money around as needed to improve performance. With this newfound flexibility, Scruggs immediately did
two simple things that would have been impossible otherwise: He eliminated 20 middle-management jobs, and he used the savings to give monthly
performance bonuses to the 500 employees who processed the workers'
compensation claims. In the first month after this change, productivity shot
up 30 percent in one unit, 50 percent in another, 60 percent in a third. By
the third month, 265 employees were earning bonus checks and the backlog was gone. At previous productivity rates, the department would have
had to hire 52 new employees to gain the same increase in output.

A similar transformation occurred in the Department of Revenue, which
also won significant freedoms from the legislature. Impressed, the legislature extended similar flexibility to several other departments, and the improvements continued. Next Chiles directed his staff to comb through the
state's 28,750 rules and eliminate half of them.

Most of the rules of bureaucracy were put in place, at some point during
the past century, for good reasons. One hundred years ago, government
reinventors known as "Progressives" mounted a decades-long crusade for
standardization and centralization in public institutions. They were desperate to banish the graft, political patronage, and cronyism that riddled public service, and they found inspiration in the systems being developed by
corporate managers to control their sprawling empires. They convinced
public leaders to adopt standardized administrative practices—particularly
budget, financial management, personnel, and procurement rules—to
keep every aspect of government under tight control.

The Progressives succeeded in most places. They curbed the power of
political bosses, limited patronage in hiring and firing, and embedded a set
of standard operating procedures into public organizations. But handing
power over day-to-day practices to civil service commissions, budget offices, purchasing offices, and headquarters staffs took control out of the
hands of the operational managers who were supposed to produce results.
This taught managers to suppress their own judgment and mindlessly follow rigid, centralized authority.

Many also internalized an excellent excuse for the poor performance
that followed: If I don't have real authority over my resources and people,
how can I be held accountable for results? But the administrative agencies
were not responsible for results, either: Their business was to control waste,
fraud, and abuse. The fact is, no one in bureaucratic governments is truly
held accountable for achieving the outcomes citizens want. And we wonder
why so few deliver them!

In an era of permanent fiscal crisis, we can no longer afford to bind our civil servants in red tape. We need to follow the path pioneered by imaginative leaders such as Lawton Chiles.

Some leaders refuse to do this because they—or their budget officers, human resources staffs, and procurement specialists—worry that managers will misuse their freedom and bring scandal down upon their heads. This happens, but very rarely. And the best defense against it is not to tie everyone up in red tape; it is to demand strict new accountability for results. The idea is not to turn government into a free-for-all. It is to trade flexibility for real accountability.

THE CHARTER SCHOOL MODEL

One of the most successful examples of this kind of freedom-for-accountability trade is charter schools, which were a major breakthrough when introduced in Minnesota in 1991. The concept was inspired in part by a British initiative that let schools secede from their districts. Minnesota let any qualified group dissatisfied with their current public schools create new ones, outside school district control and free of most district and state regulations. They would be free to innovate, but they would operate under performance contracts, called charters, that had to be renewed every five years. If they performed poorly, they would be shut down.

As we explained in Chapter 3, charter schools are public schools, created by parents, teachers, nonprofits, and occasionally even for-profit companies. They negotiate charters with the organizations that authorize them: local school boards, city councils, state boards of education, or in some states even colleges and universities. They are schools made up of students who have chosen to be there, and most of their funds normally come from the districts those students chose to leave. To stay open, charter schools must attract (and keep) enough students to finance their operations.

As of September 2003, nearly 3,000 charter schools were operating in 36 states and the District of Columbia, serving about 700,000 students. According to the Center for Education Reform, they received, on average, 20 percent less money per pupil than traditional public schools (the difference varied by state). Nonetheless, they served the same proportion of poor students as other public schools and higher percentages of minority children. And they appeared to be doing a better job.

Rock-solid data are not yet available, because no state with charter schools measured the progress students made from year to year until recently, when Texas and Florida began doing so. (Measuring annual learning gains is the only way to know how well students in charter schools are doing. Simply comparing test scores does not tell you whether one group scores higher because they were ahead to begin with, or because they are learning more.) But by September 2003, there had been 98 studies of charter school performance, and 88 of them had concluded that charter schools were fulfilling their mandates to be "innovative, accountable, and successful," according to the Center for Education Reform.

Innovation is always easier in startup organizations, whether public, private, or nonprofit, and charter schools are no exception. A California study found that 78 percent of charter schools were experimenting with new practices, compared to 3 percent of other public schools.

Parents seem to think that charter schools offer something of value. Since the Center for Education Reform began surveying these schools more than five years ago, roughly two-thirds have had waiting lists. And in a nationwide survey, 65 percent of parents rated their children's charter schools better than their former public schools, while fewer than 6 percent rated them worse.

BROADENING THE CHARTER IDEA

Charter schools are not the only example of trading accountability for flexibility. In 1990, after 15 years of frustration with rising property taxes, Oregon voters passed Measure 5, a ballot initiative that cut those taxes sharply. By requiring state government to make up local governments' and school districts' revenue losses, it forced cuts in state spending. State universities took their licks—and then the legislature froze their tuition.

Caught in a fiscal squeeze and desperate to wring far more out of every dollar, Oregon University System (OUS) chancellor Joseph Cox offered the legislature a deal: The universities would enroll 2,000 additional students at no extra cost to the general fund if the legislature would give them new and substantial freedom to manage their own affairs. According to Cox, higher education needed liberation from the state's central controls over purchasing, contracting, and personnel management, as well as other regulations that limited their ability to find creative solutions.

Some opponents made the traditional argument that greater autonomy would lead to misuse of public funds. Others feared that the system would slash wages, ignore affirmative action, and disregard minority and female vendors.

After a series of compromises, the legislature approved the Higher Education Administrative Efficiency Act, SB 271. The 1995 bill gave the university system substantial responsibility for its own labor relations, leasing, contracting for services, capital construction, and purchasing. Cox agreed not to jettison any of the state's prevailing social policies governing affirmative action, fair pay, or equity.

The universities enrolled the 2,000 additional students by the fall of 1997, while meeting or exceeding all the social policy goals, lowering class sizes, and saving $6.7 million. In 1998, a special panel created to review the results of SB271 described its impact as follows:

> With Senate Bill 271, OUS was able to delegate the authority for personnel, labor relations, purchasing, and contracting to the people responsible for managing those services at the institutions. While simple in concept, this delegation is causing a fundamental and significant change in the culture of OUS. The focus shifted from "what cannot be done" to "what can be done" and from process to results. Managers now have more ability to cause change, becoming entrepreneurs seeking best value for their customers.

In the area of procurement alone, savings were huge. The university system made arrangements with Visa to establish "procurement cards" for small purchases. Unlike similar cards authorized through the state, the university cards did not carry a $40 annual fee per card, and Visa kicked in a 0.25 percent rebate on all purchases. With the cards, small items are now billed to and paid by each institution once a month, which vastly reduces the university's "accounts payable" overhead.

New rules allowed university staff to make direct purchases of $5,000 or less. While purchases between $5,000 and $50,000 still required a competitive quote process, they were exempted from the formal competitive procurement process of requests for proposals and invitations to bid.

One small example demonstrates the impact of flexibility in purchasing. Under the old rules, the state bureaucracy took an average of 17.5 days to process a request for new carpeting and issue a contract—not a vast amount of time, except in a rental market. Those 17 days spent pushing papers were days that housing units were unoccupied and not generating revenue. By shifting its purchases to a local carpet store, Oregon State University greatly reduced the time it took to fill vacancies—keeping those rent checks coming in.

The universities were also able to streamline their hiring processes, because they no longer had to participate in the state's centralized system. The average number of days required to fill positions dropped from 63.1 to 14.1 at Portland State University and from 121 to 18.5 at the University of Oregon. And by making offers this quickly, the universities were more often able to recruit the candidates they really wanted.

CHARTER AGENCIES

Some governments have extended the flexibility-for-accountability deal to individual departments and agencies. Here, too, the idea is to give them far greater freedom to manage their own budgets, personnel, and purchasing, but in return, to demand greater accountability for results.

In 1986, after nearly eight years as prime minister, Britain's Margaret Thatcher was frustrated with the snail's pace of improvement in the British civil service. She asked her Efficiency Unit to study the problem and suggest the next steps in reform. The unit did something no blue-ribbon inquiry had done in a century and a half of attempts to improve the civil service: It asked the civil servants themselves what they thought. The answer was virtually unanimous: The key to more effective management is to let the managers manage. Untie their hands. Give them clear missions and real authority, hold them accountable for results, and free them from the constraints of hidebound rules.

The Efficiency Unit proposed what became known as the "Next Steps" initiative. It separated departments' service delivery and compliance functions into discrete units, each one called an "executive agency"; gave each agency far greater control over its budget, personnel system, and other management practices; hired chief executives for the agencies through open searches; and paid them whatever it took to get the necessary talent, including performance bonuses. They had to negotiate five-year performance agreements with their department, specifying the results to be achieved and management freedoms to be enjoyed, as well as annual performance targets. Every five years the agency was put on trial for its life, through a "quinquennial review," and the chief executive had to reapply for his or her job.

Over the first decade, Next Steps created 130 executive agencies employing almost three-quarters of the British civil service. These agencies managed to steadily improve service while shrinking the total number of employees by 15 percent. They relied on virtually every tool in the reinventor's kit: contracting out, public versus private competition, performance bonuses, group bonuses, Total Quality Management, customer surveys, Business Process Reengineering, internal markets, "one-stop shopping," and on and on.

In November 1994, Parliament's Treasury and Civil Service Committee called Next Steps "the single most successful Civil Service reform program of recent decades." And when Tony Blair and the Labor Party were elected in 1997, they honored their 1991 pledge to keep Next Steps in place. (For more on the British model, see *Banishing Bureaucracy,* Chapter 1, and *The Reinventor's Fieldbook,* Chapter 3.)

In the late 1990s, the Clinton administration copied the British model, proposing to create a series of "performance-based organizations," or PBOs. In typical fashion, Congress approved only two. The first was the Department of Education's Office of Federal Student Aid (FSA), which oversees more than $50 billion a year in federal financial aid for students in higher education, including Pell Grants, student loans, Perkins grants, work–study funds, and Educational Opportunity Grants. FSA helps more than eight million students pay for college and vocational school every year.

Congress chose FSA in part because of the volume of complaints about its services. The aid application was hard to fill out, customers said, and in peak application season, the volume occasionally overwhelmed processing capacity, leaving students hanging. Schools had to contend with a dozen balky and ever-changing computer systems to do business with FSA, and they objected to FSA's numerous obscure regulations, enforced through surprise inspections by bureaucrats with a "gotcha" mentality.

With the Higher Education Amendments of 1998, which had overwhelming bipartisan support, Congress made FSA the first PBO. The legislation called for FSA's chief operating officer (COO) to be an experienced business executive, not a political appointee or civil servant. He or she has an annual performance agreement with the secretary of education, and together, the two develop a five-year plan for the organization. The COO's compensation is determined by how well FSA performs.

In practice, the Department of Education never gave FSA all the flexibilities promised by the legislation, but the agency did gain control over its procurement processes, particularly to purchase information technology systems. It also got permission to create a financial bonus system for all employees and to hire a 24-person management team, outside the civil service, whose pay was linked to performance.

FSA's first COO was the late Greg Woods, a former Defense Department official and high-tech executive who had joined Vice President Gore's National Performance Review in 1993. Working with his employees, Woods created a new mission statement: "FSA helps put America through school." He and his team set three multiyear performance goals: to improve customer satisfaction, cut unit costs, and boost employee engagement.

Woods transformed FSA into an e-business, which offers convenient electronic transactions to all its customers and business partners. He hired Accenture to replace one of FSA's obsolete, inefficient computer systems, offering the firm no up-front pay, only a share of the savings generated by the new system. This was a first for the federal government, and it worked so well that FSA signed a series of similar contracts for other systems. In its first two years as a PBO, FSA created a Web-based financial aid application so easy to use that students began to choose it four-to-one over paper applications. It also launched a Web site for direct loan servicing that allowed borrowers to do virtually all their business with FSA online. These innovations helped the agency win the "Business Solutions in the Public Interest" award presented by the Council for Excellence in Government, *Government Executive* magazine, and the Office of Federal Procurement Policy.

As many parents know, the basic application form is called the FAFSA: Free Application for Federal Student Aid. Woods and his team set a goal of receiving five million electronic FAFSAs by 2001, then surpassed it with 5.4 million. Their goal for turning around FAFSAs was seven days, and by 2001 they were down to an average of 4.6 days. For loan consolidations, they set a turnaround goal of 50 days and a volume goal of 50 percent more electronic applications by 2001—and exceeded both.

Not surprisingly, customer satisfaction soared. To establish a benchmark, FSA relied on the American Customer Satisfaction Index, which is widely used in the private sector. The agency scored in the low 60s, below average for government and a full 15 points below average for private businesses. Woods and his team set a goal of matching the average for private financial service companies by 2002. In 2001, after less than three years as a PBO, the agency scored 74.2, just two tenths of a point below that average and far above the federal government average of 68.6.

Woods's goal for unit costs was to accommodate growth, projected to be 19 percent by 2005, with no increase in budget—hence a 19 percent decline in unit costs. Most costs declined as planned, but an unanticipated spike in direct-loan consolidations when low interest rates attracted a surge of refinancing slowed overall progress.

For employee satisfaction, Woods's goal was to rise from 38th place in a federal government survey into the top five. His team accomplished this in one year, so they raised the bar to equaling the average level of private financial services companies on a Gallup survey of employee satisfaction and engagement. By 2001 they had blown past this mark, registering the largest one-year gain ever measured by Gallup in a federal agency.

The Bush administration pushed Woods to add a fourth goal of increasing program integrity—for example, by lowering default rates on student loans. He set a goal of driving the rate below 8 percent by 2001, and that year FSA reached an all-time low of 5.6 percent. The agency nearly doubled its goal for collecting previously defaulted loans—$2.4 billion—and brought another $2.7 billion in loans back into regular repayment, all during a recession. With these results, employees received bonuses equal to 90 percent of their regular two-week paychecks in 2001.

Unfortunately, however, Greg Woods was diagnosed with pancreatic cancer early in 2002. After he resigned, the Bush administration quickly reverted to business as usual. It quit measuring customer satisfaction, employee satisfaction, and unit costs, pulled back all of FSA's significant flexibilities, and concentrated most of its attention on saving money and getting a clean audit. Secretary Rod Paige, who had championed charter schools as school superintendent in Houston, allowed his own charter agency to be neutered.

CHARTER AGENCIES IN IOWA

We call the basic tool used by FSA and pioneered by the British executive agencies a "flexible performance agreement," or FPA. It is a written agreement negotiated between a steering organization and a service or compliance organization that articulates the results expected, the flexibilities that will be granted, how performance will be measured and reported, and how that information will be used to trigger consequences, both positive and negative.

In 2002, the state of Iowa hired the Public Strategies Group (PSG) to be its official "reinvention partner," using a consulting model PSG had developed at FSA. Working with Governor Tom Vilsack and the Iowa House and Senate, PSG helped develop legislation to create "charter agencies" for the state: performance-based organizations that negotiate flexible performance agreements with the governor. These combined the usual trade of freedom for accountability with belt tightening. Six agencies—all volunteers—accepted cuts in operating costs totaling $15 million per year: the Departments of Revenue, Corrections, Natural Resources, and Human Services, plus the Alcoholic Beverages Division of the Commerce Department and the Iowa Veterans' Home. In return, they negotiated freedoms such as these, advertised in a leaflet recruiting volunteers:

- *Freedom from FTE ceilings or other employment controls.*
- *Authority to waive personnel rules and do what makes sense.*
- *Authority to waive procurement rules and buy what makes sense.*
- *Authority to waive information technology rules and buy the computers and software you want.*
- *Authority to keep half of this year's unspent money and spend it next year.*
- *Authority to keep and spend proceeds from lease or sale of capital assets.*
- *Authority to reprogram money between accounts.*
- *Authority to waive administrative rules.*
- *Access to a $3 million Transformation Grant Fund.*
- *Protection for two years from across-the-board cuts.*

Each agency worked out a five-year agreement with the governor, specifying the results it would produce, special projects it would complete, which of 40 potential freedoms it would be granted, and the consequences for its level of performance. The $3 million fund allowed charter agencies to apply for grants to finance improvements. The Revenue Department received $500,000 to hire six new staff members for two years, for example. Most were auditors, who were expected to bring in far more in revenues than they cost; the rest are working to slash the turnaround time for tax refunds, which should reduce the amount of interest Iowa owes taxpayers who get refunds.

Soon after the agreements were signed, a revenue shortfall necessitated across-the-board cuts of 2.5 percent. True to his word, Governor Vilsack exempted the charter agencies—an act that greatly enhanced the initiative's credibility. As we write, the governor is collecting proposals from the charter agencies for legislation needed to secure additional freedoms.

We have reproduced excerpts from one agency's FPA on the following pages.

INTERGOVERNMENTAL
FREEDOM-FOR-ACCOUNTABILITY TRADES

In the American system of multitiered government—with its federal, state, county, and city governments, plus special districts and school districts—some of the rules that tie managers' hands originate at a higher level of government. Each year, the federal government distributes more than a third of

CHARTER AGENCY AGREEMENT BETWEEN
THE GOVERNOR OF THE STATE OF IOWA AND
THE IOWA DEPARTMENT OF REVENUE

The Department of Revenue requests that the Governor designate the Agency as a Charter Agency, pursuant to Section 7J.1 of the Code of Iowa.

The Department commits to producing the following results in terms of performance measures and special projects:

Departmental Performance Targets

- Increase share of individual income tax returns filed electronically to 80 percent by 2007.
- 60 percent of General Fund tax revenues will be received by electronic funds transfer by 6-30-04.
- 90 percent of all individual income tax refunds will be issued within 60 days of date of receipt of a taxpayer's return.
- Process 99 percent of all transactions through centralized accounting system within one day of receipt from departments.
- Regarding productivity of audit staff, maintain a ROI [return on investment] of at least $8 for every $1 spent for enforcement.
- 95 percent of taxpayer service contacts will be responded to within 24 hours.
- Composite customer satisfaction scores for Web-based applications will average scores of four or above [on a scale of one (minimum) to five (maximum)].

Departmental Special Projects

- Develop plans for 5 new electronic services by 12-31-03. [E.g., electronic filing for income, sales, use, and other business taxes.]
- Collaborate with other agencies on successful 1) implementation of ERP system [Enterprise Resource Planning—a new system that will integrate all budget, finance, accounting, human resources, e-procurement, payroll and benefits data], 2) monitoring of tax incentive and other economic development initiatives, 3) development of improved economic and revenue forecasting processes, and 4) implementation of the DAS [Department of Administrative Services] agency.
- Generate proposals to simplify income tax system and overhaul property tax system.

(continues)

Charter Agency Benefits and Flexibilities

The Governor and Lt. Governor pledge their support to the Charter Agencies' success, and recognize the Department of Revenue and Director Michael Ralston are stepping above and beyond expectations in their willingness to become a Charter Agency. The agency will have the following benefits and flexibilities. These benefits and flexibilities do not supersede the requirements of the Accountable Government Act.

The Department of Management (DOM) will assure that Charter Agencies:

1. May apply to receive grant funds from the $3 million general fund appropriation for Charter Agency innovation projects.
2. Retain 50 percent of unspent year-end general fund appropriation (from agency operations) balance for five years, beginning with fiscal year 2004.
3. May receive support at no cost from PSG to achieve desired charter outcomes, as needs arise and resources permit.
4. May propose increases in fees that are commensurate with and directly related to improving services to citizens.
5. May reduce copying and paperwork expenses via use of electronic signatures, record keeping, and transactions.
6. Are exempted from appropriated full-time equivalent (FTE) limitations for a period of five years, beginning with fiscal year 2004.
7. May change the status of "direct report" managerial positions to "at will" positions. Affected employees must agree to the change voluntarily in writing for the change to occur.

---

a trillion dollars to state and local governments, but recipients often have to go through a bureaucratic game of Twister to use the funds.

In the early 1990s, Governor Barbara Roberts of Oregon wanted freedom from the restrictions imposed on federal grant money. Her state was measuring outcomes through its Oregon Benchmarks, and she felt that Oregon could improve those outcomes if it were allowed to use federal funds more effectively. In 1994, she managed to negotiate a memorandum of understanding between top-ranking federal officials and officials from Oregon state, county, and city governments, creating what became known as the "Oregon Option." As recorded in the National Performance Review's 1996 report, "They agreed to pilot a redesigned system that is structured, managed, and evaluated on the basis of results; oriented to customer needs and satisfaction; biased toward preventing problems, not just fixing them after-

8. May add interns to their workforces.
9. May award "exceptional job performance (performance bonus)" pay to non-contract covered employees or to contract covered employees with the approval of the labor union. This applies to individual employees as well as to employee "teams."
10. May award "special-duty" pay or "extraordinary duty" pay. Special duty pay applies when an employee is temporarily assigned to a vacant position in a higher class. Extraordinary duty pay applies when an employee is temporarily assigned work duties in a higher class.
11. May create any position in any classification provided that duties are consistent with established classification and filled in compliance with collective bargaining agreements and HRE (Human Resources Enterprise) rules.
12. May purchase goods and services outside General Services Enterprise (GSE) contracts provided the charter agency can document the cost benefit.
13. May sell or lease capital assets and retain proceeds and may utilize the GSE as an agent in the sale of capital assets.
14. May make their travel arrangements directly with vendors, with appropriate audit-worthy documentation.
15. May pay a fiscal year 2005 vehicle administrative fee (overhead) that is at least 30 percent lower than the current fee.
16. May, with appropriate audit-worthy documentation, use sole source contracts.
17. May, through addendum, extend contracts beyond the current allowable renewal term.

ward; and simplified and integrated as much as possible, delegating responsibilities for service design, delivery, and results to front-line, local-level providers."

Federal, state, and local participants would reach agreement on an outcome they desired, then isolate the barriers to achieving it and get rid of them. The idea was to give waivers to rules that got in the way and allow consolidation of different federal funding streams, so those on the ground could use the money more effectively. For instance, Oregon officials convinced the federal Centers for Disease Control to merge the six funding streams for childhood immunization we described in the opening pages of this chapter. Oregon governments, hospitals, insurance companies, and HMOs then formed a coalition and launched a public campaign to ensure that every child was getting the necessary shots, and the percentage of two-year-olds who were adequately immunized rose from 53 percent in 1994 to 74 percent by 1999. One of the biggest problems in the past had been inadequate information, so they also created a single registry for immunization records on every child in the state, called ALERT. They made sure that every doctor in every institution, both public and private, had access to the system—so when a child came through the door, the doctor could see what shots he or she still needed. As the registry came online, the numbers rose again, to 80 percent in 2000.

The Clinton administration, which called initiatives like this "Performance Partnerships," negotiated some with other states as well. Clinton also urged Congress, with only limited success, to consolidate 271 separate grant programs into 27 performance partnerships focused on results.

In 1993, Minnesota offered another model, to unshackle local governments from state restrictions that hampered performance. The state established an independent board, made up of the state auditor, the commissioners of finance and administration, two administrative law judges, and six legislators. This board gave grants to local governments to develop innovations in public service delivery, particularly innovations involving collaboration between multiple levels of government. More important, it granted three-year waivers from state rules in order to "eliminate perceived barriers to more efficient delivery of public services." The waiver program was used as a kind of test probe: If a temporary waiver heightened efficiency or effectiveness, without unintended consequences, the board and local governments worked to have the law changed permanently.

Through early 2001, the board had received more than 600 grant applications and made 113 grants. Averaging about $55,000, the awards funded innovations ranging from the merger of a city police department and county sheriff's department in Rock County to the creation of an electronic information network serving all 87 county attorneys, the state court administrator, the state attorney general, and other judicial agencies. Grantees reported $7.2 million a year in recurring savings. Unfortunately, a 50 percent budget cut in 2000 ended funding for grants, and during the fiscal crisis in 2002 the legislature eliminated the board entirely.

Of the first 84 waiver requests, 36 had been approved by 2001; 16 were disallowed because they involved federal law; the board declined 3; and 17 were withdrawn after the state agency enforcing the rule allowed the applicant to proceed without a waiver from the board. Twenty-five resulted in new legislation, enabling all local governments to benefit from the same freedoms.

For example, Hennepin County, Minnesota's most populous, found that 20 percent of its medical assistance recipients did not file the required income verification form every six months. Those recipients lost their benefits and had to reapply the next time they needed medical help—a costly and wasteful process. It turned out that most of these people were elderly citizens living on Social Security. County officials requested a waiver that would allow them to verify income simply by comparing their data with electronic data maintained by the Social Security Administration, which already tracked changes in income. The board approved the concept; subsequently, the legislature voted to allow the same process in any county willing to invest in the necessary software.

The mere existence of the board helped change the mindset of some state administrators. "State agency officials are now more receptive to new ideas for achieving desired outcomes," reported Gary Pagel, the board's executive director. Why? "If state agencies continue to rigidly enforce their rules and laws, local officials may now appeal to the board for the flexibility necessary to test new ideas." For instance, one local school district had a teenage parenting program that provided childcare for young mothers while they attended classes, but the state Department of Human Services threatened to close the center because it was not a licensed daycare provider. When the district applied for a waiver, DHS inspectors immediately changed their position and offered to grant a variance themselves.

In Iowa, Governor Vilsack wants to extend the charter agency idea to local governments. Iowa puts a real straitjacket on local governments; state laws control virtually everything they can do. To provide one small example, any local construction project that costs more than $25,000 requires a public bid, which can entail $4,000 to $5,000 in legal work alone.

So the governor has proposed to allow any group of local governments—such as a county and its cities, or multiple cities, or even multiple counties—to apply for status as a "freedom community." With that designation would come significant flexibilities: reduction of state mandates; broad authority to set their own rates for property, income, and sales taxes, surcharges, and fees; and a streamlined process for reorganization (such as merging a county and city government, or sharing services, or shifting from multiple elected positions to one appointed county executive who appoints all other management positions).

In return, the cities and/or counties would have to do two things: approve a reorganization that results in a realignment of city/county services (such as the county sheriff taking over city police responsibilities, or significant shared services between participating cities or counties) and establish accountability mechanisms, including a citizen process to set goals for the community, performance targets in key service areas, and annual performance and (simplified) financial reports, to be mailed to every citizen in the community.

Bob Rafferty, former chief of staff to Governor Terry Branstad, Vilsack's Republican predecessor, is the PSG consultant now leading this reform effort. He sees freedom communities as the catalyst to start a chain reaction in local government. They could give local leaders "the tools and leverage to create pockets of local government innovation and reform that can lead the way and make it much easier for the rest of Iowa to follow suit and reform local government," he says.

That's a formula for success in the age of permanent fiscal crisis. Every twenty-first-century government ought to trade flexibility for accountability, to give public organizations the freedom they need and citizens the accountability they expect.

TWELVE

Make Administrative Systems Allies, Not Enemies

When Peter Hutchinson became Minnesota's commissioner of finance in 1989, the state already faced a budget shortfall, and his main job was to get it under control. He used his first few weeks on the job to carefully assess the hole Minnesota had dug for itself. While the state had some options for trying to climb back out, there was no magic formula for instantly balancing the budget. Six months of the two-year budget period are already gone. The longer he stood on the edge of this financial pit, staring into it, the deeper and darker it appeared.

Then he had an inspiration. The total shortfall essentially equaled the total combined salary increases all state employees could expect in the coming year, based on past increases and existing contracts. Hutchinson's idea was to postpone normal pay raises until the economy recovered and revenues came back to their normal level.

With some urgency (and not a little naïveté), he laid out his plan for Governor Rudy Perpich. The governor seemed encouraging; he asked only that Hutchinson make a presentation the following week to a meeting of union shop stewards.

Hutchinson arrived at the meeting with a host of overheads, certain that his graphs and pie charts would convince all attending of the seriousness of the state's fiscal challenge and the wisdom of his proposal. He launched into his presentation with great enthusiasm, convinced that the logic of his argument was unassailable. But down in the front row two men kept elbowing one another and snickering. Undeterred, Hutchinson carried on, talking with a reformer's zeal about the need to win back citizen confidence by bringing the budget into line. He reached the end with a flourish, uttering his concluding thoughts with a last burst of inspiration. Then he shut off his overhead projector, turned to the two in front, and asked them what the hell was so funny.

"Well," one of them said, "that was a deluxe presentation, but it's plain as day you don't know what you're talking about."

Hutchinson, who had only been on the job for a couple of months, secretly wondered how they knew. But he replied calmly: "What makes you think that?"

Because you don't know the way it works around here. You see, it's like when we paint our buildings every spring. Just about always on opening day of fishing season, the order comes down to paint the buildings—inside and out. You talk to us about not wasting taxpayer dollars, but every year we have to miss opening day so we can paint buildings that don't need painting.

Hutchinson was stunned. "Why on earth do you paint the buildings when they don't need it?"

"You're the finance guy?" the other one chuckled, jabbing his buddy in the ribs. Then he shook his head and explained.

Look. In the spring, just before the end of the fiscal year, they add up all the money left over in the budget. They know they have to spend that money because, if they don't, your department will swoop down and take it away and then you'll cut us back by that much for next year. If we do what you want us to do—save money for the taxpayers—then our budget shrinks. It's nice what you're saying, but the real truth is, you use it or you lose it.

That was the day Hutchinson realized that the actual systems created for budgeting, accounting, purchasing, personnel, and auditing were far more powerful than all the pronouncements made by elected officials or department heads. The systems run those who govern, not the other way around. That's why government employees call the organizations that run them "control agencies." On that day, Hutchinson also realized that in the name of savings, these systems were creating colossal waste.

IT'S ABOUT STRATEGY

"For an executive," says Harvard Business School professor Robert Kaplan, "when it comes to accounting there are only two questions that matter: Do you know what the strategy is for your organization, and does your accounting system know?" We would add that your budget system, your human resource system, your purchasing system, and your auditing system need to know that strategy as well.

Most administrative systems in government were designed to facilitate bureaucracy. Bureaucracy, in turn, was devised as an antidote to the corruption and administrative chaos that preceded it. The first rule of bureaucracy is that people cheat and therefore must be controlled—that's why it often takes as many as nine signatures to release an expense check. It's also why drivers in some states can get a license renewed in 15 minutes, but it can take an employee seven weeks to get reimbursed for a travel expense.

Generally, the people who run administrative systems view them as a means of protecting taxpayers from the abuses of government employees. What these defenders of the old faith fail to see is that their administrative systems are pursuing a strategy quite different from the strategy of their organizations. Their organizations want better results, while these administrative systems want greater control. The systems are based on the assumption that compliance with process rules will produce behavior consistent with norms that citizens want—norms such as fairness, equity, lowest cost, and decisions based on merit. These norms are exactly what government lacked 100 years ago, and the resulting corruption inspired the Progressive reform movement of the early 1900s.

We can now declare the good news: victory. These systems did their job. Corruption in government today is minuscule compared to what existed in the early twentieth century. The bad news is that we are still shackled with systems from the horse-and-buggy era. Governments have changed faster on the outside than on the inside. Although there have been many successful reforms over the past decade, too many administrative systems still hamstring employees, ignore results, and generate colossal waste. In an age of permanent fiscal crisis, we need systems that unshackle employees, reward results, and promote value.

Though plenty of models now exist, reform of budget, accounting, personnel, procurement, and auditing systems remains difficult. Few politicians understand this kind of reform; it isn't politically sexy; and many of those in charge of these systems interpret every challenge as an attack on the norms of fairness, equity, lowest cost, and decisions based on merit. That is why any effort at reinvention must first explicitly acknowledge the absolute value of those norms. Administrative system reform must:

Encompass These Norms	*While Delivering These Ends*
Fairness and integrity	Timeliness
Equity	Quality

Efficiency: lowest cost   Effectiveness: results citizens value
Decisions based on merit   Cost-effectiveness: value for money
Accountability   Consequences for performance

BUDGETING

In Part I we discussed how to create budgets that deliver results citizens want at a price they are willing to pay. But budget creation is only half the job. After the budget is established, it has to be managed, in the face of all the unexpected circumstances governments face every day. Yet most budget offices keep their managers locked in the grip of systems that pre-date dial telephones. They forbid them to carry over savings from one year to the next, move money from one account to another, or change the mix of staff versus contracts without specific permission. Some budget offices go so far as to review and approve or disapprove every hiring or spending decision.

The primary tool that budget offices use to hogtie managers is the cost-based line item. They order managers to build budgets in excruciating cost detail, then use the detail to imprison them. As *Reinventing Government* reported, a decade ago in one branch of the military, base managers had 26 different accounts for housing repairs alone! The National Performance Review (NPR) illustrated the kind of waste this produces by telling the story of a base that was left without a snowplow when its equipment broke down. It had no budget line allocating money to purchase a new plow, but it did have money allocated for repair. So managers used this money to lease the plow they needed. Incredibly, the annual cost of the lease—$100,000—was the same as the purchase price of a new plow.

This is but one of many ways that budget systems actually *encourage* public managers to waste money. The most notorious example is the well-documented spending frenzy at the end of each fiscal year, when smart managers spend every penny to be sure that they get, at the very least, the same amount next time around. Many managers know where they could save 5 or 10 percent, but why endure restructuring or layoffs if you can't use the money for something else that serves your mission? Who wants to save money only to have it taken away and given to some other manager who overspent?

Managers could simply ask for permission to shift money from one account to another, you might think. But the budget office often answers such requests this way: "Thanks for asking. No, you cannot make the shift. But since you brought it up, we need the money elsewhere, so we'll take it. And thanks." Good managers seldom make that mistake twice.

As *Reinventing Government* said, old-fashioned budgets "trap managers in yesterday's priorities, which quickly become tomorrow's waste." The attempt to prevent bad management through financial rigidity has made good management impossible.

In every organization there are exceptions, of course. In times of crisis, almost all governments are able to break the rules, find the flexibilities they need, and get the job done. In an emergency everyone from the front line to the budget office is clear about the mission, the desired results, and the delegation of authority to get it done—period. That is why we get such exceptional performance after floods, blizzards, hurricanes, and earthquakes. But the fiscal condition of government today *is* a national emergency. We need to make the exceptional performance we find in times of calamity the norm every day.

To do this, governments need to adopt Budgeting for Outcomes, as we outlined in Chapter 3. Then they need to make some simple changes in budget rules, all of which have been used widely, with great success, over the past decade.

Provide real savings incentives. Let agencies that save keep some or all of the savings for employee gainsharing (see page 178) or for investments in improved performance. The State of Washington created a savings incentive program in 1997, for example. Agencies can keep half of their general-fund savings not related to entitlements or other targeted spending authority. The remaining savings (a much larger number) are directed to K–12 education for school construction and technology, and to higher education for distinguished professorships, graduate fellowships, and college faculty awards. Agencies can use their portion of the savings for any onetime investments that improve services. In 2003, for example, most such investments were in training, technology, and work-process improvements.

Since 1997, agencies have accumulated $31 million in savings and generated another $227 million for education. In the early years of the program, savings were much larger—no doubt because managers responded to the incentive by quickly squeezing the obvious fat out of their operations.

The British, Canadians, Australians, Swedes, and many American governments also let agencies share in their savings. If you do so, however, be careful not to hem in agencies with too many rules and obstacles, because managers will react with cynicism, viewing shared savings as just another bureaucratic game they will eventually lose. There are five basic features that are important to make shared savings work:

- To qualify, agencies should demonstrate that their performance has not slipped. (You don't want them saving money by cutting back on services that have value.)
- Make the share that agencies can keep meaningful. We recommend 50 percent.
- Limit the use of the savings to gainsharing bonuses and investments that do not raise the agency's long-term operating costs.
- Require that such investments be tied to improving results in some way: through service enhancements, cost reductions, boosting employee skills or morale, and so on. Otherwise, the program may be vulnerable to attack from critics who see any government spending as wasteful.
- Protect the savings from retroactive raids by budget balancers. If times get desperate and the budget office goes after the agencies' share of the savings, managers will conclude that the incentive was a false promise—and soon there will be no more savings to share.

Provide flexibility to reallocate money across budgets in response to changing circumstances. The best solution to the problems of budget rigidity is to give managers lump-sum operating budgets without line items and let them allocate resources as they see fit. Great Britain, Australia, and New Zealand have all done this, because they have created systems that hold top managers accountable for agency performance. They now focus on controlling *results*, not on controlling where agencies spend every dollar. The next best solution is to give managers the power to move money between line items and accounts without permission.

Create an innovation fund. Innovation funds are pots of money that organizations can use to invest in efforts to improve service, reduce costs, or both like Iowa's Transformation Grant Fund, described in Chapter 11. This tool has also grown quite common. The Air Combat Command managed to create a fund of $10 million. The city of Hampton, Virginia, puts 10 percent of annual shared savings into its innovation fund. These funds are most effective when every investment is connected to a specified return—whether financial, so the fund can be repaid, or in terms of improved service quality.

PURCHASING

Back when personal computers were first catching on, a resourceful community college in Minnesota decided to offer a computer course. Because the school was part of state government, professors were required to buy computers through the state's purchasing office. They placed the order two months in advance, advertised the course, and were fully subscribed almost immediately. But two days before the course was to begin they were forced to cancel it, because the purchasing office had not yet placed the order. Purchasing was still waiting for some other agency to come in with a similar order, so it could get a bulk discount. When asked why they had, in effect, sabotaged this new course, the purchasing officials said that their job was to get the lowest cost, period.

Traditional government purchasing systems are incredibly frustrating to managers, and at the same time incredibly wasteful. When Texas compared the cost of procurement in the public sector with costs in the private sector, the state discovered that governments spend 5.5 cents to process a dollar of procurement, while the private sector spends one cent per dollar. Just for technology purchases the difference would be worth $1.5 billion a year to state and local governments.

When Vice President Gore's National Performance Review (NPR) examined the federal government's procurement system, its members found similar problems. It took more than four years, for instance, to purchase a major information technology system—meaning that new systems were virtually obsolete when they arrived. One observer dubbed this "getting a 286 at a 486 price." Gore's 1993 report came down hard on the whole process:

> *History helps to explain our current system. When John Augustus Roebling built the Brooklyn Bridge, popular legend tells us that he designed it to endure stress levels more than 20 times the expected daily levels. Why? Because New York City procurement systems were supposedly so corrupt, Roebling feared that materials normally ordered for such construction would fall short of critical standards. Admittedly, federal procurement systems have never suffered the same corruption as those in patronage-plagued, late–19th-century New York City. But even today, the assumption underlying many federal procurement regulations, laws, and policies is similar to the one Roebling held about New York City—that everyone is trying to cheat the government and, thus, every possible circumstance must be controlled. . . .*
>
> *Our system of excessive laws, regulations, and overseers is premised on [the] assumption that, if given discretion, line managers and procurement employees will cheat and act with poor judgment with taxpayer money. The concept of letting managers get value for money, make smart business decisions, and be accountable for results remains foreign to our government. . . .*

Prodded by Vice President Gore, President Clinton, and Senator John Glenn, Congress passed two major procurement reform bills in the 1990s. The system is not yet perfect, but it is much improved. In 1997 the NPR reported on progress:

The entire system is being overhauled, with huge help from Congress in the form of the Federal Acquisition Streamlining Act of 1994 and the Clinger-Cohen Act of 1996. The Pentagon has gone to multiyear contracts and is using more commercial parts. That is saving $2.7 billion on the new C–17 cargo plane and $2.9 billion on new smart munitions. Smaller purchases count, too. For example, the Army now buys duffel bags for $2.29 each instead of $6.75. It all adds up.

The government used to make small purchases—a stapler, a book, a piece of software—just like it made big ones: with paperwork costing $50 or more. The cost to the government was ridiculous—a $4 stapler wound up costing $54, and it could take months for the forms to be filled out before the stapler got to the person who needed it. The vendors weren't very happy either, waiting two to three months to get their Treasury check for four dollars.

Way back in 1985, five Department of Commerce employees were working on how to streamline small purchases. They came up with an overpoweringly common-sensical idea from the private sector: a credit card. In a pilot program with Rocky Mountain BankCard System, Visa cards were issued to 500 employees. It was, not surprisingly, a success, and in 1993 the National Performance Review recommended that the program be greatly expanded. To date the government has used the cards over 10 million times to buy goods and services worth $20 billion—saving over $700 million so far and speeding delivery of needed tools to workers.

All told, reform has saved the taxpayers over $12 billion to date.

Many state and local governments have followed suit. Milwaukee issued purchase cards to make commodity purchases much easier. It also increased departments' purchasing authority (with associated auditing by purchasing staff) to $5,000, after discovering that while 41 percent of the requisitions were for less that $5,000, they represented less than 2 percent of the total dollar volume. Its purchasing department posted simplified procedure manuals on the city's intranet, so all managers had easy access to the rules. And it used digital technology to speed up the procurement process and provide better management reporting.

As a result, Milwaukee's purchasing department was able to cut its staff by nearly two-thirds and its budget by more than 55 percent. Productivity increased and transaction costs declined.

To produce more value for dollars spent, we recommend a number of basic procurement principles:

Give managers more control over purchasing—and more accountability. Increase managers' authority to purchase goods on their own, up to a sensible dollar limit. And give them purchase cards for all such transactions.

Substitute "best value" for "low cost." Too many purchasing organizations operate as if low cost were the *only* basis on which to buy. Too many purchasing laws actually require such an approach. But a cheap product that doesn't last or a cheap service that doesn't really meet the need is not a good deal. Best-value purchasing challenges all government buyers to get the most value for the dollar, not just the lowest price. It asks them to consider the total cost of ownership over the life of the product, including operational and replacement costs; the performance history of the vendor; the quality of the goods or services; and the proposed technical performance. Other significant factors include the financial stability of the vendor, the timeliness of delivery, the cost of training required, a realistic risk assessment of the proposed solution, the availability and cost of technical support, and a reasonable testing and quality assurance program.

Simplify and automate the purchase of commodities, while expanding the list of items that qualify. In government, purchasing an off-the-shelf commodity should be much simpler than purchasing other things. There is no need for an elaborate process of writing specifications, reviewing them, qualifying vendors, and so on. And there are usually enough vendors of commodities that market competition provides quality goods at reasonable prices. Think of it this way: If you could buy something at Staples or Office Depot, why waste people's time with bureaucratic complications? Use master contracts of approved commodities, create electronic catalogues, put commodity purchases online, and insist that vendors update their prices often. Continuously review what's included, since yesterday's specialty items become tomorrow's commodities. Personal computers were once a specialized purchase, for instance, but today they are definitely commodities.

California's purchasing people decided not to bother inventing their own master contracts. They looked at the federal lists put together by the General Services Administration (GSA) and decided they were good enough. So California agencies can purchase items from any company with federally approved product schedules and prices that choose to be part of California's program—up to a price of $250,000. This has broadened choices, lowered prices, and sped up the acquisition of many products and services.

Enhance competition. For commodities, managers should qualify products from multiple vendors and force continuous competition on price. For specialized procurements, ensure that multiple vendors are included, as procurement offices have traditionally done, and move toward results-based specifications (see below). This will encourage more vendors to think of themselves as possible bidders, while encouraging traditional bidders to think more creatively about how to deliver the desired results.

Create an e-commerce infrastructure. Use electronic bidding, e-Bay–like purchasing (reverse auctions), electronic catalogues and ordering, and electronic funds transfer. In effect, many governments have put their catalogues of approved commodities and services online and have asked vendors to compete with one another by adjusting their prices every day. When Missouri did this, it saved roughly $10 million in computer technology purchases alone over the first five years. The U.S. federal government has created an online shopping and ordering system, called GSA Advantage!, that lets federal managers choose from thousands of contractors and millions of services and products.

Partner with vendors and get them to share the risk and rewards. Create long-term partnerships with suppliers to harness their best thinking about productivity improvements. Especially when a project is complex or uncertain, pay them a share of savings or revenues rather than a guaranteed fee. For example, the California Franchise Tax Board formed a partnership to redesign its tax collection system. Rather than draw up detailed specifications, the Tax Board gave prescreened vendors a statement of the problem and asked for their best thinking about solutions. Once the board selected a vendor, it then negotiated a contract that paid a portion of the savings and new revenue generated. For one system installed through this partnership, the return was five times greater than the board had estimated. The vendor recouped its investment in five months rather than two years. The project took only four months, one-fifth the average time for comparable projects.

Use Requests for Proposals (RFPs) to buy results, not just to meet specifications. On particularly complex or one-of-a-kind projects, a government agency will not have the expertise it needs to create detailed specifications. The solution is to define the desired results, then use the bidding process to challenge potential partners or vendors to apply their expertise in creating solutions. Canada calls this approach "common purpose procurement";

Michigan calls its version "solutions-based" solicitation. The process usually has multiple steps. In California, for example, the state first requests a high-level concept paper from potential vendors. Purchasing officials then discuss these submissions with companies that respond, before requesting more detailed proposals based on a more detailed set of requirements. This can continue through several iterations, but vendors do not provide actual prices until their final submissions. Although this takes more time than a single-phase RFP, it helps the state tap into the expertise of vendors to define what it needs, and it helps vendors understand exactly what the state wants. It also results in far more innovative solutions.

PERSONNEL/HUMAN RESOURCES

In 1881, a disappointed job seeker shot and killed President James Garfield. Congress responded by passing a civil service bill, creating a new set of personnel rules intended to control political manipulation of public employees. At first, it was a simple system, modeled largely on the British Civil Service. But over time, Congress and the federal Office of Personnel Management (OPM) created more and more rules, in a futile attempt to squeeze out all arbitrary treatment and favoritism. By the time President Clinton was elected, there were 850 pages of federal personnel law, 1,300 pages of OPM regulations on how to implement those laws, and another 10,000 pages of rules and guidance in OPM's *Federal Personnel Manual!* (Clinton threw out the manual and started over, but Congress never passed his proposed reforms to civil service law.)

Virtually everyone who has studied traditional civil service systems over the past 20 years has called for a fundamental overhaul. The Brookings Institution called for "a complete reconstruction" of our federal civil service system.

The Massachusetts Taxpayers' Foundation labeled the commonwealth's system "a nightmare," "a scandal," and "an unmitigated disaster."

The National Academy of Public Administration said, "It is not a question of whether the federal government should change how it manages its human resources. It must change."

Clinton's National Performance Review concluded, "To create an effective federal government, we must reform virtually the entire personnel system: recruitment, hiring, classification, promotion, pay, and reward systems." At every level of government, a bureaucratic system designed for a government of clerks has become a straitjacket for a government of knowledge workers.

When most civil service systems were developed, public employees were not unionized. The courts had not yet outlawed most patronage hiring and firing, nor did they protect most employees from wrongful discharge. Civil service rules were the only protection public employees had from the whims of elected officials—who were in the habit of firing thousands of employees when a new party took power and rewarding political supporters with their jobs.

Today we have three layers of protection, and the result is often gridlock. Managers have trouble hiring the talent they need, because the centralized hiring process is so bureaucratic and slow. Thousands of job classifications divide employees into absurdly narrow categories and pay grades, frustrating managers' attempts to move them or reward them with higher pay. Within each classification, pay is determined by longevity, not performance, and when good employees reach the top of their pay grade, further raises are impossible without a promotion. When layoffs occur, employees with seniority can usually "bump" those without, causing a massive game of musical chairs down the organization chart—leaving behind unhappy people in jobs they weren't trained for and don't want. Good managers waste enormous amounts of time circumventing these rules and battling human-resource offices in a frustrating attempt to get the right people with the right skills into the right jobs.

Even firing those who can't perform seems almost impossible. It usually takes so long—and requires such a prolonged battle through multiple appeals—that most managers avoid it like the plague. Instead, they move people into make-work jobs or transfer them to unwitting colleagues. In the Minneapolis School District, for example, principals who wanted to get rid of nonperforming tenured teachers would use budget limits or program changes to "excess" them. This often meant eliminating their jobs, then recreating the same jobs with other titles in order to hire better teachers. This housecleaning always took place in the spring, and those who were "excessed" had the right to apply for openings in other buildings. While the process was technically called "bidding," it came to be known by its more colorful descriptor: "The dance of the lemons."

Everyone in a school knew who the lemons were. And everyone knew that their presence was damaging the credibility of the district. So when Peter Hutchinson became superintendent, he and union leader Louise Sundin developed a dramatically different approach and put it in the union contract. Through a new professional development process, each teacher creates a team that includes his or her supervisor and several colleagues. These teams observe, provide feedback, and review the teacher's performance, to help him or her teach more effectively. If concerns arise, they might recommend more intensive assistance, including training, in-class observation, coaching, and detailed improvement plans. Usually this helps get performance back on track. But when it doesn't, supervisors and teams can recommend outplacement and termination. Over the past five years, 300 teachers have been required to undergo intensive support and assistance, and 70 of them are no longer teaching in Minneapolis.

The integrity of the new process was established early on. Among the first teachers to leave were one with 28 years of experience and another who was a member of the union executive board. In another early case, a teacher chose to pursue the traditional hearing process, which had always frustrated attempts to remove nonperformers. She arrived at the hearing with a union-appointed representative. Across the table she found not only the school district's representative but two teaching colleagues who had been part of her performance improvement team. They were well prepared to attest to her lack of skill in the classroom. She resigned on the spot.

In 2002, the Washington State Legislature passed civil service reform and collective bargaining legislation. Because the legislation called for a complete overhaul of Washington's personnel system, the Department of Personnel conducted extensive research on trends and best practices in other human resource systems, both public and private. Their report provides a good overview of the fundamental changes that are gradually sweeping the human-resources world, as governments try to replace practices rooted in the nineteenth century with systems more appropriate for the twenty-first century:

> The overall trend in both the public and private sectors is to link human re-
> source (HR) management more directly to the strategic goals of the organiza-
> tion. This requires a flexible HR system that can adapt to changing business
> requirements and the differing needs of various segments of a large organiza-
> tion (such as separate agencies within a state system).
>
> To create this type of flexibility, organizations are decentralizing more and
> more authority for personnel actions to managers, with human resource pro-
> fessionals providing tools, services, and consultation.
>
> States and other public jurisdictions are using various methods to stream-
> line their classification systems. Many are using a broadband approach in

which large numbers of jobs or functions are grouped into broad categories based on various factors, such as type of work, level of responsibility, compensation level, occupational group, competencies, and so on.

The trend in public sector compensation is to move towards more flexible systems with broad salary bands and/or pay options that allow for recognition of labor market shortages; education, training, and skill development; and performance awards for both individuals and groups. . . .

As organizations modernize their human resource systems, they tend to place greater emphasis on performance as a key factor in all types of HR decisions, including compensation, promotion, layoff, and reemployment from layoff. Successful attainment of predefined, well-articulated goals becomes the basis for monetary and other rewards. Performance assessment is done on a regular basis and is viewed as a critical component of staff management.

To flesh out this picture, we recommend the following principles:

Give managers freedom to manage their people. Decentralize authority for hiring, firing, and promotion. Take it away from Human Resources and give it to the agencies and departments themselves, along with accountability for performance. Make the HR department a consulting or support resource. After all, if managers are on the hook for producing specific results, they need the power to assemble a team with the necessary skills and motivation.

Shift to broad job classifications to give agencies flexibility in organizing work. Reduce the number of job classifications dramatically—down to a few dozen if possible. This will give managers more flexibility to move people to new positions within the same broad classification, as needs change.

Couple this with a broadband pay system, with only three to five broad pay ranges within each job classification. Broadband systems, which have proven themselves in many places by now, allow managers to set salaries at levels required to recruit and keep the talent they need.

Streamline hiring, promotion, and discipline processes, and base all of them on objective performance expectations. Centralized HR processes in government are notoriously slow. Hiring, for example, often takes three to six months—by which time all the best candidates have found other jobs. Use performance criteria rather than seniority in personnel reductions. Put an end to "bumping": Keep high performers and let low performers go. And streamline firing processes, by allowing only one appeal, for instance.

Link compensation to performance. Eliminate automatic pay increases based on longevity. Set salaries at levels required to recruit and keep the talent you need, in your labor market, and reward performance with bonuses, awards, gainsharing, and other performance management tools. (See Chapter 8.) Allow for variable compensation rates (permanent or temporary) based on particularly challenging assignments, such as teaching in difficult schools or leading teams on complex projects. Let managers link salary increases to the acquisition of new skills, such as operating new kinds of equipment or cross-training to handle varied work assignments, as an incentive for lifelong learning and a way to offer mobility to those in low-level jobs. And reinforce the role of teams in delivering results by employing team-based rewards, such as team-based bonuses, gainsharing, and performance awards.

Invest in building the skills and capacities of employees. Invest in training and education. Major corporations spend four times what the federal government spends on developing the competence of their staffs, according to the National Commission on the Public Service. In addition:

- Institute team-based or peer-based professional development processes: annual goal setting, planning of professional development opportunities, and peer reviews as part of performance appraisals.
- Use job rotation to enhance opportunities to learn, grow, and contribute to success. See every job as a learning opportunity, and use each one as part of the process of succession planning.
- Assign every employee a coach: a trusted source of feedback on performance, advice, and encouragement regarding the challenges employees face. Coaches help even the best get better.
- Invest in leadership development. Leadership doesn't just happen.

ACCOUNTING

Traditional public accounting systems have thousands of cost codes that are used to track individual expenditures in excruciating detail. These codes were invented to ensure that not one penny of government money would go astray. There's just one problem: The detail often overwhelms the people who handle the data. In Minnesota, school districts are required to enter data using a standard set of 1,500 codes and follow a 400-page instruction manual, on the assumption that this will ensure the accuracy and comparability of entries by hundreds of districts. The legislative auditor discovered, however, that 45 percent of audited entries were inaccurate, mostly because the school district personnel could not keep track of the meanings and nuances of so many different codes. This system consumes millions of dollars to create the illusion of accuracy where it doesn't actually exist.

Accounting systems tell people what matters by telling them what to count. In too many cases, they say loud and clear that what matters is *cost*, not results. Such systems were created to control spending, after all, not to support achievement of results. Most government accounting systems, like government personnel systems, were established to prevent fraud and abuse, back in the Progressive era. Since their greatest concern was theft, the architects of these systems focused almost exclusively on current transactions—where public money might slip into a private pocket. This was called, appropriately, "cash accounting," because its main purpose was to keep track of the cash. Unfortunately, cash accounting was so focused on the short term that it neglected the long-term implications of current decisions. In a cash system, governments could grant future benefits for employees, such as pensions, without accounting for them as liabilities. So politicians could hand out goodies left and right, with little if anything showing up on the books as a budget increase.

Equally perverse was the way in which cash accounting ignored the declining value of assets. When a government builds a bridge or an aircraft carrier, it is creating something of value. But as that structure ages, its value declines, because without costly maintenance and repair it will wear out. This gradual consumption of an asset's value is a form of spending known as "depreciation." In cash accounting, established to track current transactions, it was invisible. Hence politicians could—and did—build new structures and hold ribbon-cutting ceremonies to buff their images, while neglecting the existing infrastructure. When they cut spending on maintenance in times of fiscal crisis, the tremendous future cost of that neglect would not show up on the books for years. Needless to say, this system encouraged their natural tendencies to ignore anything beyond the next election.

During the late 1970s, this kind of short-term thinking led New York City and Cleveland to the brink of bankruptcy. As a result, congressional leaders began to discuss how to impose better accounting standards on state and local governments. Afraid of congressional mandates, the National Governors Association and eight similar bodies created the Governmental Accounting Standards Board (GASB), to define "generally accepted accounting principles" (GAAP). Bond-rating agencies evaluate a government's financial management in part based on whether they meet GAAP standards.

In 1990, GASB began to move governments away from cash accounting by creating new standards requiring "modified" accrual accounting. In the late 1990s, GASB pushed further and required full accrual accounting for all government revenue and spending, including capital assets, beginning in fiscal 2002 for states and large cities and counties, 2003 for midsize jurisdictions, and 2004 for those with annual revenues under $10 million. This requires that *all* of the costs and revenues of providing a service in any year be recorded in that year, not just the cash received or paid out—to eliminate accounting illusions created by mismatched timing. It also forces governments to depreciate capital expenditures over time. Currently, GASB is moving to cover post-employment benefits beyond pensions, such as retiree health benefits, as well.

These are all important steps forward, and every government should comply with GASB's standards. But the new information will show up in year-end financial statements, not in budgets. Bond rating agencies will read them, but how many elected officials will pay attention remains an open question. Like many issues, it will probably depend on how many reporters cover them.

Other practices can also help give decisionmakers vital information necessary to deliver more results for the dollar. Full cost accounting helps managers identify both the direct and the indirect (overhead) costs of their programs and units, such as pensions and other employee benefits. Activity-based costing goes one step further and helps managers find out how much it costs to produce each unit of output. By knowing the true cost of filling a pothole, building a mile of road, or operating a program, managers can make informed judgments about the price, value, and competitiveness of their work.

Accounting systems *can* provide useful information, in other words, if they are set up to do so. But accounting systems are too often taken for granted. Rarely if ever do governments ask, What is our accounting strategy and how does it help us deliver the most results we can for the price citizens are willing to pay? In fact, we had never seen this done until our firm became involved with New York State.

New York's current accounting system was created more than 25 years ago. In those 25 years it has become increasingly complex, a patchwork of systems and subsystems, operating with technology several generations old. New York decided a few years ago that it was time for a new system. In most jurisdictions, this would mean simply adding technological sophistication to the current system. But making something electronic does not necessarily make it better. Ruth Walters, then New York's assistant comptroller, recognized that rebuilding the accounting system was an opportunity that could be strategic as well as technical. Before rushing to buy new software, she and her colleagues asked themselves what assumptions should undergird the system and what results it should produce. This strategic reflection led to some interesting conclusions, among them the following:

- *New York State's (NYS's) and the Office of the State Comptroller's (OSC's) operating strategies should be to achieve operational excellence—continuously improving the quality and cost effectiveness (value for money) of all activities. We will design CAS [the Central Accounting System] to support these strategies.*
- *NYS and OSC should accept reasonable risk in return for reasonable rewards in the form of:*

    Lower costs,
    Improved products/results, and/or
    Better customer service.

- *OSC believes that NYS's accounting strategy should support its operating and finance strategies.*
- *The core purpose of CAS is to provide information needed for effective decision-making—use of such information is intended to improve NYS's management and operations, compliance, and accountability.*
- *CAS will be designed to identify errors, omissions, and inconsistencies. In such instances the CAS will be designed to accommodate:*

    Corrections by organizations.
    Learning by organizations in response to mistakes.
    Flexibilities needed for unusual or unique situations
    Resolution of disagreements between organizations and OSC.
    Intervention by OSC in the few instances when organizations refuse to make corrections . . .

This is a unique statement of accounting strategy, because it says the core purpose of accounting is to provide information for decisionmaking, not control. At this point it is just a statement of philosophy, still being used to drive the new system's design. The proof will be in the operation of the new system, still years away. But to their credit, Walters and her colleagues asked the right questions and answered them based on what they wanted, not on what New York had always had.

In addition to GASB's new requirements and the philosophical approach outlined by New York, you can make your accounting system support your strategy by employing the following principles:

Make sure that what you account for is what really counts. Account for things at the right level of detail, and don't confuse detail with accuracy. As our Minnesota example shows, more of one may result in much less of the other.

Use accounting to gather information that managers can use to manage their finances themselves, rather than using the accounting system itself to manage. In traditional public accounting, risks are managed by creating multiple steps and checks. This creates an enormously cumbersome process. Even though a manager has a budget and a responsibility to get something done, spending any money requires certification in the accounting system of the budgeted amount; approval of a contract or purchase order by the contracting manager, the manager's supervisor (and for larger contracts the supervisor's supervisor), and the accounting department; setting aside (reserving or encumbering) the necessary funds; receipt of an invoice; approval of the invoice by the contracting manager, the manager's supervisor (and for larger contracts the supervisor's supervisor), and the accounting department; payment; and, finally, a record of the transaction. This process slows things down so much that governments have had to pass laws requiring prompt payment of invoices to put a sense of urgency in the system.

Note that recording needed financial information is only one of the steps; the rest are designed strictly to ensure that spending is kept under control. But every step and every check consume managers' time. It is far better to hold managers accountable for results, use the accounting system to give them the information they need, and let them manage their money.

Balance risk and results. Zero tolerance for risk is the wrong objective—and it is far too expensive. It requires so many steps and checks that it constipates the organization. Recognize that some risks, such as allowing managers to spend up to a certain limit without additional checks, are not only acceptable, they will reduce costs and improve service. If you design your accounting system to treat every accounting transaction the same, you will spend dollars to save pennies.

Integrate reporting of financial and performance information. Today most government managers get reports from the accounting department in great detail on their spending, reports from the budget office showing how their spending compares with the budget (and demanding explanations of variances), and reports from their staff on the work—usually on inputs (payroll, regular time, overtime, materials, and so forth) and outputs (potholes filled, transactions processed, reports issued). Then it is up to the manager to make sense of it all: to sort out the connections between one set of information and another and make corrections in the allocation of resources or the deployment of staff. It's a lot of paper, and it's frustrating.

An integrated reporting system would give managers up-to-date information on total performance: inputs consumed (money, time, materials), activities completed, outputs delivered, outcomes, and how it all compares to the organization's performance agreement and budget. In essence, the accounting system would deliver a performance scorecard to each manager once a month. This would equip managers with the information they needed to continuously improve the value they deliver.

For costs that need to be counted, use full cost accounting, activity-based costing, and accrual accounting. Together these will help managers see what it really costs to deliver their assigned results.

AUDITING

"It's a fact of life that, left alone, most people will do as little and get away with as much as they possibly can," says Mike Egan, an audit administrator with the Philadelphia City Controller's Office. He goes on to say:

> It's part of the human condition: laziness and greed come naturally, industry and honesty come with reinforcement. People need an impetus to keep their noses to the grindstone and their hands out of the till; and ever since the first government regulation was promulgated in the Garden of Eden, that impetus has been fear. It's an instinct: a hardwired drive to avoid what's bad for us and to seek what's good for us.
>
> Fear is a healthy human emotion with limitless benefits. . . .
>
> If every time a public official picked up a pen to sign a contract or to approve a voucher he felt the auditor's hot breath on his neck, the taxpayer could sleep a lot easier. . . .
>
> Please consider me an unapologetic adversary.

Egan's article demonstrates why no internal function of government is more feared than the auditor (or inspector general): In too many places auditing seems consumed by the desire to find things that are going wrong and punish them. In any system populated by human beings, with all our failings, such an auditor's work will never be done.

But any environment that is too tightly controlled is one is which there is no freedom to innovate. Without some reasonable elasticity in rules and some reasonable tolerance for noble failure, no one will take a risk. And without risk-taking, innovation stops.

The 1993 report of the National Performance Review condemned the auditors' "gotcha" mentality. It complained bitterly about the federal inspectors general, whom it found overzealous in their pursuit of any broken rule. "At virtually every agency he visited, the vice president heard federal employees complain that the IG's basic approach inhibits innovation and risk taking," it said. "Heavy-handed enforcement—with the IG watchfulness compelling employees to follow every rule, document every decision, and fill out every form—has had a negative effect in some agencies."

Fortunately, the past decade has seen a gradual revolution in public auditing. Increasingly, auditors see their roles as helping public organizations better serve their customers, while securing the confidence of the public in their integrity. The Canadian Auditor General's Office is considered a world leader in this revolution, and former auditor general Denis Desautels sums up the changes well: "The emphasis of the traditional role, in the 1950s and 1960s, was on compliance with all the financial rules and regulations. The basic objective was to determine if the departments spent within their budgets for the things they were authorized." Then, in the 1970s, some auditors began to focus on efficiency. Next:

> There was a gradual movement to concern about getting value for money. And it hasn't stopped there. More recently it has evolved into concerns about effectiveness as well. In this evolution, we have also moved towards, for one thing, the notion of best practices, benchmarking, learning from what other jurisdictions are doing. And there is more emphasis on results being achieved. It is a kind of auditing that is more broad-minded. We're supporting improvements.

This trend in auditing is evident in the 2003 edition of the U.S. General Accounting Office's "yellow book," *Government Auditing Standards*. One of its major revisions is expansion of the definition of performance audits:

> Performance audits provide information to improve program operations, facilitate decision making by parties with responsibility to oversee or initiate corrective action, and contribute to public accountability. The term performance audit is used generically to include work classified by some audit organizations as program evaluations, program effectiveness and results audits, economy and efficiency audits, operational audits, and value-for-money audits.

Auditing can contribute greatly to producing the results citizens want at the price they are willing to pay, if auditors follow these principles:

Focus on results, not just money. In public organizations driven to produce results, someone needs to help managers figure out what to measure and how to measure it. A neutral, objective body is also needed to audit the measurement process, to keep it honest. Auditors are in a perfect position to play both roles. In addition, auditors have begun to publish comparisons of performance against similar organizations. (See pp. 183–185.)

Enhance competition. In Phoenix, Arizona, the auditor's office audits competitive bids in the city's managed competition program, to ensure that both public and private bidders are including all costs and submitting honest bids. It also helps benchmark the cost and quality of services in Phoenix against those in other large southwestern cities. In the U.K., Margaret Thatcher created a new Audit Commission in the early 1980s to audit local governments. It gathers and publishes comparative data on 10 to 20 key local services—complete with simple bar graphs. When the reports come out, once a year, they fill the tabloids, prompt public discussion, and put real pressure on laggards to improve their performance. (See p. 183.)

Spread best practices. Perhaps the most advanced role auditors are beginning to play is as a source of expertise on best practices. If focused on performance, their audits can teach them a great deal about the difference between high- and low-performing organizations. The U.K. Audit Commission formally plays this role, identifying key success factors, keeping a database on the Web, running conferences, maintaining a telephone help line, and publishing guidebooks for police departments, fire services, and other local government organizations. The Phoenix auditor's office regularly does research and reports on best practices in service delivery, even leading operational managers on study trips to other cities to learn from the best and adopt their innovations.

Emphasize managing risks, not zero tolerance. As we have said, most of government operates with an extremely low tolerance for risk. Traditional auditors reinforce this tendency by slapping people's wrists when they bend the slightest rule to improve service to customers. But not all risks are equal. Small transactions carry less financial risk than large ones. Agencies with a long history of good financial management are less risky than agencies with the opposite history. Auditors need to learn how to assess risks and target those areas that pose the greatest hazard. The IRS doesn't audit everyone; it focuses on those returns that represent the highest risk.

In New York, the Office of the State Comptroller charts risks along two dimensions: likelihood (the probability of a negative outcome), and impact (the significance of a negative outcome). This type of risk assessment allows auditors to take into account an organization's experience and history (the likelihood of a problem) as well as the nature of their work (the potential impact of a problem).

WHEN SYSTEMATIC REFORM IS NOT POSSIBLE

Reform of administrative systems is not terribly controversial, but it is not politically sexy either. In parliamentary systems, as in the U.K., New Zealand, Australia, and Canada, administrative systems have already been thoroughly reinvented along the lines we advocate. But in the United States, the political system of divided executive and legislative branches makes such reform more difficult. Most proposals simply languish in legislatures that are more interested in the headline issues of the day. When full-scale reform fails to grab the politicians' attention, however, you can still adopt short-term measures that will help, while building the case for systemic change. Consider the "Bureaucracy Buster Panel" outlined in the box below, which the Public Strategies Group developed for a state government.

USING A BUREAUCRACY BUSTER PANEL TO ELIMINATE NEEDLESS RULES, REGULATIONS, PAPERWORK, AND PROCEDURES

The following is a suggested strategy for identifying and eliminating need-less or counterproductive rules. The term "rules" applies here to all *internal* rules, regulations, policies, paperwork, and procedures that form the conditions under which state employees deliver government services. The reason for doing this is twofold:

1. To save money by eliminating the cost of both complying with and enforcing rules; and
2. To put the focus of accountability on state employees producing results citizens value, while giving employees reasonable flexibility in how to produce those results.

The approach is to create a "demand" to review individual rules by (a) initiating a highly publicized invitation to employees and managers to chal-

(continues)

---

lenge needless rules; (b) assuming that the challenged rule will be waived, modified, or eliminated unless the official who authorized the rule can demonstrate its continued need and efficacy; and (c) empowering a small panel to review disputed requests for elimination and to make decisions.

Identifying Needless Rules

The Governor (to the extent he has time) and department heads should conduct "Bureaucracy Buster" meetings with large groups of employees, preferably all employees in a department. These meetings should be used to solicit employee suggestions of rules (and policies, procedures, paperwork, etc.) that should be modified, waived, or eliminated. After an introduction to explain the process and give a few examples to jump-start people's thinking, employees should develop their ideas in small groups, then report them to the entire group.

At these meetings, department heads should be empowered to immediately eliminate or modify a rule if it applies only to their department. If not, it should be sent to the authorizer (see below).

A simple and easy Web-based process should also be established to allow employees to suggest rules for elimination on a Bureaucracy Buster Web page. Employees should be encouraged to use these criteria in making their suggestions:

- The rule should be under the control of some level of state government. Rules from other jurisdictions should not be part of this particular process.
- Rules that are burdensome to follow, costly to enforce, or that adversely affect cost-effective delivery of state services should be targeted.
- There is (or was) usually a "good" reason behind every rule. If these purposes are still relevant, employees should be encouraged to suggest alternative, less costly ways of meeting the purposes behind challenged rules.

Disposing of the Challenges

Challenges to rules should be immediately forwarded to the state official responsible for the rule. (For example, if it is a statewide personnel rule, it should go to the personnel director. If it is a department-wide procedure, it should go to the department director. If it is an office-wide paperwork practice, it should go to the person in charge of the office.) This rule "*authorizer*" might be a front-line manager, a department director, or an official in one of the state's administrative support agencies. Rule authorizers should have 21 calendar days in which to respond to the challenge. The authorizer may:

1. immediately eliminate the rule;
2. seek more information before acting (with a 14-day deadline for action after they receive the information);
3. waive the rule only for the challenger or class of challengers, perhaps with conditions;
4. modify the rule; or
5. make a case to the Bureaucracy Buster Panel for keeping the rule as is.

Within 30 calendar days of the challenge, the challenger should be notified through the Web-based system of the disposition of the challenge. All dispositions should be posted on the Bureaucracy Busters Web site for all to see.

Challengers dissatisfied with the decisions of the rule authorizer could appeal to the Bureaucracy Buster panel.

Bureaucracy Buster Panel

This panel should be charged by the governor to oversee the whole process and to make decisions on appeals. The panel should have the power to modify, waive, or eliminate any internal rule or regulation, even over the objection of the rule authorizer. The panel should also identify patterns in challenged rules and periodically make recommendations to the governor on systemic changes that will reduce costs and improve service.

We recommend that the panel be limited to three people. It should not attempt to be a representative body. However, diversity in the perspective of the three panel members will improve the performance of the panel. We suggest that the panel be composed of a front-line employee, a supervisor or middle manager, and a senior manager.

The panel should receive a charter directly from the governor. It should have a full- or part-time staff person for its first year of operation. The need for staff support will diminish over time.

WHEN SCANDALS ERUPT

The most common fear voiced about administrative system reform is that employees who are given more authority will lead us back down the path of waste, fraud, and abuse. In 2001, it seemed that such a fear might be coming true.

Earlier in this chapter we reported on the use of purchase cards in the federal government. These are credit cards issued to government agencies by banks, with purchase limits of $2,500 per item. (Eager to get the business, major banks have offered the government rebates on all purchases made with cards.) In 1998, Congress also authorized credit cards to pay for federal travel.

By 2001, employees at just one department, Defense, were making almost $10 billion in annual purchases using purchase and travel cards. The department estimated cumulative savings for purchase cards alone at $954 million—a figure that was mounting at a rate of more than $200 million a year. Department personnel used purchase cards for 95 percent of eligible transactions, at a savings of $20 per transaction compared to the old purchase-order process. In addition, "Implementation of the travel charge card has allowed the department to generate savings by dramatically reducing the number of travel advances processed to support travelers, who can now use their card at an automated teller machine (ATM) to draw cash for their trip."

Then, in 2001, the General Accounting Office issued a report on abuses at DOD, and the headlines began. In testimony before Congress, GAO highlighted purchases for personal use, including home improvement items from Home Depot, DVD players, clothing, jewelry, eyeglasses, and pet supplies. Other reports turned up more than $13,000 spent at legal brothels in Nevada—without indicating whether they were for meals or other activities. At other agencies, GAO reported finding travel cards used to pay for clothes, mortgage payments, and personal trips.

Some thought the purchase and travel cards were doomed. But with more than $1 billion in savings documented, the Department of Defense was loath to give them up. So the department put together a task force, which investigated and issued a report in June 2002.

Many governments would have abandoned the program altogether. But the task force pointed out that the cards not only saved money, they improved "mission effectiveness." For example, letting organizations use cards for small purchases "dramatically improved their ability to procure relatively inexpensive, mission-critical items." The task force argued that better management was the solution, not a return to bureaucracy. It made 25 recommendations designed to heighten managers' scrutiny of purchase- and travel-card use, strengthen internal controls, block use of cards at certain types of merchants, use data-mining technologies to detect fraud and abuse, and better train employees to understand what purchases were off limits. Already, it pointed out, management attention to the travel-card problem had reduced write-offs from $1,700,000 per month to $300,000.

Today, new procedures are in place to both win and enforce compliance. Not all of the problems have disappeared; indeed, they never will. Human beings are fallible, and no compliance system works perfectly. But DOD leaders recognized that improving the ability of our soldiers, sailors, and airmen to do their jobs, even at a slightly higher risk, was far better than imposing rigidities that would cost billions and impede performance. To the surprise of some, there was no outcry from Congress or the public over DOD's decision. Apparently, people understand common sense when they see it.

THIRTEEN

Smarter Work Processes
Tools from Industry

In the 1990s, Joann Neuroth was a team leader in the Michigan Department of Commerce, trying to reduce the time it took to approve economic development grants to cities. Her team's first steps toward enhancing quality involved gathering data about current procedures, then analyzing the data to find specific targets for improvement. When they mapped the department's many-step grant-approval process, Neuroth says, "I got it in my stomach that I hadn't ever seen all of it before. The flaws in the system were huge. That was news."

In her description, the process of analysis and discovery sounds almost like a religious conversion: "The system was talking to us. When I saw the patterns emerging, I felt like we'd always been working blind before. It was like reading a mystery story—but the conclusion really mattered to me."

Neuroth and her colleagues were among thousands of public-sector teams who have embarked on the process of continuous, incremental improvement known as Total Quality Management. TQM gives teams of employees the analytic capacity and the decisionmaking power to redesign work. It enables them both to eliminate the causes of quality defects and to improve the quality of their output. And there is a good reason why TQM is so popular—it works. When the Michigan team cut grant-making time by 40 percent, Neuroth says, "The results astonished me."

While old-style government has always been the whipping boy for waste and inefficiency, these faults are not unknown in the private sector. But corporate America has made huge advances in productivity over the past 25 years, in part by adopting techniques developed to redesign the way work gets done. Reinventors can dip into this same toolbox to rethink the often antiquated work processes that drag down performance: the many forms, the endless handoffs, the interminable delays so maddening in public bureaucracies. Sometimes, improving performance involves developing new strategies, but more often it simply requires the redesign of existing work. Foremost among the many techniques to do so are three we will discuss here: TQM, "WorkOuts," and Business Process Reengineering (BPR). Total Quality Management, the most common of the three, helps you make continuous incremental improvements in your work processes. WorkOuts and BPR are for heavy lifting, when you need to make radical changes and quantum leaps in performance.

TOTAL QUALITY MANAGEMENT

Managing quality is not a twentieth-century invention. As craft guilds developed in the Middle Ages, they used specifications and performance audits to enforce product quality. The Industrial Revolution turned craftsmen into factory workers, introducing performance measurement and standardization to manage quality. Then, American business adopted Frederick Taylor's system of "scientific management," which used inspection as the primary method of quality control.

Quality inspection separates good products from bad ones, to cut down the number of defective units shipped to customers. During World War II, a few Americans, including Joseph Juran and W. Edwards Deming, began to develop ways to ensure quality from the beginning, using statistical analysis of production processes. Their ideas helped U.S. firms produce enormous amounts of high-quality armaments for the war.

After the war, the U.S. government sent Deming to Japan to help conduct a census. While there, and in subsequent visits, he taught Japanese manufacturers the new production methods. In America, manufacturers abandoned them, because a postwar boom placed a premium on volume, not quality. But the Japanese agreed to experiment with quality improvement techniques, and the results were dramatic: Industrialists reported productivity gains of 30 percent or more in just weeks. By the mid 1950s, Deming and Juran were revered figures in Japanese industry—decades before America knew of them.

The essence of TQM is to replace *inspection* for quality *after* production with *improvement* of quality *before* production. As TQM advocates never tire of saying, quality must be built in from the beginning.

There are many versions of TQM, and quality adherents avidly debate their merits. Most versions, however, share a set of core principles:

Quality is in the eye of the customer. In the bureaucratic tradition, quality is defined by producers: the professionals and managers who control the business. TQM turns this assumption on its head. As TQM pioneer Armand Feigenbaum put it, "Quality is what the customer says it is." TQM drives organizations to find out what customers want and deliver it—the first time and every time. It also recognizes that customers' expectations may change over time—one reason continuous, ongoing improvement is at its core.

External customers use the organization's final output, but most production processes involve many steps, for each of which there is an internal customer. TQM organizations use feedback from both kinds of customers to determine which features of quality to improve at any given moment.

To improve quality you must improve processes. A fundamental tenet of TQM is that all processes vary constantly in their quality; the fundamental goal of TQM is to reduce that variability while creating a consistently upward trend in quality.

Consider a state government program that makes grants to cities. Although state administrators use the same process with every grant, the amount of time it takes to approve each one may vary considerably. The first step is to determine what is behind the variation. There are two kinds of causes. One, known as *special causes*, occurs when workers make mistakes or special events interfere with the process. An employee in the state grant-making process might lose an application form, for instance, or become ill for several days. Either reason would delay the process, but neither is a part of the process itself. The other, called *common causes*, is due to faults inherent in the process. For example, if there are many sequential steps in the grant-making process, the handoffs between employees may consume too much time. Or the grant application forms might be so complicated that they are riddled with errors that cause delays in processing.

Common causes cannot be corrected by telling employees to try harder or punishing them when they don't. You have to change the processes they use—which is what TQM sets out to do.

Deming estimated that 85 to 94 percent of process problems are due to common causes. In his 1982 book, *Out of the Crisis*, he argued that management should stop blaming employees and start fixing flaws in their work processes.

Decisions about improving processes should be based on facts and data, not opinions. To improve processes you must start by analyzing data about process performance. This is a highly rational method—quite different from using intuition or opinion to guess at what is wrong. Once you identify common causes that are at work, you can decide how to change the process. Then you test the change, once again gathering data about performance. If the experimental change improves results, you institute it permanently.

Process improvement is an ongoing effort that yields incremental, continuous increases in quality. Any process is likely to be plagued by many problems. Fixing one may boost quality, but it leaves other issues unaddressed. In addition, organizations have numerous processes, each of which can be targeted for improvement. Because there are so many processes and so many potential causes of problems, the work of continuous improvement proceeds bit by bit, and it never ends.

The people who do the work should be responsible for improving work processes. In the past, managers controlled work processes. In some organizations adopting TQM, managers still decide which processes to improve and which improvements to implement. But since employees know the most about how work is actually performed, they should be the ones in charge of improving processes.

Using a team to develop improvements brings together employees with different knowledge about the process. It gets more heads analyzing problems and brainstorming about improvements, and it makes workers more open to implementing the process improvements, since they helped create them. In businesses that have won the Malcolm Baldrige Award, America's highest recognition of TQM mastery, as many as 80 percent of the employees are deeply involved in quality management.

Some reinventors greatly expand the basic definition of TQM to include the use of performance management, employee empowerment, and organizational empowerment. General Bill Creech relied on all three, plus competition, to double the U.S. Tactical Air Command's effectiveness, for instance. Indeed, Creech says that TQM's process improvement tools fell woefully short, until he added these missing ingredients, which became part of the way he defined quality in his book *The Five Pillars of TQM*.

In deepening basic TQM, Creech and others followed in the footsteps of Deming, who over the years focused less on TQM's technical side and more on creating the organizational culture and leadership necessary to support quality. All of them were expanding a technical tool into a broader management philosophy. Because the rest of this book (and past books) outlines our management philosophy, here we will stick to TQM as a tool.

Using TQM to Create Improvements

A typical TQM improvement process involves a team of 10 or fewer employees. They may target any aspect of a process's performance: the time it takes, its cost, or how well it responds to customer needs.

The steps they take, known as the continuous improvement cycle, help organizations avoid what some call the "ready, fire, aim" method of improvement, in which teams jump to conclusions before analyzing the cause of problems, tackle problems beyond the control or influence of team members, or fail to plan adequately how to implement and evaluate their solutions.

In 1992, the 50-bed hospital at Langley Air Force Base, headquarters of the Air Combat Command (a merger of Creech's Tactical Air Command and the Strategic Air Command), began using improvement teams. They all employed the same six-step improvement process (see boxed text). One team, called BRATS (for Babies Are Ready at Term), used TQM to cut the amount of time a mother and newborn baby stayed in the hospital after the birth. This increased customer satisfaction and cut the hospital's costs without putting infants at risk. By examining the work of the BRATS team, we can get a good look at the guts of an improvement process.

The process starts with the customer. The hospital's Quality Improvement Council created BRATS because mothers were complaining about having to stay at least 72 hours after giving birth.

BRATS had eight members, selected to ensure that all parts of the discharge process were represented. Team members were trained to use TQM techniques and given a coach knowledgeable in TQM and group facilitation. The team set ground rules for group behavior and a specific time to meet each week. At each meeting, they used a formal agenda, designated a timekeeper, kept minutes, and evaluated the quality of the meeting.

The team first developed a flow chart of what happened to the patients from the moment they arrived on the ward until their discharge. This identified numerous opportunities for reducing the time: streamlining the formal discharge process; conducting required laboratory tests earlier; teaching mothers breastfeeding techniques before birth; and shifting doctors' rounds so they could discharge patients in the early morning. In addition, the team studied the criteria that doctors and nurses used to determine whether an infant could be discharged.

Next, improvement teams collect and analyze data about the process. BRATS reviewed questionnaires indicating that many patients wanted to be discharged earlier than 72 hours after giving birth. It measured the length of

---

STEPS IN THE IMPROVEMENT PROCESS

The Air Combat Command's improvement process has six steps:

1. *Identify the opportunity for improvement.* Define the process to be improved and describe the improvement goal in measurable terms.
2. *Gather and analyze data.* Collect accurate, quantifiable data about process performance.
3. *Generate potential improvements.* Identify as many ways as possible to improve the process.
4. *Evaluate and select potential improvements.* Decide which improvements will be most cost-effective, efficient, and feasible.
5. *Implement the improvements.* Use a small-scale, temporary change to test them.
6. *Evaluate the process improvement.* Track performance to find out what effect the change is having. If the change works, make it permanent. If not, figure out why and try something else.

Many organizations call organization-wide implementation of the change a seventh step; hence they talk about a "seven-step improvement process."

---

patient stays, which averaged four days, including the day of birth. Since the team did not want to make improvements that jeopardized babies' health, it also researched the medical literature about early infant discharge.

Then the team performed a cost–benefit analysis of possible solutions. It discovered that breastfeeding education before birth was feasible, but would greatly increase the time spent in prenatal visits. It found that some of the discharge criteria could be satisfied with a next-day follow-up visit after discharge, and that some of the required medical tests on the infant could be performed sooner. And the team learned that bonding between mother and infant could be accomplished more quickly by increasing the time babies spent with their mothers in the hospital.

The team decided to experiment with some changes for three months. It would enhance breastfeeding education before birth, perform lab tests earlier, and complete discharge papers on the second day for infants who met discharge criteria. Patients who strongly requested an early discharge were treated in the new way. Certain babies (those with slight weight loss, for instance) were required to return for follow-up appointments the day after discharge.

TOTAL QUALITY MANAGEMENT TECHNIQUES

TQM practitioners use many statistical techniques to help teams collect information, analyze and display data about processes, generate ideas about
solutions, reach consensus, and plan actions. Most of these are relatively
simple. The specific techniques chosen are far less important than the general commitment to making decisions based on data.

- *Flow charts* are schematic diagrams or charts describing the step-by-
  step activities and decision points in a process. They give team
  members common reference points with which to understand the
  process and common language with which to describe it.

- *Cause-and-effect diagrams* show, in picture form, a list of possible
  problems and/or potential solutions. Teams use structured brainstorming sessions to identify the possible causes of a particular
  problem, or factors that would help solve it. They define the issues,
  identify major categories of causation (such as lack of information,
  specific policies, or employee mistakes), identify more detailed causes,
  and then, using data, identify the most important of these. The picture
  they produce is often called a fishbone diagram, because the final
  drawing usually looks the skeleton of a fish: The effect is the head and
  the causes branch off the backbone.

- *Run charts or time plots* measure the performance of a process over
  time, to help teams detect whether time-related changes such as delays
  affect the outputs.

- *Control charts* plot the variation in performance of a process over time:
  They are run charts with the normal upper and lower boundaries of
  variation marked. They help define where performance will fall in the
  absence of special causes, and they help teams detect whether special
  causes are interfering with the process.

- *Histograms* are bar charts that graphically display variations in data.
  They have an immediate visual impact, because the bars form certain

---

Through the test period, no mothers or babies needed to be readmitted
after an early discharge. Ninety-seven percent of the patients were satisfied
with the new process. And letting the patients leave the hospital a day earlier than usual saved an estimated $240,000.

As its final step, BRATS institutionalized the changes. This meant bringing all appropriate staff up to speed on the improvements and changing the

patterns, such as a bell curve with a single, centered peak. (For example, they might show that half of all phone calls are answered in four rings, another 25 percent in three to five rings, and very few in just one or two or in more than five rings.) By analyzing these patterns, teams can sometimes see the causes of problems.

- *Pareto diagrams* are bar charts that display all the causes contributing to the flaws in a process, with the length of each bar representing the relative importance of the cause. Joseph Juran named this technique after Vilfredo Pareto, a nineteenth-century Italian economist who said, among other things, that 80 percent of the trouble is usually caused by 20 percent of the problems. Pareto diagrams help teams identify the most important causes of a process's difficulties—hence what to work on first.

- *Scatter diagrams* show whether two variables are related by plotting them on a chart with an x- and y-axis. For instance, if one wanted to know whether a welfare client would be likely to get a job faster if she had more training, one would plot the experience of a series of people. Someone who had found a job in four weeks after 24 weeks of training would be plotted at four on one axis, 24 on the other. If the factors were unrelated, the points would be randomly scattered. If more training resulted in finding jobs more quickly, the points would group themselves around one line; if the opposite were true, they would group around another line.

- *Selection matrices* help teams make quick comparisons between alternative improvements. They select critical criteria for judging any improvement, assign them weights, and then rate each solution by each criterion. They add up the ratings using a matrix chart, then implement those improvements with the highest ratings.

(For more detail on these and other TQM techniques, we recommend *Total Quality Transformation: Improvement Tools*, published by Productivity-Quality Systems, Inc.)

hospital's monitoring and documentation processes. The hospital also began to survey early discharge mothers by phone within a week of discharge to assess whether they or their babies should be seen before their next scheduled appointments. BRATS produced a complete report on its work—and then disbanded.

The Spread of TQM in Government

As Deming and a handful of TQM consultants spread the word, they attracted certain government leaders, usually at the local level, the breeding ground of most innovation in American government. Joseph Sensenbrenner, the mayor of Madison, Wisconsin, was one of the first converts. Elected in 1983, he found his city losing revenue while demand for services soared and service systems broke down. In 1985, Sensenbrenner launched pilot TQM efforts in city government and helped start a local network of public- and private-sector quality adherents. By 1989, the city had 30 process improvement teams at work.

At about the same time, Ft. Lauderdale, Florida, committed to initiate a quality improvement process. It contracted for help from Florida Power & Light, the first American company to win Japan's prestigious Deming Prize. In the late 1980s, a handful of other cities and counties followed, including Hillsborough County, Florida, Ft. Collins, Colorado, and Phoenix, Arizona.

Schools, colleges, and universities also began to embrace quality management. In the U.S. federal government, defense agencies led the quality movement. According to the U.S. Office of Personnel Management, between 1988 and 1993 the Naval Aviation Depot in Cherry Point, North Carolina, saved $185 million through TQM. It also increased its revenues from contracted repair work—for which it competes with private firms—by 60 percent.

In 1988, TQM got a huge boost when then secretary of defense Frank Carlucci pledged to use TQM to meet the mammoth agency's productivity goals. The same year, the Reagan administration created a Federal Quality Institute to promote TQM and assist agencies in getting started.

In 1989, after Wisconsin governor Tommy Thompson held a full-day retreat on TQM for his top executives, five department heads formed a steering committee to push quality management throughout state government. In 1990, then governor Bill Clinton launched TQM in Arkansas state government, with the help of an executive on loan from private industry.

In the fiscal crisis of the early 1990s, public-sector interest in TQM exploded. By 1993, according to Myron Tribus, a leading promoter of TQM, as many as 1,500 local communities were organizing quality efforts. And in 1994, 40 states reported that they had initiated TQM in selected agencies.

The Power and Limits of TQM

What accounts for TQM's growth? Once again, the answer is simple: It works.

THE LIMITS OF TQM

TQM does not:

- Change the governance system;
- Change the administrative systems: budget, personnel, procurement, accounting, and auditing;
- Change or clarify organizational purpose;
- Introduce incentives and consequences for performance;
- Give customers the power of choice;
- Decentralize control through organizational empowerment;
- Produce breakthrough system or process redesigns; or
- Account for processes that are complex, varied, and nonlinear, like teaching.

Higher quality eliminates the need for employees to fix, replace, or redo defective products or services. Some analysts believe rework amounts to as much as 30 percent of costs in service industries, and most of government is a service industry.

Quality improvement eliminates waste and saves money, but it does far more. By improving quality, it leads to higher customer satisfaction. Madison found that many projects also improved labor–management relations and employee morale. TQM shifts some control to front-line employees, increasing their job satisfaction, and changes the culture as employees buy into teamwork and the need to adapt their work to meet their customers' needs.

Nonetheless, TQM alone cannot transform public institutions, because it gives reinventors no leverage to move the larger systems that block change. This is one reason TQM is favored mostly by institutional managers, not politicians.

Nor does TQM help organizations clarify or change their purposes. It helps them to do things right, but not to do the right things. Yet many public agencies experience the problem of confused, conflicted, or outdated purposes.

Another reason TQM falls short of organizational transformation is that it does not change the underlying incentives in public organizations. This is less important in the private sector, where competition usually creates very clear consequences for organizations and most firms use some form of performance pay. But as General Bill Creech argued, you create quality by getting the fundamentals right; you then control it by using process improvement techniques. Deep, sustained improvement requires a clear purpose, fundamental empowerment of employees, real accountability to customers, and effective incentives. (For more about these fundamentals, see *Banishing Bureaucracy.*)

The Tactical Air Command "had no shortage of sophisticated process tools and methods when I took over as commander," Creech wrote.

> *Conceptually, that previous set of quality functions, tools, and techniques in TAC was supposed to yield a do it right the first time mentality—it wasn't designed just to catch mistakes after they were made. But though they helped, they fell woefully short in instilling the quality mindset—and the level of competence and motivation needed to do it right the first time, every time. What were the missing pieces? . . . They involved new organization, new leadership, new empowerment, new ways to instill quality-consciousness, and new incentives to get every employee committed to eliminating defects at the source—and to continuous improvement in every process and every activity.*
>
> *TAC's quality—and productivity—improved dramatically only when we took those steps. And they far overshadowed the steps we also took to be smarter in our process analysis and improvement actions.*

Process-oriented TQM even falls short on employee empowerment. Creating a quality council and improvement teams gets the TQM ball rolling, but the way to keep it moving—and to accelerate it—is to shift even more power to front-line employees. If you reduce management layers, eliminate functional "silos," decentralize organizational controls, and create permanent teams, your employees will develop a real stake in managing quality.

Radical decentralization should be the permanent foundation of a TQM organization, Creech argued. Temporary improvement teams can be viewed as just another management fad. Unless employees experience real authority being shifted to them, they may see TQM as just another layer of control dressed up in new slogans.

Finally, TQM's focus on improving quality by reducing variation works with some public-sector functions, but not others. It works when a process is linear and repeated often. But what happens with a process like education, which is complex and nonlinear? As the psychologists have proven—and we all know from experience—different people learn in different ways. To standardize the learning process by eliminating variation is to condemn atypical learners to failure. Good teachers purposely build variation into the environment so that different people can learn in their own ways.

Much of the public sector's work—from welfare case management to Head Start to employment and training programs—involves human development, and human development is by its nature complex, varied, and nonlinear. The same is true of most policy work: It is not a collection of linear, oft-repeated processes that can be improved by eliminating variation. Other public-sector work, from policing to the court system, requires constant subjective judgments about how to handle different individuals. Police officers can use TQM to improve much of their information processing, scheduling, and the like, but who would try to take variation out of the process of investigating suspects or intervening in conflicts?

The TQM Journey: Lessons Learned

Becoming a "quality" organization involves a challenging exploration into unfamiliar terrain. Typically, it takes most organizations—public or private—several years to achieve significant results. The following lessons should be useful in speeding up the process:

Start at the top of the organization. TQM requires the full support of the CEO, as well as behavior that consistently demonstrates that he or she "walks the talk." Top executives need to go through intensive TQM training and visit organizations that have implemented quality management. They should make their commitment to TQM very visible throughout the organization. When he was governor of Ohio, George Voinovich personally built a labor–management partnership to push TQM with the Ohio State Employees Association, which had opposed his election. He and all his top managers went through TQM training. He hired a TQM director who reported directly to the governor and gave him an annual budget of $500,000.

Don't measure success by dollars alone. Focusing exclusively on financial savings shortchanges the potential of TQM. If you start with the assumption that TQM is a cost-cutting exercise, you risk alienating employees before you start, because many will assume quality is about making them work harder so you can downsize the organization. Others will simply go through the motions, because cost-cutting does not motivate them—they care about making the organization more effective.

The point of TQM is to raise quality. Lower cost is only one aspect of value. Many worthwhile process improvements don't save money but do improve results.

Deal the union in. TQM changes the work employees do and the responsibilities they assume in the workplace. It changes the power relationship between managers and workers. It leads to productivity gains, which have implications for employment levels. It often affects collective bargaining agreements and processes. All of this is of concern to public employee unions, and sooner or later, they will become involved—as an obstacle or as a partner.

In Ohio, Governor Voinovich agreed that 50 percent of all quality steering committee members in departments would be from the union. When the union insisted on selecting those people, management bristled—but eventually agreed. When the union wanted to ensure that TQM improvements would not cost state employees their jobs, the state agreed to a no-layoff guarantee. Workers displaced by TQM got another state job at the same pay.

Cut managers in on the deal—and change their role. Some organizations skip their middle managers and front-line supervisors when they start involving employees in TQM. According to the former U.S. Federal Quality Institute (FQI), leaving managers out of TQM implementation only increases the likelihood that they will be hostile. When Mayor Sensenbrenner launched TQM in Madison, for instance, the greatest opposition came from managers. "There were individual managers who could not tolerate the idea of bringing their employees into decisions or who resented taking time to reassess tried and true procedures," he said.

FQI recommended "cascade" training, in which you first train top management, then managers and supervisors, and finally front-line employees. Once managers are trained, you should get them involved in the initial improvement teams, so they understand how the process works. Then give them a key role in the TQM process. Have some of them facilitate and coach—but not direct—improvement processes. Have others become TQM trainers. Most important, have others form teams to improve processes that require management commitment or involve other agencies, such as budget, personnel, and procurement processes. Too often, organizations spend all their energy on minor processes and forget the most important ones, because they don't put senior managers—the only people with the clout to change some processes—on improvement teams.

Don't create a quality bureaucracy. At the outset, the organization needs someone whose role is to spearhead the quality initiative—someone driven by a passion for TQM, not by a desire to run a quality bureaucracy. But creating a special unit to "do quality" for the organization lets everyone else off the hook for making quality a part of their basic routines. It also undervalues the potential of the organization. The goal is to make quality improvement a routine part of the organization's work.

"Integrate quality with regular operations as quickly as you possibly can," advises Stan Spanbauer, former president of Fox Valley Technical College. After several years working with TQM, his college eliminated its top-management steering committee and quality coordinator position. "Every manager has to be a quality coordinator," he said.

Use just-in-time training to build TQM know-how. "Long delay times between training in TQM practices and application on the job often generate cynicism and doubt about the quality effort, a perception that it is just another management 'flavor of the month,'" according to the Federal Quality Institute. Train your people just before they begin to use TQM. Unless they immediately apply what they are learning to problems that matter to them, they are not likely to retain much of what they've learned.

WORKOUTS

Quality management is not designed to reinvent governance systems—to introduce public school choice, vouchers for public housing residents, or a competitive market for job training, for instance. It is designed only to improve existing processes. Even there, it focuses on incremental improvement, when many public systems and processes need total redesign. When reinventors are looking for a sudden jolt to the system and dramatic improvements in results, they sometimes borrow another technique from the world of business: the WorkOut.

Developed at General Electric in the late 1980s, WorkOuts are brief but intensive group sessions intended to solve problems by redesigning work processes from the ground up. The technique was designed "to get rid of thousands of bad habits accumulated since the creation of General Electric," explains former chairman Jack Welch. "We've got 112 years of closets and attics in this company. We want to flush them out, to start with a brand new house with empty closets, to begin the whole game again."

In a WorkOut, members of the organization gather to solve a particular problem. The group may be small (a few dozen) or large (100 or more); it depends on the number of people required to bring together all the knowledge about the problem. Supported by a trained facilitator, the group works together for up to one week. It moves from team building, brainstorming, and testing solutions all the way to presenting full-scale proposals to top managers. On the spot, the managers must reject or accept the recommendations. They can say they need more information, but if they do, they must charter a team to get the information by an agreed-upon date.

A WorkOut assembles people who don't usually work with or trust each other—who in fact may be blaming each other for the problem. They have to spend days together. The process breaks down barriers and promotes openness and candor. It forces long-buried problems to the surface. It challenges old ways of thinking and requires participants to take responsibility for improving the organization. It creates the opportunity—and the need—for people to be creative. And it forces people to make decisions about which changes to adopt.

In 1991, the Northeast Region of the U.S. Customs Service engaged in a WorkOut with GE to resolve a customs problem with the company. It liked the process so much that it asked GE's management center to help it run its own WorkOuts. It held 30 in 1992, then started training others in the Customs Service.

State agencies in West Virginia and North Carolina also started using WorkOuts. So did Louisville, Kentucky, after Joan Riehm, a deputy mayor, stumbled across the tool when she was looking for a way to make big changes quickly. Riehm alerted Mayor Jerry Abramson, who asked GE chairman Jack Welch if he thought the tool would work in government.

GE officials walked Abramson and his cabinet through a simulation at a two-day retreat in February 1992. What happened has been documented by David Kennedy in a case study at Harvard's John F. Kennedy School of Government:

> The subject was vacant lots and abandoned structures . . . some 4,000 vacant lots and empty houses. . . . Huge amounts of city energy and money, involving a score of departments, went into dealing with the aesthetic, health, safety, and legal problems they caused.
>
> The cabinet's WorkOut session began with small ideas. . . . Gradually, though, the tone changed. "It was obvious that there were some people there who thought, 'Oh, shit, we're going to have to get together and make like we're interested for two days,'" says Chief of Police Doug Hamilton. "But then people saw that it was serious money that was basically being thrown out the window because no one took a concerted effort toward it . . . this was a two or three million dollar chunk of money. People started to get kind of excited about it."

The group wanted to speed up the city's acquisition and redevelopment of vacant property. But the only way to get the properties was through the criminal courts, lot by lot—a process that was "slow, expensive, and subject to the whims of judges who hated dealing with such cases." The group got stuck on this problem.

The GE facilitator told them to pretend there were no legal obstacles and asked what they would do in that case. The city's lawyer objected—no surprise there—but "the rest of the group was liberated . . . a real idea emerged: Change the law to allow civil, rather than criminal, action, and mobilize the city's development arms to promote new uses for seized properties." That's what the group recommended to the mayor.

Abramson was impressed. He liked the results, and he liked seeing his cabinet so energized. He lost no time in convincing the state legislature to create an administrative court to handle the vacant lot cases. The new court opened for business that summer—at the same time Louisville began its second WorkOut.

The WorkOut is a "work stoppage," says Colonel Clayton (Dick) Frishkorn, former quality director for the Air Combat Command, which began using the tool in 1994. He says that participants set their usual work aside and, in "one intense, hard-hitting week generate high-energy creativity and innovation."

> *It cuts through the barrier of never having the time to fix things. Remember the old story about a man who sees someone sawing a tree with a dull saw and asks, "Why don't you stop and sharpen the saw?" And the guy answers, "I don't have the time." Well, a WorkOut makes the time.*

One of the ACC's first WorkOuts cut the time it took to inspect B1-B bombers by more than three and a half days, a 42 percent reduction. Another reduced the time it took to inspect an airplane engine by 65 percent, thus avoiding $5 million in costs. By 1996, the ACC had two dozen WorkOuts planned, and Frishkorn was training teams at every ACC base.

Lt. Col. Chuck Louisell ran an ACC WorkOut that tested how quickly Eglin Air Force Base in Florida could get its F-15 fighter jets ready for combat. Eglin passed with flying colors, bettering the ACC standard of 24 hours by nearly five hours. But Louisell was not satisfied. He challenged his 60th Fighter Squadron to cut the ACC standard by 50 percent—to 12 hours. "Everybody said, 'That's crazy, you can't get there from here,'" Louisell remembers. So he scheduled another WorkOut to try.

In December 1996, about 30 members of the squadron stopped doing their work and focused instead on changing how they worked. Louisell put senior managers and specialists, such as engineers, at their disposal to answer any questions or help solve problems.

To begin, the employees divided into four teams and performed their usual tasks. With the help of other base employees, outside observers, and facilitators, they videotaped and analyzed the way they did things and came up with ideas for improvements.

Almost immediately they discovered big efficiency gains. It normally took two and a half hours to perform the preflight inspection, but one team found that inspectors wasted a great deal of time walking around the planes or back and forth to their toolboxes. "One inspector walked over 4,097 feet," Louisell says. The team gave inspectors tool belts and changed the sequence of tasks, which halved the walking-around time. That and other changes reduced the inspection to 70 minutes.

Another team tackled the process for loading external fuel tanks, which took five people 97 minutes. After the team reordered the sequence of tasks and assigned specific tasks to each worker, it took four people only 12 minutes. "This team caught on fire," says Louisell. "It was like watching an Indianapolis 500 pit crew at work."

At the end of the week, the WorkOut teams assembled these and many other changes into a seamless new process for readying the F-15s. They tried it out on the last day, as pilots prepared to fly the planes on a training mission. All the planes were ready in 12 hours.

Success Factors for WorkOuts

In a WorkOut, all the action is highly compressed into just a few days, which creates enormous pressures on participants. The stakes are high. The interactions are intense. And what people actually do during a WorkOut is new work: identifying problems, brainstorming, testing ideas, and then—the crowning moment—telling managers what they should do. The WorkOut solves specific problems, but meanwhile, it changes the culture.

Practitioners in the ACC and Customs Service point to several key factors that help make sure a WorkOut works out:

Make sure top managers are committed to the process, because they will have to make the final call on recommended changes. There is no substitute for this; don't leave home without it.

Pledge to employees that any changes that reduce work will not lead to layoffs. As Colonel Frishkorn puts it, "No one suggests improvements that will cost them their job."

Prepare carefully for a WorkOut. When selecting the project to work on, make sure it is one that needs urgent attention. When selecting the WorkOut team, make sure you have all the technical knowledge you need.

Use a trained facilitator to run the process. Like TQM or BPR, a WorkOut is a highly structured process that requires leadership from someone with skills in getting groups to function as teams, to think creatively about problems, to focus in on solutions, and so on. A facilitator also brings objectivity and conflict resolution capabilities to the process.

BUSINESS PROCESS REENGINEERING

Joe Thompson, former director of the Department of Veterans Affairs office in New York City, first trained his employees in TQM, but soon decided it wasn't enough. "We found that no amount of teams solving small problems would get it done," he remembers. "A fundamental change had to be brought about." Nor would the limited scope and time frame of a WorkOut have created the kind of from-the-ground-up transformation that was necessary.

When agencies need a complete overhaul, they turn to Business Process Reengineering, a tool that shares some characteristics with TQM and Work-Outs, but aims at breakthrough change in business processes too complex to redesign in a few days.

Some organizations reengineer first, then turn to TQM. They recognize that although redesigned business processes yield dramatic improvements, they can still be continually improved after they are transformed.

Reengineering also focuses on customer satisfaction and performance improvement, but it is more a onetime event than a continuous process. It is a project, while quality management—at its best—is a philosophy, a way of doing business.

Michael Hammer and James Champy, authors of *Reengineering the Corporation*, describe Business Process Reengineering as "the fundamental rethinking and radical redesign of business processes to achieve dramatic improvements in critical, contemporary measures of performance, such as cost, quality, service, and speed." By redesigning an organization's large-scale work processes, in one fell swoop, BPR eliminates or alters the work many people do and changes the organizational structure of functional divisions and units. Usually it injects a megadose of advanced information technology into the organization as well.

Like TQM, reengineering lets the customer define quality, and it targets work processes for redesign. But while TQM attacks one by one the hundreds or even thousands of subprocesses in an organization, BPR redesigns complex, large-scale business processes: the process of determining applicants' eligibility for benefits; the process of collecting taxes or child-support payments; the process of approving new facilities or purchases.

Some organizations reengineer because they need to modernize their information systems. Instead of automating their inefficient bureaucratic processes—"paving the cow paths," Hammer and Champy call it—they reengineer their key processes, *then* redesign their information systems.

BPR is not a tool for all reasons. Organizations usually have 10 to 20 broad business processes, says Thomas Davenport, author of *Process Innovation.* A reengineering project is inherently unsettling and usually discomforting. Between its promise and its payoff lies the peril of a risky, complex, lengthy, disruptive, and unfamiliar task. "Reengineering," say Hammer and Champy, "should be brought in only when a need exists for heavy blasting."

The payoff is huge leaps in performance. For instance:

- The Arizona Department of Transportation used BPR to cut the time it took to issue a driver's license from an average of 21 days to 5 days.
- Arizona's Department of Economic Security doubled collections of child-support payments.
- The state's Family Assistance Administration cut the time it took to determine welfare eligibility from 26 days to 1.
- The U.S. Postal Service cut the time it took to approve major facilities projects from eight months to three.
- The U.S. Department of Defense reduced its medical inventories by about two-thirds, saving $3 billion over 12 years.
- The U.S. Social Security Administration cut the time it took to determine disability eligibility from 155 days to 40.

Reengineering the Collection of Sales Taxes

Most people are not tax cheaters; they are willing to pay the right amount of taxes at the right time. But their efforts to do the right thing are often stymied by indecipherable tax forms and Byzantine procedures.

In 1991, top managers in Minnesota's Department of Revenue decided to change this state of affairs. They decided to shift the department's focus from *catching* taxpayers after they broke the law to *winning* their compliance with the law.

To many of the department's accountants, attorneys, auditors, and other employees, this new goal did not make sense. For years, agency officials had assumed that most businesses wanted to pay as little as they could, even when it meant breaking the law. So they spent half the budget on auditors and tax collectors. Among themselves, employees routinely referred to businesses that paid regularly as "cash cows" and those that didn't as "scumbags."

But the agency's new leaders believed the change would generate even more revenue for the state. "The department's old system focused on the 5 percent of the population that didn't pay," says Connie Nelson, then an assistant commissioner. "We wanted to build a new system that focused on making it easy for people to pay. The goal was 100 percent voluntary compliance."

To accomplish this, they would have to help businesses do a better job of determining their correct tax liability, filing accurate returns, and paying on time. But the system was hardly designed to do this. The state treated all businesses alike: Different businesses got the same tax information and forms, even though the tax laws affected them quite differently. Often the information was out of date, because the department took up to six months to incorporate changes in the tax code. The 20-year-old computer system couldn't keep up with the more than one million annual tax returns, so it took employees months to identify problems with tax returns—and even longer to collect the taxes due. When they audited a business, it could take three years.

Minnesota had created its sales tax 22 years earlier, as a temporary tax. At that time, the department had just added administration of the new tax to its other work, without putting much thought into the design. Two decades later, the tax had settled in as permanent. "It was time to rethink this entirely," Nelson concluded.

One root of these problems was the department's separation into functional silos. Six different divisions, reporting to three different assistant commissioners, shared responsibility for administering the sales tax system. Each "owned" just a single function: One provided information to taxpayers, another processed returns, a third audited returns, and so on. These isolated units rarely coordinated with each other, much less worried about the whole system's performance. No one owned *that* problem.

Nelson and her colleagues identified eight business processes used to administer the sales tax, each with numerous subprocesses. One alone—receiving tax returns and entering the information in agency computers—took 40 days on average. But when the reengineers examined what happened during that time, they found that only *14 hours* was actual "task time." The rest was consumed in handoffs between units and employees.

They realized that no matter how much they tweaked the existing system, it couldn't produce the improved compliance they wanted, because it had not been designed to win compliance. They decided instead to scrap it and start over: to *reengineer* the sales tax. They asked employees to help create and implement a new design, starting with a clean slate.

The reengineers set seemingly impossible goals: The new system should tailor tax returns and information to each business's individual situation and needs; be substantially faster in serving businesses, processing returns, and collecting payments; reduce filing burdens on taxpayers; and turn audits into positive experiences for taxpayers. All of this would lead to an increase in compliance, they believed.

To achieve these goals, Minnesota's reengineers redesigned six major work processes from top to bottom, customized tax returns and filing procedures for individual businesses, replaced functional silos with integrated process teams, empowered front-line employees to make decisions, trained them in customer service, revamped the personnel system, deployed substantial new computer technologies, amended state laws, and marketed the new system to businesses.

After a lengthy implementation period, the new design began to prove itself. Businesses now got customized information and service. They could file electronically. They could get problems solved quickly over the phone. The majority of new sales tax payers could register in an hour—down from six weeks. Nearly all the rest could register in two days or less. They could file and pay their state and local sales taxes together, with one check.

Even businesses that were *audited* now gave the agency high marks for service. In late 1995, the St. Paul *Pioneer Press* reported the results of a state survey. Of more than 500 businesses audited between 1992 and 1994, 97 percent of respondents reported being treated fairly by the service. The department also scored in the 80's and 90's when rated for their consideration of taxpayer's time and their effectiveness in conveying information, including an understanding of taxpayer rights.

Greg Tschida, a department financial analyst who helped lead the reengineering effort, explained why the agency tried to turn audits into an educational experience. "We're looking for future compliance rather than dollars," he says. "I can audit you and get $10,000 this year. But if I teach you to comply the right way, for the next 40 years I get the money up front without any effort on my part."

It was hard to prove whether taxpayer compliance had improved, since there was no scientific way to measure it. But in 1995, the department's traditional backlog of collection cases disappeared.

The Three Phases of BPR

BPR is driven from the top down. Senior managers guide projects from start to finish. Their clout is necessary to authorize the radical changes that emerge. Their expertise and perspective are necessary because middle managers and front-line employees usually only know about their own specialized functions and units, not about larger process flows. In addition, it takes leadership from the top to overcome the inertia and resistance of employees.

Typically, a team of senior managers selects processes for reengineering and establishes performance targets. One member of the steering team serves as the project *sponsor:* the high-level leader who ushers the project through turf wars, protects it from attack, maintains top management's commitment, secures resources for the team, and manages communications with the rest of the agency. A second member serves as the *project manager,* who drives the project and sets up teams of employees to develop process changes.

"You look for risk-takers when filling these and other key roles," says Minnesota's Nelson, who is now our colleague in the Public Strategies Group. "People who, even in bureaucracies, have moved around a lot and had a lot of experience. Don't pick them on the basis of their title, but on their attributes."

No two reengineering initiatives are the same. However, most go through three classic phases: research, redesign, and implementation. Minnesota's reengineers called these stages "Get Curious, Get Crazy, and Get Real."

Phase I: Get Curious
The goal of the research phase is to determine the performance of your current work processes, decide which ones should be reengineered, and set performance targets for the redesigned processes.

Just identifying business processes is often difficult, because they are typically hidden from view—they have been fragmented into those infamous functional silos. This causes "headaches, because it requires people to think across the organizational grain," note Hammer and Champy. "It's not a picture of the organization . . . but a depiction of the work that is being done."

In its research phase, the Minnesota reengineering team interviewed compliers to learn what they went through in complying with the department's requirements. The team met with key legislators and agency managers to determine their goals for the state sales tax. And it questioned fi-

---

PHASES AND STEPS IN A TYPICAL REENGINEERING PROJECT

Phase I: Research ("Get Curious")

1. Identify the organization's mission and goals.
2. Identify existing business processes that support the mission.
3. Assess the performance of existing business processes.
4. Select one or more business processes for reengineering.
5. Establish performance targets for the new business processes.

Phase II: Redesign ("Get Crazy")

1. Start with clean-slate thinking to develop new ideas for design.
2. Select key ideas for the new design; integrate them into a whole-process design.
3. Address related systems such as information technology and human resources.
4. Plan the "migration" to the new process design.

Phase III: Implementation ("Get Real")

1. Secure signoff on the new design by top management.
2. Test key changes on a small scale.
3. Roll out changes in a carefully coordinated sequence.

---

nancial businesses and other state revenue agencies to identify their best practices and performance levels. Groups of employees from different functional units also met to describe their work to each other.

Finally, the team identified the system's major work processes, among them registration, information and education, filing and paying, processing payments, ensuring compliance, and collection enforcement. Then it mapped the flow of work in each one, identifying the sequence of all the steps. No employee or manager knew all of the steps that the work followed—only the steps involved in their special function. As they put together a detailed flow chart, Nelson says, they found out that "a lot of the work they were doing wasn't even used at the next step."

Next, teams decide which processes to reengineer. They look for leverage points: ways to create dramatic improvements for customers and stakeholders. This decision often involves a difficult judgment. If the scope of the project becomes too large, the effort can overwhelm the organization. But if the scope is not sufficiently aggressive, BPR will not produce big results. The trick, says Nelson, is to make the project "large enough to achieve radical breakthroughs, small enough to manage through implementation." Reengineering veterans advise organizations to select processes that are critical to achieving the organization's mission and strategies, that will have the greatest impact on the most customers, that are most urgently in need of repair, and that are most feasible to change radically.

Minnesota's reengineering crew chose to focus on six processes:

- **Registering and profiling taxpayers:** Businesses register to do business in the state; the department collects information about their operations and issues a tax ID number.
- **Filing of tax returns and payments:** Businesses file returns and payments with the agency.
- **Providing taxpayer information and service:** The department helps taxpayers understand sales tax laws, rules, and procedures by giving them information and assistance.
- **Processing business filings:** The department captures information on returns for its electronic databases.
- **Ensuring accuracy of compliance:** The department checks returns to identify taxpayers needing assistance in complying accurately.
- **Ensuring payment and collections:** The department notifies taxpayers of delinquencies and collects overdue payments.

Finally, the team picked stretch targets for the performance of these business processes. "This was the hardest part of the project," says Nelson. "We didn't have any kind of base to work against. Thinking about what performance should be was brand new."

But setting seemingly impossible targets is crucial. "It forces the reengineering design teams to consider alternatives to today's practices," says Nelson. "This aids in the breakthrough thinking process." The targets also give different divisions and units an incentive to lower their walls and coordinate their thinking; otherwise, they can't achieve the ambitious goals.

In setting targets, Nelson says, "you want much more than a 20 to 30 percent improvement—you want at least 100 percent." But the revenue team didn't know how much better performance could get. "We had to go by the seat of our pants," says Nelson. The team developed targets shown in the box on the next page by asking itself what level of performance would satisfy compliers and stakeholders, while helping the organization achieve its overall goal of 100 percent voluntary compliance.

KEY STRETCH TARGETS OF SALES TAX REENGINEERING PROJECT

Process Performance Indicator	Previous Results	Stretch Target
• Time required to process returns completely and accurately	40 days	7 days
• Time required to change forms and instructions after legislative action	180 days	60 days
• Time required to make information about filing available to agency employees	40 days	1 day
• Time required to resolve payment delinquencies	600 days	90 days
• Percentage of taxpayers for whom electronic filing and payment are available	0 percent	90 percent
• Percentage of taxpayers with customized tax returns	0 percent	100 percent

---

Phase II: Get Crazy

Minnesota's steering group created redesign teams for each of the six key processes. Teams had up to 12 members and were led by people assigned to the project full time. The employees attended a three-day training session that kicked off this second phase. Then they began to redesign business processes, identify costs and benefits of the changes, and develop a "migration" plan for moving from old to new processes.

An important part of their orientation was a culture-changing tool we call "surfacing the givens." It helps employees let go of unwritten, often unspoken assumptions about how their organization should function. For example, one of the most important assumptions that surfaced concerned what it meant to be "fair" to taxpayers. Most employees thought it meant treating them all in exactly the same way. Some, including Nelson, argued that processes should be tailored to meet compliers' differing needs. "If someone does not understand what is expected," says Nelson, "you don't just give them the same piece of information you've given everyone else. What if they can't read it or understand it?"

The idea of customizing services challenged yet another assumption: that agency employees were just supposed to follow procedures and rules, not to make their own judgments. If service to compliers were a priority, employees would need the discretion to decide what to do in order to serve them better. Rules couldn't cover every possible situation.

"We threw out all but a few of these assumptions and beliefs," says Nelson. This gave the design teams the freedom to think anew.

Then they brainstormed for ideas that might help achieve the stretch targets. Many involved ways to eliminate steps that were duplicative, time-consuming, or error-prone. Because they were designing ideal processes, not just trying to improve existing processes, they came up with "different and more dramatic ideas," says Nelson. They drew on key principles for design that have been developed by reengineering experts, including:

Organize around outcomes, not tasks. To determine the right outcomes, ask customers (or in this case, compliers) what deliverables they want, then organize processes to create them. See through the customers' eyes. "The customer's voice is the strongest motivator to get people to change," says Nelson. "People want to do a good job. When they hear about customer problems they can fix, they fix them."

Use parallel, not sequential, processes. Abandon step-by-step, assembly-line design; identify activities that can be performed concurrently or on parallel tracks. As Russell Linden points out in *Seamless Government:*

> *The more steps in a process, the greater likelihood of errors, delays, and information falling through the cracks. When each unit works on one aspect of a product and then sends it on to the next unit, there is little ownership and a lot of finger pointing when errors occur. A parallel process speeds up the outcome and allows errors to be caught much sooner.*

Finally, the teams put their ideas together, integrating them into a coherent whole. They rested on two pillars. First, taxpaying businesses would be treated according to their different needs and their past payment performance. Second, "Employees will have more responsibility to resolve taxpayer issues, and the resources needed to do so." They will have "greater authority and opportunity . . . to work a given job through to completion. People will be able to solve problems on the spot instead of sending cases on to another unit."

Then the team tackled the related issues that their redesign surfaced: how best to use information technology, the design of new jobs, personnel system changes needed to make the new process work, and the development of a system to measure their performance.

Last, they developed a migration plan that spelled out the pace, sequence, and cost of the changes. They also specified how the system should transition to new job designs, information and communications systems, and technologies, and how the agency should let compliers know about changes.

In August 1992 the reengineers presented department executives with a 67-page redesign proposal. It identified scores of specific changes necessary to bring the new design to life, including:

- development of customized tax returns and forms, procedures, instruction booklets, and self-assessment kits for taxpayers;
- extensive training in customer service skills, dispute resolution, information gathering, new sales tax procedures, new technologies, and new job skills;
- creation of a new job classification, a "revenue tax specialist," to provide particular taxpayers with information, education, and services;
- first-time use of networked computer workstations, extensive new software and database capacity, two-way electronic communications systems, and scanning and imaging technologies;
- elimination of numerous filing requirements;
- new methods for employee evaluations;
- amendments to a handful of state laws;
- a marketing campaign to sell the new processes to business associations and individual taxpayers; and
- special education classes for tax professionals.

The team was proposing an enormous amount of change for the sales-tax employees, and they knew it. They estimated that the transformation would cost $3.2 million, not including employee time.

Phase III: Get Real

The Minnesota reengineers realized that they had taken on more changes than the revenue agency could swallow in one bite. They broke down implementation of the redesign into 14 separate "releases," each of which put one important change in place, over a period of about two years.

A half-dozen implementation teams, often meeting daily, worked on getting ready for the releases. They tested several key changes on a small scale first to make sure they would work.

Gradually, they reconfigured the agency's organization chart, replacing most functional divisions and units with streamlined, integrated work processes. They redesigned jobs and helped employees and managers adjust to new assignments. They relocated most staffers whose jobs were eliminated, although a few were laid off. The teams conducted training, bought new technology, and developed a computerized communications network that 300 employees used to swap ideas and keep up on progress. They fixed glitches with the new information technology—the document scanner had trouble with the forms for sales-tax returns, for instance—and they worked with legislators to ensure political and financial support for the changes.

In August 1993, the agency installed its new registration and profiling process, the first big implementation step. By late 1995, all six new processes were hitting most of their once unthinkable targets.

Each taxpaying business had an individual profile and a return customized to its unique situation, which cut by 70 percent the time it took to electronically process the information. Payment problems were resolved within 90 days. Nearly 60 percent of new business registrations—which had formerly taken six weeks—now took an hour. The agency implemented four changes in sales-tax law, not over a period of months, but in just a few days.

For the first time, new businesses could register by telephone or fax—an option more than half of them used. Taxpayers had to file 400,000 fewer returns each year, a 35 percent reduction. They could pay 28 state and local taxes with one form and one check. And the accuracy of information they filed had increased to 98 percent.

BPR Projects in Government: Lessons Learned

Reengineering is difficult work. It's tough to start with a clean slate in government. Some legislative, executive, or judicial mandates may be unavoidable. Lawmakers who like to micromanage agencies will get in the way. Often several agencies share pieces of a business process, but won't cooperate in reengineering it. Because their tenure is limited, political appointees who run agencies are on the lookout for short-term initiatives, and they shy away from risky, drawn-out reengineering efforts.

Any one of many different stakeholders—middle managers, unions, interest groups, central agency officials, and legislators—can block a project or throw it off course. Since top managers often hop to new jobs, it's hard to keep an organization's leadership focused on top-to-bottom transformation.

Our research into government experience with BPR identified a set of key lessons successful reengineers have learned, all of which help overcome these potential roadblocks.

Secure—and maintain—top management buy-in. "Don't begin without top executive support," says Connie Nelson. Only they can secure resources and political support for the project. It is only their visible enthusiasm that will convince managers and employees to take risks. And make sure they understand reengineering. Take them to visit sites that have used it. As the project unfolds, keep them in the information loop.

Anticipate employee anxiety about downsizing. Half of the companies in the 1994 *State of Reengineering Report* by CSC Index reported that the most difficult part of reengineering was employee anxiety about losing one's job. The same problem occurs in government. Some agencies combat it by pledging that there will be no layoffs for those employees whose jobs are eliminated; instead, they will be retrained and transferred.

Anticipate the need to redesign administrative systems. As Minnesota's revenue reengineers learned, to redesign work processes you must often re-design the personnel and information systems. "We started with the work flow and ended up saying that everything has to change," remembers Joe Thompson, director of New York City's regional veterans' office. "If you don't change the way you compensate and measure performance, if you just try to change work flow, you'll fall short."

Secure political support. Organizations can't hide reengineering projects from elected officials; the work involves too many people and is too disrup-tive. It's best to develop political support at the front end of the project, so it is in place when radical changes come to the table. Managers normally have to ask elected officials for the resources they need to reengineer, anyway. The Minnesota team built key legislators into their project from the begin-ning, by treating them as important stakeholders. They asked the politi-cians what their goals for the sales tax system were, then included those ob-jectives as part of the project. They briefed legislators every 90 days on the project's progress. Few politicians will turn up a chance to take credit for dramatic improvements in government's performance, so it also helps to produce some short-term improvements, so elected officials don't have to wait two or three years before they can claim success.

Involve the union. To smooth the way for reengineering, seek union par-ticipation at the beginning of the project and, if you're dealing with reason-able union leaders, let them share in decisionmaking. At a minimum, keep them well informed of where the project is heading and how it will get there. Typically, unions will be most concerned about how the project will change job descriptions and classifications and whether it will lead to lay-offs. At the start of the project, no one knows the answer to those questions, so be candid. If union leaders don't trust the managers, they will suspect the worst—and resist.

Use outsiders—consultants, customers, legislators, and employees in other agencies—to help your organization think outside the box. Hammer and Champy say a ratio of one outsider to every two or three insiders is about right, so bring in people with a fresh perspective who are willing to challenge the status quo, and make them part of your reengineering teams. Encourage them to ask naive questions and to shatter assumptions. Each of Minnesota's redesign teams included human "yeast"—someone with no knowledge of the existing process.

Imagine that the slate is clean, even if it's not. In *Seamless Government*, Linden advises that even if you cannot escape the constraints of laws and rules, you should imagine you have a clean slate. "The point is to unleash as much creativity as possible and allow seemingly outlandish ideas to flourish," he says. "If the design team can brainstorm in the most freewheeling and playful way possible, it will find breakthrough ideas lurking within apparently ludicrous ones."

When the reengineering team in New York's veterans' office launched its project, Director Joe Thompson set the stage for new thinking. "I gave them this proposition: If you were a company and had to compete against other companies to provide the same service, what would you design? I said, reality will temper you from ideal design, but let's start out with ideal design."

As Linden says, brainstorm first, then check ideas carefully against possible constraints.

Communicate to the whole organization about BPR. A reengineering project is a big, sustained, and frightening event in the life of an organization. Rumors and misinformation will fly. Put good information into employees' hands through newsletters, expert presentations, project briefings, and other forums through which people can get questions answered. Nelson's reengineers adopted a communications philosophy they called "the Three O's": make it "Open, Often, and 'Onest." They used electronic bulletin boards to share information and to identify questions and issues that employees had.

But even these efforts couldn't satisfy everyone's needs for information. "The most frequent question from the employees was, 'What will happen to my job?'" Nelson says. "We were not able to answer that question during Phase II. That inability was sometimes heard as 'hiding the truth,' rather than the fact that it was the truth." Again, one solution is to pledge, if you can honestly do so, that reengineering will not lead to layoffs. Another is to put rank-and-file workers on the steering team, so that they can see for themselves that leaders are being honest when they say that they don't know what will happen to jobs.

Watch out for "paralysis by analysis." Reengineering depends on a great deal of analysis. But reengineering consultants and experienced practitioners caution that most organizations go overboard trying to produce detailed models of their current processes. "Extensive analysis," say Hammer and Stanton, "is a profound waste of time":

> *Through analysis you will create a huge, detailed description of how the existing process operates, which you will then proceed to throw away. . . . Too much time spent on analysis and documentation can cripple the imagination. You become so focused on the old way of doing things that you can no longer conceive of any other way.*

Minnesota's revenue reengineers adopted a rule of thumb: Understand enough about existing processes to make decisions. "Further work gives you greater precision, but doesn't add additional value to the decision-making process," Nelson says.

Hammer and Stanton advise reengineers to put a limit—a "time box"—on how long they will analyze existing processes. Four to six weeks is usually "enough time to achieve the level of understanding necessary for reengineering," they say.

Keep up the pace. Because reengineering takes a relatively long time, the risk of losing momentum is high. "If a project slows down too much," says Nelson, "the agency may get tired of being bold; it may lose courage."

Hammer and Stanton say that a project should not take more than a year before producing some results. "If you let a reengineering effort drag on for more than a year" without some concrete business benefits, they warn, "it will die. Executive management will lose faith and begin to withdraw its funding."

When Minnesota's BPR project began in 1991, Don Trimble, then a division manager, worried that it was just another management fad. "I'm the type of person that questions things when [top managers] make too much of a big deal about it," he explains. "There was a whole lot of drum beating going on back then." At staff meetings, Trimble openly expressed skepticism.

Yet he was involved in the project's first phase. That's when he began to agree that a total redesign was needed. "The case made sense to me," he says. "But the goals and outcomes seemed fairly aggressive. . . . It scared me."

Still, when a project co-leader left the agency, Trimble took the position and steered the BPR team through Phase II. It wasn't easy. "Putting everything on paper is one thing; when you start doing it is another. Even when we signed off on the design, I don't think anybody had in mind how the reorganization—the new look—was going to occur."

By 1996, though, the radical process designs and impossible performance targets of 1991–1992 had become the accepted way of doing business. The agency had taken a huge leap forward, and its members now understood what it meant to "work smarter." Trimble summed it up well: "Reengineering prepared us for the future."

And that may be the most valuable thing smarter work processes do.

PART FIVE

SMARTER LEADERSHIP

Managing Change
from the Radical Center

FOURTEEN

Leadership for a Change

When Peter Hutchinson was superintendent of the Minneapolis public schools, his favorite activity was visiting classrooms. One day, in a fourth grade classroom, the teacher stopped the class to introduce him. She explained that he was the superintendent of schools and asked the class if anyone knew what a superintendent was.

Hands flew into the air. (Fourth graders are so enthusiastic about learning that they will take a stab at any question.) The teacher called on an eager young man who proudly announced that the superintendent was the guy in charge of Super Nintendo. The teacher allowed as how that was a very creative answer, then explained that the superintendent was the leader of the schools.

"Does anyone know what a leader is?" she asked. Hands flew again. The teacher called on a young girl in the back who was raising her hand so hard and high that Peter was afraid it might become detached from her body. She stood very straight and tall as she answered, "A leader is someone who goes out and changes things to make things better." Hutchinson was stunned: A fourth grader had articulated perfectly what government needs—and what people expect.

If the path to "making things better" were not strewn with so many obstacles, more people might rise to the challenge. But today, our public institutions are mired in the worst fiscal crisis since World War II, citizens are cynical and the media is worse, the political process alternates between banalities and vicious personal attacks, and many politicians actively campaign against the very institutions they say they want to lead. Costs are rising out of control, but the price of government is limited. Who in his or her right mind would want the job of leader?

Unfortunately, too many of those who step forward are driven either by ego or ideology. They come in a number of flavors. There are those who want to *be* something more than they want to *do* something. They have had a burning desire to be a "leader" since they were lunchroom monitors in grade school. The trouble is, this type will rarely risk their political popularity to actually reform the systems they lead.

Others are more complacent. They have secured a comfortable position of leadership and they want to keep it, so they say that government is good enough, or that we're working as hard as we can, or that the problems are someone else's fault. They are in serious denial. Their objective is to further secure their own position, but every day they let down that fourth grader, along with everyone else who looks to leaders to "make things better."

Then there are the traditional liberals who promise to make things better but aren't willing to do what it takes to change them. They are motivated by their concern for others, but they won't take on their friends in the teachers' unions and public employee unions, who so often block change. Nor will they risk alienating voters who benefit from programs that work poorly or waste money. They fight tooth and nail against reform of programs—like public housing and the old welfare system—that are clearly producing terrible outcomes, for fear that reform will hurt some of the poor. We do not question their motives, but they too are in denial: They don't recognize that the system is fundamentally flawed. Many still believe that throwing money at the system and trying harder will produce results. They too let down that fourth grader, by talking about big dreams, then not being willing to shake off their liberal straitjackets to get results.

Finally, there are the ideological conservatives. Many of them want to change the system, but they don't want to make it better, for fear that people will want more of what government has to offer. They let down that fourth grader by telling her that government is the enemy. They urge us to "starve the beast" financially, so that it will be too weak to impinge on private enterprise. They are in denial about the essential role of government as the referee in a market economy. They are so fixated on the ideas of individual initiative and freedom that they ignore the equally compelling role of community and collective support in a market economy. With 20/20 tunnel vision, they disparage the contributions made by public education, public health, Social Security, Medicare, Medicaid, and environmental protection in maintaining a decent society. At the same time, they take for granted—and therefore vastly undervalue—the essential role of government in creating and maintaining our roads and highways, our air travel system, our legal system, our banking system, our system of corporate finance, and the other regulatory systems that help sustain the economy by tempering its excesses.

In the end, all of these "leaders" merely perpetuate the crisis, because perpetuating the crisis is in each of their interests.

To get ourselves out of this mess, we need leaders who abhor the status quo but are not prisoners of ideology; leaders who are driven to deliver better results at a price citizens are willing to pay; leaders who are willing to charge citizens the real price of government in return for real value; leaders who have the common sense to dismount the dead horse of bureaucracy but the courage to search out a stronger steed.

The kind of leadership we need comes from the "radical center." Ideologically neither left nor right, this is not split-the-difference centrism. The leaders we need do not inhabit the mushy middle. They have staked out an entirely new political paradigm—the "Third Way" that President Clinton, Prime Minister Tony Blair, and other modern leaders have popularized. They take a commonsense view of the world but have the gumption to foment radical change. To deliver on government's traditional ends, they are willing to fundamentally alter the means: the structure and operation of public systems.

Public leadership has never been easy, and in the days ahead it will only get more difficult. Fortunately, there are examples in our midst of leaders who have succeeded, or who are succeeding. These leaders can serve as sources of hope and guidance. From them we can learn essential lessons about winning the battle for public support in an age of permanent fiscal crisis.

FIRST, TELL THE TRUTH

Twenty-five years of spin doctors, pollsters, and thoroughly managed media has only increased the public's appetite for the truth. Voters are sick of platitudes, weasel words, equivocations, and outright lies. In 1976, after the lies of Watergate, Jimmy Carter was the first modern candidate who won by pledging to tell the truth ("I will never lie to you"). In 1992, both independent Ross Perot and Democrat Paul Tsongas positioned themselves as leaders who brought us the hard truth, unvarnished. In 2000 it was John McCain's turn, with his "Straight Talk Express" in the Republican primaries. The same phenomenon occurred in state and local politics: Jesse Ventura in Minnesota, Angus King in Maine, and Lowell Weicker in Connecticut all won governorships as independent candidates who rose above politics-as-usual to confront the hard realities. The late Minnesota Senator Paul Wellstone became a hero to some for saying things politicians normally don't say. And in the run-up to the 2004 primaries, Howard Dean surged beyond far better known candidates because of his straight talk and outsider status. Only when the other candidates began to imitate him did they catch up.

The carefully manicured phrasing of typical political discourse has become so pervasive, and so numbing, that voters respond with eager delight to the novelty of a candidate simply speaking his mind. Americans crave leaders who will speak to them as mature and thoughtful adults. They do not want their leaders to flinch from open discussion of fiscal reality when voters are "in the room." They can deal with bad news. They simply want leaders who will level with them. And more often than not, they can tell when talk is on the level and when it is smoke and mirrors.

"Never fall into the trap of selling the public short," says Roger Douglas, a radical centrist leader in New Zealand. As finance minister for New Zealand's Labor Party, Douglas faced a fiscal crisis that makes ours pale by comparison. His nation had been in decline for a generation. In 1950, New Zealanders had the third-highest per capita income in the world; by 1984, they were twenty-first. Their national budget alone consumed more than 40 percent of GDP. Heavy borrowing had driven annual inflation up to 15 percent, and interest on the national debt ate up almost 20 percent of the budget. Upon coming to power in 1984, Douglas's Labor government came within a hair's breadth of defaulting on the national debt. The Reserve Bank of New Zealand had to suspend foreign-exchange transactions, and the government had to devalue the national currency by 20 percent. Over the next six years it proceeded to lead the most radical transformation of a modern democratic government ever undertaken.

And yet Douglas and his colleagues did not gild the lily, sweeten the medicine, or soften the blow. As Douglas advises:

> *Structural reform does not become possible until you trust, respect, and inform the electors. You have to put them in a position to make sound judgments about what is going on.*
>
> *Tell the public, and never stop telling them, right up front:*
>
> - *What the problem is and how it arose.*
> - *What damage it is doing to their own personal interests.*
> - *What your own objectives are in tackling it.*
> - *What the costs and the benefits of that action will be.*
> - *Why your approach will work better than the other options.*

Ordinary people may not understand the situation in all its technical detail, but they have a lifetime of experience at work and at home to help them sift the wheat from the chaff. They know when key questions are being evaded. They can sense when they are being patronized or conned, and do not like it. They respect people who front up honestly to their questions.

As Douglas suggests, the ways of government can be arcane. The numbers politicians talk about are huge, and the programs are often clouded by jargon and acronyms. But if you can't state your case in plain language, citizens will believe that you don't know what you are talking about—or worse, that you don't want them to know.

Most citizens have what Ernest Hemingway once called a "crap detector." It operates according to a very simple algorithm:

Do I understand what the politicians are saying?

Does it mean anything?

And if so, do they mean what they say?

Telling the truth in plain language is how we communicate that we have a grip on what we are facing. Getting a grip is the first step in changing things to make them better. Without a grip on the facts—even the brutal facts—leaders fall back on unwarranted hopes or outright deception. If you don't have a grip, you shouldn't be leading.

MAKE YOUR PURPOSE CLEAR AND PURSUE IT RELENTLESSLY

On January 18, 1994, Peter Hutchinson was returning from the movies with his wife. A month earlier he and his colleagues at PSG had been appointed superintendent of the Minneapolis public schools. A private company leading a school district under a contract that paid them only if student achievement actually improved? This had never been done before. And the jury was still out.

As they drove home the radio announced that it was cold—record cold—with a wind chill that made it feel 60 to 70 degrees below zero. Hutchinson said to his wife, "I wonder what superintendents do when it's this cold?" He found the answer when he got home: 54 messages demanding that he close schools the next day, with more calls coming in by the minute.

PSG had been hired for one simple reason: The school district was in trouble. Achievement gains were shrinking and finances were in a shambles. PSG was expected to fix both—and fast. As Hutchinson and his colleagues prepared for this work, the question of how to decide whether to close or open schools had never come up. Luckily, they got a reprieve when the governor ordered every school in the state closed.

The next day was another matter. Hutchinson made his way to the superintendent's office and spent several hours answering the phones—first from the police, who reported hundreds of immigrant children waiting for buses without coats or mittens, because they had not gotten the word. Thanks to the police, these kids were already on their way home. Then more calls from parents, students, and teachers clamoring for another day off tomorrow, since the record cold was forecast to continue. Then calls from the press, who wanted to know if the schools were being led by a bunch of wimps. Closing school in Minnesota because it's *cold?*

As the day wore on, the mix of calls began to change. Increasingly, Hutchinson heard from distressed parents who expected him to "get these damned kids back in school." By the end of the day the calls were split, and emotions were high. One faction saw opening the schools in such hostile weather as something only a fool would do, while the other saw keeping kids home for another day as an attack on parental sanity and a huge hassle for those without daycare alternatives.

As Hutchinson contemplated what to do, he had an epiphany. It didn't matter what he decided; either way he was going to be ripped apart. In that realization was his liberation. He saw clearly that in the face of polarized opinion, a leader is free to do what he or she believes is right, since criticism will follow regardless of the choice. All that really matters are the eventual results of his or her decision.

This is not a license to act arbitrarily; quite the opposite. It requires that leaders embody the mission and goals of the organization they serve—and reinforce them with every decision they make.

On his second day at the district, Hutchinson had asked his assistant to get him a copy of the mission statement. A couple of weeks later, someone had unearthed it from a dusty file. It was several pages long, and to Hutchinson's dismay, it lacked focus: Nowhere did it say what difference the schools would make for the children they served. With the support of the school board, PSG crafted a new statement of purpose: "The mission of the Minneapolis Schools is to ensure that all children learn." That mission statement became the foundation for *every* action that PSG took. Hutchinson and his colleagues repeated it and interpreted it relentlessly for three and a half years. They challenged everyone—teachers, custodians, bus drivers, aides, administrators, board members, parents, and community leaders—to figure out how *they* would, in fact, ensure that all students learn.

This relentless focus on "ensuring that all children learn" produced a turnaround in student achievement. The average annual gain in reading scores, for example, was on the decline when the mission statement was written. Students were still gaining ground, but the rate was slowing. On norm-based tests, if a student starts the year at the 50th percentile, it takes a year's worth of growth to stay in the 50th percentile by year's end. Minneapolis students were gaining about two percentiles a year, on average, which was not bad for an urban district. But given that they were starting out below the national average, it was not good enough for the board or the community. Four years later the rate had tripled, to a six percentile gain. Attendance rates were up, and suspension rates were down. On a 1996 referendum to increase property taxes by $160 million for the schools, 70 percent voted yes.

So on that cold day in January, what first appeared as a tough choice was, in fact, very easy. If ensuring that all students learn was the mission, being in school was the means to that end. School would be open for business.

FRAME EVERYTHING IN TERMS OF RESULTS

After defining their mission, leaders need to flesh out that statement by identifying the key outcomes they are trying to produce, as we discussed in Part I. They need to ensure that progress on those outcomes is measured, and they need to frame everything they do in terms of that mission and those results. In the Minneapolis school district, PSG's contract was based on results: All but $65,000 a year depended upon improving student achievement, public confidence in the schools, and other outcome goals. At Hutchinson's prodding, the district created a set of high learning standards for all students; testing aligned to those standards; reports on achievement gaps between students of different racial and socioeconomic groups (something done in few other places but essential for accountability); and quarterly reports on performance in the areas of student achievement, the learning climate, family involvement, community confidence, the attraction and retention of students, instructional effectiveness, suspensions and disciplinary events, graduation and dropout rates, and management. Every school got an annual performance report, spelling out its students' average annual gain in reading and math, its suspension and disciplinary rates, its graduation and dropout rates (for high schools), and its turnover rate for students. All of this was public information, and Hutchinson talked about it constantly.

To be effective in today's world, leaders have to go beyond good intentions, wishes, and excuses that there isn't enough money. Virtually every government and every school district is squeezed for money—and will continue to be. Budget cuts and tax increases are the currency of the day. As a consequence, the public is cranky, and incumbent executives are at great risk—whether they are elected or appointed by elected officials.

The only way out of this trap is through a door labeled *results*. Leaders need to frame every debate and every decision in terms of the results they are trying to achieve—not needs, not wants, not the way it has always been, but *results*. Framing the discussion this way lets everyone know—both citizens and government insiders—what is most important. It also reinforces a culture of accountability throughout the public sector.

Governor Locke learned this lesson in Washington State, as we have explained. After six years in which he had earned an image more as a technician than a leader, he confronted the fiscal crisis head on. The tool he used was an Outcomes Budget, framed around the 10 results he felt were most important to the citizens of Washington. This act, and the decisions that flowed from it, changed his image, gave him new stature with the public and new power with the legislature, and reinvigorated his administration.

Beverly Stein spent *eight years* focusing on results as county executive and chair of the Multnomah County Board of Commissioners. As a Democratic state legislator, Stein had been a leader in creating the Oregon Progress Board and the Oregon Benchmarks, a set of long-term outcome goals for the state. When she was elected county commissioner and executive in 1993, she was determined to do the same for Multnomah County—but also to *use* those benchmarks to transform the entire county government. As we reported in Chapter 3, Stein and her fellow commissioners first chose 85 county benchmarks, then narrowed it down to 12 "urgent benchmarks," then narrowed it further to three real priorities, called "long-term benchmarks": increasing high school completion rates, reducing the percentage of children living in poverty, and reducing crime.

Stein redesigned the budget around the benchmarks, presenting outcome data on every program and identifying which programs aligned with each benchmark. She cut every department's budget, but told them they could earn money back by developing new strategies to achieve the benchmarks. She launched a quality initiative with the acronym RESULTS, which we will describe in the next section. She hired coordinators to focus on specific benchmarks, such as teen pregnancy. She convened meetings between the board and department heads to help choose "key results" for all 300 county programs. She published reports on progress against the benchmarks in her budgets. She asked each of her fellow commissioners to take ownership of one long-term benchmark, in partnership with a larger group (the County Commission on Children and Families, the Community Action Commission, and the Public Safety Coordinating Council). She and they sponsored public forums on each of the three benchmarks, at which board members, staff, and others reviewed current strategies to achieve the benchmark; examined information about best practices elsewhere, demographic data, and other research; and discussed new strategies for the county.

When a tax limitation initiative forced budget cuts, she and the board targeted their cuts on programs making the least contributions to the benchmarks. She also moved money into new strategies to achieve long-term benchmarks, such as a major initiative that was successful in boosting school attendance. She and her fellow commissioners even used the benchmarks to develop criteria for granting tax abatements to recruit and retain businesses.

For eight years Stein framed everything in terms of the results she was trying to achieve. In virtually every speech, she talked about the county's three most important benchmarks. And when she resigned in 2001 to run for the Democratic nomination for governor, the Portland *Oregonian*, the state's largest-circulation newspaper, summed it up this way:

> *In eight years running the county government, Stein has increased its efficiency, effectiveness, and sensitivity to its children in particular. She achieved this at a time when Oregon's counties took the biggest hit from Measure 5 of any level of government.*
>
> *. . . Stein can fairly claim to have given county taxpayers more for their money—and more for their children.*
>
> *Wherever she goes next, Multnomah County residents can be glad Bev Stein was here.*

Multnomah County has 1.5 million residents. New York City has 8 million—and a decade ago it was widely considered almost ungovernable. But Republican Mayor Rudy Giuliani proved otherwise. "I tried to run the city as a business, using business principles to impose accountability on government," he says in the preface to his book, *Leadership*. "Objective, measurable indicators of success allow government to be accountable, and I relentlessly pursued that idea."

Giuliani's excellent book is organized around 14 lessons about leadership. The third is, "Everyone's Accountable, All of the Time." In his career, Giuliani says, accountability for performance "is the cornerstone." In trying to build an accountable government, he "decided to start with the highest profile agency, one whose performance could be measured not just in the savings of dollars, but in the saving of lives." Those who have read Chapter 8 will recognize his method: "The centerpiece of our efforts," he writes, "was a process called Compstat."

> *This combined two techniques, neither of which had previously been implemented. First, crime statistics were collected and analyzed every single day, to recognize patterns and potential trouble before it spread. At the Compstat meetings, we used that data to hold each borough command's feet to the fire—a hundred police at a time, from brass to officers, joined by others from throughout the criminal justice system, would be convened in a big room in which every one of that command's statistics faced scrutiny. . . .*
>
> *Even after eight years, I remain electrified by how effective those Compstat meetings could be. It became the crown jewel of my administration's push for accountability.*

Giuliani talked constantly about Compstat. It became the best-known public management initiative in the country. And he replicated it in 20 city agencies.

In September 1990, three years before Giuliani was elected, *Time* magazine had run a cover story with the headline, "The Rotting of the Big Apple." It reported that according to polls, 59 percent of residents would leave the city if they could.

When Giuliani left office, things were different. The crime rate was down by 57 percent, shootings by 75 percent, robbery by 62.5 percent. Inmate-on-inmate violence in the jails was down 93 percent. The welfare rolls had fallen by 60 percent. The rate of home ownership had risen by more than 10 percent. Citizens rated 85 percent of city streets "acceptably clean." The city had reduced or eliminated 23 city taxes, saving individuals and businesses a total of $8 billion. The city payroll was down by 20,000 full-time employees, but the number of teachers and uniformed police were both up. Tourist visits had risen from 25.8 million a year to 37.4 million, and *Zagat's* had named New York as the best city to visit in the nation. More than 200 new businesses had opened in Harlem. In 2000, for the second time in four years,

Fortune magazine had named New York City the number one place for business in North America. And despite the September 11 terrorist attacks, every city resident we know felt there had been a renaissance.

That renaissance happened because Mayor Giuliani focused relentlessly on results. If it can be done in New York, it can be done anywhere.

GET BACK TO THE CORE

In a time of crisis, whether fiscal or otherwise, smart leaders bring everyone's focus back to what really matters.

Mission creep is endemic in government. The job of the legislature, in the eyes of legislators, is to pass laws. So they do. A good way to help people—and distinguish oneself as an effective legislator—is to create new programs, so they do that, too. For a political résumé, passing laws and creating programs is far more appealing than repealing laws and killing programs, so the statute books thicken. Often, if one program is not quite working, the response is to add another, and another, and another. But each new law and each new program adds new work.

While no single change may be that dramatic, the accumulation of add-ons can cause an organization to completely lose focus. It can end up creating a flurry of activity but missing the central point.

As we described in the Introduction, Washington State faces permanent limits on revenue and spending growth and rising costs for the core activities of the state: "education, medication, and incarceration." Governor Locke decided the time had come to ask the big question: What should state government do and what should it stop doing? He and his staff defined 10 outcomes most important to the citizens, decided which state activities contributed the most to those outcomes, and left the rest out of the budget. They made some hard choices, but because they chose clear priorities rooted in results, the public, the media, and the legislature supported most of their decisions. Most citizens understood that it was time to define the state's priorities and let the rest fall away.

Mayor Giuliani puts it well:

The reality is that there's only so much a city government can do—or should do. A dollar spent on a benevolent-sounding program is a dollar not spent somewhere else. A good leader establishes priorities and sticks to them, backing them with resources to carry them out. Sometimes the best way to fulfill those priorities is to remove the distractions—and expenses—that keep them

from being fulfilled. . . . One of my immediate goals was to streamline the
government to allow us to focus on our major priorities.

BE INTENSELY DRIVEN BY A PASSION
FOR YOUR CUSTOMERS

Any serious consideration of core purpose leads leaders back to the question: Who are our customers and what do they want from us?

Some people are still thrown by the use of "customer" in the context of government. Obviously, government has very few instances in which a consumer comes in with five dollars, hands it to the person behind the cash register, and walks out with a loaf of bread, a carton of milk, and a dozen eggs. And we agree that the concept of "citizen" is more important, in a democracy, than the concept of "customer." Citizens are government's owners; by voting, they elect representatives to steer the ship of state. But citizens are also government's customers, when they use public services or benefit from compliance activities. Voting rarely gives them much leverage over the quality of those services and activities. The truth is that leaders can fully address the needs of their citizens only if they also pay attention to what the customers of specific services want.

In government, as we discussed in Chapter 6, the primary customers of an organization are the *principal intended beneficiaries* of its work. If you are a schoolteacher, your primary customers are your students and their parents. If you are in law enforcement or environmental protection, your primary customers are the public at large. While you may spend your time interacting with criminals or businesses, these are not your customers. They are, instead, *compliers:* those who must abide by the laws and regulations that you enforce.

Organizations that lose sight of their customers inevitably will lose sight of their core purpose as well. Organizations also lose their way when they put the needs of other stakeholders—contractors, unions, special interest groups, politicians—ahead of the needs of their customers. They have lost their way:

- when a school board spends more time on union issues than reading scores;
- when a Department of Transportation's employees think their customers are the contractors who build the roads rather than the people who drive on them; or

- when a city builds plush new offices but cannot repair its streets or
  pick up its garbage.

When organizations lose sight of their primary customers, they also lose
sight of their core passion. Given that the driving force for public employees
is not profit but a desire to serve, few losses could be more devastating.

When this happens, the solution is to reestablish focus on and connec-
tion with customers: to listen to them, provide the quality they demand,
and give them the control and choices they want, as we explained in Chapter 9. We cannot win the competition for public support if we lose sight of
the public we are supposed to serve.

Early on in his tenure at General Electric, CEO Jack Welch described his
company as one "with its face to the CEO and its ass to the customer." The
Office of Federal Student Aid was a public-sector organization with much
the same orientation. As we explained in Chapter 11, FSA runs the student
loan and grant programs of the federal government. When Greg Woods took
over FSA, in late 1998, it was struggling with high defaults, high costs, and
low morale. As the federal government's first "performance-based organization," it had been granted freedom from some internal rules in return for increased accountability. For Woods and his team, that meant a five-year contract to perform.

Early on, Woods recognized that the central problem at FSA was confusion over whom it served. For many employees, it looked and felt as if the
banks were the customers and the students were a pain in the organization's posterior. Almost immediately, Woods created a customer service task
force to develop a strategy to transform the organization. The task force
struggled until its leader, Stephen Blair, decided to load all 50 members on a
bus and take them to some nearby college campuses. He told them to go
talk with students about their experience with the financial aid system.
They heard some scathing responses, and they learned firsthand the power
of financial aid to change a student's life. They came back highly energized,
with scores of ideas about how to improve the system. Five years later,
many of them still pointed to that bus trip as a seminal moment.

The task force developed a series of recommendations to improve service by making the loan and grant process more customer-friendly. As we described in Chapter 11, the tools included Web-based applications, simplified forms, readable language, and help desks.

Woods launched the new strategy in a huge auditorium, with FSA employees on folding chairs, facing a stage. He took the stage and began the
traditional talk-fest that passes for a strategy session within a bureaucracy.

He hadn't gotten far when he told the assembled staff that the key to FSA's "turnaround" was to . . . turn around . . . and see their customers. He literally asked them to stand up and turn their chairs around. When they did so, they faced the real front of the room, where a panel of students sat ready to talk about how student loans could change a life and how the loan process could be improved. The effect was electric.

Thus began years of hard work, challenging every aspect of FSA to make it serve its customers. The results, as we saw in Chapter 11, have been as dramatic as the "turning point" Woods staged in that auditorium.

BE WILLING TO CHANGE EVERYTHING BUT YOUR VALUES

If the job of a leader is to "change things to make them better," everything must be open to question—everything but the organization's basic values.

This is easy to say but hard to do. Resistance to change can be fierce; it is deeply embedded in every organization. The first law of organizational inertia proclaims that an organization will stay as it is unless compelled to change—whether by inspired leadership, stepped-up competition, dramatic economic decline, the encroachment of a disruptive technology, or some other external threat.

Much of this resistance is driven by people's fears that their values are being threatened. As we said in Chapter 12, citizens and those who serve them expect that governments will be fair, honest, equitable, efficient, and accountable, and that they will make decisions based on merit, not favoritism. These are the core values on which public services are based. Employees will accept and, in fact, initiate much more change if they can see how it will both make the customers better off and preserve these values. If serving customers is what ignites someone's passions, then maintaining integrity with core values sustains the burn.

To drive change, effective leaders seize on—and sometimes even invent—external threats. The most powerful of these, of course, is the threat of extinction. The University of Minnesota's campus at Crookston, a two-year agricultural school 100 miles south of the Canadian border, resisted change until the statewide system closed one of its other satellite campuses and the university president began eyeing Crookston with the same notion. In the twinkling of an eye in university time, Crookston embraced change and remade itself into a high-tech outpost at which every student had a laptop computer. It was so successful that it dramatically increased its enrollment even while it raised its price. Once known affectionately as Moo U, it soon had a new nickname: Thinkpad U.

But while it was the threat to the school's existence that made this transformation possible, it was an entrepreneurial chancellor who led it. The chancellor was Don Sargeant, and his key concept was "self-directed learning." His key innovation—the disruptive technology—was the laptop computer. In 1993, Sargeant and his colleagues required every student to lease a laptop for $750 a year—a 25 percent increase in the price students paid. Nonetheless, in three years the number of full-time students increased by 22 percent—from 927 to 1,133.

Pervasive use of computers required that Crookston remodel classrooms to include power sources and network connections at each seat and provide all dorm rooms and common rooms with network access. But the true transformation took place in the minds and methods of the staff. Upon realizing that their students would be armed with laptops come fall, faculty members spent the summer "cramming" about computers. When the students showed up, the faculty was about a week ahead of them. All year they sprinted to stay ahead of their customers—a process that had a huge impact on the culture.

On surveys completed in 1996, more than 80 percent of the faculty said that the laptops had stimulated changes in how they taught and the resources they used, and nearly 60 percent said that they had become better teachers as a result. But perhaps the most fundamental change was in how faculty viewed their students and the learning process. "Where before they tended to think teaching was about them doing the best job of presenting information to the student—it was in their control—now they realize a lot of the process is actually in the student's control," Sargeant told us. "It requires more projects, more interactivity."

But change need not always be compelled by threat. It can also be powered by reigniting an organization's passion for its customers, within the crucible of its core values. When the customers demand improvement, those who care about serving them will drive the change themselves. That's the energy that Greg Woods galvanized when he put FSA's staff face-to-face with their customers.

CREATE AN ORGANIZATION OF LEADERS

Leadership is not just about the top of an organization. Obviously, the more power the top leader has, the easier it is to make changes. But top leaders can't move organizations unless they have leaders throughout who buy in and help them. The late General Bill Creech, who reinvented the U.S. Tactical Air Command, called this "distributed, bottom-up leadership."

Effective leaders champion and support leaders at every level of their organization. They en"courage" them, they coach them, they remove the obstacles that stand in their way, and they help them when they have trouble. Again Creech said it best: You have to "find the way, show the way, and pave the way."

When Beverly Stein was elected chair of the Multnomah County Board of Commissioners, she was determined to transform the county's dysfunctional politics and bureaucracy. The first thing she did was ask one of her staff to research what made initiatives to improve quality successful. Her staff member reported back that the literature on change identified "leadership from the top" as the most important ingredient.

Stein took that to heart; for the next eight years managers and line workers had no doubt that quality and results were her priorities. But Stein also understood that leadership meant more than just her—that she needed leaders everywhere in the organization committed to change. So she created a steering committee, made up of a diagonal slice of the organization, to develop a five-year transformation plan she called her "Results Roadmap." At the committee's suggestion, she convened the first ever meeting of 200 top managers from across department lines to explain the roadmap and enlist their help.

Stein launched a quality initiative called RESULTS (Reaching Excellent Service Using Leadership and Team Strategies). From the beginning, she stated that it would be her *only* slogan. For the next eight years she used it to drive her focus on results down through the organization to line workers, the grassroots of the organization.

RESULTS was built around Total Quality Management. (See Chapter 13 for more on TQM.) The first step was a $50,000 mini-grant program, in which teams of county employees could apply for grants to buy the training and technical assistance they needed to learn TQM methods. "What this did was get the message down to the line level that something was happening, and you could participate," says Stein. Some 200 "process improvement teams" (PITs) were given training while they worked on improving work processes, and Stein visited many of them to show her interest and support. Dozens of improvements resulted:

- A team figured out how to retrofit a building to temporarily hold prisoners for $25,000, rather than the $200,000 that had been quoted by contractors.

- Community and Family Services redesigned the county's contracting process, bringing down the number of contract specialists from nine to five while decreasing the error rate by 22 percent.
- Central Stores cut the number of required forms for purchasing from 14 to 5.
- The Health Department reduced the two- to four-hour waiting time to speak to a nurse to three minutes or less, while reducing the number of triage nurses from 13 to 7.

To maintain support for the initiative among her fellow commissioners, Stein asked that a process improvement team report on its efforts to the board every three weeks. This gave board members concrete information on what was happening, but it also publicly recognized the leadership of employees. "Our consultant would teach them how to present it in a clever way," remembers Stein. "We often had skits that showed how they saved money and were more efficient. For most of these line workers, it was the only time they had ever presented before the Board of Commissioners, so they were very nervous."

Knowing that the initiative could be undermined by any sign that it was just another flavor of the month, Stein worked hard to "walk her talk." She brought the unions in as partners, for instance. Though AFSCME, the main union, had not supported her candidacy, she doubted RESULTS would ever really penetrate the organization if the unions opposed it. So she approached the AFSCME local president and told him what she wanted to do. His initial reaction was defensive: He said that county workers were already doing a good job. But he agreed to read some books Stein suggested. He came back and told her that he thought his members would benefit if public perceptions of government workers improved, so he would help. From then on, RESULTS was a labor–management project.

Stein agreed to give union stewards paid release time to attend a quality management conference. She met with the union president monthly to troubleshoot any emerging issues. And the union inserted a statement of support for RESULTS in its collective bargaining agreement. "AFSCME also sponsored me to go to work sites to hear directly from employees about their concerns," she says. " I would always talk about RESULTS and quality when I did that. And it gave employees direct access to me."

At some point, the top leader has to hand other leaders real power and step back, so they can lead. Stein did this with her department heads. When the Results Roadmap was done she disbanded the steering committee and gave responsibility for deploying it to her department heads:

I met with department heads every other week. One of the agenda items was always a rotating report from one of the seven department heads on how they were deploying RESULTS in their department. There was a RESULTS committee in every department—a committee of employees responsible for leading this.

Another big part of empowering leaders throughout an organization is teaching them—training them, helping them find coaches, and helping them learn from failure. To sharpen leadership skills, Stein had the county's training programs redesigned around the RESULTS goals and dramatically increased their budget. She engaged a coach to hone her own effectiveness and recommended that department heads do the same. She and her chief of staff coached those who chose not to.

Distributed leadership also involves celebrating when your leaders succeed—both to reward them and to publicize the behavior you want. Stein wrote congratulatory notes to employees who demonstrated effective leadership, and whenever a department held an event to recognize employees, she appeared and spoke. But she learned, from a regular employee survey, that employees wanted more recognition, so she put a team together to develop more systematic efforts. And when the organization itself won a big award, she threw a huge party:

We went through a year-long process of applying for the Oregon Quality Award, which used the Baldrige criteria. When we won, we had a big party. I remember going to that party, and my face hurt from smiling so long. People felt really acknowledged because we had it in a Hilton Hotel ballroom. The message was that government isn't second class—we can have a party in a nice hotel, too.

At some point, enabling leaders throughout your organization also means protecting them at unhappy moments. The leader is like the point bird in a formation of geese, hitting the wind first and breaking the path for others. When bad news hit the press, Stein knew she had to support her troops:

If something went wrong, we would immediately talk to all the commissioners and give them all the context, so they wouldn't battle us back. The care and feeding of commissioners is really critical. I tried my best to back the employees up without being an apologist for stupid things. When really bad things happened, I said they were mistakes and we were going to learn from them and move on.

Over eight years, Stein says, she learned just how indispensable creating an organization of leaders is:

> I learned that this was the bottom line, if you're really serious about making changes. The research we had done that said you had to have leadership at the very top is really true; that's where distributed leadership starts—you have to distribute it from the very top. And that person has to constantly send waves down through the organization—otherwise it falls down people's list of priorities.
>
> It's like oil and water: To get that oil emulsified and down into the water takes really hard work. But it's the only way that transformation will really work, because you have to change the hearts and minds of every employee, down to the janitors.
>
> It has to be an organized deployment. It's not enough to just have meetings and tell employees this and that. You have to have a strategy. How are you going to engage the department heads? Then they have to engage their second level, and they have to figure out how their second level is going to engage the middle managers, and the middle managers have to figure out how to engage the employees. It has to be a thought-out engagement strategy; it can't just be a bunch of different activities.

Ultimately, Stein says, "the goal is to transform the culture of the organization, so it's just the way we do things—so everyone feels like this is important, that 'I want to be doing this.'"

"One of the things I am most proud of is hearing that a janitor in one of our facilities told the director, who was praising his work, that his goal was improving customer service. That day I knew we were different in fact—not just in theory."

FIFTEEN

Politics

Truth, Lies, and the Campaign
for Public Support

Five centuries ago, Machiavelli articulated a difficult truth about political reform: "There is no more delicate matter to take in hand, nor more dangerous to conduct, nor more doubtful in its success, than to set up as a leader in the introduction of changes. For he who innovates will have for enemies all those who are well off under the existing order of things, and only lukewarm supporters in those who might be better off under the new."

Unfortunately, the permanent fiscal crisis makes the "introduction of changes" a necessity. Effective leaders have little choice but to master the delicate and dangerous art of reform.

Consider Steve Goldsmith, who served as the Republican mayor of Indianapolis from 1992 through 1999, during which time he was one of the most successful reinventors in the world. Formerly a county prosecutor, Goldsmith is a cool, cerebral, intellectual politician—by personality, the opposite of a Bill Clinton. He is not a gifted campaigner, and he is not a natural politician. Yet, by keeping his mind open, he mastered the politics of reinvention.

When Goldsmith ran for mayor in 1991, he promised to privatize up to 25 percent of city services (excluding the police and fire departments). The public employee union in town, AFSCME, opposed him bitterly. He decided to start the privatization process with something easy: the city's sewer billing process. The city spent nearly $3 million a year to collect $40 million, while the private water utility mailed out very similar bills to the very same customers every month. Goldsmith had his staff contact that utility, thinking it could simply bill for both services. The utility looked at the city's costs, then offered to perform the work for *5 percent* less than it was costing the city.

Goldsmith was disappointed. He asked his staff to make the same offer to every private utility in the state. Faced with competition, the local water company now bid *30 percent* below current costs—saving the city more than $1 million a year. And Goldsmith drew the appropriate lesson: "The key issue . . . was not whether tasks were performed by public or private institutions. . . . Competition, not privatization, made the difference."

Goldsmith also recognized that in going forward he could fight city workers all the way, or he could try to harness their self-interest to the interests of the city. So he decided to let the employees in on the action. He instituted managed competition—a competitive bidding process in which public agencies are allowed to bid against private firms for the right to keep their work. (See Chapter 7 for more on this approach.) When he turned to the second proposed privatization—filling potholes and repairing streets in a 10-block section on the northeast side of the city—he asked city workers to bid for the job. But the workers involved "thought we were setting them up for failure," Goldsmith remembers:

> The workers complained they could not possibly compete while carrying unreasonable overhead in the form of managers' salaries. For a mere ninety-four workers in the street repair division there were thirty-two politically appointed supervisors—an absurd ratio, especially considering that most of the supervisors were relatively highly paid. In part to call my bluff, union employees told us that if we were serious about competition we would eliminate several of these supervisors to give the union a real chance to compete.

When they raised this issue, AFSCME's Steve Fantauzzo told us, "We felt that we had thrown a grenade back into [the administration's] lap."

"By normal political standards the union's demand would have been a show stopper," Goldsmith agrees.

> The supervisors were all registered Republicans. I was a Republican mayor. These managers, and their patrons in the party, had supported my election. The union had supported the opposition and campaigned strongly against me. Now the union wanted me to fire politically connected Republicans to help a Democratic union look good.
>
> We did it. We had to. If I had blinked and shielded my fellow Republicans, the message would have been clear: We were not serious about competition.

Goldsmith laid off half the 32 supervisors. Local Republicans were aghast, but union leaders sat up and took notice. "When the mayor actually laid off the middle managers," said Fantauzzo, "it was a positive message to our local leadership." AFSCME agreed to work with the slimmed-down management team to put together a competitive bid; the city agreed to pay for a consultant to help them—and the workers actually won.

"Simply empowering these workers transformed them into efficiency experts overnight," Goldsmith says. "They became incredibly creative in imagining how they could do their work more cost-effectively."

Goldsmith's political supporters pressured him again, demanding that he cancel the award. Some felt that awarding the bid to city workers would damage his credibility with the business community. Others worried that the city team had underestimated its costs and would not stay on budget—a potential embarrassment. But the mayor held firm.

Over the next seven years Indianapolis successfully bid out more than 70 services, some of them multiple times. Of the first 64 competitions, city employees won 16 outright and split 13 more with private contractors. The city saved more than $120 million over seven years, and the Indianapolis International Airport saved another $100 million by competitively bidding out its management.

Having learned he could work with the unions, Goldsmith agreed when union stewards asked that savings their members were generating be shared with the workers. He authorized gainsharing programs, under which city workers took home bonus checks as high as $1,750 a year.

By 1995, Fantauzzo was partnering with city officials to explain the city's managed competition process at conferences. His union remained neutral in the mayoral campaign, and Goldsmith won reelection with almost 60 percent of the vote. Meanwhile, union officials were quietly approaching managers and suggesting functions that could be outsourced, to reduce costs. Since their members could now share in the savings, their interests were aligned with the mayor's.

By 1997, Goldsmith reports, he had cut the city's general-fund budget from about $460 million in 1992 to $428 million. "For the purpose of comparison, if the budget had continued to grow at the rate it did through the 1980s, the 1997 budget would have topped $547 million, about 36 percent higher than our actual budget."

Goldsmith exemplified many of the principles of leadership we have already outlined, which apply as well to politics:

- *He told the truth.* Even if it hurts, leveling with voters and interest groups is, in the long run, the only way to earn the trust a leader must have to make big changes. Trust the public with the truth and they will trust you.

- *He made his purpose clear and pursued it relentlessly.* Goldsmith's core purpose for eight years was to lower the cost of government in Indianapolis while improving services, a goal he talked about constantly.
- *He framed everything in terms of results.* Goldsmith understood that citizens cared about lower spending and taxes and better services, not about a process of managed competition. He sold results, not process—then explained why changes in process were necessary to deliver those results. He forced the union, which naturally tried to protect its members' jobs, to prove that they could deliver the results citizens wanted at a lower price than anyone else.
- *He cut back to the core.* Goldsmith focused on things that really mattered to citizens and got city government out of other businesses. "Over the years," he says, "even the prudently managed city of Indianapolis had ventured far afield. The city ran golf courses, tree nurseries, and even a window-washing service. We had done these things for so long that they seemed like obvious government functions, even though to an outside observer they might seem absurd."
- *He questioned everything except city government's values.* The voters didn't want business as usual, but they didn't want wholesale destruction of city government either. Goldsmith protected core public-sector values—reducing employment outside the police and fire departments by more than 40 percent, for example, with very few layoffs.

Goldsmith's story illustrates other political lessons as well. There are many pieces of advice we could pass on, but we have tried to distill them into our top 10 lessons for leaders who want to master the politics of reinvention.

1. Get focused and stay focused.

To get big things done, political leaders must focus public attention on only one or two themes. Their administrations may accomplish many other tasks, but if they try to communicate about all of it, the voters will have trouble identifying what really matters. Their accomplishments will get lost in the media noise, which is at ear-splitting volume these days.

Bill Clinton learned this when he was governor of Arkansas. In his first term he was an aggressive young reformer, working on a dozen different fronts. But when reelection day came in 1980, voters turned him out. Five years later, David Osborne asked him what he had learned from this experience:

> *I learned that if you do a lot of things, and you talk about a lot of different things while you're doing it, the perception may be that you haven't done anything. You have to be able to give a little clearer sense of direction. If you want to get broad, popular support for what you're doing, people have to be able to understand or explain it in a sentence or two. And I think to the folks out there a lot of what I did came across just as a lot of good government things that didn't have any unifying theme that people could really buy into.*

After winning back the governorship two years later, Clinton focused for the next ten years on just two themes: first education reform, then economic development.

2. Reframe the issue: If you want a different answer, ask a different question.

If your opponents get to frame the issue, they win. When opponents of charter schools accuse them of hurting existing public schools by taking away students and money, shift the debate from the welfare of *schools* to the welfare of *students*. Bring charter school students and parents together to talk to the media about how these new schools have changed their lives. Ask how anyone could propose to take this opportunity *away* from the state's children? That is a debate which cannot be lost.

The political leader who brought public school choice to America was Rudy Perpich, the Democratic governor of Minnesota through much of the 1980s. (For that story, see *Banishing Bureaucracy,* pp. 157–174.) When Perpich and his allies were pushing for statewide public school choice, the teachers' unions and school-board association blocked them. Perpich then pulled 61 people representing 24 different groups into a Governor's Discussion Group, where he asked them to hammer out a consensus proposal. The reformers quickly reframed the debate. One of them, Verne Johnson, summarized the argument they made this way:

> *You can go to a private school, or you can move your place of residence to another district, and people in fact do this all the time. So choice exists. But it's related to your personal family wealth. It costs money to move into a different kind of suburb, to get a different kind of house; it costs money to pay tuition.*

You can even go to a different public school without moving, if you're willing to pay tuition. If you have a lot of money you have a lot of choice. If you don't have a lot of money, you don't have a lot of choice.

Johnson and his colleagues let the unions know that this would be their argument with the public. The unions and school boards could fight it, but they would be fighting to deny equal opportunity to poor and working families. "I think it became clear to the unions for the first time how vulnerable they were," says Ted Kolderie, another of the reformers.

Governor Gary Locke reframed the issue in Washington State, with his Priorities of Government. He recognized early in the budget process that if he kept asking the same question he would get the same answer. If the question was, "What programs should we cut?" the answer, from all across the state, would be "Not mine!" So instead he asked different questions: "What outcomes are most important to the people of Washington, and how can we best spend our limited resources to produce those outcomes?"

Those who disagreed with his choices had to explain why their programs would deliver better results at the same (or a lower) price. With the debate framed this way, Locke won before it even started, because if someone could prove that different choices would produce better results at the same price, he was happy to go along. As the Tacoma *News Tribune* put it, "If you want to change where a debate in the Legislature ends, change where it starts."

3. Mobilize the general interest.

The reforms we advocate help citizens immensely, but they are often opposed by interest groups, whether public employee unions or private contractors with cushy contracts. And in politics, interest groups tend to be organized, their skills at capturing media attention well honed, while the general interest is unorganized and voiceless. It is up to leaders to give the general interest a powerful voice.

Most citizens are neither left nor right, neither particularly conservative nor particularly liberal. Most citizens are not politically active, not a part of any organized interest group. They are, quite simply, citizens. They pay taxes, and they want governments (schools, communities, states, and a nation) of which they can be proud. Leaders must make the benefits of change crystal clear, then take their case directly to these citizens, mobilizing public sentiment so the general interest can defeat the special interests during the legislative process. If the media refuses to take that public sentiment seriously, leaders can commission opinion polls to prove their case. In 1995, for instance, the media publicized complaints about Boston's school choice plan by white parents frustrated that they couldn't get their children into their preferred schools. To defend school choice, the mayor and the Private Industry Council had a customer survey done of attitudes toward the choice plan. It showed that 80 percent of parents were satisfied with the assignment system and almost 90 percent got their first or second choice.

When Governor Perpich first proposed statewide choice, with districts competing for students and dollars, it was a radical new idea, and only a third of Minnesotans expressed support for it in a public opinion poll. But he kept after it for four years, educating the public.

Perpich liked to tell his staff, "Once you get the legislature pinned down in St. Paul, leave town." He would get in his car and start driving, visiting small towns, walking into a café or restaurant downtown, having coffee with people and talking. Then he would drive to the next town. Since he was governor, the media would follow him around. He would explain that while the legislature was in the state capitol listening to special interest groups, he was out listening to the citizens. He would occasionally take his entire cabinet out of St. Paul for a day's meeting with citizens. He would tell his staff, "Don't get pinned down in St. Paul. That's not where the real politics are—the real politics are out where the people are. You can't win in St. Paul until you first win with the citizens. Once you do that, the legislature will come along."

4. Build and mobilize constituencies that support the changes you want to make.

To make change you need power, and to get power you need constituencies. Sometimes you literally have to organize citizens who would benefit from change, to overcome the already organized opposition. The Minnesota reformers started with two small organizations, People for Better Schools and the Citizens League. Next they recruited the support of the Minnesota Business Partnership. Then they turned to minority communities, where parents were eager for choice because they felt trapped in inner-city public schools and could not afford private schools. Later, they organized the students and parents who had benefited from Minnesota's first small choice program, which let high school juniors and seniors take college courses for dual credit.

5. Neutralize interest groups that might otherwise oppose you by creating visible benefits for them.

In Indianapolis, city council members from poor, inner-city neighborhoods were mostly liberals, who often allied themselves with public employee unions to fight for more government spending. Their instincts would have been to vote with their labor allies against managed competition. But

Mayor Goldsmith announced that the savings from managed competition would be used to fund the largest infrastructure investment program in the city's history, targeted squarely on seven poor, inner-city neighborhoods. As the savings started to roll in, he accelerated the process by borrowing against future savings to launch the investments. Called Building Better Neighborhoods, his initiative spent $1 billion over five years to rebuild curbs and sidewalks, repair sewer lines, repave streets, and improve parks, public housing, and fire and police stations—$750 million of it in those seven inner-city neighborhoods. It converted a number of city councilors into staunch supporters of managed competition.

6. Make elected officials an offer they can't refuse.

Goldsmith's tactic is one example of converting legislators by offering them something they want. But there are plenty of others. Foremost among them is delivering savings that legislators need to balance the budget. In Iowa, for example, Governor Tom Vilsack had to cut spending for the third straight year when preparing the 2004 budget. Yet to do so without undermining critical services, he negotiated two "smarter spending" line items in the budget: $83 million in savings, to be generated by a series of reinvention initiatives; and $5 million in investment to make those savings possible. The net savings of $78 million helped the legislature stave off draconian cuts, while also giving Vilsack the legislative commitment to reinvention he wanted.

Another common tactic is to deliver early, visible improvements in important public services, then share the credit with legislators. Early victories are critical in the politics of reform: They give politicians positive exposure, generate enthusiasm among reformers, and give reform efforts credibility with the press and the public. "Whenever I started a new endeavor, I looked to have a clear, decisive victory as early as I could," says Mayor Giuliani.

7. Never compromise the fundamentals.

While it is often necessary to cut deals, it is never worth compromising the fundamentals of reform. The small group of education reformers who succeeded in bringing public school choice to Minnesota—and thus to America—cited this as one of their 10 fundamental rules of change. Verne Johnson, Ted Kolderie, and their allies said it this way: "Don't play the 'Washington game' by trading away the fundamental elements of the plan. Compromise may yield bad policy. Say 'no' rather than give up the fundamentals of what you really want."

Real reform is about changing the way *systems* work: budget systems, personnel systems, education systems, child-welfare systems—systems of all kinds. It is about clarifying their purposes and changing their incentives, accountability structures, and power structures to produce different behavior. If you cannot change these things, you will not get fundamental improvement. It is a mistake to compromise away any of these fundamental elements.

Roger Douglas, the former New Zealand finance minister who led the most sweeping reinvention effort in the world, agrees: "The problem with compromise policies is simple," he says. "They do not produce the right outcome for the public at the end of the day. So they come back to haunt the politicians responsible for them."

You may not be able to get all the fundamentals in place in one fell swoop. You may have to settle for winning one piece of system change at a time, as the Minnesota reformers did. It took them four years of legislative battles and partial victories to implement statewide public school choice, and several more years to add charter schools. But at each step, they won a piece of the fundamental system reform they wanted. They were never willing to accept a compromise that did not deliver a piece of system reform— or worse, that gave up on a crucial element. Nancy C. Roberts and Paula J. King, the authors of a book about the role these reformers played in changing education in Minnesota, quoted one of them about this:

> *"Understand," he said, "that the great reform problem is a system problem, not a program problem. That is what distinguishes us—pushing for change in the way the system worked." If you keep that in mind, no way could you settle for less—better grading, class size improvement, even devolving responsibility to the school level. "We wouldn't have been satisfied until the relationships and incentives were changed and there were some reasonable expectations that the system would perform differently."*

8. Stay on offense: Don't play defense.

When you are trying to make fundamental changes in systems, speed and momentum are critical. A rapidly moving target is harder for opponents to hit. Once you build up momentum, don't lose it by playing defense when the opposition counterattacks. Reiterate your goals clearly and then move on to the next element of your change strategy. Don't let your opponents force *you* to play defense: Force *them* to react to your next offensive.

Roger Douglas is eloquent on this point:

> *Define your objectives clearly and move towards them by quantum leaps. Otherwise, the interest groups will have time to mobilize and drag you down. . . . Speed is essential, and it is impossible to go too fast . . .*

If action is not taken fast enough, the consensus that supports reform can collapse before the results become evident, while the government is still only part-way through its reform program . . .

Once you start the momentum rolling, never let it stop until you have completed the total program. The fire of opponents is much less accurate if they have to shoot at a rapidly moving target.

If you take your next decision while they are still struggling to mobilize against the last one, you will continually capture the high ground of national interest and force them to fight uphill.

9. Campaign every day.

The campaign for public support is just that—a campaign. The big difference is that there is a "vote" every day—not just every second or fourth November. Every time citizens interact with their government, and every time they read about or hear about their government, is a moment of truth. Leaders must campaign relentlessly for public support.

10. Stay committed for the long haul.

"It was a surprise to me," says former Multnomah county executive Beverly Stein, "but my commitment to staying for eight years [the maximum allowed] was very important in securing the commitment of others to my change agenda."

Fundamental change takes a long time. If leaders think they are embarked on a one- or two-year project, they will never succeed. The opposition will outlast them, and those sitting on the fence will quickly figure out that the leaders are not committed enough to accomplish what they have set out to do—so they will stay on the fence. A small band of reformers may charge the barricades, but when they find the leader absent in year three, they too will give up and depart.

Citizen expectations, fed by rapid innovation in the private sector, are rising dramatically. At the same time, the problems we confront are becoming ever more complex. Consider a few of the challenges we face today: building stable governments in Iraq and Afghanistan; combating terrorism; slowing global warming; regulating financial transactions in a global, digital economy; ensuring the safety of thousands of new medicines; deciding on the ethics of cloning and recombinant DNA research. . . .

Meanwhile our "old" problems are not going away. Forty-four million Americans still have no health insurance. Our public schools still lag behind those of other nations. Traffic gets more congested every year. The cost of health care and Social Security threatens to crowd out *50 percent* of the federal budget within the next 25 years. As the baby boomers retire, Social Security, public pensions, and health care will converge to create a fiscal "perfect storm," at all levels of government.

Most of our leaders offer one of two unpalatable choices: a higher price to support the government of the past—bureaucracies, red tape, and all—or a lower price for a shrunken government that gives up on some of the values the public holds dearest. But there is an alternative: delivering ever more value at the price citizens are willing to pay. To cope with the fiscal storm, we must relentlessly reinvent our public institutions. And then we must reinvent them again . . . and again.

None of us has a crystal ball. None of us knows what choices the American people will make. Will we decide to fund universal health care and raise the price of government? Or will we contain health care costs by limiting coverage for the poor and aged? Will we find major areas of public spending to reduce, as we did with the defense budget after 1970? Will we change our crime-fighting strategies and keep fewer people in prison, for example? Or will we make a societal decision to change the way we provide health care at the end of life? And what about technology? Will breakthroughs allow us to fundamentally change the costs and quality of basic services?

We have embraced fundamental change before, many times. Within the price limit imposed by citizens over the last 50 years, we built the interstate highway system, educated the baby boom generation, put a man on the moon, created Medicare and Medicaid, and won the Cold War.

Some of the options available to us will be impossible if we fail to embrace fundamental change today. The positive use of government to tackle our biggest problems—whether global warming, nation-building in Iraq, traffic congestion, or the millions of Americans without health insurance—founders on the rock of public distrust. Major new public initiatives will remain virtually impossible until the majority of Americans believe their governments are providing more value for their tax dollars.

If we fail to win that battle for public support, we will one day face a painful choice: give up much that we value—our current levels of Social Security, Medicare, and Medicaid benefits, our current levels of police protection, our current levels of commitment to public education—or pay a significantly higher price of government than we have for the past 50 years.

Can we live up to a fourth grader's expectations? Can we "change things to make things better?" Given what is at stake, do we have any other choice?

NOTES

All quotations that are not attributed in the text or in these endnotes are from interviews with the authors or their associates. Only in cases where there might be some confusion about the source of a quotation have we indicated in a note that it came from an interview.

INTRODUCTION

1 *Seattle Times* quote: "The First Steps Toward Living Within Our Means," *Seattle Times,* November 17, 2002.

1 "On April 7, 2003 . . . ,": Jennifer Steinhauer, "New York to Lay Off 3,400 as Fiscal Crisis Grows," *New York Times,* April 8, 2003, p. A23.

1 "The following day . . . ,": Jennifer Medina, "New York City Adds 3,200 School Jobs to Its List of Layoffs," *New York Times,* April 9, 2003.

1 "Nationwide, 16 percent of cities . . . in 2002:" National League of Cities, "Fiscal Conditions Force One in Four Cities to Consider Police Cuts," press release, February 12, 2003.

1 "38 percent of large cities predicted cuts": National League of Cities, "Homeland Security Duties Hurt Ability to Provide Normal Public Safety and Will Lead to Cuts in Services in Many Cities," press release, December 5, 2002.

1 "Portland, Oregon's largest city . . . up sharply": Fox Butterfield, "As Budgets Shrink, Cities See an Impact on Criminal Justice," *New York Times,* June 7, 2003, p. A1.

1 "Many school districts in Oregon . . .": Andrew Reschovsky, "State Government Fiscal Crises and the Effect on Local Government and Schools," *La Follette Policy Report,* Robert M. La Follette School of Public Affairs, Vol. 14, No. 1 (Spring 2003), p. 5.

1 "Oklahoma City had to close . . . to save money": Sam Dillon, "State Cutbacks Put Schools and Federal Law to the Test," *New York Times,* March 31, 2003.

2 "Collectively, the states faced a . . . :" National Governors Association, "The State Fiscal Crisis," www.nga.org, February 22, 2003.

2 Ray Sheppach quotation: Quoted in David Rosenbaum, "States Balance Budgets with Blue Smoke and Mirrors," *New York Times,* August 24, 2003, p. 4.

2 "In fiscal 2002, 38 states . . .": *Fiscal Survey of the States 2003,* National Governors Association, www.nga.org, December 2003, p. 1.

2 "In 2003, 40 states . . .": Ibid., p. ix.

2 "Connecticut laid off prosecutors . . .": Jason White, "Governors Scramble for Soundbites to Decry Budget Crisis," *Stateline.org.,* March 23, 2003.

2 "Every state in the Union . . .": Alan Greenblatt, "Making Do," *Governing,* December 2003, pp. 31–33. For more specifics see: Pamela M. Prah, "Human Impact of State's Budget Cuts," *Stateline.org,* March 25, 2003.

2 "Texas cut 275,000 children . . .": Timothy Egan, "States, Facing Budget Shortfalls, Cut the Major and the Mundane," *New York Times,* April 21, 2003, p. A1.

2   "As a result, the University of Arizona . . .": Jason White, "More States Cut Spending to
     Balance Budgets," *Stateline.org*, July 23, 2003.

2   "Massachusetts, Missouri, Iowa, and Texas . . .": Pamela M. Prah and Jason White,
     "Education Feels State's Financial Squeeze," *Stateline.org*, March 26, 2003.

2   "Meanwhile programs are disappearing . . .": Greg Winter, "As State Colleges Cut
     Classes, Students Struggle to Finish," *New York Times*, August 24, 2003.

2   Scheppach quotation on "perpetual fiscal crisis": Quoted in Neal Peirce, "'Perpetual
     Fiscal Crisis' for States?" Washington Post Writers Group, January 22, 2002.

2   Scheppach quote on perfect storm: National Governors Association, "The State Fis-
     cal Crisis," February 22, 2003.

2   "The 2004 deficit is expected . . .": Office of Management and Budget, "Overview of
     the President's 2005 Budget," Executive Office of the President, www.whitehouse.
     gov/omb/budget/fy2005/overview.html, February 2004.

2   "Federal revenues in 2003 . . .": See Figure 2.1, on p. 421.

2   "In January 2004 . . . living American:" *The Budget and Economic Outlook*, (Washing-
     ton, D.C.: Congressional Budget Office, January 26, 2004). The Census Bureau reports
     that the U.S. population is 291 million (Jennifer C. Kerr, Associated Press, "South,
     West Growth Pushes U.S. Population Near 300 Million," *Boston Globe*, December 19,
     2003, p. A8). The CBO report cited here says that gross federal debt at the end of fiscal
     2003 was $6.8 trillion. With $4.1 trillion added, this would bring the total to $10.9 tril-
     lion in 2014, which would be $37,457 for every living American.

3   "In fiscal 2002, . . .": National Governors Association, "The State Fiscal Crisis;" and
     Nicholas W. Jenny and Richard P. Nathan, "Sizing Up the Shortfalls: The States in
     Straits," *Government Finance Review*, April 2000, pp. 10–14. The exact figure was 9.4
     percent.

3   "Total revenues . . .": Nicholas W. Jenny, "Tax Increases Shore Up State Revenue,"
     State Revenue Report No. 53, The Rockefeller Institute of Government, September
     2003, available at www.rockinst.org/.

3   Our tax base is "deteriorating": National Governors Association, "The State Fiscal
     Crisis."

3   "Most states don't tax services . . .": Robert Tannewald, "Are State and Local Revenue
     Systems Becoming Obsolete?" *Government Finance Review*, February 2003, pp.
     20–24. Services accounted for 58 percent of consumer spending by 2000, up from 41
     percent in 1960. If the proportion continued to rise at the same rate, it would be al-
     most 60 percent by 2004. This conclusion is supported by calculations from Bureau
     of Economic Analysis, NIPA Table 1.1.5, "Gross Domestic Product," at http://www.
     bea.gov/ (January, 2004).

3   First sales taxes imposed in 1930s: Andrew Welsh-Huggins, "From Tattoos to Walker,
     Levies Spread Across the Land," Associated Press, in *Boston Globe*, April 13, 2003, p.
     A18.

3   "In 1975, Social Security and Medicare . . .": "Historical Budget Data" and "Current
     Budget Projections," Congressional Budget Office, http://www.cbo.gov.

3   "The Congressional Budget Office projects . . . past 50 years": *The Long Term Budget
     Outlook*, (Washington, D.C.: Congressional Budget Office, December 2003).

4   "Thanks to the baby boom . . . ,": Ibid., p. 19.

4   "By 2003, reserves plus . . . $14 trillion": Howell Jackson, "It's Even Worse than You
     Think," *New York Times*, October 9, 2003, p. A37.

4   "Of the 123 largest funds . . . seven years": John Mauldin, "Unintended Conse-
     quences: Iraq, Pensions and Index Funds," *Investors Insight* (http://www.investors
     insight.com/), March 15, 2003.

4   "With all other state . . .": John Mauldin, "The Real Old Europe," *Investors Insight*
     (http://www.investorsinsight.com/), March 21, 2003.

4   "But the real time bomb . . .": "Table 1: National Health Expenditures Aggregate and
     per Capita Amounts, Percent Distribution, and Average Annual Percent Growth, by

Source of Funds: Selected Calendar Years 1980–2002," U.S. Centers for Medicare & Medicaid Services (formerly the Health Care Financing Administration), http://www. cms.hhs.gov/statistics/nhe/historical/t1.asp, January 2004. The exact average annual increase in total spending on health care from 1960–2002 was 10.19 percent.

4   "It now eats up . . . :" Ibid. The exact number for 2002 was 14.9 percent; given historical trends, it was clearly higher than 15 percent by 2004.

4   ". . . and governments pay 45 percent . . ." : Ibid. The exact number for 2002 was 45.9 percent; 32.5 percent was federal spending, 13.4 percent was state and local government spending.

4   "In 1985, Medicaid cost $40 billion . . .": John D. Klemm, "Medicaid Spending: A Brief History," *Health Care Financing Review*, Vol. 22, No. 1 (Fall 2000).

4   ". . . consumed 11 percent of state budgets . . .": Interview with Nick Samuels at National Association of State Budget Officers, April 2003.

4   ". . . today it costs $230 billion . . .": National Governors Association, "The State Fiscal Crisis."

4   ". . . consumes 20 percent . . . another 10 percent," "NASBO Analysis: Medicaid to Stress State Budgets Severely into 2003," National Association of State Budget Officers, March 2002; and "The Fiscal Survey of States: November 2002," National Association of State Budget Officers, November 2002, p. 4.

4   "The elderly made up less . . .": *The Long Term Budget Outlook*, Congressional Budget Office.

4   "Medicare, which is exclusively for the elderly . . .": Ibid., p. 29.

5   "Education spending has risen . . .": National Governors Association, "The State Fiscal Crisis."

5   "In an effort to reduce crime . . .": Fox Butterfield, "Prison Rates Among Blacks Reach a Peak, Report Finds," *New York Times*, April 7, 2003, p. A11. Butterfield cited a Justice Department report.

5   "At least 20 states . . .": David E. Rosenbaum, "States Balance Budgets with Blue Smoke and Mirrors," *New York Times*, August 24, 2003, p. 4.

5   Frenzel quotation: in Roben Farzad, "Ten Things Your Politician Won't Tell You," *SmartMoney.com* (http://www.SmartMoney.com), October 15, 2002.

5   *Seattle Times* quotation: "The First Steps Toward Living Within Our Means," *Seattle Times*, November 17, 2002.

6   Most of the information about the Washington State budget process is based on the authors' personal experience. Their firm, the Public Strategies Group, helped the governor and his staff design and run this process.

8–9   Locke quotations: Governor Gary Locke, Budget Development Remarks delivered at "Priorities of Government" news conference, November 14, 2002.

11   The *Seattle Times* quotation: "The Right Pieces to Locke's Budget," *Seattle Times*, December 20, 2002.

11   Tacoma *News Tribune* quotation: "For Painful Times, Locke Offers a Painful, but Rational, Budget," Tacoma *News Tribune*, December 18, 2002.

11   Carlson quotation: Locke's "'budget for the next two years . . .'": John Carlson, "The Emerging Leadership of Gov. Gary Locke," *Eastside Journal*, December 29, 2002.

11   Carlson quotation: "He is willing to face down . . .": David Postman, Locke's Plan to Fix Budget Puts Legacy on the Line, Seattle *Times*, January 13, 2003.

11   Late January survey: *Washington Voters & Gary Locke*, Moore Information Public Opinion Research, January 2003; and "Voters Support Locke Leadership On Budget," press release from Washington Roundtable, February 11, 2003, available at http://www.waroundtable.com/press/.

12   Everett *Daily Herald* quotation: "Our Views," Everett *Daily Herald*, December 2, 2002.

14   Pinellas County Juvenile Welfare Board: See notes for Chapter 5, pp. 118–121.

14   Iowa Department of Transportation: See notes for Chapter 6, pp. 132–133.

14   Indianapolis: See notes for Chapter 15, p. 328.

15   Gainsharing at Seattle area's wastewater treatment operation: David Osborne and
      Peter Plastrik, *The Reinventor's Fieldbook* (San Francisco: Jossey-Bass: 2000, pp.
      215–216.

15   "During the 1990s, Minnesota's . . . county saved money": Personal communica-
      tion from Lyle Wray, former county executive of Dakota County, January 23, 2004.

15–16 Occupational Safety and Health Administration information: See notes to Chapter
      10, pp. 215–216.

16   "The payoff is dramatic savings . . .": Vice President Al Gore, B*usinesslike Govern-
      ment: Lessons Learned from America's Best Companies* (Washington, DC: National
      Performance Review, October 1997), p. 49.

16–17 Milwaukee purchasing reforms: personal communication from Anne Kinney, for-
      mer Milwaukee budget director.

17   "Montgomery County, Maryland . . .": Interview with Montgomery County Finance
      Director Timothy L. Firestine by our PSG colleague Anne Kinney.

17   "Nothing is more important . . .": National Assessment of Educational Progress,
      "2003 Mathematics and Reading Results," National Center for Education Statistics,
      available at http://www.NCES.ed.gov (January 2004). Specifically, 37 percent of
      fourth graders and 26 percent of 8th graders are not up to the basic level in read-
      ing, while 23 percent of 4th graders and 32 percent of 8th graders don't reach that
      level in math.

17   "Yet America's cities and states . . .": Butterfield, "As Budgets Shrink, Cities See an
      Impact on Criminal Justice"; Ralph Ranalli, "'Hazmat' Temas Say Budget Cuts Hurt
      Terror-Response Role," *Boston Globe*, April 8, 2003, p. B4; National League of Cities,
      "Fiscal Conditions Force One in Four Cities to Consider Police Cuts"; and National
      League of Cities, "Homeland Security Duties Hurt Ability to Provide Normal Public
      Safety and Will Lead to Cuts in Services in Many Cities."

19   "President Bush and the Republican Congress . . .": See Figure 2.1, on p. 42.

CHAPTER 1: GETTING A GRIP ON THE PROBLEM

23   "The story begins . . . grow to $2.5 billion": "November Forecast," Minnesota De-
      partment of Finance, November 2001.

23   "The plan would trim . . . $667 million in budget reserves": Patricia Lopez, "Short-
      fall Puts the Heat on Returning Legislators," Minneapolis *Star Tribune*, January 27,
      2002.

23   "Included in this tough medicine . . .": "Who Would Feel the Pain," Minneapolis
      Star Tribune, January 13, 2002.

23   "The remedy included . . . tax increases of a comparable size:" Lopez, "Shortfall
      Puts the Heat on Returning Legislators

23   "The sleights of hand included . . .": "The Second Half," Minneapolis *Star Tribune*,
      March 1, 2002.

24   "With a straight face . . . robbing from tomorrow": Dane Smith, "Are Politics at
      Play? No Way, Say Architects of the Budget Deal," Minneapolis *Star Tribune*, Febru-
      ary 20, 2002.

24   Moody's quotation: Patricia Lopez, "Bond Rating Moody's Warns the Legislature,"
      Minneapolis *Star Tribune*, June 24, 2002.

24   "But Moe and Pawlenty . . . *after* the November election:" Patricia Lopez, "Candi-
      dates Cautiously Tackle Budget," Minneapolis *Star Tribune*, September 23, 2002.

25   Minneapolis *Star Tribune* quotation: Patricia Lopez, "State Gets $4.56 Billion Jolt,"
      Minneapolis *Star Tribune*, December 5, 2002.

25   "New York helped balance its budget in 1992 . . .": "Tourists Return to Explore New
      York's Resurgent Erie Canal," CNN.com, November 2, 2000, available at http://
      www.cnn.com/2000/travel/pursuits/outdoors/11/02/erie.canal/.

25 "Similarly, in 2003, Massachusetts . . . $175 million:" Rick Klein, "Legislators' Plan Keeps Health, Drug Programs," *Boston Globe*, June 20, 2003.

26 *Government Finance Review* quotation: James E. Burnham, "Risky Business: Evaluating the Use of Pension Obligation Bonds," *Government Finance Review*, June 2003.

26 "Chicago *Tribune* columnist quotation: John McCarren, "Unraveling Blagojovich's Amazing Budget of Trickery," *Chicago Tribune*, June 6, 2003.

26 "In 2003, after months of stalemate . . . passed a $99 billion budget": Tom Chorneau, "Schwarzenegger Declares a Fiscal Crisis," *Boston Globe*, December 19, 2003.

26 ". . . with *$10.7 billion* of borrowing . . . appeared to be unconstitutional:" Nicholas W. Jenny and James Orsi, "Budget Balancing Tactics," *Rockefeller Institute State Fiscal News*, Vol. 3, No. 7 (August 2003).

27 "In 1996, the city of Pittsburgh . . . the next hand": Burnham, "Risky Business," *Government Finance Review*.

27 "Standard and Poor's . . . junk bond status:" Penelope Lemov, "Pittsburgh's Fiscal Problems Run It Down," *Governing*, December 2003, p. 58.

27 "Wisconsin, which had been . . .": Neal R. Peirce, "State Fiscal Woes May Last Years," *Stateline.org*, July 12, 2002.

27 "By April 2003, 34 states . . .": Richard Lehman, "The Great Tobacco Bond Scam," Forbes.com *Advisor Soapbox*, April 9, 2003 (at www.forbes.com/columnists/2003/ 04/09/cz_rl_0408soapbox.html), January 2004.

27 Rowan Miranda quotation: "Special Report: Pittsburgh in Crisis: One shot deals prop up shaky finances," *PittsburghLIVE.com* (Pittsburgh *Tribune-Review*), http:// pittsburghlive.com/x/tribune-review/specialreports/pghincrisis/illusion.html (January, 2004).

28 "In his memoirs, Stockman . . . was a fraud:" David Stockman, *The Triumph of Politics: Why the Reagan Revolution Failed* (New York: Harper and Row, 1986).

28 "In Missouri . . . light bulb in government buildings be unscrewed:" Rosenbaum, "States Balance Budgets with Blue Smoke and Mirrors," *New York Times*.

28 "In Portland, Oregon . . . executing warrants": Butterfield, "As Budgets Shrink, Cities See an Impact on Criminal Justice," *New York Times*.

29 Quotation from Alaska: From Department of Administration, "State of Alaska Capital Project Summary FY 2003 Deferred Maintenance Bonds," January 29, 2002, p. 2, available at http://www.gov.state.ak.us/omb/03omb/budget/alldefermaint.pdf.

29 Pawlenty quotation: Patricia Lopez and Dane Smith, "Pawlenty's 2004–05 Budget Proposal Getting Back to Black," Minneapolis *Star Tribune*, February 19, 2003.

32 "In 1983, Massachusetts . . . amnesty to bring in $84 million: Massachusetts Department of Revenue, "Voluntary Compliance: The $564 Million Story," December 1985.

32 "Voluntary compliance shot up . . . by roughly 5 percent:" Ibid., and interview with John Sasso, then chief of staff to governor Dukakis, February 1985.

32 "By 1986, 17 states had copied the Massachusetts program:" Anne Swardson, "States Test Idea of Tax Amnesty," *Washington Post*, March 4, 1986.

32 "When President Bush cut income tax rates . . .": Michael Kranish, "Dean's Tax Claims Bring Skepticism," *Boston Globe*, December 7, 2003, p. A1.

33 "In 2002, while forced to raise tuition . . .": Fox Butterfield, "Politics and Economics Join in University Crisis," *New York Times*, July 22, 2003, p. A10.

33 "In New York City, Mayor Michael Bloomberg . . .": Jennifer Steinhauer, "In Fiscal Pain, New York Leans on Private Sector," *New York Times*, April 30, 2003, p. A29.

33 "Huge variations exist in government revenue sources . . . revenue from gambling": Based on data from the U.S. Bureau of the Census for State and Local Government Finances, available at http://www.census.gov/govs/www/estimate.html (January 2004), and from the Nelson A. Rockefeller Institute of Government's Gate-

way to State and Local Government Information, at http://stateandlocalgateway. rockinst.org/ (January, 2004).

34   Table 1.4 is based on two sources. Federal government information is from Executive Office of the President, *A Citizen's Guide to the Federal Budget: Budget of the United States FY 2001*, Chart 2–3, available at http://w3.access.gpo.gov/usbudget/ fy2001/guide02.html. State and local information is from the U.S. Bureau of the Census data on State and Local Government Finances, available at http://www. census.gov/govs/www/estimate.html (January 2004).

35   "Economists from . . . by 2006": Donald Bruce and William F. Fox, *State and Local Tax Revenue Losses from E-Commerce: Updated Estimates* (Knoxville: Center for Business and Economic Research, September 2001).

35   "Yet services have increased from 40 to 60 percent . . .": See endnote to p. 3 on this point.

37   Louisiana forecasting conference: *Fundamentals of Sound State Budgeting Practices* (Denver: Foundation for State Legislatures and National Conference of State Legislatures, 1995), p. 20.

38   Ruth Richardson quotation: Public Management Service, *Budgeting for the Future* (Paris: Organization for Economic Cooperation and Development, 1997), p. 19.

38   "The Parliament and public of New Zealand . . .": Ibid., p. 20.

38   Pawlenty quotation: Dane Smith, "Governor Calls Budget Opposition Worrisome," Minneapolis *Star Tribune*, January 19, 2003.

38   "Of the $4.2 billion shortfall . . .": Dane Smith, "DFLers Drop Bid to Raise Taxes," Minneapolis *Star Tribune*, May 17, 2003.

38   "Then, suddenly, the Democrats capitulated": Ibid.

39   John Gunyou article: John Gunyou, "10 Things You Should Know About the State Budget," Minneapolis *Star Tribune*, June 15, 2003. Used with permission.

CHAPTER 2: SETTING THE PRICE OF GOVERNMENT

The charts and tables in this chapter are based on analysis of data from the following sources:

- Personal income data is from the U.S. Bureau of Economic Analysis web page on National Personal Income and Outlays, National Income and Product Accounts (NIPA) Table 2.1: "Personal Income and Its Disposition," available at http://www. bea.gov/bea/dn/nipaweb/index.asp (January 2004).

- Personal income data for individual states and localities is from the U.S. Bureau of Economic Analysis web page on Regional State and Local Personal Income, "State Annual Estimates" and "Local Area Annual Estimates," available at http://www. bea.gov/bea/regional/statelocal.htm (January 2004).

- Data on uses of personal income for the U.S. is from the U.S. Bureau of Economic Analysis, National Personal Income and Outlays, NIPA Table 2.3.5: "Personal Consumption Expenditures by Major Type of Product," http://www.bea.gov/ bea/dn/nipaweb/index.asp (January 2004).

- Federal current receipts and current receipts as a percent of GDP are from the Office of Management and Budget, *Budget of the United States Government, Fiscal Year 2004, Historical Tables*, Table 1.3: "Summary of Receipts, Outlays, and Surpluses or Deficits (–) in Current Dollars, Constant (FY 1996) Dollars, and as Percentages of GDP: 1940–2008," http://www.whitehouse.gov/omb/budget/ fy2004/hist.html (January 2004).

- State and local government own source general revenue data is from the U.S. Bureau of the Census, *Federal, State, and Local Governments: State and Local Government Finances*, http://www.census.gov/govs/www/estimate.html (January 2004).

- State population data and per capita income is from the U.S. Bureau of the Census, *United States Census 2000*, http://www.census.gov (January 2004).
- Denver price of government is from data prepared by the City of Denver.

46   "In 1970 health care . . . total government spending": U.S. Bureau of Economic Analysis web page on National Personal Income and Outlays, NIPA Table 3.16: "Current Government Expenditures by Function" (November 2003).

50   "In 1973 alone, revenues increased by nearly 14 percent": U.S. Bureau of the Census, *Federal, State, and Local Governments: State and Local Government Finances*, http://www.census.gov/govs/www/estimate.html (January, 2004).

CHAPTER 3: SETTING THE PRIORITIES OF GOVERNMENT

62   Pawlenty quotation: "the Mount Everest of budget deficits": Patricia Lopez and Dane Smith, "Pawlenty Plan Cuts to the Chase," Minneapolis *Star Tribune*, January 15, 2003.

62   "His ally, the House speaker . . .": Laurie Blake, "State's Budget Crisis May Kill Popular Service," Minneapolis *Star Tribune*, December 15, 2002.

68   Oakland goals: City Manager Robert C. Bobb, *Budget Briefing: The Mayor's Proposed Policy Budget Fiscal Year 2003–2005* (Oakland, Calif.: City of Oakland, May 2003), p. 3, available at http://www.oaklandnet.com/budget/BudgetBriefingMay2003.pdf.

69   Goals for the Broward County Public Schools: Dr. Frank Till, "Superintendent's Annual Evaluation of District Outcomes 2002–2003," Broward County Public Schools, www.broward.k12.fl.us/studentassessment/District%20Outcomes.pdf.

70   San Diego information: *Final FY 2000 Budget* (San Diego: City of San Diego, 2000).

70   Prince William County information: *FY 2002 Fiscal Plan, Vol. I, Executive Summary* (Prince William, Va.: Prince William County, 2001).

72   Charlotte's quality of life index: *The Charlotte Story: Public Service Is Our Business–Charlotte's Roadmap to Change and Improving Performance* (Charlotte: City of Charlotte, April 2000), p. 32; and *Charlotte Neighborhood Quality of Life Study 2002* (Charlotte: UNC Charlotte Department of Geography and Earth Sciences, July 1, 2002).

72   Washington State's Indicators: Guidance Team, "Report to the Governor: Purchasing Results That Matter Most," November 2003, pp. 5–6.

73–82 Budget development process in Washington State: authors' personal experience; their firm, the Public Strategies Group, helped the governor and his staff design and run this process.

76   The Price of the Priorities in Washington State: Ibid., p. 7.

78   The Washington Health Team's Cause-and-Effect Map: Ibid., p.17.

89   "To deal with this problem, New Zealand . . .": See for instance the "Managing for Outcomes," Web page of New Zealand's State Services Commission: http://www.ssc.govt.nz/display/document.asp?navid=208.

CHAPTER 4: STRATEGIC REVIEWS

98   Samuel Johnson quotation: John Bartlett, *Bartlett's Familiar Quotations*, sixteenth edition (Boston: Little Brown, 1992), p. 317.

99   Brad Mallon quotation: in Charles Mahtesian, "Why the Sun Rarely Sets on State Bureaucracy," *Governing*, June 1992, p. 25.

99   "By 2003 . . .": Texas Sunset Advisory Commission, "Frequently Asked Questions," http://www.sunset.state.tx.us/faq.htm, January 2004.

100   "Yet the General Accounting Office reports . . . .": Elizabeth Becker, "Administra-

tion to Urge Congress to Close More Military Bases," *New York Times*, January 26, 1999.

104   John Kost quotation: John M. Kost, *New Approaches to Public Management: The Case of Michigan* (Washington, D.C.: The Brookings Institution, July 1996), pp. 19–21.

105   Donald Kettl quotation: Donald F. Kettl: "Reinventing Government, Part II," *The New Democrat*, November 1994, p. 26.

105   "In 1993, President Clinton's mandate . . . ideas that went nowhere": From personal experience; David Osborne was a senior advisor to Vice President Gore during the 1993 performance review.

110   Treasury Department Web site quotation: HM Treasury: "Spending Reviews," www.hm-treasury.gov.uk/spending_review/spend_index.cfm, January 2004.

100   Treasury Department quotation about "basic elements" of PSAs: *Public Service Agreements 2002* (London: HM Treasury, January 2004), "Introduction," http://www.hmtreasury.gov.uk/Spending_Review/spend_sr02/psa/spend_sr02_psa intro.cfm.

110   Information on Local Government PSA: Ibid.

110–111 Quotations re: Strategy Unit: Prime Minister's Strategy Unit, "Strategy Unit," www.strategy.gov.uk/output/Page77.asp, January 2004.

CHAPTER 5: CONSOLIDATION

112   "The new Department of Health . . . innumerable restructurings since": Interviews with Buddy MacKay and Robert S. O'Leary, his deputy at HRS.

113   "It has 23,000 employees and a $4 billion budget": Telephone conversation with Bill Spann, Director of DCF Office of Communications, December 19, 2003; and DCF web page: www.state.fl.us/cf_web/.

114   "In October, 2003 . . . 'unmanageable and inefficient . . . '": Associated Press, "DCF to Cut Jobs, Restructure, and Consolidate Itself," Ocala *Star-Banner*, October 8, 2003, p. 4A.

114–115 Information on Department of Homeland Security: Tanya N. Ballard, "Homeland Security Organized Along Administration's Proposal," *Government Executive*, November 20, 2002.

115   David Walker quotation: David Walker, *Highlights of a GAO Forum, Mergers and Transformation: Lessons Learned for a Department of Homeland Security and Other Federal Agencies*, GAO-03-293SP (Washington, D.C.: U.S. General Accounting Office, November 2002).

115   Frank Dobbin quotation: Louis Jacobson, "Merging Cultures of Homeland Security Agencies Will Be Big Challenge," *Government Executive Daily Briefing*, www.governmentexecutive.com/, June 13, 2002.

116   "But integrating agents . . . decisions by management:" Brian Fiel, "All for One," *Government Executive*, May 1, 2003.

116   "Even Customs and INS agents . . . I practice in:" Shawn Zeller, "Border Blues," *Government Executive*, September 2003, pp. 9–11.

116   Harvey Johnson quotation: Jason Peckenpaugh, "Under One Roof," *Government Executive*, May 1, 2003.

117   Drucker quotation: Peter F. Drucker, *The Age of Discontinuity* (New York: Harper Torchbooks, 1978), p. 233.

118–119 Historical background on Pinellas County Juvenile Welfare Board: Corporation for Enterprise Development, "Human Investment Model #1," unpublished paper prepared for Governor Chiles's Commission on Government by the People, July 1991; and Juvenile Welfare Board Web page, www.jwbpinellas.org/home/home.htm.

119   Quotation from Juvenile Welfare Board leaders: www.jwbpinellas.org/home/home.htm.

119   Children's Service Councils: interview with Juvenile Welfare Board Executive Director James E. Mills.

119   Juvenile Welfare Board spends $46 million a year: Ibid.

119   "It funds almost 60 different providers . . . referral service": Ibid.

121   Information on decategorization boards: Bill Rust, "Decat in the Hat: Iowa's Successful First Step Toward Devolving Resources, Responsibility, and Accountability for Child and Family Outcomes," *Advocasey*, Vol. 1, No. 1, Spring 1999, pp. 4–12 (published by Annie E. Casey Foundation.); and interview with Jesse Rasmussen, former director of Iowa Department of Human Services.

122   Gary Lippe quotation: Rust, "Decat in the Hat."

122   Human Services Research Institute quotation: Ibid.

123   Ted Kolderie quotation: Ted Kolderie, "The States Will Have to Withdraw the Exclusive," *Public Services Redesign Project* (newsletter published by the Center for Policy Studies, in St. Paul), July 28, 1990, p. 3.

125   Fremont-Winema National Forest and Lakeview Bureau of Land Management District: Interview with Dede Domingos, interagency administrative officer; and memo from Russell Linden based on interviews on site.

125–126 Information on Regional Computer Center in Cincinnati area: *What Works: Management Applications of Performance Measurement in Local Government* (Washington, D.C.: Center for Performance Measurement, International City/County Management Association, 2001), p. 10.1.

126   "In 2002, the agency returned . . .": Interview with Paul Taylor, Center for Digital Government.

126   "By late 2003, 18 states and eight cities . . . for the state": Ibid.

127   InforME: *Paying IT Forward: Doing the Public's Business With Digital Technologies While Reducing Pressure on the General Fund* (Folsom, Calif.: Center for Digital Government, 2003), p. 39.

127   National Association of State Insurance Commissioners: Ibid., p. 30.

127   Iowa County Treasurers Association: Ibid., p. 31.

127–128 Portland-Multnomah County Call Center: Interview with Dr. David Lane.

128   Bush administration e-government initiatives: Executive Office of the President, *E-Government Strategy: Implementing the President's Management Agenda for E-Government* (Washington, D.C.: April 2003).

129–130 Quotations from survey of 100 public school superintendents: Howard Fuller with Christine Campbell, Mary Beth Celio, James Harvey, John Immerwahr, and Abigail Winger, *An Impossible Job? The View from the Urban Superintendent's Chair* (Seattle: Center on Reinventing Public Education, University of Washington, July 2003), available at http://www.crpe.org/.

129–130 National Commission on Governing America's Schools report: National Commission on Governing America's Schools, *Governing America's Schools: Changing the Rules* (Denver: Education Commission of the States, November 1999).

130   Milwaukee schools: See Osborne and Plastrik, *The Reinventor's Fieldbook*, pp. 279–284.

130   Houston schools: Donald R. McAdams, *Fighting to Save Our Urban Schools . . . and Winning! Lessons from Houston* (New York: Teachers College Press, 2000).

130   Minneapolis schools: personal knowledge from work as superintendent.

130   "Washington, D.C. has a separate . . .": District of Columbia Public Charter School Board Web site: http://www.dcpubliccharter.com/communityint/schools/schools.htm.

130–131 "Philadelphia's school district . . . outside its boundaries": "Charter Districts: The State of the Field," *State Notes*, April 2003 (published by the Education Commission of the States, www.ecs.org).

CHAPTER 6: RIGHTSIZING

132–133   Information on Iowa: From personal experience of authors and their colleagues as consultants for Governor Vilsack; interviews with and personal communications from Cynthia P. Eisenhauer, director of Iowa Department of Management; Jim Chrisinger, Department of Management; Jesse Rasmussen, former director, Department of Human Services; Bob Kurtter, senior vice president, State Ratings Group, Moody's Investors Service; and letter and attached report (untitled) from Cynthia P. Eisenhauer and Dr. Steven Gleason, then director of Department of Public Health, to Senator Jeff Lamberti and Representative David Millage, chairmen of the Legislative Fiscal Committee, August 16, 2002, outlining restructuring taken in every department as a result of "Improving Government" review.

133   Mary Christy quotation: Eisenhauer and Gleason letter to Senators Lamberti and Millage.

134–141   Charlotte information: From City of Charlotte web pages; *The Charlotte Story: Public Service Is Our Business, Charlotte's Roadmap to Change and Improving Performance* (Charlotte, N.C.: City of Charlotte, April 2000); Charlotte's *Corporate Performance Reports* for fiscal years 1999, 2000, 2001, 2002, and 2003; Neal Peirce and Curtis Johnson, "The Peirce Report: Shaping a Shared Future," *The Charlotte Observer,* reprint, September 17-October 8, 1995; and interviews with City Manager Pam Syfert and staff members Rick Davis, Ruffin Hall, and Lisa Schumacher.

134   Quotation from rightsizing blueprint: *The Charlotte Story*, p. 10.

135   Quotation re: "four fundamental questions": Ibid., p. 12.

137   "PSG recommended a design . . .": Information on the Better Results for Kids redesign is available at the Web site established to share information with all stakeholders. It is at http://www.dhs.state.ia.us/BetterResultsforKids/default.asp (January 2004).

139   Oakerson and Svorny quotation: Ronald Oakerson and Shirley Svorny, "Reform, L.A. Style: The Theory and Practice of Urban Governance at Century's Turn," unpublished paper presented at the John Randolph Haynes and Dora Haynes Foundation Conference, University of Southern California, School of Policy, Planning and Development, September 19–20, 2002.

142–143   Human capital planning done at GAO: David Walker, *Managing for Results Using Strategic Human Capital Management to Drive Transformational Change*, GAO 02–940T (Washington, D.C.: U.S. General Accounting Office, July 15, 2002).

143–144   World Bank quotation and information on Peru's rightsizing: "Strengthening Peru's Tax Agency," *PREM Notes* No. 60, November 2001 (published by the World Bank).

143   "Charlotte tells a similar story . . . 44 percent in 1999: *The Charlotte Story*, p. 10; *1999 City Services Survey Presentation of Results* (Charlotte: Market Wise, Inc., April 20, 1999); *City of Charlotte 2003 Evaluation of City Services May/June 2003* (Charlotte: Market Wise, Inc., 2003). The latter two documents were provided by the Office of the City Manager.

CHAPTER 7: BUYING SERVICES COMPETITIVELY

149–152   "Bid to Goal" initiative in San Diego: All information is from interviews with Joe Harris; *Final FY 2000 Budget* (San Diego: City of San Diego, 2000), pp. 177–183; Metropolitan Wastewater District, semifinalist application for the Innovations in American Government 2002 Awards Program, October 23, 2002; and Robert Mallet, "Site Visit Report," Innovations in American Government 2002 Awards Program, March 11, 2003.

153   Managed competition in Phoenix: Osborne and Gaebler, *Reinventing Government*, pp. 76–78.

153   "During the second Clinton . . . the entire government": Jason Peckenpaugh, "Tough Competition," *Government Executive*, March 2003, pp. 35–44; and Jason Peckenpaugh, "Tall Order," *Government Executive*, June 2003, p. 9–20.

154   "In the late 1980s, New Zealand . . . Labor Party government!": Jonathan Boston, John Martin, June Pallot, and Pat Walsh, *Public Management: The New Zealand Model* (Auckland: Oxford University Press, 1996), p. 193.

154   "During that same era, the British government ordered . . .": Osborne and Plastrik, *Banishing Bureaucracy*, p. 31.

154   "Partnerships UK": William Eggers and Stephen Goldsmith, "Networked Government," *Government Executive*, June 2003, pp. 28–33.

155   East Lansing, Michigan, strategy to lower wastewater treatment costs: Osborne and Plastrik, *The Reinventor's Fieldbook*, pp. 183–185.

155   The Center for Naval Analysis study: Jacques S. Gansler, "Six Myths of Competitive Sourcing," *Government Executive*, June 2003.

155   "Indianapolis saved 25 percent on average . . .": Interviews with Skip Stitt, then deputy mayor of Indianapolis.

155   "The British national government saved 21 percent . . .": *Next Steps Review: 1995*, Cm. 3164 (London, HMSO, 1996) p. v.

155   "The U.S. General Accounting Office reports . . .": Peckenpaugh, "Tall Order," *Government Executive*, June 2003.

156   Central Stores in the Minnesota Department of Administration: Several of our colleagues in the Public Strategies Group were high-level officials in the department when this occurred, including CEO Babak Armajani, who was deputy commissioner.

156   Robert Mallet quotation: Mallet, "Site Visit Report."

157   Robert J. Dilger et al. survey: cited in Gansler, "Six Myths of Competitive Sourcing," *Government Executive*, June 2003.

157   Tacoma-Pierce County Health Department: Bob Williams & Lynn Harsh, *The Stewardship Project* (Olympia, Wash.: Evergreen Freedom Foundation, June 2003), pp. 3–3, 3–4.

158   Sunnyvale Leisure Services unit: Interviews with managers in Sunnyvale. Data on share of budget from tax dollars: Personal communications from Tom Lewcock, former city manager, and Robert Walker, parks and recreation director.

159   Fox Valley Technical College: interviews with former Fox Valley President Stanley Spanbauer and other staff.

160   "Of 320 competitions at the Department of Defense . . .": Brian Fiel, "Playing Defense," *Government Executive*, June 2003, p. 81–84.

160   "In the United Kingdom . . .": Interview with John Oughton, then head of the Efficiency Unit and Market Testing Program, June 1994.

161   "A 1997 study by the Center for Naval Analysis . . . laid off": Gansler, "Six Myths of Competitive Sourcing," p. 86.

161   "A 1989 U.S. Department of Labor study . . . retired": Governor Peter Wilson, *Competitive Government: A Plan for Less Bureaucracy, More Results* (Sacramento: Office of the Governor, April 1966), p. 29. This publication cited *The Long-Term Employment Implications of Privatization*, NCEP, March 1989.

161   "A 2001 study by the U.S. General Accounting Office . . .": Gansler, "Six Myths of Competitive Sourcing," p. 86.

161   "In Phoenix, Philadelphia, and the U.K. . . .": Re. Philadelphia and Phoenix, ibid. Re. the U.K.: Audit Commission, *Realising the Benefits of Competition: The Client Role for Contracted Services* (London: HMSO,1993), p. 22.

161   "In the U.K., European Community . . .": Audit Commission, *Realising the Benefits of Competition*, p. 22.

161–162   Swedish transition fund: John Kamensky, "Summary of Information on Sweden," memo prepared for U.S. National Performance Review, June 1996.

162   Privatization of Office of Personnel Management's Investigative Services unit: U.S. Office of Personnel Management, semifinalist application for Innovations in American Government 2000 Awards Program, March 30, 2000; and John D. Donohue, "Site Visit Report," Innovations in American Government 2000 Awards Program, July 17, 2000.

CHAPTER 8: REWARDING PERFORMANCE

163   Description of Citistat meetings: Visit to Citistat; Lenneal J. Henderson, *The Baltimore CitiStat Program: Performance and Accountability* (Arlington, Va: The IBM Endowment for the Business of Government, May 2003); Phineas Baxandall and Charles C. Euchner, *Can CitiStat Work in Greater Boston?* (Cambridge, Ma.: Rappaport Institute for Greater Boston and National Center for Digital Government at John F. Kennedy School of Government, Harvard University, October 22, 2003); Paul E. O'Connell, *Using Performance Data for Accountability: The New York City Police Department's CompStat Model of Police Management* (Arlington, Va.: The PricewaterhouseCoopers Endowment for the Business of Government, August 2001); Christopher Swope, "O'Malley Restless for Results," *Governing* magazine, April 2001; Bill Schiller, "Accountability: In Baltimore, Things Get Done," *Toronto Star*, Feb. 23, 2001; and Sam Allis, "Baltimore Tutorials," *Boston Globe*, Sept. 29, 2002, p. A2. Quotations from Schlanger, Gallagher, and Kolodziejski are from interviews conducted by our Public Strategies Group colleague, Camille Barnett.

164   O'Malley quotation, "If we only looked at performance . . .": Swope, "O'Malley Restless for Results," *Governing*.

164   Marvin Billups quotation: Ibid.

165   "Baltimore had been a city in decline . . . metropolitan area": Henderson, *The Baltimore CitiStat Program: Performance and Accountability*, p. 10.

165   "Mayor O'Malley has fired two agency heads for poor performance . . .": Interviews with CitiStat participants conducted by Camille Barnett.

165   "In the first year of CitiStat alone . . .": Schiller, "Accountability: In Baltimore, Things Get Done," *Toronto Star*.

165   "Some 1,500 reports are phoned in . . .": Baxandall and Euchner, *Can CitiStat Work in Greater Boston?* p. 10; and Schiller, "Accountability: In Baltimore, Things Get Done."

165   Problem with illegal dumping: Baxandall and Euchner, p. 12.

165   "CitiStat also revealed . . . Public Health": Ibid., p. 13.

165   "Because so many problems cross . . . social services": Ibid., p. 10.

166   Lead abatement: Ibid., p. 12.

166   Results of first year of Citistat: Martin O'Malley speech, quoted in Henderson, *The Baltimore CitiStat Program: Performance and Accountability*, p. 14; and Schiller, "Accountability: In Baltimore, Things Get Done."

166   "By the end of fiscal year 2003 . . .": Baxandall and Euchner, *Can CitiStat Work in Greater Boston?* p. 5.

166   "Meanwhile services had improved": Henderson, *The Baltimore CitiStat Program*, p. 23.

166   ". . . violent crime was down 29 percent . . . were copying CitiStat": Baxandall and Euchner, *Can CitiStat Work in Greater Boston?*, p. 5.

166   "O'Malley summed it up this way for the *Toronto Star:*" Bill Schiller, "Accountability: In Baltimore, Things Get Done."

167   Michael Enright quotation: Baxandall and Euchner, *Can CitiStat Work in Greater Boston?* p. 10.

167   O'Malley quotations . . .": Henderson, *The Baltimore CitiStat Program*, p. 15.

168   "In New York City, CompStat began . . .": Rudolph Giuliani, "Rudolph W. Giuliani on Restoring Accountability to City Government," *The Business of Government*, Summer 2000, published by PricewaterhouseCoopers, p. 5.

168   Giuliani quotation: Ibid.

169   O'Connell quotation: O'Connell, *Using Performance Data for Accountability*, pp. 11–12.

169   "Every time Compstat expanded . . . 'we could Compstat it'": Rudolph W. Giuliani, *Leadership* (New York: Hyperion, 2002), p. 79.

169   "As for getting his huge police force . . . 'line of work'": Ibid., p. 72.

170   ". . . Mayor Giuliani called CompStat 'the centerpiece'": Ibid.

170   Giuliani quotation, "'The core of it . . .'": Giuliani, "Rudolph W. Giuliani on Restoring Accountability to City Government," *The Business of Government*, p. 5.

170   New York City crime statistics: Giuliani, *Leadership*, pp. 77, 380.

170   Quotation from site visit report: Liz O'Connor, "Site Visit Report," Innovations in American Government 2000 Awards Program, April 6, 2000, p. 1.

171   Information on TEAMS: Ibid.; Total Efficiency Accountability Management System, semifinalist application for the Innovations in American Government 200 Award Program, April 6, 2000; and Giuliani, *Leadership*, pp. 82–88.

172   New York's Department of Corrections quotation: semifinalist application for the Innovations in American Government 2000 Award Programs.

173–176 Information on Charlotte: From City of Charlotte web pages; *The Charlotte Story*; and interviews with City Manager Pam Syfert and staff members Rick Davis, Ruffin Hall, and Lisa Schumacher. Quotations on p. 173: *The Charlotte Story, p. 30.*

175   Herzberg study: Frederick Herzberg, *Work and the Nature of Man* (New York: World Publishing, 1966).

176   ". . . ten states tied at least": *Workforce Policies: State Activities and Innovations* (Washington, D.C.: National Association of State budget Offices, 1995), p. 43.

176   ". . . performance *bonuses go to groups of teachers . . .": Kevin Bushweller, "Eyes on the Prize," American School Board Journal*, August 1999, pp. 18–22; "Idea of the Week: Paying Teachers for Performance," *The DLC Update*, published by the Democratic Leadership Council, December 11, 1999.

176   "Florida state law requires . . .": Bushweller, "Eyes on the Prize"; Thomas Dawson, "Tie Teacher Pay to Student Performance," *Los Angeles Times*, March 30, 2000, p. A 15.

176   1998 survey: Bushweller, "Eyes on the Prize."

176   Diane Smith quotation: Ibid.

177   Performance bonuses in Texas state government: Blaine Liner et al., *Making Results-Based State Government Work* (Washington, D.C.: The Urban Institute, 2001), p.17.

177   Performance bonuses in Postal Service: See David Osborne, "Paying for Results," *Government Executive*, February 2001, pp. 61–67.

177–178 Performance bonuses in Veterans Benefits Administration: Interviews with Michael Walcoff, associate undersecretary for operations.

178–179 Gainsharing in Charlotte: *The Charlotte Story*, pp. 56–57, and interviews with Pam Syfert, Rick Davis, Ruffin Hall, and Lisa Schumacher.

181–182 Information on Vermont Energy Efficiency Utility: Vermont Energy Efficiency Utility, Innovations in American Government 2002 Supplementary Application, Oct. 18, 2002; and Keon Chi, "Site Visit Report," Innovations in American Government 2002 Awards Program, 2002.

182   Adoption and Safe Families Act and adoptions from foster care: Administration on Children, Youth, and Families, semifinalist application for Innovations in American Government Award 2001, April 12, 2001; and Robert A. Stone, "Site Visit Report," Innovations in American Government 2001 Awards Program.

182   Ben Franklin Partnership: David Osborne, *Laboratories of Democracy* (Boston: Harvard Business School Press, 1988), p. 50.

183   U.K. Audit Commission: See Osborne and Plastrik, *The Reinventor's Fieldbook*, pp. 211–212.

183–184 Florida school performance reports: See Florida Department of Education Web sites, such as the home page, http://www.fldoe.org/; "Florida School Grades—School Accountability Reports," at http://www.firn.edu/doe/schoolgrades/; and "Education Information and Accountability Services," at http://www.firn.edu/doe/eias/.

184–185 Prince William County *Service Efforts and Accomplishments Report:* "Service Efforts and Accomplishments Report 1997 to 2002, Executive Summary," Prince William County, http://www.pwcgov.org/docLibrary/PDF/000461.pdf (January 2004).

185   Florida Secretary of Environmental Protection: Environmental Performance Measurement System, semifinalist application for the Innovations in American Government 1999 Awards Program, April 16, 1999; and Robert D. Behn, "Site Visit Report," Innovations in American Government 1999 Awards Program, July 1999.

186   IRS problems: David E. Rosenbaum, "Audit Confirms Abusive I.R.S. Practices, *New York Times*, January 14, 1998, p. A13.

187   2002 Office of Personnel Management survey: Brian Friel, "The Rating Game," *Government Executive*, August 2003, pp. 46–52.

187   Joe Chandler quotation: in "Daily Briefing: Rating Employee Performance Appraisal Systems," *GovExec.com*, November 29, 1999, http://www.governmentexecutive.com/dailyfed/1199/112999b2.htm.

189   "The city of Baltimore . . . city facilities": Baxandall and Euchner, *Can CitiStat Work in Greater Boston?*, p. 11.

189   "In New York . . . insider trading": Giuliani, *Leadership*, p. 74.

189   Chattanooga, Tennessee: Baxandall and Euchner, *Can CitiStat Work in Greater Boston?* p. 11.

189   Texas annual review of sample indicators: Liner et al., *Making Results-Based State Government Work*, p. 81–82.

189   Illinois's child welfare system: Illinois Department of Children and Family Services, semifinalist application for Innovations in American Government 2000 Awards Program, April 4, 2000; and Robert D. Behn, "Site Visit Report," Innovations in American Government 2000 Awards Program, July 2000.

CHAPTER 9: SMARTER CUSTOMER SERVICE

193   "Choice makes a difference in parent satisfaction . . .": *Trends in the Use of School Choice 1993 to 1999: Statistical Analysis Report*, NCES 2003031 (Washington, D.C.: National Center for Education Statistics, U.S. Department of Education, May 2003). Available at http://nces.ed.gov/pubsearch/pubsinfo.asp?pubid=2003031.

195   "Both expansions were accomplished without . . .": Peter Hutchinson and Babak Armajani, *Enterprise Management* (Minneapolis: The Center of the American Experiment, 1991).

195   "By 1996, almost two . . . exam had tripled": *Postsecondary Enrollment Options Program* (St. Paul: Program Evaluation Division, Office of the Legislative Auditor, State of Minnesota, March 1996).

195–196   Jay Greene's analysis: Jay Greene, *2001 Education Freedom Index*, Civic Report
          No. 24 (New York: Manhattan Institute for Policy Research, January 2002).

196   "Other studies have proven . . .": See, for example, Eric Rofes, *How Are School
          Districts Responding to Charter Laws and Charter Schools?* (Berkeley: Policy
          Analysis for California Education, U.C. Berkeley, April 1998); David J. Armor and
          Brett M. Peiser, *Competition in Education: A Case Study of Interdistrict Choice*
          (Boston: Pioneer Institute, 1997); and *Charter Schools: A Progress Report, Part
          III: The Ripple Effect—A Cresting Wave* (Washington, D.C.: Center for Education
          Reform, July 1999). For a summary of other studies, see *What the Research Re-
          veals About Charter Schools: Summary and Analyses of the Studies* (Washington,
          D.C.: Center for Education Reform, September 2003), available at http://www.
          edreform.com/_upload/research.pdf.

196   Minneapolis *Star Tribune* quotation: Allie Shah, "Minneapolis Schools Prepare
          to Compete for Students," Minneapolis *Star Tribune*, November 4, 2003.

197   "A few years back . . . to serve 33 percent more people:" Consolidated Chemical
          Dependency Treatment Fund, Minnesota Department of Human Services, pre-
          liminary application for Innovations in American Government Award 1993, p. 2.

197–199   Information on Chicago's 311 system: 311 City Services, Supplementary appli-
          cation for Innovations in American Government 2002 Awards Program, October
          25, 2002; Steven E. Miller, "Site Visit Report," Innovations in American Govern-
          ment 2002 Awards Program, February 21, 2003; and interviews with 311
          spokespersons during final competition, May 7, 2003.

198–199   Miller quotations: Miller, "Site Visit Report."

199–200   Bloomberg quotations: Winnie Hu, "New Yorkers Love to Complain, and Hotline
          Is Making the Most of It." *New York Times*, December 1, 2003.

199   Data on New York City 311 system: Ibid.

199–200   Menchini, Weinshall, and Frieden quotations: Ibid.

200   "According to *American Demographics* . . .": Alison Stein Wellner, "The End of
          Leisure," *American Demographics*, July 1, 2000.

200   "A study from the Department of Labor . . .": Cited in "Booming Economy Tak-
          ing Its Toll on American Worker's Leisure Time: Recent Online Roper Starch Sur-
          vey Shows Stressed Out, Overworked Americans Say Time Is Worth Money," *Cir-
          cles News*, http://doit.circles.com/corp/ne_press_release_page2000.asp?Press
          Release=Aug2000_01, August 24, 2000.

200   Mary Jean Raab quotation: in Jason Fry, "What's in Store," *The Wall Street Jour-
          nal*, December 31, 1999.

200–201   National Governors Association quotation: "Building Better eGovernment:
          Tools for Transformation," *Center Online*, National Governors Association Cen-
          ter for Best Practices, http://www.nga.org/center/egovernment/, January 2004.

201   Travis County, Texas, I-Jury system: Michelle Gamble-Risley, "I-Jury Simplifies
          Summons Process," *Government Technology*, October 14, 2003.

201–202   New York State Council on the Arts: the authors' firm, PSG, was a consultant on
          this project.

202   *Pay IT Forward* quotation: *Pay IT Forward*, p. 13.

203   *Citizen 2010* quotation: *Citizen 2010*, p. 10.

203   Bush administration strategy document quotation: Executive Office of the Pres-
          ident, *E-Government Strategy: Implementing the President's Management
          Agenda for E-Government* (Washington, D.C.: April 2003), p. 5.

203   Information on federal government sites: Ibid., pp. 11–12.

203   "In 2003, the American Customer Satisfaction Index . . .": "ACSI Scores for U.S.
          Federal Government," American Customer Satisfaction Index Web page,
          http://www.theacsi.com/government/govt-03.html, December 15, 2003.

203   "The Center for Digital Government identified the 10 most common online
          services . . .": *Citizen 2010*, p. 16.

204   "According to *Pay IT Forward*, by 2003 the leading adoption rates by customers
          . . .": *Pay IT Forward*, p. 13.

204   "The savings are huge . . .": *Citizen 2010*, p. 18.

204   "In a 2003 survey done by Darrell West . . .": Darrell M. West, *State and Federal E-
          Government in the United States 2003* (Providence: http://www.insidepolitics.
          org/egovt03us.html, September 2003).

206   ServiceArizona information: Penny Martucci, National Association of State In-
          formation Resource Executive (NASIRE) Awards Nomination, 1999.

206–207   Kansas Department of Human Resources information: William Sanders, Na-
          tional Association of State Chief Information Officers (NASCIO) Awards Nomi-
          nation, 2002.

207–208   Minnesota sales tax reengineering: Our colleague at PSG, Connie Nelson, was
          one of the leaders of this effort. See notes to Chapter 13 for more documenta-
          tion.

208   ACSI quotation: "The voice of the Consumer," ACSI, www.theacsi.org/overview.
          htm, February, 2004.

208   "According to ACSI, customer satisfaction with public services . . .": Professor
          Claes Fornell, "User Satisfaction with Government Services Differs Widely
          Across Departments," ACSI, http://www.theacsi.org/government/govt-o2c/
          html, December 16, 2002.

208–209   Quotation from Canadian Institute for Citizen Centered Service and Institute of
          Public Administration study: *Citizens First 3*, pp. 13, 90.

CHAPTER 10:
DON'T BUY MISTRUST—ELIMINATE IT

210   Epigraph: President Bill Clinton and Vice President Al Gore, *The Blair House Pa-
          pers* (Washington, D.C.: National Performance Review, 1997), p. 27.

211   Quote from National Performance Review report: Vice President Al Gore, *From
          Red Tape to Results: Creating a Government That Works Better and Costs Less*
          (Washington, D.C.: National Performance Review, 1993), pp. 11–12, 22.

213   "More than 90 percent . . . alcohol to minors" Tax law compliance: Minnesota
          Department of Revenue, "1998 Annual Performance Report," p. 8. Seat belt use
          compliance: Office of Traffic Safety, "Minnesota Motor Vehicle Crash Facts,
          1998" Minnesota Department of Public Safety, p. 52. Liquor store compliance:
          "Fact Sheet: Stopping Illegal Alcohol Sales to Teens," Action on Alcohol and
          Teens—A Citizen's Group, http://www.winternet.com/AAT/ (January 2004).

213   "In the early 1990s, for instance . . .": Interview with Babak Armajani, former
          deputy Commissioner of Revenue.

215   "When Madison, Wisconsin, reformed its purchasing system . . .": Osborne and
          Plastrik, *The Reinventor's Fieldbook*, pp. 420–421.

215   Environmental Protection Agency Common Sense Initiative: *Reinvention at
          EPA* (Washington, D.C.: Environmental Protection Agency, 1999), downloaded
          February 8, 2000, www.epa.gov/reinvent/taskforce/report99/commit.htm. This
          document is no longer on EPA's Web site.

215   Quote from Christine Todd Whitman: Christine Todd Whitman, speech deliv-
          ered at the National Environmental Policy Institute, March 8, 2001, downloaded
          in 2001 from EPA website, www.epa.gov/.

215–216   OSHA experience: Clinton and Gore, *The Blair House Papers*, p. 16; James E.
          Roughton and Lawrence J. Grabiak, "Reinventing OSHA: Is It Possible?" *Profes-
          sional Safety*, December 1996, pp. 29–33; Brian Friel, "OSHA: Cooperative Com-
          pliance," *GovExec.com*, December 8, 1997; Brian Friel, "Uncooperative Compli-
          ance," *GovExec.com*, March 11, 1998; "Here's How We Measured Up in FY 1996,"

OSHA Web page, www.osha.gov/vanguard/customer/cusmeas.htm, downloaded February 8, 2000.

216 Joe Dear quote: in Susannah Zak Figura, "The New OSHA," *Government Executive*, May 1997, p. 38.

216 "For example, EPA's metal finishing committee adopted performance goals . . .": Alison Maxwell, "EPA Reports on Reinvention," *GovExec.com*, March 31, 1998.

216 "OSHA shifted its performance goals for area offices . . .": "Here's How We Measured Up in FY 1996," OSHA Web page.

216 The Massachusetts Environmental Results Program: Massachusetts Department of Environmental Protection, semifinalist application for Innovations in American Government 2001 Awards Program, April 23, 2001; Shelley Metzenbaum, "Site Visit Report," Innovations in American Government 2001 Awards Program, 2001; Massachusetts Department of Environmental Protection, "The Massachusetts Environmental Results Program: Protecting the Environment and Helping Small Businesses," paper prepared for National Environmental Innovations Symposium, December 6–7, 2000.

217 "In a paper summarizing its reinvention efforts, the EPA concluded . . .": EPA Innovations Task Force, *Aiming for Excellence: Actions to Encourage Stewardship and Accelerate Environmental Progress*, EPA 100-R-99-006 (Washington, D.C.: U.S. Environmental Protection Agency, July 1999), p. 15.

217 Dennis Murphy quotation: in Peter Hutchinson and David Osborne, "Winning Compliance," *Government Executive* (June 2000).

217 "When the Minnesota Department of Revenue realized . . .": Interview with Babak Armajani, former deputy commissioner of the Revenue Department.

218 "The Minnesota Department of Revenue radically simplified its short form . . .": Ibid.

218 "In Winnipeg, Manitoba, the City Council was concerned . . .": Ibid.

219 "After Congress hauled them on the carpet in 1998, IRS leaders have struggled . . .": Gary M. Stern, "Pay Your Taxes, Please," *Government Executive*, December 1999; Vice President Al Gore, Secretary of the Treasury Robert E. Rubin, *Reinventing Service at the IRS: Report of the Customer Service Task Force* (Washington, D.C.: National Performance Review, 1998), pp. 4–8.

219 "The 1998 IRS reform law dipped a toe . . . collection plummeted": Brian Friel, "IRS Tries to Stop the Reform Pendulum," *GovExec.com*, February 3, 2000.

220 "Over the first four years . . . 'doing the worst'": Ed Finkel, "Permits On Time, or Money Back," *The Public Innovator* No. 24 (March 16, 1995), pp. 1–3 (published by the National Academy of Public Administration's Alliance for Redesigning Government).

220 "According to a U.S. Department of Justice report . . .": Michael S. Scott, *Speeding in Residential Areas: Problem-Oriented Guides for Police*, Problem-Specific Guide Series No. 3 (Washington, D.C.: U.S. Department of Justice Office of Community Policing, 2003), p. 18.

220 "Before its late-1990s reforms . . . installment plan": Stern, "Pay Your Taxes, Please," *Government Executive*.

221 "The Kansas Department of Revenue . . . greatly accelerated": David Cay Johnston, "A Kinder, Smarter Tax System for Kansas," *New York Times*, June 22, 1998.

221 "Iowa changed the rules so that . . .": Interview with Bob Rafferty, PSG consultant in Iowa.

221 Consumer Product Safety Commission information: U.S. Consumer Product Safety Commission, semifinalist application for Innovations in American Government 1998 Award Program, April 13, 1998; John D. Donohue, "Site Visit Report," Innovations in American Government 1998 Award Program, 1998.

221 "The Interior Department's Fish and Wildlife Service . . . foot the bill": Jeffrey P. Cohn, "Negotiating Nature," *Government Executive*, February 1998.

222   "Oregon's Green Environmental Management Systems Permit Program . . .", *The Oregon Green Permits Program Guide,* Oregon Department of Environmental Quality, January 14, 2000.

222   "West Virginia has instituted a similar program . . .": Office of Innovation, "Environmental Management Systems," West Virginia Department of Environmental Protection Web page, www.dep.state.wv.us/item.cfm?ssid=21&ss1id=473, October 2003.

222   "In Maine's Top 200 initiative, for instance . . ." Clinton and Gore, *The Blair House Papers*, p. 16.

CHAPTER 11: USING FLEXIBILITY TO GET ACCOUNTABILITY

227   "In Houston it's called . . .": Donald McAdams, *Fighting to Save Our Urban Schools . . . and Winning!" Lessons from Houston* (New York: Teachers College Press, 2000), p. 88.

227   McAdams quotations and story: Ibid., pp. 89–91.

229   Tillamook County story and Cameron quotations: in Al Gore, *The Best Kept Secrets in Government,* p. 56.

229   Florida's Division of Worker's Compensation: David Osborne, "Raise Taxes? Slash Services? Is There Another Choice?" *Governing,* March 1992, p. 55.

230   "A similar transformation . . . half of them": Osborne and Plastrik, *The Reinventor's Fieldbook,* pp. 396–397, 450–451.

231   "As of September, 2003, nearly 3,000 . . .": Center for Education Reform, http://www.edreform.com/.

232   "But by September, 2003, there had been 98 studies . . .": *What the Research Reveals About Charter Schools: Summary and Analyses of the Studies* (Washington, D.C.: Center for Education Reform, September 2003), available at http://www.edreform.com/_upload/research.pdf.

232   "A California study found that 78 percent . . .": R.G. Corwin and J. Flaherty, *Freedom and Innovation in California's Charter Schools* (Los Alamitos, Calif.: SWRI, 1995), cited in Chester E. Finn, Jr., Bruno V. Manno, and Gregg Vanourek, *Charter Schools in Action* (Princeton: Princeton University Press, 2000), pp. 90–91.

232   Charter school waiting lists: The Center for Education Reform, which does an annual survey of charter schools, provided this number.

232   "And in a nationwide survey 65 percent . . .": Finn et. al., *Charter Schools in Action,* p. 85.

232–234 Discussion of Oregon University System: Senate Bill 271 Review Panel, *Final Report* (Salem, Oregon: Oregon University System Department of Administrative Services, July 1998); and Terrence J. MacTaggart and James R. Mingle, *Pursuing the Public's Agenda* (Washington, D.C.: Association of Governing Boards of Universities and Colleges, Center for Public Higher Ed Trusteeship and Governance, 2002), pp. 26–27.

235–237 Information on U.S. Office of Federal Student Aid: Our company, the Public Strategies Group, worked as the official "transformation partner" of FSA from 1999 through 2003. Much of our information comes from our colleagues who did this work. In addition, we have used a number of briefing documents put together by the Student Financial Assistance Transition Team: "PBO Origins and Organization," U.S. Department of Education briefing paper, 2001; and "SFA Does E-Business," U.S. Department of Education briefing paper, 2001.

236–237 Data on FSA performance: Greg Woods, "Letter to Employees," Office of Federal Student Aid, December 2001.

238   "Each year the federal government distributes . . .": U.S. Census Bureau, *Consolidated Federal Funds Report for Fiscal Year 2002: State and County Areas* (Wash-

ington, D.C.: U.S. Government Printing Office, 2003), available at www.census. gov/prod/2003pubs/cffr02.pdf.

241–242   Quotation from National Performance Review report: Al Gore, *The Best Kept Secrets in Government*, p. 57

241–242   Immunization campaign in Oregon: interviews with Connie Revel, former director of the Oregon Option, and other participants in the campaign; and Howard M. Leichter and Jeffrey Tryens, *Achieving Better Health Outcomes: The Oregon Benchmark Experience* (New York: Millbank Memorial Fund, 2002), pp. 24–27.

242   "Clinton also urged Congress . . .": Gore, *Best Kept Secrets in Government*, p. 57, and personal communication from John Kamensky, former deputy director of the National Performance.

242   Discussion of Minnesota's Board of Government Innovation and Cooperation and quotations: Board of Government Innovation and Cooperation, semifinalist application for Innovations in American Government 2001 Award; and Charles C. Euchner, "Site Visit Report," Innovations in American Government 2001 Awards Program, 2001.

243   Information on freedom communities in Iowa: interviews with Bob Rafferty.

CHAPTER 12: MAKE ADMINISTRATIVE SYSTEMS ALLIES, NOT ENEMIES

246   Robert Kaplan quote: From a lecture on accounting for the Advanced Management Program 102, which Peter Hutchinson attended in the spring of 1988.

248   "As *Reinventing Government* reported . . .": Osborne and Gaebler, *Reinventing Government*, p. 118.

248   "The National Performance Review (NPR) illustrated . . .": Gore, *From Red Tape to Results*, p. 18.

249   "As *Reinventing Government* said, old-fashioned budgets . . .": Osborne and Gaebler, *Reinventing Government*, p. 117.

249   Washington State Incentive Savings Program: Office of Financial Management, *Report of Fiscal Year 2003 Savings, Incentive Account Expenditures*, Rcw 43.79.460 (Olympia: State of Washington, 2003).

250   "The British, Canadians, Australians, Swedes, and many American governments . . .": See, for instance, Allen Schick, *Modern Budgeting* (Paris: Organization for Economic Cooperation and Development, 1997), pp. 22–23.

250   "Great Britain, Australia, and New Zealand have all done this . . .": Ibid., and Office of the Auditor General of Canada, *Toward Better Governance: Public Service Reform in New Zealand (1984–94) and Its Relevance to Canada* (Ottawa: Office of the Auditor General of Canada, 1995).

250   "This tool has also grown quite common . . . innovation fund": Osborne and Plastrik, *The Reinventor's Fieldbook*, pp. 409–410.

251   "When Texas compared the cost of procurement . . . local governments": Joint Task Force of the National Association of State Purchasing Officials and the National Association of State Information Resource Executives, *Buying Smart: State Procurement Saves Millions* (Lexington, Ky.: NASPO/NASIRE Joint Task Force on Information Technology Procurement Reform, September 1996).

251   Gore report quotation: Vice President Al Gore, *Reinventing Federal Procurement: Accompanying Report of the National Performance Review* (Washington, D.C.: National Performance Review, September 1993).

252   "In 1997 the NPR reported on progress . . . $12 billion to date": Vice President Al Gore, *Businesslike Government* (Washington, D.C.: National Performance Review, October 1997), pp. 48–49.

252   "Milwaukee issued purchase cards . . . transaction costs declined": Interview
       with Cheryl Oliva, director of purchasing, City of Milwaukee, conducted by
       Anne Kinney of the Public Strategies Group, June 2002.

253   "Best-value purchasing challenges all government buyers . . . quality assurance
       program": Joint task force of the National Association of State Purchasing Offi-
       cials, the National Association of State Information Resource Executives and the
       National Association of State Directors of Administration and General Services,
       Buying Smart: Blueprint for Action (Joint Information Technology Procurement
       Project, September 1998).

253   "California's purchasing people decided . . . of many products and services":
       Joint Task Force, *Buying Smart: State Procurement Saves Millions.*

254   "When Missouri did this . . .": Joint Task Force, *Buying Smart: Blueprint for
       Action.*

254   "For example, the California Franchise Tax Board formed a strategic partnership
       . . . for comparable projects": Joint Task Force, *Buying Smart: State Procurement
       Saves Millions.*

255   "In California, for example, the state first requests . . . innovative solutions":
       Joint Task Force, *Buying Smart: Blueprint for Action.*

255   ". . . modeled largely on the British Civil Service": Donald J. Savoie, *Thatcher,
       Reagan, Mulroney: In Search of a New Bureaucracy* (Pittsburgh: University of
       Pittsburgh Press, 1994), pp. 49–53; Frederick Mosher, *Democracy and the Public
       Service,* (New York: Oxford University Press, 1968); and Paul Van Riper, *History of
       the United States Civil Service* (Chicago, Ill.: Row Peterson and Company, 1958).

255   "By the time President Clinton was elected . . .": Gore, *From Red Tape to Results,*
       pp. 20–21.

255   Brookings quotation: Donald F. Kettl, Patricia W. Ingraham, Ronald P. Sanders,
       and Constance Horner, *Civil Service Reform: Building a Government That Works*
       (Washington, D.C.: Brookings Institution Press, 1996), pp. 3–6.

255   Massachusetts Taxpayers' Foundation quotation: Chris Black, "Civil Service
       Feels the Strain," *Boston Globe,* August 26, 1987, pp. 1, 83.

255   National Academy of Public Administration quotations: in Gore, *From Red Tape
       to Results,* p. 22.

255   National Performance Review quotation: Ibid.

257   "Over the past five years . . .": Data provided by Minneapolis Public Schools for
       1998–2003.

257–258 "In 2002, the Washington State Legislature . . . *staff management*": Washington
       State Department of Personnel, *Human Resource Systems Research Report*
       (Olympia, Department of Personnel, November 2002).

259   "Major corporations spend four times . . .": *Leadership for America: Rebuilding
       the Public Service* (Washington, D.C.: National Commission on the Public Ser-
       vice, 1989) quoted in Al Gore, *Reinventing Human Resource Management: Ac-
       companying Report of the National Performance Review* (Washington, D.C.: Na-
       tional Performance Review, 1992), p. 43.

259   "The legislative auditor discovered, however . . .": *School District Spending* (St.
       Paul, Minn.: Office of the Legislative Auditor, February 1990), p. 88.

262   "This strategic reflection led to some interesting conclusions . . . *make correc-
       tions* . . .": New York Office of the State Comptroller, "FOCAS Strategic Direc-
       tion," working document of New York's redesign of its accounting system. Used
       with permission of the State of New York.

264   Mike Egan quotation: Mike Egan, "The Auditor—Partner or Adversary?" *Local
       Government Auditing Quarterly,* September 2003.

265   Quotation from 1993 report of the National Performance Review: Gore, *From
       Red Tape to Results,* p. 32.

265   Quotation from former Canadian Auditor General Denis Desautels: in Osborne and Plastrik, *The Reinventor's Fieldbook*, p. 423.

265   Quotation from Government Accounting Office "yellow book": Comptroller General of the United States, *Government Auditing Standards*, GAO 03-673G (Washington, D.C.: U.S. General Accounting Office, June 2003), Sections 1.14 and 1.15.

266   "In Phoenix, Arizona, the auditor's office audits competitive bids . . .": Interviews with former auditor Jim Flanagan.

266   "In the U.K., Margaret Thatcher created a new Audit Commission . . .": For more, see Osborne and Plastrik, *Fieldbook*, pp. 318–319, 424–425.

266   "In New York . . . impact of a problem": Office of the State Comptroller, *Standards for Internal Control in New York State Government* (Albany: State of New York, February 1999).

269   "Earlier in this chapter . . . federal travel": Background material on the use of purchase cards is from *Joint Report of the Purchase Card Financial Management Team and the Purchase Card Integrated Product Team to the Under Secretary of Defense (Acquisition and Technology) and the Under Secretary of Defense (Comptroller)* (Washington, D.C.: Department of Defense, February 1997), pp. 3–5.

270   "By 2001, employees at just one department . . .": *Charge Card Task Force Final Report* (Washington, D.C.: Department of Defense, June 2002), p. 1-1.

270   "The department estimated cumulative savings . . . for their trip": Ibid., pp. 2-1, 3-2.

270   "Then, in 2001, the General Accounting Office . . . or other activities": Caroline Polk, "Not in the Cards, " *Government Executive*, July 2003, pp. 74–76.

270   Quotation from task force: *Charge Card Task Force Final Report*, pp. 1–2.

270   "Already, it pointed out, management attention . . .": Ibid., pp. –4.

CHAPTER 13: SMARTER WORK PROCESSES

273   "Managing quality is not . . . quality control": J. M. Juran, *Juran on Leadership for Quality: An Executive Handbook* (New York: The Free Press, 1989).

273   Deming and Juran experiences in Japan: Department of Revenue, *History of Quality Improvement* (Madison, Wis. Department of Revenue, January 1989).

274   Armand Feigenbaum quotation: in Marshall Shaskin and Kenneth J. Kiser, *Putting Total Quality Management to Work* (San Francisco: Berrett-Koehler, 1993), p. 56.

275   "In businesses that have won . . .": Jerry Bowles and Joshua Hammond. *Beyond Quality: New Standards of Total Performance That Can Change the Future of Corporate America* (New York: Berkley Publishing Group, 1987).

275   "Indeed, Creech says that TQM's process . . .": Bill Creech, *The Five Pillars of TQM: How to Make Total Quality Work for You* (New York: Dutton, 1994), p. 315.

280   Joseph Sensenbrenner's experience as mayor of Madison, Wisconsin: Joseph Sensenbrenner, "Quality Comes to City Hall," *Harvard Business Review* (March-April 1991).

280   "According to the U.S. Office . . . 60 percent": *Federal Quality News*, Volume 2, Number 2, U.S. Office of Personnel Management, June 1993.

280   "By 1993, according to Myron Tribus . . .": Myron Tribus, *Community Quality Councils, Part I,* newsletter from Statistical Process Controls, Inc., & SPC Press, Inc., winter 1993.

280   "And in 1994, 40 states reported . . .": Keon S. Chi, *Total Quality Management in State Government: Trends and Issues,* paper presented at American Society for Public Administration national conference, July 22–26, 1995.

281   Madison, Wisconsin, TQM results: James J. Kline, "Total Quality Management in
       Local Government," *Government Finance Review*, August 1992.

281   "TQM shifts some control to . . .": Shaskin and Kiser, *Putting Total Quality Man-
       agement to Work.*

282   Bill Creech quotation: Creech, *The Five Pillars of TQM*, pp. 203–204.

283   Governor George Voinovich and Ohio State Employees Association: interviews
       with Steve Wall, then TQM director for Governor Voinovich.

284   "According to the former U.S. Federal . . .": Federal Quality Institute, *Education
       and Training for Total Quality Management in the Federal Government*, Federal
       Total Quality Management Handbook Series (Washington: U.S. Government
       Printing Office).

284   Sensenbrenner quotation: Sensenbrenner, "Quality Comes to City Hall."

284   "FQI recommended 'cascade' training . . . :" Federal Quality Institute, *Education
       and Training for Total Quality Management in the Federal Government.*

285   "Long delay times between training in TQM . . ." Ibid., p. 12.

285   Jack Welch quotation: In David Kennedy, *Meeting for a Need: Jerry Abramson
       and CityWork in Louisville, Kentucky*, case study C16-92-1155.0 (Cambridge,
       Ma.: Kennedy School of Government, Harvard University, 1992).

286   Northeast Region of the U.S. Customs Service WorkOut: Philip Spady, *Managing
       Change and Innovation in the U.S. Customs Service*, unpublished internal report
       provided by Philip Spady, then director of Northeast Region; and Buffalo Dis-
       trict Personnel Office, *WorkOut — What Is It?* videotape (Buffalo: U.S. Customs
       Service, September 1993).

286   West Virginia and North Carolina WorkOuts: David Parkhurst, "GE and States
       Work It Out," *The Public Innovator*, Issue No. 1 (published by the Alliance for Re-
       designing Government at the National Academy of Public Administration),
       March 31, 1994.

286   Louisville WorkOuts: Kennedy, *Meeting for a Need: Jerry Abramson and CityWork
       in Louisville, Kentucky.*

287   "One of the ACC's first WorkOuts . . . in costs": Background Paper on ACC Head-
       quarters Action WorkOut (AWO) Initiative, provided by Air Combat Command,
       February 1996.

289   Hammer and Champy quotation: Michael Hammer and James Champy, *Reengi-
       neering the Corporation* (New York: HarperBusiness, 1993), p. 32.

290   Hammer and Champy quotation: Ibid., p. 33.

290   Data on payoffs for reengineering: Sharon L. Caudle, *Reengineering for Results:
       Keys to Success from Government Experience* (Washington, D.C.: National Acad-
       emy of Public Administration, August 1994).

290   Minnesota sales tax reengineering: "Sales Tax Re-engineering: Overview," Min-
       nesota Department of Revenue, June 1993; Connie Nelson, *Practitioner's Guide*,
       unpublished manuscript, 1993; *Sales Tax Re-engineering: Business Process Re-
       designs* (St. Paul: Minnesota Department of Revenue, July 1992); and interviews
       with Connie Nelson, Greg Tschida, and Don Trimble.

293   Hammer and Champy quotation: Hammer and Champy, *Reengineering the Cor-
       poration*, p. 121.

297   Russell Linden quotation: Russell Linden, *Seamless Government* (San Francisco:
       Jossey-Bass, 1994), p. 95.

300   "Half of the companies in the 1994 . . .": *State of Reengineering Report* (Cam-
       bridge, Mass.: CSC Index, 1994).

301   Linden quotation: Linden, *Seamless Government*, p. 172.

302   Hammer and Stanton quotations: Michael Hammer and Steven A. Stanton, *The
       Reengineering Revolution: A Handbook* (New York: HarperBusiness, 1995), pp.
       19–21, 28.

CHAPTER 14: LEADERSHIP FOR A CHANGE

310   "Never fall into the trap of selling the public short . . .": Roger Douglas, "The Politics of Successful Structural Reform," unpublished manuscript, p. 27.

310   New Zealand economic crisis and reforsm. See Osborne and Plastik, *Banishing Democracy,* pp. 75–90.

310   "Structural reform does not become possible until you trust . . .": Douglas, "The Politics of Successful Structural Reform," p. 27.

315   Portland *Oregonian* quotation: "Stein's Time Counted at County," *The Portland Oregonian,* March 18, 2001.

315   Giuliani quotation: "I tried to run the city as a business . . ." Rudolph Giuliani, *Leadership,* p. xiii.

316   "In his career, Giuliani says . . .": Ibid., pp. 69–71.

316   "The centerpiece of our efforts . . .": Ibid., pp. 72, 79.

316   "In September 1990, . . . if they could": Ibid., p. xi.

316–317 "The crime rate was down . . . North America": Ibid., pp. 381–387.

317   Giuliani quotation: "The reality is that there's only so much . . .": *Leadership,* p. 318.

318   "They are, instead, *compliers . . .*": For a full discussion of this, see Osborne and Plastik, *Banishing Bureaucracy,* pp. 179–181.

319   Jack Welch quotation: Jerry Useem, "Tyrants, Statesmen, and Destroyers (A Brief History of the CEO)," *Fortune,* November 18, 2002; available at Fortune.com: www.fortune.com/fortune/specials/2002/ceos/timeline6.html.

319–320 Greg Woods at the Office of Federal Student Aid: Our firm, PSG, was FSA's "transformation partner" through this period.

320–321 Information on the University of Minnesota's campus at Crookston: Our firm consulted with Chancellor Sargeant during this transformation; in addition, we have relied on interviews with Chancellor Sargeant and documents he provided.

322   Creech quotations: Creech, *The Five Pillars of TQM,* pp. 281, 292.

322–325 Beverly Stein experience: interviews with Beverly Stein.

CHAPTER 15: POLITICS

326   Machiavelli quotation: Niccolo Machiavelli, *The Prince* (New York: Dover Publications, 1992), p. 13.

326–329 Steve Goldsmith experience in Indianapolis: See Osborne and Plastik, *Banishing Bureaucracy,* pp. 115–130.

327–329 Goldsmith quotations: Stephen Goldsmith, *The Twenty-First Century City: Resurrecting Urban America* (Washington, D.C.: Regnery Publishing, 1997), pp. 18–21.

328   "Over the next seven years Indianapolis successfully bid . . .": Ibid., p. 31.

328   "Of the first 64 competitions . . .": Osborne and Plastrik, *Banishing Bureaucracy,* p. 124; see endnote to p. 124 for sources.

328   "The city saved more than $120 . . . its management": Ibid., pp. 124–125, 128.

328   "By 1995, Fantauzzo was partnering with city officials . . .": Ibid., pp. 126–127.

328   "By 1997, Goldsmith . . . 'actual budget'": Goldsmith, *The Twenty-First Century City,* pp. 79–80.

329   Goldsmith quotation: "Over the years": Ibid., p. 27.

330   Clinton quotation: in Osborne, *Laboratories of Democracy,* p. 92.

331   "If you want to change where a debate in the Legislature ends . . .": Peter Callaghan, "Locke Changed This Year's Budget Debate Before It Began," Tacoma *News Tribune,* June 8, 2003.

331   "In 1995, for instance, the media publicized complaints . . . second choice":
        Karen Avenoso, "Most Parents Back School Choice Plan, Says Boston Survey,"
        Boston Globe, December 14, 1995, p. 40.

332   "Perpich liked to tell his staff . . . will come along'": Peter Hutchinson served for
        a time as Perpich's finance commissioner.

333   "Called Building Better Neighborhoods . . . managed competition": Goldsmith,
        The Twenty-First Century City, pp. 86, 155; and personal communication from
        Goldsmith.

333   "In Iowa, for example, Governor Tom Vilsack . . .": Our firm, PSG, is Vilsack's
        "reinvention partner" in these efforts.

333   Giuliani quotation: Giuliani, *Leadership*, p. 40.

333   "Don't play the 'Washington game' . . .": Nancy C. Roberts and Paula J. King,
        *Transforming Public Policy: Dynamics of Policy Entrepreneurship and Innova-
        tion* (San Francisco: Jossey-Bass, 1996), p. 100.

334   "The problem with compromise policies is simple . . .": Douglas, "The Politics of
        Successful Structural Reform," p. 6.

334   "Understand," he said, "that the great reform problem is a system problem . . .":
        Roberts and King, *Transforming Public Policy*, pp. 219–220.

335   Douglas quotation: Douglas, "The Politics of Successful Structural Reform," pp.
        17–20.

336   "The cost of health care and Social Security . . ." *The Long Term Budget Outlook*
        (Washington, D.C.: Congressional Budget Office, December 2003). The CBO
        projects that under current law, even if the historical growth of Medicare slows a
        bit, Medicaid, Medicare and Social Security will rise from 8.1 percent of GDP in
        2003 to 17.4 percent by 2030. Total federal spending has averaged about 20 per-
        cent of GDP for the past 50 years, as the CBO points out; at this level an increase
        from 8.1 to 17.4 percent—an increase of 9.4 percentage points—would con-
        sume 46.5 percent of the federal budget in the next 26 years.

INDEX